OXFORD ENGLISH DRAMA

General Editor: MICHAEL CORDNER
Associate General Editors: PETER HOLLAND · MARTIN WIGGINS

FOUR REVENGE TRAGEDIES

THE REVENGE TRAGEDY flourished in Britain in the late Elizabethan and Jacobean period for both literary and cultural reasons. Thomas Kyd's *The Spanish Tragedy* (1587) helped to establish the popularity of the genre, and it was followed by *The Revenger's Tragedy* (1606), published anonymously and ascribed first to Cyril Tourneur and then to Thomas Middleton. George Chapman's *The Revenge of Bussy D'Ambois* and Tourneur's *The Atheist's Tragedy* were written between 1609 and 1610. Each of the four plays printed here defines the problems of the revenge genre, often by exploiting its conventions in unexpected directions. All deal with fundamental moral questions about the meaning of justice and the lengths to which victimized individuals may go to obtain it, while registering the social strains of life in a rigid but increasingly fragile social hierarchy.

KATHARINE EISAMAN MAUS is Professor of English at the University of Virginia. Her publications include *Ben Jonson and the Roman Frame of Mind* (1985), *Soliciting Interpretation: Literary Theory and Seventeenth-Century English Poetry*, ed. with Elizabeth D. Harvey (1991), and *Inwardness and Theater in the English Renaissance* (1995).

MICHAEL CORDNER is Ken Dixon Professor of Drama at the University of York. He has edited George Farquhar's *The Beaux' Stratagem*, the *Complete Plays* of Sir George Etherege, and, for Oxford English Drama, *Four Restoration Marriage Plays* and Sheridan's *The School for Scandal and Other Plays*.

PETER HOLLAND is McMeel Family Professor in Shakespeare Studies at the University of Notre Dame.

MARTIN WIGGINS is a Fellow of the Shakespeare Institute and Lecturer in English at the University of Birmingham.

OXFORD ENGLISH DRAMA

J. M. Barrie
Peter Pan and Other Plays

Aphra Behn
The Rover and Other Plays

George Farquhar
The Recruiting Officer and Other Plays

John Ford
'Tis Pity She's a Whore and Other Plays

Ben Jonson
The Alchemist and Other Plays

Ben Jonson
The Devil is an Ass and Other Plays

D. H. Lawrence
*The Widowing of Mrs Holroyd and
Other Plays*

Christopher Marlowe
Doctor Faustus and Other Plays

John Marston
The Malcontent and Other Plays

Thomas Middleton
Women Beware Women and Other Plays

*A Mad World, My Masters and
Other Plays*

Richard Brinsley Sheridan
*The School for Scandal and
Other Plays*

J. M. Synge
*The Playboy of the Western World and
Other Plays*

John Webster
*The Duchess of Malfi and
Other Plays*

Oscar Wilde
*The Importance of Being Earnest and
Other Plays*

William Wycherley
The Country Wife and Other Plays

Court Masques
ed. David Lindley

Eighteenth-Century Women Dramatists
ed. Melinda Finberg

Five Romantic Plays
ed. Paul Baines and Edward Burns

Four Jacobean Sex Tragedies
ed. Martin Wiggins

Four Restoration Marriage Plays
ed. Michael Cordner

Four Revenge Tragedies
ed. Katharine Maus

*London Assurance and Other Victorian
Comedies*
ed. Klaus Stierstorfer

*The New Woman and Other
Emancipated Woman Plays*
ed. Jean Chothia

*The Roaring Girl and Other City
Comedies*
ed. James Knowles and Eugenen
Giddens

OXFORD WORLD'S CLASSICS

——

Four Revenge Tragedies

The Spanish Tragedy · *The Revenger's Tragedy*
The Revenge of Bussy D'Ambois
The Atheist's Tragedy

——

Edited with an Introduction and Notes by
KATHARINE EISAMAN MAUS

OXFORD
UNIVERSITY PRESS

OXFORD
UNIVERSITY PRESS

Great Clarendon Street, Oxford OX2 6DP

Oxford University Press is a department of the University of Oxford.
It furthers the University's objective of excellence in research, scholarship,
and education by publishing worldwide in

Oxford New York

Auckland Bangkok Buenos Aires Cape Town Chennai
Dar es Salaam Delhi Hong Kong Istanbul Karachi Kolkata
Kuala Lumpur Madrid Melbourne Mexico City Mumbai Nairobi
São Paulo Shanghai Taipei Tokyo Toronto

Oxford is a registered trade mark of Oxford University Press
in the UK and in certain other countries

Published in the United States
by Oxford University Press Inc., New York

© Katharine Eisaman Maus 1995

The moral rights of the author have been asserted
Database right Oxford University Press (maker)

First published as a World's Classics paperback 1995
Reissued as an Oxford World's Classics paperback 1998
Reissued 2008

British Library Cataloguing in Publication Data

Data available

Library of Congress Cataloging in Publication Data

Four revenge tragedies / edited with an introduction by Katharine Eisaman Maus.
p. cm.—(Oxford world's classics)
Contents: The Spanish tragedy—The revenger's tragedy—The
revenge of Bussy d'Ambois—The atheist's tragedy.
1. English Drama (Tragedy). 2. English Drama—17th century.
2. Revenge—Drama. I. Maus, Katharine Eisaman, 1955– .
II. Series. 822'.051208'09032—dc20 PR1257.F68– 1995 94–8005

ISBN 978–0–19–954053–2

6

Printed in Great Britain by
Clays Ltd, St Ives plc

In memory of
ERIC HUANG WEFALD
1957–1989
and
MARY CLARE MANSFIELD
1960–1989

CONTENTS

ACKNOWLEDGEMENTS

I AM grateful to Sarah Wright and M. J. Kidnie for help in checking the modernized texts back against the quartos, to Gordon Braden for conversations about revenge tragedy, and to Jerome McGann for conversations about editing. Series editor Michael Cordner, whose interest and expertise were crucial in the preparation of this edition, deserves especially fervent thanks.

K.E.M.

INTRODUCTION

THE revenge plays of the English Renaissance mark neither the beginning nor the end of a tradition. Their forbears are Greek and Latin tragedies which derive their plots from still more ancient legends. Their modern descendants are film Westerns and detective thrillers in which a man (the revenger is usually but not always male) hunts down the killer of his partner or family, assuming some of his adversary's most sinister traits in the process.

Revenge tragedy is not, however, now or in the past, merely a collection of durable clichés. There are infinite ways to elaborate the basic plot: *The Spanish Tragedy* and *The Revenger's Tragedy*, as we shall see, exploit the conventions to quite different ends. The other two plays in this volume, *The Atheist's Tragedy* and *The Revenge of Bussy d'Ambois*, might even be called 'anti-revenge' plays, interesting less for the ways they instantiate the norms of their genre than for the ways they dissent from them. None the less, it is easier to recognize the idiosyncrasies of individual works if some typical characteristics of this perennially fascinating kind of play are kept in mind.

Revenge tragedies feature someone who prosecutes a crime in a private capacity, taking matters into his own hands because the institutions by which criminals are made to pay for their offences are either systematically defective or unable to cope with some particularly difficult situation. Such plays testify to an apparently ineradicable yearning for justice—a yearning that abides even, or especially, in the most unfairly victimized persons. But at the same time, they register a troubling discrepancy between the desire for equity and the means of fulfilling that desire.

Usually the deficiencies of the world presented in the play antedate the action we see on stage. Indeed the defectiveness of the status quo is virtually a precondition of the genre; for by definition revenge occurs after a crime has been perpetrated, as a response to some previous outrage. Often an initial scene or speech retrospectively describes the original transgression. The importunate ghosts who haunt revenge tragedies remind characters and audience of constraints the past places upon the present, of obligations the living bear to the departed. Remains of the dead serve similar purposes, simultaneously commemorative and hortatory. The revenger preserves and cherishes the skull, the blood-stained handkerchief—even, at times, an entire corpse.

The structure of revenge tragedy thus complicates the issues of justice with which it is so deeply concerned. The protagonist must confront a dreadful situation not of his own making. His initial blamelessness is strongly emphasized. In *The Spanish Tragedy*, Hieronimo does nothing to bring about Horatio's death, and Horatio himself is innocent of any wrongdoing. In *The Revenger's Tragedy*, Vindice and his family are accidental casualties of the Duke's misgovernment, not deserving targets of his wrath. Clermont d'Ambois is so far from identifying his interests with his slain brother's that he remains on intimate terms with one of Bussy's most virulent foes. In *The Atheist's Tragedy*, Charlemont is betrayed by an uncle whom he has every reason to trust.

How, then, are we to evaluate the actions of the revenger? Does the protagonist's victimization exonerate him, partially or fully? Do we condone crimes that retaliate for previous crimes? On the one hand, both Christianity and some classical moral codes popular in the Renaissance prescribed patience and non-aggression. ' "Vengeance is mine," saith the Lord'—an all-knowing, all-powerful God was supposed to compensate for failures of human justice, in the future if not in the present, in the next world if not in this one. On the other hand, a man's 'honour' in early modern England required him to retaliate swiftly for slights to himself, and to refuse to tolerate the abuse of his kin or dependants.

Revenge, then, evokes mixed moral feelings. On the one hand, vengeance seems a form of savage but appropriate repayment. In Renaissance English, the word that captures this conception is 'quit', which means 'revenge' as well as 'pay back' or 'have done with'. 'Quit' suggests a welcome finality to the revenger's action, as if countering murder with murder somehow cancels both crimes out. On the other hand, in revenge tragedy visions of restored equilibrium almost always turn out to be mirages. 'Wreak', another archaic synonym for the taking of vengeance, can simply signify the doing of any serious injury. In so far as revenge contributes to a spiral of violence, its horrors exacerbate the agony it attempts to alleviate.

In revenge plays, the conflict between these two ways of thinking about revenge sometimes breeds arguments between characters, as in the dispute between Charlotte and Clermont in *The Revenge of Bussy d'Ambois*; sometimes causes the revenger to vacillate, as Hieronimo does in *The Spanish Tragedy*; and sometimes operates more implicitly, inducing ambivalence about the revenger's behaviour in the theatre audience. Moreover, a revenge that begins as a carefully regulated exaction of eye for eye often veers into uncontrolled excess. Vindice and Hieronimo repay their enemies with compound interest, gleefully embellishing their victims' deaths and involving innocent bystanders in the final bloodbath. The revenger seems compelled to take purgative action—to cleanse his world of a terrible wrong—but the only way to do so magnifies the original atrocity.

Revenge tragedy, then, places an innocent individual in a quandary and provides him no entirely satisfactory way out. From the protagonist's point of view, he is simply the random victim of appalling misfortune. In order for his predicament to interest an audience, however, it must somehow pertain to the audience's own concerns. The revenger's problem must be shared, albeit in an attenuated form, by the spectators to his tragedy; or, to put it the other way around, his dilemma must condense some more widely experienced anxiety into an artistically persuasive form.

The insupportable situations in which revengers find themselves therefore tend to reflect contradictions in which their entire society, or some large subsection of it, participates: points at which its self-conception is perniciously inconsistent, or at which it makes conflicting demands upon its members. Individual revengers do not reject the principles of their society but attempt to live them out, fulfilling difficult obligations to friends and kin. In order to do so, however, they sacrifice other pressing responsibilities. In Aeschylus' *Oresteia*, Orestes is bound both to honour his mother and to revenge his father's death: what is he to do, then, when his mother murders his father? Literary critics have shown how Orestes' dilemma reflects unresolved issues about gender roles and family structure in ancient Greece. Twentieth-century revenge tragedies often depict the norms of civilized custom colliding with the brutal amorality of the American frontier or the modern city.

Elizabethan and Jacobean revenge tragedies explore the particular stresses and incongruities produced by the highly stratified society of late sixteenth- and early seventeenth-century England. Throughout Renaissance Europe, social order was thought to depend upon a traditional network of obligations and privileges that bound patrons to dependants, sovereigns to subjects, aristocrats to retainers. Monarchs demanded that their nobles help them wage war; in turn they delegated the nobles' authority over certain territories or enterprises. Aristocratic landowners expected specific kinds of service and materials from their tenants; the tenants for their part felt entitled to traditionally fixed rents. Overt displays of dominance and submission marked degrees of rank: and everyone, of course, except the monarch at the apex of the pyramid, had to humble himself before someone else. Renaissance revenge tragedy taps the repressed frustrations of such situations, presenting the delicious spectacle of subjects hood-winking and finally annihilating their superiors.

Revenge tragedy reflects, however, not merely the predictable strains of life in a hierarchical society, but the less calculable effects of a hierarchy in the process of transformation. To many in Renaissance England, the ancient system of authority and deference seemed to be deteriorating. In the past, they thought, people had 'known their places', whether those places were high or low. The knowing of one's place is often not a legally enforceable or even a very explicit affair, however, but rather a matter of custom. Pedringano relies upon such tradition in *The Spanish Tragedy*, expecting after his arrest that his master Lorenzo will 'stand good lord, and help him in distress' (3.4). Pedringano is paid to murder Serberine, but he is not merely a mercenary. As a long-time family servant, he expects protection and reward for carrying out his master's commands.

Pedringano's faith is, of course, grossly misplaced. And although he is a rascal, his bitter experience reflects the fundamental dilemma with which English Renaissance revenge tragedy struggles. In *The Spanish Tragedy*, *The Revenger's Tragedy*, and *The Revenge of Bussy d'Ambois*, the hero is wronged by persons who conspicuously outrank him. Even in *The Atheist's Tragedy*, where the characters are close relatives, Charlemont is the villainous D'Amville's generational subordinate. In a system in which power is inherited, the vicious or incompetent master poses a seemingly intractable problem, for there is no institutionally legitimate way to dismiss him.

What is to be done when a powerful individual refuses to acknowledge the claims an inferior has upon him? One response is lament: in *The Spanish Tragedy*, Hieronimo's complaints about the indifference of kings and gods; in *The Revenge of Bussy d'Ambois*, the disgust voiced by Renel in the opening scene; in *The Revenger's Tragedy*, Vindice's yearning for a lost golden age, expressed from the margins of a decadent court. In this genre, dismay over the irresponsibility of rulers is so potent a sign of rectitude that villains hypocritically mouth such sentiments to gain their victims' confidence. In *The Revenge of Bussy d'Ambois*, the double agent Baligny excoriates the modern aristocracy in conversation with Renel; likewise D'Amville, in *The Atheist's Tragedy*, denounces baronial cowardice to Charlemont.

Revenge might even be thought of as lament provoked to action. Subjects may not vote their evil superiors out of office, but they may kill them. On the one hand, the revolt of the subordinate constitutes treason—in a hierarchically ordered society, the most heinous of crimes. On the other hand, in so far as the revenger aims not to overturn the social hierarchy but to restore its proper functioning, he is a conservative, not a revolutionary figure. Caught in a double bind, the revenger seems simultaneously an avatar and enemy of social order.

The complexities of the revenger's endeavour correlate with several important social changes in early modern England. In the sixteenth and seventeenth centuries there was more to the perception of a breakdown in class relations than the nostalgia that always makes the past seem nobler, simpler, and happier than the present. The period witnessed cataclysmic economic change. Rapid inflation, an increasingly sophisticated money economy, and sharp alterations in the relative profitability of different kinds of agricultural and mercantile enterprises, all encouraged a keener sense among the powerful classes of where their self-interests lay, and how those interests might conflict with their role as it had traditionally been defined. As they adapted to new circumstances—limiting, for instance, the number of retainers they employed or the kinds of hospitality they extended—those beneath them who had benefited from the older arrangements could suffer serious dislocation. Economic change created, moreover, anomalies in the social hierarchy, individuals whose wealth was out of proportion to their inherited positions. D'Amville, in *The Atheist's Tragedy*, is one kind of example: hoarding has made him richer than the younger brother of a baron ought to be. Renel in *The Revenge of Bussy d'Ambois*, or Vindice in *The Revenger's Tragedy*, is another kind of example: the destitute gentleman whose poverty debars him from the positions of authority to which he had assumed himself to be born.

Another significant change is the increasingly nationalist organization of much of Western Europe. Medieval monarchs had wielded relatively limited power. Many governmental tasks were performed by local magnates or their powerful functionaries, who operated with considerable impunity within their spheres of influence. In the sixteenth century, however, monarchs in England, France, and Spain consolidated their supremacy at the expense of the aristocracy. This consolidation affected not merely the members of that small group, but the prospects of the much larger class of people who would expect employment from them. From the point of view of those displaced by transformations in the system of patronage, newly powerful Renaissance monarchs seemed to be arrogating to themselves tyrannical power, riding roughshod over the restraints that had characterized an earlier era. Others, particularly university-educated men from the middling classes, found their opportunities improved in a national state, which needed competent administrators for its complex bureaucracy.

The three revenge tragedies in this volume that concern themselves with life at court—*The Spanish Tragedy*, *The Revenger's Tragedy*, and *The Revenge of Bussy d'Ambois*—all view with alarm a system that concentrates power in a single crowned head. In all three plays, the ruler's inattentiveness or outright corruption contributes to disaster, so that the line blurs between personal retaliation and political coup. Monarchical government traditionally claims as its duty and sole prerogative the prosecution and punishment of serious crimes, on the grounds that any felony committed against one of the king's subjects is automatically an offence against the king himself. Persons who take justice into their own hands implicitly proclaim their lack of faith in this system: either because, in their view, the monarch fails to dispense justice fairly or because the monarch himself is the offending party. Blood vengeance, in other words, almost automatically subverts the power of the crown.

None the less, the critique of monarchy differs from play to play. In a sense Kyd, who pioneers English revenge tragedy in the late 1580s, understands its premisses more radically than do many of his successors. His heroes are not aristocrats. Hieronimo is a civil servant who holds his position by virtue of expertise and hard work—the kind of person who in England had, in fact, benefited from nationalizing trends.

> There is not any advocate in Spain
> That can prevail, or will take half the pain
> That he will, in pursuit of equity. (3.13.52–4)

As knight-marshal, Hieronimo administers a legal code in which rewards are supposedly commensurate with deeds, not with social status; his zeal for 'equity' is entirely consistent with his meritocratic values. Likewise Horatio prevails on the battlefield, an arena in which strength and courage matter more than pedigree. In the opening scenes, demonstrated excellence and the patronage of a benign king are apparently enabling father and son to engineer their own advancement. They seem to have realized a dream of upward mobility shared by many able men of undistinguished origins, including Kyd himself.

This appearance, however, is deceiving. Birth rather than worth remains decisive in a Renaissance court, and the rare meritocrat finds himself awkwardly situated. The social strains are finely captured at the royal banquet: Horatio, who has captured Prince Balthazar in battle, waits upon the table where the King's erstwhile enemy is welcomed as a guest. As the action unfolds we realize, sooner than do Horatio or Hieronimo, that for the most powerful men in the play caste loyalties override the national interests for which Horatio fought and Don Andrea died. Lorenzo, the king's nephew, finds the foreign Prince Balthazar a fitter companion than his fellow-countryman Horatio. The King cultivates the good will of his Portuguese counterpart, swiftly forgetting his recent intransigence.

The international cohesiveness of the upper classes puts their hard-working subalterns at a social disadvantage; but were the aristocrats to honour their traditions of patronage, their snobbery would matter little. In Lorenzo, however, fierce class exclusivity combines lethally with a ruthless willingness to disregard *noblesse oblige*. Like the Duke or Lussurioso in *The Revenger's Tragedy*, like the King or Monsieur in *The Revenge of Bussy d'Ambois*, he exploits to the full the freedoms of his station without accepting its usual constraints. His blithe assumption that might makes right conflicts sensationally with the legal order that Hieronimo champions by virtue of his office, temperament, and social circumstances.

The casually murderous Lorenzo and the more passive but equally unprincipled Balthazar meet resistance not only from Hieronimo but from Bel-imperia. For Kyd, the high-born woman and the meritorious retainer seem natural allies. As the marriageable female most closely related to the Spanish king, Bel-imperia is a precious asset. Like Horatio or Hieronimo, though for different reasons, she occupies an apparently privileged position; but her entitlements, like theirs, turn out to be largely illusory. Balthazar goes through the motions of courtship, motions that pretend to honour her right of refusal. But when Bel-imperia continues to rebuff him, her desires are simply overridden. Her marriage is meant to gratify her male relatives and to cement a truce among nations, not to accommodate her preferences:

'young virgins', as the King says, 'must be rulèd by their friends' (2.3.43). Bel-imperia's simultaneous power and disability is expressed in her ambiguous name, 'beautiful dominion'. Is she a ruler, free to act upon her own desires, or a realm, a piece of valuable property to be bought and sold?

Like Hieronimo, Bel-imperia rebels against her superiors' assumption that people can be manipulated like things. Her spirited refusal to comply with the dictates of a patriarchal system makes her an attractive character. There is a strong family resemblance, however, between Bel-imperia and Lorenzo. Like her brother's, Bel-imperia's patrician self-assertion is unchecked by sentiment or moral scruple. Since beauty is her only weapon, she deploys it with great calculation.

> Yes, second love shall further my revenge.
> I'll love Horatio, my Andrea's friend,
> The more to spite the prince that wrought his end. (1.4.66–8)

Ignoring conventions of feminine reticence and pre-marital chastity, Bel-imperia takes lovers from the classes below her. In the power dynamics of these relationships, her exalted social rank more than compensates for the normally weaker female position. 'I reaped more grace than I deserved or hoped,' exclaims the dazzled Horatio when she favours him with her glove (1.4.103). Bel-imperia's taste in men would infuriate Lorenzo and Balthazar even if one of them were not Horatio's rival: for sexual involvement across class lines annuls the distinction between blueblood and upstart, implying that high birth need not correlate with gifts of mind or body.

At the beginning of the last act Lorenzo and Balthazar believe themselves to have subdued Bel-imperia and propitiated Hieronimo. Shortly thereafter all four characters are dead, slain in what had seemed a strange but trifling amusement. Though Kyd derives the revenge plot and the revenger's heightened rhetoric from classical models, the idea of making the revenge itself a *coup de theatre* is probably his innovation, and certainly one of the ways *The Spanish Tragedy* most influences later Renaissance dramatists.

What is the connection between revenge and theatrical display? Legally prescribed punishments were themselves popular spectacles throughout Renaissance Europe. Beheadings, hangings, whippings, and pilloryings occurred on raised platforms before large crowds. Many such penalties had symbolic dimensions. Adulterers were paraded in bedsheets; traitors disembowelled to signify the exposure of their secret malice. The revenger's methods, in other words, do not deviate as markedly as a modern audience might assume from the normal routines of Renaissance justice. The effects of public punishments upon their audiences were, moreover, akin to some of the purposes of tragedy as Renaissance literary theorists construed them: rousing horror and pity, emphasizing the affinity between sin and its castigation, heightening awareness of the mutability of fortune.

Hieronimo's conflation of revenge and theatre, however, goes beyond simple analogy. He wants not merely to extract fitting compensation for Horatio's death, but to educate his royal audience in the meaning of his vengeance. The revenger uses his power over his enemies to force them, or their surviving kin, to see things from his perspective. 'See here my show, look on this spectacle!' exclaims Hieronimo at the end of *Spanish Tragedy*.

> Speak, Portuguese, whose loss resembles mine:
> If thou canst weep upon thy Balthazar,
> 'Tis like I wailed for my Horatio.
> And you, my lord, whose reconcilèd son
> Marched in a net, and thought himself unseen,
> And rated me for brainsick lunacy,
> With 'God amend that mad Hieronimo!'—
> How can you brook our play's catastrophe? (4.4)

Neglected by those who would amplify the differences between those who command and those who obey, Hieronimo defiantly insists upon the similarities between king and subject, aristocrat and commoner. To prove that identical losses produce identical grief he uses theatre, the most powerful tool the Renaissance had to assert the resemblances among human beings, and to induce empathetic identification. The resources of theatre are, moreover, peculiarly available to Hieronimo, whose career as lawyer and court poet depend upon his literacy.

Certainly it is easy to imagine that Thomas Kyd—talented, impoverished, spurned by the great men whose patronage he sought—invested some of his own resentments in the terms of Hieronimo's appalling triumph. At any rate, the reception of his play suggests that Hieronimo's insistence upon the value of his point of view resonated with the theatre audience if not with his onstage foes. Contemporaries most often call the play simply 'Geronimo' after the name of its hero. The unknown writer who contributed the 'additions' to Kyd's play for a revival staged in the late 1590s or early 1600s seems likewise to have assumed that the interest of *The Spanish Tragedy* resided largely in its depiction of the revenger. Rather than elaborating the plot, or delving into the motivations of other characters, the additions augment Hieronimo's role.

The culminating example of revenge-tragedy-as-character-study is Shakespeare's *Hamlet*, itself a revision of a lost play by Kyd, with its overwhelming concentration upon the hero's tormented complexity. This is not the only direction, however, in which revenge tragedy might develop. *The Revenger's Tragedy*, first performed in 1606 or 1607, represents a self-conscious departure from the models provided by the revised *Spanish Tragedy* or the Shakespearean *Hamlet*. Highly sensitive to the theatrical ingenuity of *Hamlet*—it appropriates, for instance, the striking detail of the hero musing upon a skull—*The Revenger's Tragedy* deliberately eschews its psychological intricacy. Its flat, extravagant characters and their allegorical names recall the medieval morality play rather than the complex characterological portraits of its recent predecessors. In its artistic self-consciousness, its forthright repudiation of naturalism, and its witty satiric irreverence, *The Revenger's Tragedy* has seemed to some twentieth-century artists, like the French surrealist Antonin Artaud, an uncanny precursor of their own sensibility.[1]

In political terms, however, *The Revenger's Tragedy* is more conservative in its implications than *The Spanish Tragedy*. We learn early on that Vindice's destitution is the result of the Duke's unconscionable neglect of his well-born father. Unlike Hieronimo, in other words, Vindice is not presented as a meritorious parvenu, but as the head of a traditionally respected family struggling to regain his proper social place. The play's satiric commentary—from Vindice, from Hippolito, from Castiza, even from Gratiana—persistently contrasts modern depravity with a more virtuous past. After the two dukes are eliminated, Antonio's government is described not as the triumph of novelty but as the welcome renewal of an older order.

Not surprisingly, then, the disruptive alliance Kyd suggests between the male subordinate who forges his own political agenda, and the female aristocrat who chooses her own lovers, is not repeated in *The Revenger's Tragedy*. Instead the play depicts a contest among men over the possession of women defined as the passive objects of male transactions: 'Wives are but made to go to bed and feed' (1.1). Because

---

[1] Artaud claims that *The Revenger's Tragedy* 'completely agrees with what we mean and want to be . . . [it] is very close to our *angst*, our rebelliousness, our aspirations' (*The Alfred Jarry Theatre*, in *Collected Works*, trans. Victor Corti (London: Calder and Boyars, 1968)).

Vindice derives his sense of identity and purpose from his place as head of a family, he resists not only those who hurt or kill his kinfolk, but anything that tends to disrupt the kinship system in the abstract, even apart from its particular consequences to his own case. Adultery, incest, rape, and prostitution confuse the paternity of children, making it unclear who one's kin really are. Such sins undermine the principles upon which Vindice grounds his sense of self and his concept of social order.

In *The Revenger's Tragedy* specific male privileges—supervision of daughters and sisters, access to wives and fiancées—become synecdoches for political rights in general. The members of the ruling family prove themselves tyrants by intruding upon their subordinates' sexual prerogatives. The connection between concupiscence and misgovernment is clarified, for the classically-minded Renaissance audience, by an incident in Roman history: when Tarquin, the son of the Roman king, raped Lucretia, the wife of one of his generals, she committed suicide and touched off a revolution which ended in the expulsion of the royal family from Rome. This story is deliberately recapitulated in *The Revenger's Tragedy*'s subplot, in which Junior Brother's violation of Antonio's unnamed lady precipitates a coup. Its terms also inform the main plot, in which Vindice clashes with the Duke over the possession of Gloriana, and with Lussurioso over the possession of Castiza. As prospective bridegroom in the first case and head of the family in the second, it is *his* right, not merely that of the women involved, which exercises his passion.

The Revenger's Tragedy is obsessed with the possibility of whoredom, because the whore—whether outright prostitute or mere adulterous woman—generates pleasure and profit on her own behalf rather than yielding her body to the interests of husband or father. Unlike land or objects, women have wills of their own and may elude male control, endangering the implicit but fundamental analogy between women and property, and between sexual and political prerogatives. Vindice connects female unreliability with the perilous 'openness' of the female anatomy, its susceptibility to invasion through its apertures. 'That woman is all male, whom none can enter,' he comments (2.1), using the word 'enter' to mean both 'persuade' and 'penetrate sexually'.

Little in the play challenges Vindice's assumptions. All the sexually experienced women are polluted in one way or another, intentionally or against their will. Gratiana is corrupted by a bawd, Antonio's lady tainted by rape. The scheming Duchess cuckolds her husband with his bastard. The extremely high value Vindice places on virginity is one corollary of his particular form of misogyny: only the woman who has not been 'entered' may escape the usual female frailties. Moreover, even while female vice seems deeply subversive, there seems little scope for active female virtue: the good women in the play are either victims or potential victims rescued by their male relations. The resolute Castiza, sequestered at home, has no part in or knowledge of her brothers' conspiracies, and her only strength is in simple resistance. She plays no political role, simply vanishing with her mother from the play once the men have forcibly restored Gratiana to the path of virtue.

If the gender and class politics of *The Revenger's Tragedy* are less daring than Kyd's, however, its theatrical technique is even more original. It invents uniquely clever solutions to some of the formal and generic problems raised by the revenge plot. If revenge plays are to consist of more than two scenes, their authors must devise plausible excuses for temporarily suspending the action. Some inhibition or accident must interfere between the initial demand for revenge and its execution. Thus Kyd's Hieronimo does not initially know the identity of his son's murderers and has reason to doubt the information he does receive. Chapman's Clermont, whose moral scruples require him to conduct his revenge in an above-board manner, is temporarily frustrated by a reclusive opponent and by his own unexpected arrest for treason. The hero's temperamental indecisiveness and evidentiary difficulties occupy the middle of *Hamlet*.

The Revenger's Tragedy, however, takes a different tack. Vindice, whose name means 'revenger' and who has two offences to requite, is only one among many agents of retaliation in the play. The Duchess and Spurio think of their incest as revenge upon the Duke, revenge that in Spurio's case is meant to spite the Duke and Duchess's legitimate children as well. The Duchess's sons plot against Lussurioso and against one another. Hippolito, Antonio, and others plan reprisals for the rape of Antonio's wife. With so many plots afoot, the conspirators get in one another's way. Lussurioso, told of his stepmother's affair with Spurio, abandons his plan to seduce or rape Castiza in order to expose the adulterers; but he misses the bastard, who has gone to ambush him outside Castiza's house. Meanwhile Ambitioso and Supervacuo disastrously bungle their schemes against Lussurioso. That the Duke eventually perishes is not surprising: rather it is surprising, in this welter of inept intrigue, that he lives long enough to receive his death-blow from Vindice. Likewise

Lussurioso, surrounded by malice he is too stupid to notice, almost miraculously survives until the middle of the last act, when not one but two groups of revengers arrive to finish him off.

In such unsettled circumstances, Vindice's success depends upon a talent for improvisation. His opportunistic, manipulative intelligence is a trait more commonly associated with comic than with tragic characters: and this is not the play's only affinity with comedy or farce. *The Revenger's Tragedy* emphasizes the artificiality, even the silliness, of many of the familiar procedures of English revenge tragedy. The outraged-but-witty revenger, the unspeakable villains, the maniacally complicated forms of retaliation, the revenge-as-theatrical-performance: all are overstated to the point of caricature. Gloriana's skull, the revenger's *memento mori*, is employed so bizarrely that it loses most of its intrinsic dreadfulness: the Duke's poisoning has some of the campy black humour of a Halloween caper. At other points potentially chilling turns of plot are openly played for laughs, as when the incorrect head is delivered to Ambitioso and Supervacuo, or when the second masque of revengers find to their bewilderment that their murderous work has already been done.

Often such playfulness subverts the austere morality of the revenge-play genre. It is standard, for instance, for revengers to muse upon the relationship between their actions and God's justice, and to seek some transcendental sign of divine collaboration or approval. In *The Revenger's Tragedy*, Vindice exclaims with exasperation upon Lussurioso's gross hypocrisy:

> Is there no thunder left, or is't kept up
> In stock for heavier vengeance? (4.2.196–7)

Just at that moment, thunder conveniently sounds. 'There it goes!' remarks Vindice, drawing attention to the theatrical contrivance. When thunder rolls again at Lussurioso's death, the self-conscious jest is even clearer: 'Dost know thy cue?' The emphasis upon the stage-trick tends to sabotage any serious allusion to heavenly wrath.

The end of the play provides yet another example of the way *The Revenger's Tragedy* questions the logic of revenge-play conventions even while seeming to employ them. The death of the revenger is a virtually unbreakable rule in English Renaissance revenge plays: the success of his plot incurs a blood-guilt for which his life must satisfy. Often, like Hieronimo, he has no desire to outlive his vengeance, and his suicide suggests his own acceptance of the stern law by which he is judged. By contrast, Vindice commits not one but two perfect crimes. Nothing about the conduct of his vengeance necessitates his death. His exposure and execution do not suggest the ineluctable workings of fate, the wrath of an unappeased deity, or the torment of agonized conscience. Rather they are consequences of Vindice's effervescent inability to keep his mouth shut, and of Antonio's priggish eagerness to distance himself from the actions that bring him to power.

Revenge for Vindice, as for Hieronimo, is itself a kind of theatre. Vindice shares Hieronimo's didactic zeal. Careful choreography allows plenty of time to instruct the Duke in the meaning of his death; the dying Lussurioso must also be apprised of his assailant's identity. In both *The Spanish Tragedy* and *The Revenger's Tragedy* successful revenge is thus connected with the moment of revelation that Aristotle claims is the end to which all tragedy moves. None the less, the two works reflect upon theatricality in different ways and for different ends. In *The Spanish Tragedy* the frame episodes ironically imply that human beings are, like actors in a play, working through scripts they have not themselves written. Just as Balthazar and Lorenzo unwittingly put themselves at the mercy of Hieronimo's malevolent authorial imagination, so Hieronimo unknowingly carries out the plans of the gods. The characters' sense of freedom and control is a wishful delusion, as empty as the box that supposedly contains Pedringano's non-existent pardon. Kyd uses theatrical metaphors to suggest drastic limitations upon what people know and hence upon their capacity for self-direction. *The Revenger's Tragedy* by contrast emphasizes not the determinism of the theatrical situation, but the duplicity of theatrical disguise. Looking at the skull he has 'dressed in tires', Vindice wonders:

> Does every proud and self-affecting dame
> Camphor her face for this? and grieve her Maker
> In sinful baths of milk, when many an infant starves,
> For her superfluous outside—all for this? (3.5.83–6)

His grotesque puppet, he implies, is little different from the live woman she counterfeits: a 'superfluous outside', ornamental and misleading, concealing the rotten truth within.

Both *The Spanish Tragedy* and *The Revenger's Tragedy* are deeply pessimistic, even nihilistic works. In neither play do the consolations of religion seem at all compelling. In *The Spanish Tragedy*, the Christian sentiments erratically expressed by Isabella and Hieronimo appear simply misplaced, since the afterworld we see authoritatively presented in the frame episodes is a pagan one. Moreover, the dispensations of divine justice are hardly reassuring. In the induction Minos, Rhadamanth, and Aeacus, stymied by a simple classification difficulty, subject Andrea to onerous bureaucratic delays. When the case finally comes before Pluto, the king of Hades responds not to the logic of Andrea's circumstances but to Proserpine's flirtatious intercession. At the end of the play, the fate of the other characters is left in Andrea's partial hands. He places Bel-imperia incongruously with the vestal virgins, punishes Lorenzo (not Balthazar) as an aspiring lover, and treats Castile as severely as Horatio's murderers, although his only conceivable offence has been his disapproval of Bel-imperia's affair. Kyd's Hades seems as capricious and nepotistic as the court of Spain: it reproduces rather than compensates for the defects of this world.

If *The Spanish Tragedy* suggests that the structure of the universe is irretrievably faulty, *The Revenger's Tragedy* suggests that it is radically mysterious. Parodying, as we have seen, the way the revenge genre represents the workings of Providence, the play perhaps mocks as well the very idea of divine intervention in human affairs. Lacking the usual revenge-tragedy ghost, it remains agnostic even on the basic issue of life after death. In this mysterious universe, the transcendental source of justice is obscure. Amoral self-assertion replaces allegiance to a divine power: the only sanction Vindice respects is his own. 'We have enough | I' faith, we're well,' he proclaims triumphantly on his way to execution (5.3).

As I mentioned earlier, *The Revenge of Bussy d'Ambois*, first performed in 1610 or 1611, and *The Atheist's Tragedy*, published in 1611 and probably first performed in the previous year, might be considered 'anti-revenge plays'. While employing some mechanisms of the traditional plot, they distance themselves more emphatically than their two predecessors from the principle of retaliation. Since ambivalence about the ethics of revenge is built into the form already, however, the moral qualms Chapman and Tourneur express are not their most important innovation. Rather, each play attempts to domesticate some of the genre's disruptive energies, suggesting constructive alternatives to the supposedly necessary atrocities of vengeance. Readers and audiences who find *The Spanish Tragedy* or *The Revenger's Tragedy* pointlessly bleak may welcome this development. Those who relish the disturbing ironies of the earlier revenge plays are likely to find their successors wishful or simplistic.

In both *The Revenge of Bussy d'Ambois* and *The Atheist's Tragedy* traditional codes of belief and behaviour, however threatened, have a certain explanatory value and practical efficacy. This is not to say that the virtuous necessarily triumph. *The Revenge of Bussy d'Ambois* ends with the suicide of the hero, as he contemplates a world from which, with the assassination of his patron, all moral good seems to have vanished, 'and I left negligent | To all the horrors of the vicious time':

> Shall I here survive,
> Not cast me after him into the sea,
> Rather than here live, ready every hour
> To feed thieves, beasts, and be the slave of power? (5.5.185–92)

But despite Clermont's well-founded disgust for the French court, he earns praise from both enemies and friends. Similarly, in *The Atheist's Tragedy* even D'Amville acknowledges Charlemont's generosity and courage. In both plays those who do not practice virtue appreciate it when they see it, a form of discernment unthinkable for the villains of *The Spanish Tragedy* or *The Revenger's Tragedy*.

In these morally more clear-cut worlds, it seems likely that villains will receive their just deserts even without the heroes' intervention. *The Revenge of Bussy d'Ambois* ends with King Henry still in control, but members of Chapman's audience conversant with recent French history would have known that his downfall occurred only a few months later, just as Guise predicts in his dying minutes. In *The Atheist's Tragedy*, D'Amville's collapse requires no action on Charlemont's part: 'atheism' is simply unsustainable given the way the world works in this play.

In neither of the later plays is the wronged hero an enthusiastic revenger. In *The Revenge of Bussy d'Ambois* Clermont takes minimal vengeance, challenging his brother's murderer to a duel. By dispassionately observing the protocols regulating such disputes, he avoids the typical revenger's excesses. In *The Atheist's Tragedy*, Charlemont remains almost entirely passive in the face of outrageous provocation. When he is once tempted to retaliate, the ghost of his murdered father orders him to desist. Old Montferrers is meant to contrast vividly with the typical, vindictive revenge-play phantom.

Despite these similarities, the plays employ revenge-play conventions to drastically dissimilar ends. *The Revenge of Bussy d'Ambois*, loosely based on recent events in France, concerns itself overtly and at length with political themes that, as we have seen, are revenge-tragedy stock-in-trade, but which the other plays by comparison subordinate to the development of the plot and character. The problems of tyranny so dominate Chapman's play that they threaten to derail the story of vengeance. Clermont's abortive arrest for treason is causally unrelated to his role as Montsurry's nemesis; for Chapman, however, it seems thematically appropriate to connect even reluctant revenge with suspected resistance to a central authority. Likewise the historically specific, nearly contemporary setting, so different from Kyd's inaccurate Spain or the fantasy Italy of *The Revenger's Tragedy*, supports Chapman's thematic agenda. Like England, France developed into a true nation-state in the sixteenth century, but across the Channel the concentration of power in the sovereign was far more thorough. Along with imperial Rome—another authoritarian, centralized regime often mentioned in *The Revenge of Bussy d'Ambois*—the French example attracted those in England who welcomed such concentration of power and dismayed those who did not.

Chapman's techniques of characterization are consistent with his conception of revenge tragedy as political theatre. His characters define their individual interests in terms of a larger communal framework. The difference between the virtuous and the vicious lies in how they define that explanatory context. For the worldly Maillard and Baligny, the amoral court provides the only standards for their actions: both men justify perjury and fraud on the basis of their expediency for the king's faction. Clermont, by contrast, sees himself as participating in an orderly universe under the auspices of what he calls the Great Cause. From this wider perspective, he is able to condemn local perversions of the world order instead of capitulating to them.

Clermont derives his philosophy from classical Stoics, mainly Epictetus and Seneca. The Stoic tries to achieve a happiness defined as internal to his own state of mind, detached from the vicissitudes of the external world:

> To love nothing outward
> Or not within our own powers to command,
> And so being sure of everything we love,
> Who cares to lose the rest? (4.5.4–7)

Since Clermont's equanimity cannot be shaken by any afflictions his enemies can visit upon him, he is not susceptible to injuries that demand retaliation. Revengers like Hieronimo or Vindice, nursing their sense of intolerable wrong, seem to the Stoic to have grievously misconstrued the sources of true happiness.

Clermont's reluctance to take revenge, then, follows from what he believes to be true of the universe and the human mind. His attitude had much to recommend it in the turbulent world of sixteenth-century Europe, where in fact Stoicism underwent a revival in the face of protracted religious warfare and economic distress. None the less, such detachment is costly. Clermont's friendship with the Guise elicits ridicule from the Monsieur, who insultingly calls Clermont a 'minion' or homosexual favourite. Monsieur, however, misconstrues the situation: Clermont prefers male friendships to relationships with women not because the former permit secret sexual indulgence, but because they seem to escape it. The Stoic's denigration of dependency encourages contempt for the needy body and a deep suspicion of sexual love, in which emotional satisfaction depends upon another person's co-operation. In a chilling passage about the Countess, whose sorrow on his behalf has blinded her, Clermont insists upon the difference between sexual lust, a purely carnal affair, and chaste 'masculine' love that requires no sexual expression. Marriage, in his view, is merely a socially sanctioned outlet for sordid impulses.

Clermont's dismissiveness towards sexuality, an attitude which the play as a whole seems to endorse, has unfortunate consequences for the women characters. In most Renaissance plays—certainly in the four collected here—women's roles are determined by their sexual connection to the male characters. But in cases where that sexual sphere is assumed to be a pre-eminently significant one for both men and women, women are allotted certain limited powers. Thus in *The Spanish Tragedy*, as we have seen, Bel-imperia is a force to be reckoned with; and in *The Revenger's Tragedy* Vindice's nervous misogyny backhandedly acknowledges the disruptive possibility of female initiative. In *The Revenge of Bussy d'Ambois*, by contrast, women become virtually irrelevant. Tamyra, an impetuous descendant of Bel-imperia, defiantly makes her own sexual choices but in a context which renders her peripheral. The Countess's feminine emotional susceptibility, although touching, precipitates just the kind of over-reaction to misfortune that the Stoic wisely eschews; she weeps herself blind for what turns out to be no reason at all. Since the brave, self-reliant behaviour the Stoic admires as virtuous is culturally coded as 'masculine', the virago Charlotte seems the woman most likely to take effective action, and indeed she attempts to avenge Bussy in male disguise. But her subterfuge comes to nothing as she, too, ends up a mere spectator to her brother's duel. As an alternative to heroic endeavour, all Clermont offers her is a sarcastic invitation to worry about cosmetics: superficial matters beneath the notice of the philosophical male.

Another problem Chapman must confront is the difficulty of translating the Stoic's resolute inwardness into a theatrical form necessarily committed to external display. Clermont's defence of theatre is telling: in his view, it teaches audiences to view with indifference the variety and unpredictability of worldly fortune. Thrilling depictions of spectacular adventures would undermine rather than reinforce this indifference. Throughout *The Revenge of Bussy d'Ambois*, Chapman refuses to exploit the dramatic possibilities of his material. When Clermont is ambushed he performs courageous feats, but these are reported to us rather than acted out. Likewise the Guise tells Clermont in 5.1 that he has been accosted by an apparently supernatural voice, but we see nothing of this on stage; nor are we ever shown a clear confrontation between Guise's forces and the King's. Chapman suggests that the radically undramatic quality of *The Revenge of Bussy d'Ambois* was a subject of criticism in his own time, admitting in his preface that 'in the scenical presentation it might meet with some maligners'. But however perverse the play's priorities may seem from a theatrical point of view, they are fully consistent with the ethical ideals to which Clermont subscribes: his Stoic conviction that truth is invisible, interior, and undisplayable.

Like *The Revenge of Bussy d'Ambois*, *The Atheist's Tragedy* presents the 'necessity' for revenge as unreal. The idea that revenge sets right an unjust universe is once again shown to be delusive. But Tourneur's case for quietism is profoundly different from Chapman's; and in a variety of ways his play differs significantly, too, from *The Spanish Tragedy* and *The Revenger's Tragedy*. *The Atheist's Tragedy* does not concern itself with the relation between rulers and their subjects, but with a family rivalry. Moreover, the threat to social order in the play comes not from above, from a tyrant's absolutist aspirations, but from below. D'Amville, the villain of the play, is a younger brother, by law and by custom the eldest brother's subordinate in social status and in his claims on the family estate. From Nature, defined as the 'low' material processes of the observable world, he derives a model of unprincipled struggle for selfish goals. D'Amville's aggressive acquisitiveness is consistent with the entrepreneurial instincts of the incipient capitalist classes of sixteenth- and early seventeenth-century Europe.

Certainly he makes wealth his idol: Tourneur never tires of reiterating the irony that 'atheism' does not mean freeing oneself from the adoration of a deity, but merely substituting a false and debased god for the true one. Predictably his materialist villain allies himself with Languebeau Snuffe, the hypocritical innovator in religious matters, just as in real-life London, merchants impatient with archaic ways of conducting business tended to find common cause with Puritan iconoclasts. Tourneur's deviations from the revenge-tragedy format have important consequences. When kings and powerful aristocrats abuse their authority, as we have seen, their inferiors have reason to feel that existing social institutions cannot remedy the situation. But in *The Atheist's Tragedy*, where danger is imagined as erupting from below, it can be handled by the authoritative reintroduction of traditional hierarchies. In this play nothing is systematically the matter with the status quo—with the institutions of marriage or of primogeniture, for instance. Things merely go temporarily awry.

Villainy in *The Atheist's Tragedy* tends to take the form of fraud; and interestingly, being an imposter means cynically ventriloquizing the conventions of revenge tragedy. The handkerchief Borachio exhibits to support his false report of Charlemont's death is a stage descendant of Bel-imperia's ill-starred 'favour' in *The Spanish Tragedy*, which Horatio takes from the dead Andrea's arm, and which Hieronimo later cherishes in memory of Horatio. Similarly, when Charlemont arrives unexpectedly from France in 3.3—having been visited by a real ghost—D'Amville 'counterfeits to take him for a ghost', a pretence which in the grammar of revenge tragedy puts him inappropriately in the place of a victim of injustice, rather than in the place of the villain. D'Amville knows, too, how to deploy a particular kind of bombast, originally derived from Seneca, which Renaissance dramatists used as the mark of the distraught revenger.

> Drop out
> Mine eye-balls, and let envious Fortune play
> At tennis with 'em. (2.4.27–9)

The extravagant terms in which Hieronimo expresses grief in the original or the revised *Spanish Tragedy* is meant to indicate utter lack of calculation. D'Amville, however, realizes that unpremeditated over-reaction can be feigned, and he uses it successfully to assert his innocence at Montferrers's death. In the final scene, unhinged by his sons' deaths, he speaks 'revenger's rhetoric' again, this time condemned to use it sincerely.

The way D'Amville's counterfeiting tends to become genuine marks an important innovation of Tourneur's play. Whereas the usual structure of the revenge play separates its outright villains, roundly condemned, from the ambivalently-handled retaliating victim, *The Atheist's Tragedy* combines the disturbing aspects of a Lorenzo and a Hieronimo, or a Duke and a Vindice, in the same character. D'Amville is his own worst enemy: it is as if after he wrongs Charlemont he then revenges the iniquity upon himself. His futility is represented in ways that seem contrived to a modern reader and probably seemed contrived in their own time, but which certainly emphasize his self-destructiveness.

What makes revenge unnecessary in *The Atheist's Tragedy* is the existence of the God whom D'Amville repudiates, a God who punishes wrongdoing and compensates for apparent injustices. The virtuous man confidently turns over his case to the monarch of heaven as, in this world, he was supposed to rely upon the Crown to punish felonious assaults. *The Atheist's Tragedy* salvages the absolute power other revenge tragedies condemn, by associating it not with fallible human authorities but with a beneficent deity. Like *The Revenge of Bussy d'Ambois*, Tourneur's play takes issue not merely with the morality of revenge, but with the plausibility of the worlds in which revenge tragedies typically imagine their action taking place.

Against D'Amville's subversiveness, Tourneur pits the profoundly conventional virtues of Charlemont and Castabella: respect for parents, fear of God, love of one another, courage in adversity. Sometimes Charlemont's expressions of contempt for externals can sound almost Stoic:

> I've lost a signory
> That was confined within a piece of earth,
> A wart upon the body of the world.
> But now I am an emp'ror of a world,
> This little world of man. (3.3)

Charlemont's virtue, however, is structured quite differently from Clérmont's. In fact, Tourneur decisively parts company from Chapman on the issue of what counts as meritorious, and the disparities here go to the heart of the differences between the two plays.

The Stoic Cause or Necessity that Clermont invokes is an entirely impersonal force, and Chapman rigorously insists, in orthodox Stoic fashion, that the 'happiness' achieved by submitting to Necessity is very much its own reward. Although Clermont may be worthier than the other characters, he ends up dead none the less. Because Stoicism spurns everything most human beings desire, it is almost by definition the practice of an élite—in *The Revenge of Bussy d'Ambois*, even Guise cannot maintain the correct attitude consistently. By contrast, 'rank custom' is imagined to be incapacitating: blindly imitating one another's folly, ordinary people wander in a moral labyrinth without even realizing that they are lost.

The Stoic's main weapon against custom is philosophical disputation. Clermont's virtue manifests itself largely in reasoned argument—certainly we see him talking more than we see him acting, though Chapman would resist separating the two enterprises. Since classical times Stoicism has expressed itself in terms of paradox and conundrum, and Clermont's arguments, challenging received ideas, are often radically counterintuitive. His eccentric justification of theatre, his strange defence of Guise's role in the Massacre, and his odd choice of suicide, all astonish either his interlocutors or the theatre audience, or both.

In *The Atheist's Tragedy*, by contrast, custom rightly understood is the path to happiness. Few behave as well as Charlemont and Castabella, but everyone understands the widely endorsed principles behind their behaviour. Moreover, the world is structured in such a way that faith is eventually rewarded in easily comprehensible terms: with happy marriage, wealth, titles. The 'custom' to which Charlemont and Castabella adhere is closely related to their piety: they refuse on principle to subject basic rules of conduct to the scrutiny of human reason. For D'Amville, the apparent irrationality of the incest taboo is reason to break it; but Castabella replies:

> I could confute
> You, but the horror of the argument
> Confounds my understanding. (4.3.140–2)

Similarly when Charlemont, imprisoned and deprived of his birthright and his beloved, begins to question the wisdom of the divine plan, he swiftly stops himself with a resolution to avoid 'profane conceit' (3.3.13). Charlemont and Castabella are not stupid, but they practise a virtue for which intellection is superfluous. The perfervidly clever D'Amville, by contrast, kills himself by a blow to the brain.

Tourneur's conviction that the universe is ultimately congenial to virtuous human beings has important dramaturgical consequences. *The Atheist's Tragedy* prominently features emblematic or allegorical

moments that assert the correspondence between spiritual and material truths, between heavenly and mundane realms, between God and
human beings. In this respect Tourneur's method diverges sharply
from Chapman's, and functions quite differently as well from the
superficially similar technique of *The Revenger's Tragedy*. In *The
Revenger's Tragedy*, for instance, the roll of thunder is handled so as
to make the possible intervention of a deity seem a mere stage device.
In *The Atheist's Tragedy*, however, when thunder sounds after Montferrers's murder, it quite straightforwardly signifies divine displeasure, and D'Amville's attempts to reassure Borachio ring hollow.

In *The Atheist's Tragedy* emblematic devices acquire complexity not
because they are used ironically, but because the same symbol
resonates in a variety of directions, all of them quite orthodox. Much
of the fourth act, for instance, takes place in a graveyard. In the often
very funny scenes between Languebeau and Coquette, the setting
functions as a reminder of the mortal corruption their sexual relation
both exemplifies and attempts to ignore. Later, however, the same
graveyard reinforces the *contemptus mundi* of Charlemont and Castabella, found together using a death's head as a pillow. Elsewhere, too,
dramatic events, places, and appearances work to reinforce the play's
moral lesson. Act 5 opens upon the spectacle of D'Amville's ill-gotten
gains, a pile of gold derived from Montferrers's estate. By the scene's
end, the biers of Rousard and Sebastian are juxtaposed with it, a
tableau vividly illustrating the collapse of D'Amville's materialist
ambitions. While the Stoic claims of *The Revenge of Bussy d'Ambois*
inhibit its theatrical effectiveness, the piety of *The Atheist's Tragedy*
enhances its forcefulness onstage.

The four markedly varied plays in this volume participate in and
help create a living tradition of representing revenge in the theatre.
The highly self-conscious ways they respond to and refract the
tensions of the society in which they were created still speak to
audiences and readers today.

NOTE ON THE TEXTS

IN this edition, spelling and punctuation have been modernized to a British standard. Names of characters have been silently standardized in the speech headings and stage directions. The Latin stage directions favoured by Chapman have been translated. Stage directions have been added, in brackets, to clarify the action for a reader.

The notes elucidate difficult wording, note puns and *double entendres*, provide information on staging, fill out historical context, indicate verbal references to other literary works, and very occasionally point out the significance of scenes or exchanges likely to be obscure to a non-specialist reader. Words and phrases whose difficulty is dependent upon context are paraphrased in the notes. Obsolete words, mythological names, and so forth, are listed in the glossary.

The plays as printed here are based upon the following texts: *The Spanish Tragedy*: 1592 quarto; additions from the 1602 quarto; *The Revenger's Tragedy*: 1607/8 quarto; *The Revenge of Bussy d'Ambois*: 1612/13 quarto; *The Atheist's Tragedy*: 1611 quarto.

The following modern editions have been consulted: *The Spanish Tragedy*, ed. J. R. Mulryne (New York: Norton, 1989); *The First Part of Hieronimo and The Spanish Tragedy*, ed. Andrew Cairncross (Lincoln: University of Nebraska Press, 1967); *The Spanish Tragedy with Additions: 1602*, ed. W. W. Greg (Oxford: Malone Society Reprints, 1925); *The Works of Thomas Kyd*, ed. Frederick Boas (Oxford: Clarendon, 1901); *The Works of Cyril Tourneur*, ed. Allardyce Nicoll (London: Fanfrolico Press, 1930); *The Revenger's Tragedy*, ed. Lawrence J. Ross (Lincoln: University of Nebraska Press, 1966); *The Revenger's Tragedy*, ed. R. A. Foakes (Cambridge, Mass.: Harvard University Press, 1966); *The Plays of George Chapman: The Tragedies*, ed. Allan Holaday and Robert J. Lordi (Cambridge: D. S. Brewer, 1987); *The Revenge of Bussy d'Ambois*, ed. Robert J. Lordi (Salzburg: Institute für Englische Sprache, 1977); *The Atheist's Tragedy*, ed. Irving Ribner (Cambridge, Mass.: Harvard University Press, 1964); *The Atheist's Tragedy*, ed. Brian Morris and Roma Gill (New York: Norton, 1976); *Classics of the Renaissance Theater*, ed. J. Dennis Huston and Alvin B. Kernan (New York: Harcourt Brace and World, 1969).

SELECT BIBLIOGRAPHY

THERE are few book-length studies of revenge tragedy *per se*. The most readable comprehensive survey of the genre is still Fredson Bowers, *Elizabethan Revenge Tragedy* (Princeton, NJ: Princeton University Press, 1940). The poet T. S. Eliot discusses the influence of the Roman playwright Seneca upon English revenge plays in two essays, 'Seneca in Elizabethan Translation' and 'Cyril Tourneur', in *Essays on Elizabethan Drama* (New York: Harcourt, Brace, and World, 1932). Gordon Braden, in *Renaissance Tragedy and the Senecan Tradition: Anger's Privilege* (New Haven, Conn.: Yale University Press, 1985), shows that Seneca provides Renaissance dramatists not merely a stylistic model but a world-view and mode of conceiving character that resonates powerfully with their own experience.

More general discussions of tragedy often have interesting implications for revenge plays. For instance, although Antonin Artaud's *Theater and Its Double*, trans. Mary Caroline Richards (New York: Grove Press, 1958), does not discuss revenge plays directly, it remains a provocative manifesto of theatrical anti-naturalism, full of implications for the ritual mayhem of *The Spanish Tragedy* and *The Revenger's Tragedy*. Several critics of Renaissance tragedy have found the theological scepticism of *The Spanish Tragedy* and *The Revenger's Tragedy* congenial, and the plays' stylized characters and plots grounds for enthusiasm rather than dismay. Jonathan Dollimore, *Radical Tragedy: Religion, Ideology, and Power in the Drama of Shakespeare and his Contemporaries* (Brighton, Sussex: Harvester Press, 1984), discusses the 'anti-humanism' of *The Revenger's Tragedy* in terms of Renaissance concepts of politics and characterization. Catherine Belsey, arguing from a similar theoretical position in *The Subject of Tragedy: Identity and Difference in Renaissance Drama* (Methuen: London and New York, 1985), has helpful comments on the way gender is conceptualized in Renaissance drama.

Since each of the plays in this volume has generated its own set of critical problems, however, it would be misleading to suggest that they have produced a unified tradition of 'revenge tragedy' interpretation. A favourite topic for Kyd's critics is his irony. G. K. Hunter's 'Ironies of Justice in *The Spanish Tragedy*', *Renaissance Drama*, 8 (1965), 89–104, is a far-reaching exploration of the moral problem. Barry Adams shows how irony pervades Kyd's stagecraft in 'The

Audiences of *The Spanish Tragedy*', *Journal of English and Germanic Philology*, 68 (1969), 221–36. Barbara Baines discusses the relationship between Kyd's irony and Renaissance scepticism in 'Kyd's Silenus Box and the Limits of Perception', *Journal of Medieval and Renaissance Studies*, 10 (1980), 41–51. C. L. Barber's essay on Kyd in *Creating Elizabethan Tragedy* (Chicago: University of Chicago Press, 1988), deftly combines psychoanalytic and socio-historical perspectives. Katharine Eisaman Maus expands on some of the issues discussed in the introduction to this volume, concentrating especially upon Kyd's unusual conception of political and theatrical duplicity, in *Inwardness and Theater in the English Renaissance* (Chicago: University of Chicago Press, 1995).

Many critics of *The Revenger's Tragedy* have struggled with the question of its authorship. The play was published anonymously in 1607, and attributed to Cyril Tourneur half-a-century later, in a playlist published in 1656. Some modern editors accept this attribution; others believe that the play is actually by Thomas Middleton. Samuel Schoenbaum provides a balanced account of the controversy in *Internal Evidence and Elizabethan Dramatic Authorship* (Evanston, Ill.: Northwestern University Press, 1966); D. J. Lake makes the case for Middleton in *The Canon of Thomas Middleton's Plays: Internal Evidence for the Major Problems of Authorship* (Cambridge: Cambridge University Press, 1975). The most interesting interpretive criticism of the play has attempted to come to terms with the implications of its overtly theatrical presentation of character, and its elaborately patterned savagery. In 'Acting and Violence: *The Revenger's Tragedy* and Its Departures from *Hamlet*', *Studies in English Literature*, 24 (1984), 275–91, Scott McMillan explores the disorientation that attends what he calls the problem of 'double identities of things, characters, and language' in the play. Francis Barker, *The Tremulous Private Body* (New York: Methuen, 1984) and Peter Stallybrass, 'Reading the Body: *The Revenger's Tragedy* and the Jacobean Theater of Consumption', *Renaissance Drama*, 18 (1987), 121–48, both argue that the play exemplifies a distinctively pre-modern form of subjectivity, which cannot be assimilated to 'our' accepted notions of selfhood or personality.

There is far less criticism published on *The Revenge of Bussy d'Ambois* and *The Atheist's Tragedy*. Chapman's critics argue over whether Clermont was meant to be perceived as failure or as a paragon: Suzanne F. Kistler, 'The Strange and Far-Removed Shores: A Reconsideration of *The Revenge of Bussy d'Ambois*', *Studies in*

Philology, 77 (1980), 128–44, argues the former case; Richard S. Ide, 'Exploiting the Tradition: The Elizabethan Revenger and Chapman's "Complete Man" ', *Medieval and Renaissance Drama in English*, 1 (1984), 159–86, argues the latter. Two excellent essays on *The Atheist's Tragedy* discuss aspects of its stagecraft: Huston Diehl, 'Reduce Thy Understanding to Thine Eye: Seeing and Interpreting in *The Atheist's Tragedy*', *Studies in Philology*, 78 (1981), 47–60, and William Gruber's 'Building a Scene: Text and Its Representation in *Atheist's Tragedy*', *Comparative Drama*, 19 (1985), 193–208.

CHRONOLOGY

PROVIDING a chronology for English Renaissance revenge plays is difficult for two reasons. First, it is hard to define clearly the limits of the genre. Political tyranny and retaliation for personal injury are ubiquitous tragic problems in the theatre of the age: thus John Webster's *White Devil* (1612), Thomas Middleton's *Women Beware Women* (1621), Shakespeare's *Macbeth* (1606), and John Ford's *'Tis Pity She's A Whore* (1632) all display some features of revenge tragedy, but are not usually considered under that rubric. Similarly the plot of John Marston's *Malcontent* (1604) involves revenge, but the play is a comedy. The second problem is that precise dating of Renaissance plays is often difficult or impossible. The dates given here, which all refer to dates of first performance, are taken from *The Revels History of Drama in English*, vols. 3 and 4 (Methuen: New York, 1975, 1981); the chronology in that volume is itself based upon Samuel Schoenbaum's revision of Alfred Harbage, *Annals of English Drama 975–1700* (Philadelphia: University of Pennsylvania Press, 1965). It is worth remembering that popular plays, like *The Spanish Tragedy* or *Hamlet*, were often revived and thus exerted a continuous influence upon later practitioners in the genre.

1587   Thomas Kyd, *The Spanish Tragedy*.
1589   Kyd, *Hamlet* (lost).
1594   William Shakespeare, *Titus Andronicus*.
1598–99 *The Spanish Tragedy* presented in revival, probably with the 'additions' that have survived in the 1602 quarto.
1600   John Marston, *Antonio's Revenge*.
1601   William Shakespeare, *Hamlet*.
1602   Henry Chettle, *Hoffman*.
1604   George Chapman, *Tragedy of Bussy d'Ambois* (the prequel to *The Revenge of Bussy d'Ambois*).
1606   Anonymous, *The Revenger's Tragedy*.
1609–10 George Chapman, *The Revenge of Bussy d'Ambois* and Cyril Tourneur, *The Atheist's Tragedy*.
1611   Francis Beaumont and John Fletcher, *The Maid's Tragedy*.
1614   John Fletcher, *Valentinian*.
1619   John Fletcher, *The Bloody Brother*.

THE SPANISH TRAGEDY

THOMAS KYD

[DRAMATIS PERSONAE

Ghost of Andrea, a Spanish courtier
Revenge
King of Spain
Don Cyprian, Duke of Castile, his
    brother
Lorenzo, the duke's son
Bel-imperia, Lorenzo's sister
Hieronimo, marshal° of Spain
Isabella, Hieronimo's wife
Horatio, their son
Viceroy of Portugal
Balthazar, his son
Don Pedro, the Viceroy's brother
Alexandro and Villuppo,
    Portuguese noblemen
Spanish General
Deputy
Bazulto, an old man
Three citizens
Portuguese ambassador
Two Portuguese
Pedringano, Bel-imperia's servant
Christophil, Bel-imperia's custodian
Lorenzo's page
Serberine, Balthazar's servant

Isabella's maid
Messenger
Hangman
Three Kings, Three Knights, and
    a Drummer in the first dumb
    show
Hymen and Two Torch-Bearers in
    the second dumb show

in Hieronimo's play:

Soliman, Sultan of Turkey
    (Balthazar)
Erasto, Knight of Rhodes (Lorenzo)
The Bashaw (Hieronimo)
Perseda (Bel-imperia)

in the additions to the play:

Bazardo, a painter
Pedro and Jaques, Hieronimo's
    servants

Army, Portuguese Nobles, Spanish
    Nobles, Halberdiers, Officers,
    Three Watchmen, Trumpeters,
    Servants]

[1.1]

Enter the Ghost of Andrea, and with him Revenge

GHOST When this eternal substance of my soul
  Did live imprisoned in my wanton flesh,
  Each in their function serving other's need,
  I was a courtier in the Spanish court.
  My name was Don Andrea; my descent,   5
  Though not ignoble, yet inferior far
  To gracious fortunes of my tender youth:
  For there in prime and pride of all my years,°
  By duteous service and deserving love,
  In secret I possessed a worthy dame,   10
  Which hight sweet Bel-imperia by name.
  But in the harvest of my summer joys
  Death's winter nipped the blossoms of my bliss,
  Forcing divorce betwixt my love and me.°
  For in the late conflict with Portingale°   15
  My valour drew me into danger's mouth
  Till life to death made passage through my wounds.
  When I was slain, my soul descended straight
  To pass the flowing stream of Acheron;°
  But churlish Charon, only boatman there,°   20
  Said that, my rites of burial not performed,
  I might not sit amongst his passengers.
  Ere Sol had slept three nights in Thetis' lap°
  And slaked his smoking chariot in her flood,
  By Don Horatio, our Knight Marshal's son,   25
  My funerals and obsequies were done.
  Then was the ferryman of hell content
  To pass me over to the slimy strond
  That leads to fell Avernus' ugly waves:°
  There, pleasing Cerberus with honeyed speech,°   30
  I passed the perils of the foremost porch.
  Not far from hence, amidst ten thousand souls,
  Sat Minos, Aeacus, and Rhadamanth,°
  To whom no sooner 'gan I make approach
  To crave a passport for my wand'ring ghost,   35
  But Minos, in graven leaves of lottery,°

Drew forth the manner of my life and death.
'This knight', quoth he, 'both lived and died in love,
And for his love tried fortune of the wars,
And by war's fortune lost both love and life.'   40
'Why then,' said Aeacus, 'convey him hence,
To walk with lovers in our fields of love,
And spend the course of everlasting time
Under green myrtle trees and cypress shades.'°
'No, no,' said Rhadamanth, 'it were not well   45
With loving souls to place a martialist.
He died in war and must to martial fields,
Where wounded Hector lives in lasting pain,°
And Achilles' Myrmidons do scour the plain.'°
Then Minos, mildest censor of the three,°   50
Made this device to end the difference:
'Send him', quoth he, 'to our infernal king,°
To doom him as best seems his majesty.'°
To this effect my passport straight was drawn.
In keeping on my way to Pluto's court,   55
Through dreadful shades of ever-glooming night,
I saw more sights than thousand tongues can tell,
Or pens can write, or mortal hearts can think.
Three ways there were: that on the right-hand side
Was ready way unto the 'foresaid fields,   60
Where lovers live, and bloody martialists,
But either sort contained within his bounds.
The left-hand path, declining fearfully,
Was ready downfall to the deepest hell,
Where bloody Furies shakes their whips of steel,   65
And poor Ixion turns an endless wheel;°
Where usurers are choked with melting gold,
And wantons are embraced with ugly snakes,
And murderers groan with never-killing wounds,
And perjured wights scalded in boiling lead,   70
And all foul sins with torments overwhelmed.
'Twixt these two ways I trod the middle path,
Which brought me to the fair Elysian green,°
In midst whereof there stands a stately tower,
The walls of brass, the gates of adamant.   75
Here finding Pluto with his Proserpine,
I showed my passport, humbled on my knee;

Whereat fair Proserpine began to smile,
And begged that only she might give my doom.
Pluto was pleased, and sealed it with a kiss.   80
Forthwith, Revenge, she rounded thee in th'ear,°
And bade thee lead me through the gates of horn,°
Where dreams have passage in the silent night.
No sooner had she spoke but we were here,
I wot not how, in twinkling of an eye.   85
REVENGE Then know, Andrea, that thou art arrived
Where thou shalt see the author of thy death,°
Don Balthazar, the Prince of Portingale,
Deprived of life by Bel-imperia.
Here sit we down to see the mystery,°   90
And serve for Chorus in this tragedy.°
    [*Revenge and Andrea seat themselves*]

[1.2]

Enter King of Spain, [attended], General, Castile, Hieronimo
KING Now say, Lord General, how fares our camp?
GENERAL All well, my sovereign liege, except some few
    That are deceased by fortune of the war.
KING But what portends thy cheerful countenance,
    And posting to our presence thus in haste?   5
    Speak, man, hath fortune given us victory?
GENERAL Victory, my liege, and that with little loss.
KING Our Portingales will pay us tribute then?
GENERAL Tribute and wonted homage therewithal.°
KING Then blessed be heaven and guider of the heavens,   10
    From whose fair influence such justice flows.
CASTILE *O multum dilecte Deo, tibi militat aether,*
    Et conjuratae curvato poplite gentes
    Succumbunt: recti soror est victoria iuris.°
KING Thanks to my loving brother of Castile.   15
    But, General, unfold in brief discourse
    Your form of battle and your war's success,
    That, adding all the pleasure of thy news
    Unto the height of former happiness,
    With deeper wage and greater dignity°   20

5

We may reward thy blissful chivalry.°
GENERAL   Where Spain and Portingale do jointly knit
  Their frontiers, leaning on each other's bound,°
  There met our armies in their proud array;
  Both furnished well, both full of hope and fear,   25
  Both menacing alike with daring shows,
  Both vaunting sundry colours of device,°
  Both cheerly sounding trumpets, drums, and fifes,
  Both raising dreadful clamours to the sky,
  That valleys, hills, and rivers made rebound,   30
  And heaven itself was frighted with the sound.
  Our battles both were pitched in squadron form,°
  Each corner strongly fenced with wings of shot;°
  But ere we joined and came to push of pike,°
  I brought a squadron of our readiest shot   35
  From out our rearward to begin the fight:
  They brought another wing to encounter us.
  Meanwhile our ordnance played on either side,
  And captains strove to have their valours tried.
  Don Pedro, their chief horsemen's colonel,   40
  Did with his cornet bravely make attempt
  To break the order of our battle ranks;
  But Don Rogero, worthy man of war,
  Marched forth against him with our musketeers,
  And stopped the malice of his fell approach.   45
  While they maintain hot skirmish to and fro,
  Both battles join, and fall to handy blows,
  Their violent shot resembling th'ocean's rage
  When, roaring loud and with a swelling tide,
  It beats upon the rampires of huge rocks,   50
  And gapes to swallow neighbour-bounding lands.
  Now, while Bellona rageth here and there,
  Thick storms of bullets rain like winter's hail,
  And shivered lances dark the troubled air.
  Pede pes et cuspide cuspis;   55
  Arma sonant armis, vir petiturque viro.°
  On every side drop captains to the ground,
  And soldiers, some ill-maimed, some slain outright:
  Here falls a body scindered from his head,
  There legs and arms lie bleeding on the grass,   60
  Mingled with weapons and unbowelled steeds,

6

That scattering overspread the purple plain.
In all this turmoil, three long hours and more,
The victory to neither part inclined,
Till Don Andrea with his brave lanciers   65
In their main battle made so great a breach,
That, half dismayed, the multitude retired;
But Balthazar, the Portingales' young prince,
Brought rescue and encouraged them to stay.
Here–hence the fight was eagerly renewed,   70
And in that conflict was Andrea slain,
Brave man-at-arms, but weak to Balthazar.
Yet while the prince, insulting over him,°
Breathed out proud vaunts, sounding to our reproach,
Friendship and hardy valour, joined in one,   75
Pricked forth Horatio, our knight marshal's son,°
To challenge forth that prince in single fight.
Not long between these twain the fight endured,
But straight the prince was beaten from his horse,
And forced to yield him prisoner to his foe.   80
When he was taken, all the rest they fled,
And our carbines pursued them to the death,°
Till, Phoebus waning to the western deep,
Our trumpeters were charged to sound retreat.
KING Thanks, good Lord General, for these good news;   85
   And for some argument of more to come,°
   Take this and wear it for thy sovereign's sake.
        Give[s] him his chain
   But tell me now, hast thou confirmed a peace?
GENERAL No peace, my liege, but peace conditional,
   That if with homage tribute be well paid,   90
   The fury of your forces will be stayed;
   And to this peace their viceroy hath subscribed,
        Give[s] the King a paper
   And made a solemn vow, that during life
   His tribute shall be truly paid to Spain.
KING These words, these deeds, become thy person well.   95
   But now, Knight Marshal, frolic with thy king,°
   For 'tis thy son that wins this battle's prize.
HIERONIMO Long may he live to serve my sovereign liege,
   And soon decay unless he serve my liege.
        A tucket° [sounds] afar off

7

KING Nor thou, nor he, shall die without reward.—   100
    What means this warning of this trumpet's sound?
GENERAL This tells me that your grace's men of war,
    Such as war's fortune hath reserved from death,
    Come marching on towards your royal seat
    To show themselves before your majesty;   105
    For so I gave in charge at my depart.
    Whereby by demonstration shall appear°
    That all, except three hundred or few more,
    Are safe returned, and by their foes enriched.°
        The army enters; Balthazar between Lorenzo and Horatio,
        captive
KING A gladsome sight! I long to see them here.   110
        [*The army*] *pass*[*es*] *by*
    Was that the warlike Prince of Portingale,
    That by our nephew was in triumph led?
GENERAL It was, my liege, the Prince of Portingale.
KING But what was he that on the other side
    Held him by th'arm as partner of the prize?   115
HIERONIMO That was my son, my gracious sovereign,
    Of whom though from his tender infancy
    My loving thoughts did never hope but well,
    He never pleased his father's eyes till now,
    Nor filled my heart with over-cloying joys.°   120
KING Go, let them march once more about these walls,
    That, staying them, we may confer and talk°
    With our brave prisoner and his double guard.
        [*Exit attendant*]
    Hieronimo, it greatly pleaseth us
    That in our victory thou have a share,   125
    By virtue of thy worthy son's exploit.
        Enter [*the army*] *again*
    Bring hither the young Prince of Portingale.
    The rest march on; but ere they be dismissed,
    We will bestow on every soldier
    Two ducats, and on every leader ten,   130
    That they may know our largess welcomes them.
        Exeunt all [*the army*] *but Balthazar, Lorenzo, Horatio*
    Welcome, Don Balthazar. Welcome, nephew.
    And thou, Horatio, thou art welcome too.
    Young prince, although thy father's hard misdeeds,

In keeping back the tribute that he owes, 135
Deserve but evil measure at our hands,°
Yet shalt thou know that Spain is honourable.
BALTHAZAR The trespass that my father made in peace
Is now controlled by fortune of the wars;°
And cards once dealt, it boots not ask why so.° 140
His men are slain, a weakening to his realm;
His colours seized, a blot unto his name;°
His son distressed, a corsive to his heart:
These punishments may clear his late offence.
KING Aye, Balthazar, if he observe this truce, 145
Our peace will grow the stronger for these wars.
Meanwhile live thou, though not in liberty,
Yet free from bearing any servile yoke;
For in our hearing thy deserts were great,
And in our sight thyself art gracious. 150
BALTHAZAR And I shall study to deserve this grace.
KING But tell me—for their holding makes me doubt—
To which of these twain art thou prisoner?
LORENZO To me, my liege.
HORATIO   To me, my sovereign.
LORENZO This hand first took his courser by the reins. 155
HORATIO But first my lance did put him from his horse.
LORENZO I seized his weapon and enjoyed it first.°
HORATIO But first I forced him lay his weapons down.
KING Let go his arm, upon our privilege.°
    [*Lorenzo and Horatio*] *let him go*
Say, worthy prince, to whether didst thou yield?° 160
BALTHAZAR To him in courtesy, to this perforce.°
He spake me fair, this other gave me strokes;
He promised life, this other threatened death;
He wan my love, this other conquered me,°
And truth to say, I yield myself to both. 165
HIERONIMO But that I know your grace for just and wise,
And might seem partial in this difference,°
Enforced by nature and by law of arms,
My tongue should plead for young Horatio's right.
He hunted well that was a lion's death, 170
Not he that in a garment wore his skin;
So hares may pull dead lions by the beard.°
KING Content thee, Marshal, thou shalt have no wrong;

And for thy sake, thy son shall want no right.°
Will both abide the censure of my doom?°   175
LORENZO I crave no better than your grace awards.
HORATIO Nor I, although I sit beside my right.°
KING Then by my judgement, thus your strife shall end:
You both deserve, and both shall have reward.
Nephew, thou took'st his weapon and his horse;   180
His weapons and his horse are thy reward.
Horatio, thou didst force him first to yield;
His ransom therefore is thy valour's fee.
Appoint the sum as you shall both agree.
But, nephew, thou shalt have the prince in guard,   185
For thine estate best fitteth such a guest:°
Horatio's house were small for all his train.
Yet, in regard thy substance passeth his,°
And that just guerdon may befall desert,
To him we yield the armour of the prince.°   190
How likes Don Balthazar of this device?
BALTHAZAR Right well, my liege, if this proviso were,
That Don Horatio bear us company,
Whom I admire and love for chivalry.
KING Horatio, leave him not that loves thee so.   195
Now let us hence to see our soldiers paid,
And feast our prisoner as our friendly guest.
        Exeunt

[1.3]

Enter Viceroy [of Portugal], Alexandro, Villuppo, [and attendants]

VICEROY Is our ambassador dispatched for Spain?
ALEXANDRO Two days, my liege, are passed since his depart.
VICEROY And tribute payment gone along with him?
ALEXANDRO Aye, my good lord.
VICEROY Then rest we here awhile in our unrest,   5
And feed our sorrows with some inward sighs,
For deepest cares break never into tears.
But wherefore sit I in a regal throne?
This better fits a wretch's endless moan.

[*Kneels*]
Yet this is higher than my fortune's reach,   10
And therefore better than my state deserves.
Falls to the ground
Aye, aye, this earth, image of melancholy,°
Seeks him whom fates adjudge to misery.
Here let me lie; now am I at the lowest.
Qui iacet in terra, non habet unde cadat.   15
In me consumpsit vires fortuna nocendo;
Nil superest ut iam possit obesse magis.°
[*Removes his crown*]
Yes, Fortune may bereave me of my crown:
Here, take it now; let Fortune do her worst,
She will not rob me of this sable weed.°   20
O no, she envies none but pleasant things:
Such is the folly of despiteful chance!
Fortune is blind, and sees not my deserts;
So is she deaf, and hears not my laments;
And could she hear, yet is she wilful-mad,°   25
And therefore will not pity my distress.
Suppose that she could pity me, what then?
What help can be expected at her hands
Whose foot [is] standing on a rolling stone,°
And mind more mutable than fickle winds?   30
Why wail I then, where's hope of no redress?
O yes, complaining makes my grief seem less.
My late ambition hath distained my faith,
My breach of faith occasioned bloody wars,
Those bloody wars have spent my treasure,   35
And with my treasure, my people's blood,
And with their blood, my joy and best beloved,
My best beloved, my sweet and only son.
O wherefore went I not to war myself?
The cause was mine; I might have died for both.   40
My years were mellow, his but young and green;
My death were natural, but his was forced.
ALEXANDRO No doubt, my liege, but still the prince survives.
VICEROY Survives! Aye, where?
ALEXANDRO In Spain, a prisoner by mischance of war.   45
VICEROY Then they have slain him for his father's fault.
ALEXANDRO That were a breach to common law of arms.

VICEROY They reck no laws that meditate revenge.

ALEXANDRO His ransom's worth will stay from foul revenge.

VICEROY No, if he lived, the news would soon be here.   50

ALEXANDRO Nay, evil news fly faster still than good.

VICEROY Tell me no more of news, for he is dead.

VILLUPPO [*kneels*] My sovereign, pardon the author of ill news,°
    And I'll bewray the fortune of thy son.

VICEROY Speak on, I'll guerdon thee, whate'er it be.   55
    Mine ear is ready to receive ill news;
    My heart grown hard 'gainst mischief's battery.°
    Stand up, I say, and tell thy tale at large.°

VILLUPPO Then hear that truth which these mine eyes have seen.
    When both the armies were in battle joined,   60
    Don Balthazar, amidst the thickest troops,
    To win renown did wondrous feats of arms.
    Amongst the rest I saw him, hand to hand,
    In single fight with their lord general;
    Till Alexandro, that here counterfeits   65
    Under the colour of a duteous friend,°
    Discharged his pistol at the prince's back
    As though he would have slain their general;
    But therewithal Don Balthazar fell down;
    And when he fell, then we began to fly;   70
    But had he lived, the day had sure been ours.

ALEXANDRO O wicked forgery! O traitorous miscreant!

VICEROY Hold thou thy peace!—But now, Villuppo, say,
    Where then became the carcass of my son?

VILLUPPO I saw them drag it to the Spanish tents.   75

VICEROY Aye, aye, my nightly dreams have told me this.
    Thou false, unkind, unthankful, traitorous beast,
    Wherein had Balthazar offended thee,
    That thou shouldst thus betray him to our foes?
    Was't Spanish gold that bleared so thine eyes   80
    That thou couldst see no part of our deserts?
    Perchance, because thou art Terceira's lord,°
    Thou hadst some hope to wear this diadem,
    If first my son and then myself were slain;
    But thy ambitious thought shall break thy neck.   85
    Aye, this was it that made thee spill his blood;
        Take[s] the crown and put[s] it on again
    But I'll now wear it till thy blood be spilt.

ALEXANDRO Vouchsafe, dread sovereign, to hear me speak.
VICEROY Away with him, his sight is second hell;
    Keep him till we determine of his death.   90
    If Balthazar be dead, he shall not live.
        [*Exeunt Attendants with Alexandro*]
    Villuppo, follow us for thy reward.
        Exit [*Viceroy*]
VILLUPPO Thus have I with an envious, forgèd tale°
    Deceived the king, betrayed mine enemy,
    And hope for guerdon of my villainy.   95
        Exit

[1.4]

    Enter Horatio and Bel-imperia
BEL-IMPERIA Signior Horatio, this is the place and hour
    Wherein I must entreat thee to relate
    The circumstance of Don Andrea's death,
    Who, living, was my garland's sweetest flower,
    And in his death hath buried my delights.   5
HORATIO For love of him and service to yourself,
    I nill refuse this heavy doleful charge;
    Yet tears and sighs, I fear, will hinder me.
    When both our armies were enjoined in fight,
    Your worthy chevalier amidst the thick'st,   10
    For glorious cause still aiming at the fairest,
    Was at the last by young Don Balthazar
    Encountered hand to hand. Their fight was long,
    Their hearts were great, their clamours menacing,
    Their strength alike, their strokes both dangerous.   15
    But wrathful Nemesis, that wicked power,°
    Envying at Andrea's praise and worth,
    Cut short his life, to end his praise and worth.
    She, she herself, disguised in armour's mask,
    As Pallas was before proud Pergamus,°   20
    Brought in a fresh supply of halberdiers,
    Which paunched his horse, and dinged him to the ground.°
    Then young Don Balthazar with ruthless rage,
    Taking advantage of his foe's distress,

Did finish what his halberdiers begun,   25
And left not till Andrea's life was done.
Then, though too late, incensed with just remorse,°
I with my band set forth against the prince,
And brought him prisoner from his halberdiers.
BEL-IMPERIA Would thou hadst slain him that so slew my love.   30
But then was Don Andrea's carcass lost?
HORATIO No, that was it for which I chiefly strove,
Nor stepped I back till I recovered him.
I took him up and wound him in mine arms,°
And welding him unto my private tent,   35
There laid him down, and dewed him with my tears,°
And sighed and sorrowed as became a friend.
But neither friendly sorrow, sighs, nor tears
Could win pale Death from his usurpèd right.
Yet this I did, and less I could not do: 40
I saw him honoured with due funeral.
This scarf I plucked from off his lifeless arm,
And wear it in remembrance of my friend.
BEL-IMPERIA I know the scarf; would he had kept it still.
For had he lived, he would have kept it still,   45
And worn it for his Bel-imperia's sake:
For 'twas my favour at his last depart.°
But now wear thou it both for him and me;
For after him thou hast deserved it best.
But for thy kindness in his life and death,   50
Be sure, while Bel-imperia's life endures,
She will be Don Horatio's thankful friend.
HORATIO And, madam, Don Horatio will not slack
Humbly to serve fair Bel-imperia.
But now, if your good liking stand thereto,°   55
I'll crave your pardon to go seek the prince;
For so the duke, your father, gave me charge.
      Exit [Horatio]
BEL-IMPERIA Aye, go, Horatio, leave me here alone;
For solitude best fits my cheerless mood.
Yet what avails to wail Andrea's death,   60
From whence Horatio proves my second love?
Had he not loved Andrea as he did,
He could not sit in Bel-imperia's thoughts.
But how can love find harbour in my breast

Till I revenge the death of my beloved?   65
Yes, second love shall further my revenge.
I'll love Horatio, my Andrea's friend,
The more to spite the prince that wrought his end;
And where Don Balthazar, that slew my love,
Himself now pleads for favour at my hands,   70
He shall, in rigour of my just disdain,°
Reap long repentance for his murderous deed.
For what was't else but murderous cowardice,
So many to oppress one valiant knight,
Without respect of honour in the fight?   75
And here he comes that murdered my delight.
     Enter Lorenzo and Balthazar
LORENZO Sister, what means this melancholy walk?
BEL-IMPERIA That for a while I wish no company.
LORENZO But here the prince is come to visit you.
BEL-IMPERIA That argues that he lives in liberty.°   80
BALTHAZAR No, madam, but in pleasing servitude.
BEL-IMPERIA Your prison, then, belike, is your conceit.°
BALTHAZAR Aye, by conceit my freedom is enthralled.
BEL-IMPERIA Then with conceit enlarge yourself again.°
BALTHAZAR What if conceit have laid my heart to gage?°   85
BEL-IMPERIA Pay that you borrowed, and recover it.°
BALTHAZAR I die if it return from whence it lies.
BEL-IMPERIA A heartless man, and live? A miracle!
BALTHAZAR Aye, lady, love can work such miracles.
LORENZO Tush, tush, my lord, let go these ambages,   90
  And in plain terms acquaint her with your love.
BEL-IMPERIA What boots complaint when there's no remedy?°
BALTHAZAR Yes, to your gracious self must I complain,
  In whose fair answer lies my remedy,
  On whose perfection all my thoughts attend,   95
  On whose aspect mine eyes find beauty's bower,°
  In whose translucent breast my heart is lodged.
BEL-IMPERIA Alas, my lord, these are but words of course,°
  And but device to drive me from this place.°
     She, in going in, lets fall her glove,° which Horatio, coming
     out, takes up
HORATIO Madam, your glove.   100
BEL-IMPERIA Thanks, good Horatio; take it for thy pains.
    [Exit Bel-imperia]

BALTHAZAR Signior Horatio stooped in happy time.
HORATIO I reaped more grace than I deserved or hoped.
LORENZO My lord, be not dismayed for what is past;
 You know that women oft are humorous.   105
 These clouds will overblow with little wind;
 Let me alone, I'll scatter them myself.°
 Meanwhile let us devise to spend the time
 In some delightful sports and revelling.
HORATIO The king, my lords, is coming hither straight, 110
 To feast the Portingale ambassador;
 Things were in readiness before I came.
BALTHAZAR Then here it fits us to attend the king,
 To welcome hither our ambassador,
 And learn my father and my country's health.   115
   Enter [attendants, bringing in] the banquet, trumpet[er]s,
   the King, [Castile, Nobles,] and Ambassador
KING See, Lord Ambassador, how Spain entreats
 Their prisoner Balthazar, thy viceroy's son.
 We pleasure more in kindness than in wars.°
AMBASSADOR Sad is our king, and Portingale laments,
 Supposing that Don Balthazar is slain.   120
BALTHAZAR [*aside*] So am I slain, by beauty's tyranny!
 [*To the Ambassador*] You see, my lord, how Balthazar is slain:
 I frolic with the Duke of Castile's son,
 Wrapped every hour in pleasures of the court,
 And graced with favours of his majesty.   125
KING Put off your greetings till our feast be done;
 Now come and sit with us, and taste our cheer.°
   [*King, Balthazar, Castile, Lorenzo, Ambassador, Nobles*]
   sit to the banquet
 Sit down, young prince, you are our second guest;
 Brother, sit down; and nephew, take your place.
 Signior Horatio, wait thou upon our cup,°   130
 For well thou hast deservèd to be honoured.
 Now, lordings, fall to; Spain is Portugal,
 And Portugal is Spain; we both are friends;
 Tribute is paid, and we enjoy our right.
 But where is old Hieronimo, our marshal?   135
 He promised us, in honour of our guest,
 To grace our banquet with some pompous jest.°
   Enter Hieronimo, with a Drum,° three Knights, each [with]

his scutcheon; then he fetches three Kings; [the three Knights]
take their crowns and them captive

Hieronimo, this masque contents mine eye,
Although I sound not well the mystery.°

HIERONIMO The first armed knight that hung his scutcheon up   140
        He takes the scutcheon and gives it to the King
Was English Robert, Earl of Gloucester,
Who, when King Stephen bore sway in Albion,°
Arrived with five-and-twenty thousand men
In Portingale, and by success of war
Enforced the king, then but a Saracen,°   145
To bear the yoke of the English monarchy.

KING My lord of Portingale, by this you see
That which may comfort both your king and you,
And make your late discomfort seem the less.°
But say, Hieronimo, what was the next?   150

HIERONIMO The second knight that hung his scutcheon up
        He doth as he did before
Was Edmund, Earl of Kent in Albion,
When English Richard wore the diadem.
He came likewise and razèd Lisbon walls,
And took the King of Portingale in fight;   155
For which, and other such-like service done,
He after was created Duke of York.

KING This is another special argument
That Portingale may deign to bear our yoke
When it by little England hath been yoked.   160
But now, Hieronimo, what were the last?

HIERONIMO The third and last, not least in our account,
        Doing as before
Was as the rest a valiant Englishman,
Brave John of Gaunt, the Duke of Lancaster,
As by his scutcheon plainly may appear.   165
He with a puissant army came to Spain
And took our King of Castile prisoner.

AMBASSADOR This is an argument for our viceroy
That Spain may not insult for her success,
Since English warriors likewise conquered Spain,   170
And made them bow their knees to Albion.

KING (*takes the cup of*° *Horatio*)
Hieronimo, I drink to thee for this device,

Which hath pleased both the ambassador and me:
Pledge me, Hieronimo, if thou love the king.°
    [*King gives the cup to Hieronimo, who drinks*]
[*To the Ambassador*] My lord, I fear we sit but overlong,   175
Unless our dainties were more delicate;°
But welcome are you to the best we have.
Now let us in, that you may be dispatched;
I think our council is already set.
    Exeunt

[1.5]

    [*Ghost of Andrea and Revenge*]
GHOST Come we for this from depth of underground,
    To see him feast that gave me my death's wound?
    These pleasant sights are sorrow to my soul:
    Nothing but league, and love, and banqueting!°
REVENGE Be still, Andrea; ere we go from hence,   5
    I'll turn their friendship into fell despite,
    Their love to mortal hate, their day to night,
    Their hope into despair, their peace to war,
    Their joys to pain, their bliss to misery.

[2.1]

Enter Lorenzo and Balthazar

LORENZO My lord, though Bel-imperia seem thus coy,
Let reason hold you in your wonted joy.
In time the savage bull sustains the yoke,°
In time all haggard hawks will stoop to lure,°
In time small wedges cleave the hardest oak,   5
In time the flint is pierced with softest shower,
And she in time will fall from her disdain,
And rue the sufferance of your friendly pain.°

BALTHAZAR No, she is wilder and more hard withal
Than beast, or bird, or tree, or stony wall.   10
But wherefore blot I Bel-imperia's name?
It is my fault, not she, that merits blame.
My feature is not to content her sight;°
My words are rude and work her no delight.°
The lines I send her are but harsh and ill,°   15
Such as do drop from Pan and Marsyas' quill.°
My presents are not of sufficient cost,
And being worthless, all my labour's lost.
Yet might she love me for my valiancy:
Aye, but that's slandered by captivity.°   20
Yet might she love me to content her sire:
Aye, but her reason masters his desire.
Yet might she love me as her brother's friend:
Aye, but her hopes aim at some other end.
Yet might she love me to uprear her state:°   25
Aye, but perhaps she hopes some nobler mate.
Yet might she love me as her beauty's thrall:
Aye, but I fear she cannot love at all.

LORENZO My lord, for my sake leave these ecstasies,
And doubt not but we'll find some remedy.   30
Some cause there is that lets you not be loved;°
First that must needs be known and then removed.
What if my sister love some other knight?

BALTHAZAR My summer's day will turn to winter's night.

LORENZO I have already found a stratagem   35
To sound the bottom of this doubtful theme.°

My lord, for once you shall be ruled by me;
Hinder me not, whate'er you hear or see.
By force or fair means will I cast about
To find the truth of all this question out.   40
Ho, Pedringano!
PEDRINGANO [*offstage*] Signior!
LORENZO   *Vien qui presto.*°
        Enter Pedringano
PEDRINGANO Hath your lordship any service to command me?
LORENZO Aye, Pedringano, service of import;
    And, not to spend the time in trifling words,
    Thus stands the case: it is not long, thou know'st,   45
    Since I did shield thee from my father's wrath
    For thy conveyance in Andrea's love,°
    For which thou wert adjudged to punishment.
    I stood betwixt thee and thy punishment;
    And since, thou knowest how I have favoured thee.   50
    Now to these favours will I add reward,
    Not with fair words, but store of golden coin,
    And lands and living joined with dignities,°
    If thou but satisfy my just demand.
    Tell truth, and have me for thy lasting friend.   55
PEDRINGANO Whate'er it be your lordship shall demand,
    My bounden duty bids me tell the truth,
    If case it lie in me to tell the truth.°
LORENZO Then, Pedringano, this is my demand:
    Whom loves my sister Bel-imperia?   60
    For she reposeth all her trust in thee.
    Speak man, and gain both friendship and reward.
    I mean, whom loves she in Andrea's place?
PEDRINGANO Alas my lord, since Don Andrea's death
    I have no credit with her as before,   65
    And therefore know not if she love or no.
LORENZO Nay, if thou dally then I am thy foe;
        [*Draws his sword*]
    And fear shall force what friendship cannot win.
    Thy death shall bury what thy life conceals:
    Thou diest for more esteeming her than me.   70
PEDRINGANO O stay, my lord!°
LORENZO Yet speak the truth, and I will guerdon thee,
    And shield thee from whatever can ensue,

And will conceal whate'er proceeds from thee.
But if thou dally once again thou diest.   75
PEDRINGANO If Madam Bel-imperia be in love—
LORENZO What, villain! ifs and ands?
      [*Offers to kill him*]
PEDRINGANO [*kneels*] O, stay, my lord! She loves Horatio.
      Balthazar starts back
LORENZO What, Don Horatio, our knight marshal's son?
PEDRINGANO Even him, my lord.   80
LORENZO Now say but how knowest thou he is her love,
And thou shalt find me kind and liberal.°
Stand up, I say, and fearless tell the truth.
PEDRINGANO She sent him letters, which myself perused,
Full-fraught with lines and arguments of love,°   85
Preferring him before Prince Balthazar.
LORENZO Swear on this cross that what thou sayest is true,°
And that thou wilt conceal what thou hast told.
PEDRINGANO I swear to both, by Him that made us all.
LORENZO In hope thine oath is true, here's thy reward.   90
      [*Gives Pedringano gold*]
But if I prove thee perjured and unjust,°
This very sword whereon thou took'st thine oath
Shall be the worker of thy tragedy.
PEDRINGANO What I have said is true, and shall, for me,°
Be still concealed from Bel-imperia.   95
Besides, your honour's liberality
Deserves my duteous service, even till death.
LORENZO Let this be all that thou shalt do for me:
Be watchful when and where these lovers meet,
And give me notice in some secret sort.°   100
PEDRINGANO I will, my lord.
LORENZO Then shalt thou find that I am liberal.
Thou know'st that I can more advance thy state°
Than she; be therefore wise and fail me not.
Go and attend her as thy custom is,   105
Lest absence make her think thou dost amiss.
      Exit Pedringano
Why so, *tam armis quam ingenio*:°
Where words prevail not, violence prevails;
But gold doth more than either of them both.
How likes Prince Balthazar this stratagem?   110

BALTHAZAR Both well, and ill; it makes me glad, and sad:
  Glad that I know the hinderer of my love;
  Sad that I fear she hates me whom I love;
  Glad that I know on whom to be revenged;
  Sad that she'll fly me if I take revenge.   115
  Yet must I take revenge or die myself,
  For love resisted grows impatient.
  I think Horatio be my destined plague!
  First in his hand he brandishèd a sword,
  And with that sword he fiercely wagèd war,   120
  And in that war he gave me dangerous wounds,
  And by those wounds he forcèd me to yield,
  And by my yielding I became his slave.
  Now in his mouth he carries pleasing words,
  Which pleasing words do harbour sweet conceits,   125
  Which sweet conceits are limed with sly deceits,°
  Which sly deceits smooth Bel-imperia's ears,
  And through her ears dive down into her heart,
  And in her heart set him where I should stand.
  Thus hath he ta'en my body by his force,   130
  And now by sleight would captivate my soul;°
  But in his fall I'll tempt the Destinies,
  And either lose my life, or win my love.
LORENZO Let's go, my lord; your staying stays revenge.
  Do you but follow me and gain your love: 135
  Her favour must be won by his remove.°
      Exeunt

[2.2]

      Enter Horatio and Bel-imperia
HORATIO Now, madam, since by favour of your love
  Our hidden smoke is turned to open flame,
  And that with looks and words we feed our thoughts
  (Two chief contents, where more cannot be had),°
  Thus, in the midst of love's fair blandishments,   5
  Why show you sign of inward languishments?
      *Pedringano showeth all to the Prince and Lorenzo, placing
      them in secret [on the upper stage]*

BEL-IMPERIA My heart, sweet friend, is like a ship at sea:°
　　She wisheth port, where riding all at ease
　　She may repair what stormy times have worn,
　　And leaning on the shore may sing with joy　　　　　　10
　　That pleasure follows pain, and bliss annoy.
　　Possession of thy love is th'only port,
　　Wherein my heart, with fears and hopes long tossed,
　　Each hour doth wish and long to make resort,°
　　There to repair the joys that it hath lost,　　　　　　15
　　And, sitting safe, to sing in Cupid's choir
　　That sweetest bliss is crown of love's desire.
BALTHAZAR (*above*) O sleep, mine eyes, see not my love profaned;
　　Be deaf, my ears, hear not my discontent;
　　Die, heart; another joys what thou deservest.°　　　　20
LORENZO [*above*] Watch still, mine eyes, to see this love disjoined;
　　Hear still, mine ears, to hear them both lament;
　　Live, heart, to joy at fond Horatio's fall.°
BEL-IMPERIA Why stands Horatio speechless all this while?
HORATIO The less I speak, the more I meditate.　　　　　25
BEL-IMPERIA But whereon dost thou chiefly meditate?°
HORATIO On dangers past, and pleasures to ensue.
BALTHAZAR On pleasures past, and dangers to ensue.
BEL-IMPERIA What dangers and what pleasures dost thou mean?
HORATIO Dangers of war, and pleasures of our love.°　　30
LORENZO Dangers of death, but pleasures none at all.
BEL-IMPERIA Let dangers go, thy war shall be with me,
　　But such a war as breaks no bond of peace.
　　Speak thou fair words, I'll cross them with fair words;
　　Send thou sweet looks, I'll meet them with sweet looks;　35
　　Write loving lines, I'll answer loving lines;
　　Give me a kiss, I'll countercheck thy kiss:°
　　Be this our warring peace or peaceful war.
HORATIO But, gracious madam, then appoint the field
　　Where trial of this war shall first be made.　　　　　40
BALTHAZAR Ambitious villain, how his boldness grows!°
BEL-IMPERIA Then be thy father's pleasant bower the field,
　　Where first we vowed a mutual amity:
　　The court were dangerous; that place is safe.
　　Our hour shall be when Vesper 'gins to rise,　　　　　45
　　That summons home distressful travellers.
　　There none shall hear us but the harmless birds;

Happily the gentle nightingale°
Shall carol us asleep ere we be 'ware,
And, singing with the prickle at her breast,°   50
Tell our delight and mirthful dalliance.
Till then each hour will seem a year and more.
HORATIO But, honey sweet and honourable love,
Return we now into your father's sight;
Dangerous suspicion waits on our delight.   55
LORENZO Aye, danger mixed with jealous despite
Shall send thy soul into eternal night.
Exeunt

[2.3]

*Enter King of Spain, Portingale Ambassador, Duke of
Castile, [and attendants]*

KING Brother of Castile, to the prince's love
What says your daughter Bel-imperia?
CASTILE Although she coy it as becomes her kind,°
And yet dissemble that she loves the prince,
I doubt not, I, but she will stoop in time.°   5
And were she froward, which she will not be,
Yet herein shall she follow my advice,
Which is to love him or forgo my love.
KING Then, Lord Ambassador of Portingale,
Advise thy king to make this marriage up,°   10
For strengthening of our late-confirmèd league;
I know no better means to make us friends.
Her dowry shall be large and liberal:
Besides that she is daughter and half-heir
Unto our brother here, Don Cyprian,   15
And shall enjoy the moiety of his land,
I'll grace her marriage with an uncle's gift;
And this it is: in case the match go forward,°
The tribute which you pay shall be released;°
And if by Balthazar she have a son,   20
He shall enjoy the kingdom after us.
AMBASSADOR I'll make the motion to my sovereign liege,°
And work it, if my counsel may prevail.°

KING Do so, my lord, and if he give consent,
    I hope his presence here will honour us   25
    In celebration of the nuptial day;
    And let himself determine of the time.
AMBASSADOR Will't please your grace command me aught beside?
KING Commend me to the king, and so farewell.°
    But where's Prince Balthazar to take his leave?   30
AMBASSADOR That is performed already, my good lord.
KING Amongst the rest of what you have in charge
    The prince's ransom must not be forgot:
    That's none of mine, but his that took him prisoner;
    And well his forwardness deserves reward.   35
    It was Horatio, our knight marshal's son.
AMBASSADOR Between us there's a price already pitched,°
    And shall be sent with all convenient speed.
KING Then once again farewell, my lord.
AMBASSADOR Farewell, my Lord of Castile and the rest.   40
        Exit [Ambassador]
KING Now, brother, you must take some little pains
    To win fair Bel-imperia from her will.°
    Young virgins must be rulèd by their friends.°
    The prince is amiable and loves her well;°
    If she neglect him and forgo his love   45
    She both will wrong her own estate and ours.
    Therefore, whiles I do entertain the prince
    With greatest pleasure that our court affords,
    Endeavour you to win your daughter's thoughts:
    If she give back, all this will come to naught.°   50
        Exeunt

[2.4]

       Enter Horatio, Bel-imperia, and Pedringano
HORATIO Now that the night begins with sable wings
    To overcloud the brightness of the sun,
    And that in darkness pleasures may be done,
    Come, Bel-imperia, let us to the bower,
    And there in safety pass a pleasant hour.   5
BEL-IMPERIA I follow thee, my love, and will not back,

Although my fainting heart controls my soul.°
HORATIO Why, make you doubt of Pedringano's faith?
BEL-IMPERIA No, he is as trusty as my second self.
Go, Pedringano, watch without the gate,°   10
And let us know if any make approach.
PEDRINGANO [*aside*] Instead of watching, I'll deserve more gold
By fetching Don Lorenzo to this match.
          Exit Pedringano
HORATIO What means my love?
BEL-IMPERIA   I know not what myself;
And yet my heart foretells me some mischance.   15
HORATIO Sweet, say not so; fair Fortune is our friend,
And heavens have shut up day to pleasure us.
The stars, thou seest, hold back their twinkling shine,
And Luna hides herself to pleasure us.
BEL-IMPERIA Thou hast prevailed; I'll conquer my misdoubt,°   20
And in thy love and counsel drown my fear.
I fear no more; love now is all my thoughts.
Why sit we not? for pleasure asketh ease.
HORATIO The more thou sit'st within these leafy bowers,
The more will Flora deck it with her flowers.   25
BEL-IMPERIA Aye, but if Flora spy Horatio here,
Her jealous eye will think I sit too near.
HORATIO Hark, madam, how the birds record by night,°
For joy that Bel-imperia sits in sight.
BEL-IMPERIA No, Cupid counterfeits the nightingale,   30
To frame sweet music to Horatio's tale.°
HORATIO If Cupid sing, then Venus is not far;°
Aye, thou art Venus, or some fairer star.
BEL-IMPERIA If I be Venus, thou must needs be Mars;°
And where Mars reigneth, there must needs be wars.   35
HORATIO Then thus begin our wars: put forth thy hand,
That it may combat with my ruder hand.°
BEL-IMPERIA Set forth thy foot to try the push of mine.
HORATIO But first my looks shall combat against thine.
BEL-IMPERIA Then ward thyself: I dart this kiss at thee.°   40
HORATIO Thus I retort the dart thou threw'st at me.°
BEL-IMPERIA Nay then, to gain the glory of the field,
My twining arms shall yoke and make thee yield.
HORATIO Nay then, my arms are large and strong withal:
Thus elms by vines are compassed till they fall.°   45

BEL-IMPERIA O let me go; for in my troubled eyes
 Now may'st thou read that life in passion dies.°
HORATIO O stay awhile, and I will die with thee;
 So shalt thou yield, and yet have conquered me.
BEL-IMPERIA Who's there, Pedringano? We are betrayed!   50
   Enter Lorenzo, Balthazar, Serberine, Pedringano, disguised
LORENZO My lord, away with her, take her aside.
   [*Balthazar restrains Bel-imperia*]
 [*To Horatio*] O sir, forbear; your valour is already tried.°
 Quickly dispatch, my masters.
HORATIO   What, will you murder me?
   [*Pedringano and Serberine*] *hang him in the arbour*°
LORENZO Aye, thus, and thus! These are the fruits of love.°
   They stab him
BEL-IMPERIA O save his life, and let me die for him!   55
 O save him, brother; save him, Balthazar!
 I loved Horatio, but he loved not me.
BALTHAZAR But Balthazar loves Bel-imperia.
LORENZO Although his life were still ambitious, proud,
 Yet is he at the highest now he is dead.   60
BEL-IMPERIA Murder! Murder! Help, Hieronimo, help!
LORENZO Come, stop her mouth; away with her.
   Exeunt, [leaving Horatio's body hanging in the arbour]. Enter
   Hieronimo in his shirt°
HIERONIMO What outcries pluck me from my naked bed,°
 And chill my throbbing heart with trembling fear,
 Which never danger yet could daunt before?
 Who calls Hieronimo? Speak, here I am.   65
 I did not slumber, therefore 'twas no dream.
 No, no, it was some woman cried for help,
 And here within this garden did she cry,
 And in this garden must I rescue her.   70
   [*Sees the body*]
 But stay, what murd'rous spectacle is this?
 A man hanged up, and all the murderers gone,
 And in my bower, to lay the guilt on me!
 This place was made for pleasure, not for death.
   He cuts him down
 Those garments that he wears I oft have seen—   75
 Alas, it is Horatio, my sweet son!
 O no, but he that whilom was my son!

O, was it thou that call'dst me from my bed?
O speak, if any spark of life remain!
I am thy father. Who hath slain my son?   80
What savage monster, not of human kind,
Hath here been glutted with thy harmless blood,
And left thy bloody corpse dishonoured here,
For me, amidst this dark and deathful shades,
To drown thee with an ocean of my tears?   85
O heavens, why made you night to cover sin?
By day this deed of darkness had not been.
O earth, why didst thou not in time devour
The vile profaner of this sacred bower?
O poor Horatio, what hadst thou misdone°   90
To leese thy life, ere life was new begun?
O wicked butcher, whatsoe'er thou wert,
How could thou strangle virtue and desert?
Aye me most wretched, that have lost my joy
In leesing my Horatio, my sweet boy!   95
    Enter Isabella
ISABELLA My husband's absence makes my heart to throb.
  —Hieronimo!
HIERONIMO Here, Isabella, help me to lament,
For sighs are stopped, and all my tears are spent.
ISABELLA What world of grief—my son, Horatio!   100
O where's the author of this endless woe?
HIERONIMO To know the author were some ease of grief,
For in revenge my heart would find relief.
ISABELLA Then is he gone? And is my son gone too?
O gush out, tears, fountains and floods of tears;   105
Blow, sighs, and raise an everlasting storm;
For outrage fits our cursèd wretchedness.
HIERONIMO Sweet, lovely rose, ill-plucked before thy time,
Fair, worthy son, not conquered but betrayed,
I'll kiss thee now, for words with tears are stayed.   110
ISABELLA And I'll close up the glasses of his sight,°
For once these eyes were only my delight.
HIERONIMO Seest thou this handkercher besmeared with blood?°
It shall not from me till I take revenge.
Seest thou those wounds that yet are bleeding fresh?   115
I'll not entomb them till I have revenged.
Then will I joy amidst my discontent;

Till then my sorrow never shall be spent.°

ISABELLA The heavens are just; murder cannot be hid.
Time is the author both of truth and right,   120
And time will bring this treachery to light.

HIERONIMO Meanwhile, good Isabella, cease thy plaints,
Or at the least dissemble them awhile;
So shall we sooner find the practice out,°
And learn by whom all this was brought about.   125
Come, Isabel, now let us take him up,
        [*Hieronimo and Isabella*] *take him up*
And bear him in from out this cursèd place.
I'll say his dirge; singing fits not this case.
O aliquis mihi quas pulchrum ver educat herbas,
        Hieronimo sets his breast unto his sword
Misceat, et nostro detur medicina dolori;   130
Aut, si qui faciunt annorum oblivia, succos
Praebeat; ipse metam magnum quaecunque per orbem
Gramina Sol pulchras effert in luminis oras;
Ipse bibam quicquid meditatur saga veneni,
Quicquid et herbarum vi caeca nenia nectit: 135
Omnia perpetiar, lethum quoque, dum semel omnis
Noster in extincto moriatur pectore sensus.
Ergo tuos oculos nunquam, mea vita, videbo,
Et tua perpetuus sepelivit lumina somnus?
Emoriar tecum: sic, sic iuvat ire sub umbras.   140
At tamen absistam properato cedere letho,
Ne mortem vindicta tuam tam nulla sequatur.°
        Here he throws [*the sword*] *from him and bears the body*
        away, [*accompanied by Isabella*]

[2.5]

[*Ghost of Andrea and Revenge*]
GHOST Broughtst thou me hither to increase my pain?
I looked that Balthazar should have been slain,°
But 'tis my friend Horatio that is slain;
And they abuse fair Bel-imperia,
On whom I doted more than all the world,   5
Because she loved me more than all the world.

REVENGE Thou talkest of harvest when the corn is green.
    The end is crown of every work well done:
    The sickle comes not till the corn be ripe.
    Be still; and ere I lead thee from this place,   10
    I'll show thee Balthazar in heavy case.°

[3.1]

Enter Viceroy of Portingale, Nobles, Villuppo

VICEROY Infortunate condition of kings,
    Seated amidst so many helpless doubts!°
    First we are placed upon extremest height,
    And oft supplanted with exceeding heat,
    But ever subject to the wheel of chance: 5
    And at our highest never joy we so
    As we both doubt and dread our overthrow.
    So striveth not the waves with sundry winds
    As Fortune toileth in the affairs of kings,
    That would be feared, yet fear to be beloved,   10
    Sith fear or love to kings is flattery.
    For instance, lordings, look upon your king,
    By hate deprivèd of his dearest son,
    The only hope of our successive line.
NOBLEMAN I had not thought that Alexandro's heart   15
    Had been envenomed with such extreme hate;
    But now I see that words have several works,°
    And there's no credit in the countenance.°
VILLUPPO No; for my lord, had you beheld the train
    That feignèd love had coloured in his looks,   20
    When he in camp consorted Balthazar,°
    Far more inconstant had you thought the sun
    That hourly coasts the centre of the earth,°
    Than Alexandro's purpose to the prince.
VICEROY No more, Villuppo; thou hast said enough,   25
    And with thy words thou slayest our wounded thoughts.
    Nor shall I longer dally with the world,
    Procrastinating Alexandro's death.—
    Go some of you, and fetch the traitor forth,
    That as he is condemnèd, he may die.   30
        [Exit several Nobles.] Enter Alexandro with a Nobleman and
        [Soldiers with] Halberts°
NOBLEMAN In such extremes will naught but patience serve.°
ALEXANDRO But in extremes what patience shall I use?
    Nor discontents it me to leave the world,
    With whom there nothing can prevail but wrong.

NOBLEMAN Yet hope the best.
ALEXANDRO   'Tis heaven is my hope.   35
    As for the earth, it is too much infect°
    To yield me hope of any of her mould.°
VICEROY Why linger ye? Bring forth that daring fiend,
    And let him die for his accursèd deed.
ALEXANDRO Not that I fear the extremity of death   40
    (For nobles cannot stoop to servile fear)
    Do I, O king, thus discontented live.
    But this, O this, torments my labouring soul,
    That thus I die suspected of a sin
    Whereof, as heavens have known my secret thoughts,   45
    So am I free from this suggestion.°
VICEROY No more, I say! To the tortures! When!°
    Bind him, and burn his body in those flames
        They bind him to the stake
    That shall prefigure those unquenchèd fires
    Of Phlegethon, preparèd for his soul.°   50
ALEXANDRO My guiltless death will be avenged on thee,
    On thee, Villuppo, that hath maliced thus,°
    Or for thy meed hast falsely me accused.
VILLUPPO Nay, Alexandro, if thou menace me,
    I'll lend a hand to send thee to the lake°   55
    Where those thy words shall perish with thy works,
    Injurious traitor, monstrous homicide!°
        Enter Ambassador
[AMBASSADOR] Stay, hold a while!
    And here, with pardon of his majesty,
    Lay hands upon Villuppo.
VICEROY   Ambassador,   60
    What news hath urged this sudden entrance?
AMBASSADOR Know, sovereign lord, that Balthazar doth live.
VICEROY What sayest thou? Liveth Balthazar our son?
AMBASSADOR Your highness' son, Lord Balthazar, doth live;
    And, well entreated in the court of Spain,°   65
    Humbly commends him to your majesty.°
    These eyes beheld, and these my followers,
    With these, the letters of the king's commends,
        Gives him letters
    Are happy witnesses of his highness' health.
        The Viceroy looks on the letters, and proceeds

VICEROY 'Thy son doth live, your tribute is received,   70
    Thy peace is made, and we are satisfied.
    The rest resolve upon as things proposed
    For both our honours and thy benefit.'
AMBASSADOR These are his highness' farther articles.
        He gives the Viceroy more letters
VICEROY [*to Villuppo*] Accursèd wretch, to intimate these ills°   75
    Against the life and reputation
    Of noble Alexandro! Come, my lord, unbind him.
    [*To Alexandro*] Let him unbind thee that is bound to death,
    To make a quital for thy discontent.°
        They unbind Alexandro
ALEXANDRO Dread lord, in kindness you could do no less°   80
    Upon report of such a damnèd fact;°
    But thus we see our innocence hath saved
    The hopeless life which thou, Villuppo, sought
    By thy suggestions to have massacred.
VICEROY Say, false Villuppo, wherefore didst thou thus   85
    Falsely betray Lord Alexandro's life?
    Him whom thou knowest that no unkindness else,
    But even the slaughter of our dearest son,
    Could once have moved us to have misconceived.°
ALEXANDRO Say, treacherous Villuppo, tell the king!   90
    Wherein hath Alexandro used thee ill?
VILLUPPO Rent with remembrance of so foul a deed,
    My guilty soul submits me to thy doom;
    For not for Alexandro's injuries,
    But for reward, and hope to be preferred°   95
    Thus have I shamelessly hazarded his life.
VICEROY Which, villain, shall be ransomed with thy death;
    And not so mean a torment as we here°
    Devised for him who, thou saidst, slew our son,
    But with the bitterest torments and extremes   100
    That may be yet invented for thine end.
        Alexandro seems to entreat
    Entreat me not. Go, take the traitor hence.
        Exit Villuppo [*guarded*]
    And, Alexandro, let us honour thee
    With public notice of thy loyalty.
    To end those things articulated here°   105
    By our great lord, the mighty King of Spain,

We with our council will deliberate.
Come, Alexandro, keep us company.
          Exeunt

[3.2]

          Enter Hieronimo
HIERONIMO O eyes, no eyes, but fountains fraught with tears;
     O life, no life, but lively form of death;°
     O world, no world, but mass of public wrongs,
     Confused and filled with murder and misdeeds;
     O sacred heavens! If this unhallowed deed,   5
     If this inhuman and barbarous attempt,
     If this incomparable murder thus
     Of mine, but now no more my son,
     Shall unrevealed and unrevengèd pass,
     How should we term your dealings to be just,   10
     If you unjustly deal with those that in your justice trust?
     The night, sad secretary to my moans,°
     With direful visions wake my vexèd soul,
     And with the wounds of my distressful son
     Solicit me for notice of his death.   15
     The ugly fiends do sally forth of hell,°
     And frame my steps to unfrequented paths,°
     And fear my heart with fierce inflamèd thoughts.°
     The cloudy day my discontents records,
     Early begins to register my dreams   20
     And drive me forth to seek the murderer.
     Eyes, life, world, heavens, hell, night, and day,
     See, search, show, send some man, some mean, that may—
          A letter falleth°
     What's here? A letter? Tush, it is not so!—
     A letter written to Hieronimo!   25
          Red ink
     [*Reads*] 'For want of ink, receive this bloody writ.°
     Me hath my hapless brother hid from thee;
     Revenge thyself on Balthazar and him:
     For these were they that murderèd thy son.
     Hieronimo, revenge Horatio's death,   30

And better fare than Bel-imperia doth.'
What means this unexpected miracle?
My son slain by Lorenzo and the prince!
What cause had they Horatio to malign?°
Or what might move thee, Bel-imperia,   35
To accuse thy brother had he been the mean?°
Hieronimo, beware; thou art betrayed,
And to entrap thy life this train is laid.
Advise thee therefore; be not credulous.
This is devisèd to endanger thee,   40
That thou, by this, Lorenzo shouldst accuse:
And he, for thy dishonour done, should draw
Thy life in question and thy name in hate.
Dear was the life of my belovèd son,
And of his death behoves me be revenged;   45
Then hazard not thine own, Hieronimo,
But live t'effect thy resolution.
I therefore will by circumstances try°
What I can gather to confirm this writ;
And, heark'ning near the Duke of Castile's house,   50
Close, if I can, with Bel-imperia,°
To listen more, but nothing to bewray.
  Enter Pedringano
Now, Pedringano!
PEDRINGANO Now, Hieronimo!
HIERONIMO Where's thy lady?
PEDRINGANO   I know not; here's my lord.
  Enter Lorenzo
LORENZO How now, who's this? Hieronimo?
HIERONIMO   My lord.   55
PEDRINGANO He asketh for my Lady Bel-imperia.
LORENZO What to do, Hieronimo? The duke my father hath
 Upon some disgrace awhile removed her hence;
 But if it be aught I may inform her of,
 Tell me, Hieronimo, and I'll let her know it.   60
HIERONIMO Nay, nay, my lord, I thank you, it shall not need.
 I had a suit unto her, but too late,°
 And her disgrace makes me unfortunate.
LORENZO Why so, Hieronimo? Use me.
HIERONIMO O no, my lord, I dare not; it must not be.   65
 I humbly thank your lordship.

LORENZO   Why then, farewell.
HIERONIMO [*aside*]
  My grief no heart, my thoughts no tongue can tell.
    Exit [Hieronimo]
LORENZO Come hither, Pedringano, seest thou this?
PEDRINGANO My lord, I see it and suspect it too.
LORENZO This is that damnèd villain Serberine   70
  That hath, I fear, revealed Horatio's death.
PEDRINGANO My lord, he could not, 'twas so lately done;
  And since, he hath not left my company.
LORENZO Admit he have not, his condition's such°
  As fear or flattering words may make him false.   75
  I know his humour, and therewith repent°
  That e'er I used him in this enterprise.
  But, Pedringano, to prevent the worst,
  And 'cause I know thee secret as my soul,
  Here, for thy further satisfaction, take thou this   80
    Gives Pedringano more gold
  And hearken to me; thus it is devised:
  This night thou must (and prithee, so resolve)
  Meet Serberine at Saint Luigi's Park—
  Thou knowest 'tis here hard by behind the house—°
  There take thy stand, and see thou strike him sure,   85
  For die he must, if we do mean to live.
PEDRINGANO But how shall Serberine be there, my lord?
LORENZO Let me alone, I'll send to him to meet
  The prince and me, where thou must do this deed.
PEDRINGANO It shall be done, my lord, it shall be done;   90
  And I'll go arm myself to meet him there.
LORENZO When things shall alter, as I hope they will,
  Then shalt thou mount for this. Thou knowest my mind.°
    Exit Pedringano
  Che le Ieron!°
    Enter Page
PAGE My lord?
LORENZO   Go, sirrah, to Serberine,   95
  And bid him forthwith meet the prince and me
  At Saint Luigi's Park, behind the house,
  This evening, boy.
PAGE   I go, my lord.
LORENZO But sirrah, let the hour be eight o'clock.

Bid him not fail.
PAGE   I fly, my lord.   100
          Exit [Page]
LORENZO Now to confirm the complot thou hast cast°
          Of all these practices, I'll spread the watch,°
          Upon precise commandment from the king,
          Strongly to guard the place where Pedringano
          This night shall murder hapless Serberine.   105
          Thus must we work that will avoid distrust;
          Thus must we practice to prevent mishap,
          And thus one ill another must expulse.
          This sly enquiry of Hieronimo
          For Bel-imperia breeds suspicion,   110
          And this suspicion bodes a further ill.
          As for myself, I know my secret fault,
          And so do they; but I have dealt for them.°
          They that for coin their souls endangerèd,
          To save my life, for coin shall venture theirs;   115
          And better it's that base companions die°
          Than by their life to hazard our good haps.°
          Nor shall they live for me to fear their faith:°
          I'll trust myself, myself shall be my friend;
          For die they shall—   120
          Slaves are ordainèd to no other end.
                    Exit

[3.3]

          Enter Pedringano with a pistol
PEDRINGANO Now, Pedringano, bid thy pistol hold,
          And hold on, Fortune! once more favour me;°
          Give but success to mine attempting spirit,
          And let me shift for taking of mine aim.°
          Here is the gold: this is the gold proposed;   5
          It is no dream that I adventure for,°
          But Pedringano is possessed thereof.
          And he that would not strain his conscience
          For him that thus his liberal purse hath stretched,
          Unworthy such a favour, may he fail,°   10

And wishing, want, when such as I prevail.°
As for the fear of apprehension,
I know, if need should be, my noble lord
Will stand between me and ensuing harms.
Besides, this place is free from all suspect.°   15
Here, therefore, will I stay and take my stand.
    Enter the Watch
FIRST WATCH I wonder much to what intent it is
That we are thus expressly charged to watch.
SECOND WATCH 'Tis by commandment in the king's own name.
THIRD WATCH But we were never wont to watch and ward°   20
So near the duke his brother's house before.
SECOND WATCH
Content yourself; stand close; there's somewhat in't.°
    [*The Watch conceal themselves.*] *Enter Serberine*
SERBERINE Here, Serberine, attend and stay thy pace;°
For here did Don Lorenzo's page appoint
That thou by his command shouldst meet with him.   25
How fit a place, if one were so disposed,
Methinks this corner is to close with one.°
PEDRINGANO Here comes the bird that I must seize upon.
Now, Pedringano, or never, play the man!°
SERBERINE I wonder that his lordship stays so long,   30
Or wherefore should he send for me so late?
PEDRINGANO For this, Serberine! And thou shalt ha't.
    [*Pedringano*] *shoots the dag* [*at Serberine, who falls*]
So, there he lies; my promise is performed.
FIRST WATCH Hark, gentlemen, this is a pistol shot!
SECOND WATCH And here's one slain; stay the murderer!   35
PEDRINGANO Now by the sorrows of the souls in hell,
Who first lays hand on me, I'll be his priest.°
    [*Pedringano*] *strives with the Watch,* [*who subdue him*]
THIRD WATCH Sirrah, confess, and therein play the priest:
Why hast thou thus unkindly killed the man?
PEDRINGANO Why? Because he walked abroad so late.   40
THIRD WATCH Come, sir, you had been better kept your bed
Than have committed this misdeed so late.
SECOND WATCH Come, to the marshal's with the murderer!
FIRST WATCH On to Hieronimo's! Help me here
To bring the murdered body with us too.   45
PEDRINGANO Hieronimo? Carry me before whom you will.

Whate'er he be, I'll answer him and you.
And do your worst, for I defy you all.
  Exeunt

[3.4]

  Enter Lorenzo and Balthazar
BALTHAZAR How now, my lord, what makes you rise so soon?
LORENZO Fear of preventing our mishaps too late.°
BALTHAZAR What mischief is it that we not mistrust?
LORENZO Our greatest ills we least mistrust, my lord,
 And inexpected harms do hurt us most.   5
BALTHAZAR Why, tell me, Don Lorenzo, tell me, man,
 If aught concerns our honour and your own.
LORENZO Nor you nor me, my lord, but both in one;
 For I suspect—and the presumption's great—
 That by those base confederates in our fault,°   10
 Touching the death of Don Horatio,
 We are betrayed to old Hieronimo.
BALTHAZAR Betrayed, Lorenzo? Tush, it cannot be.
LORENZO A guilty conscience, urgèd with the thought
 Of former evils, easily cannot err.   15
 I am persuaded—and dissuade me not—
 That all's revealèd to Hieronimo.
 And therefore know that I have cast it thus—
  [*Enter Page*]
 But here's the page. How now? What news with thee?
PAGE My lord, Serberine is slain.   20
BALTHAZAR Who? Serberine, my man?
PAGE Your highness' man, my lord.
LORENZO Speak, page, who murdered him?
PAGE He that is apprehended for the fact.
LORENZO Who?   25
PAGE Pedringano.
BALTHAZAR Is Serberine slain, that loved his lord so well?
 Injurious villain, murderer of his friend!
LORENZO Hath Pedringano murdered Serberine?
 My lord, let me entreat you to take the pains   30
 To exasperate and hasten his revenge°

With your complaints unto my lord the king.
This their dissension breeds a greater doubt.

BALTHAZAR Assure thee, Don Lorenzo, he shall die,
  Or else his highness hardly shall deny.°   35
  Meanwhile I'll haste the marshal-sessions,
  For die he shall for this his damnèd deed.
    Exit Balthazar

LORENZO Why so, this fits our former policy,
  And thus experience bids the wise to deal.
  I lay the plot, he prosecutes the point.   40
  I set the trap, he breaks the worthless twigs
  And sees not that wherewith the bird was limed.
  Thus hopeful men that mean to hold their own°
  Must look like fowlers to their dearest friends.°
  He runs to kill whom I have holp to catch,   45
  And no man knows it was my reaching fatch.°
  'Tis hard to trust unto a multitude,
  Or any one, in mine opinion,
  When men themselves their secrets will reveal.
    Enter a Messenger with a letter
  Boy!

PAGE My lord.

LORENZO   What's he?   50

MESSENGER I have a letter to your lordship.

LORENZO From whence?

MESSENGER From Pedringano that's imprisonèd.

LORENZO So he is in prison then?

MESSENGER   Aye, my good lord.

LORENZO What would he with us? He writes us here,   55
  To stand good lord, and help him in distress.°
  Tell him I have his letters, know his mind;
  And what we may, let him assure him of.°
  Fellow, begone; my boy shall follow thee.
    Exit Messenger
  This works like wax; yet once more try thy wits.°   60
  Boy, go convey this purse to Pedringano;
  Thou knowest the prison; closely give it him,
  And be advised that none be thereabout.°
  Bid him be merry still, but secret;
  And though the marshal-sessions be today,   65
  Bid him not doubt of his delivery.°

Tell him his pardon is already signed   10
And thereon bid him boldly be resolved;
For, were he ready to be turnèd off—°
As 'tis my will the uttermost be tried—°   70
Thou with his pardon shalt attend him still.
Show him this box; tell him his pardon's in't.   15
But open't not, an if thou lovest thy life;°
But let him wisely keep his hopes unknown:°
He shall not want while Don Lorenzo lives.   75
Away!
PAGE   I go, my lord, I run.
LORENZO But, sirrah, see that this be cleanly done.°
        Exit Page
Now stands our fortune on a tickle point,
And now or never ends Lorenzo's doubts.
One only thing is uneffected yet,   80
And that's to see the executioner.
But to what end? I list not trust the air°
With utterance of our pretence therein,
For fear the privy whisp'ring of the wind
Convey our words amongst unfriendly ears,   85
That lie too open to advantages.°
E quel che voglio io, nessun lo sa,
Intendo io: quel mi basterà.°
        Exit

[3.5]

Enter Page with the box
[PAGE] My master hath forbidden me to look in this box, and by my
    troth 'tis likely, if he had not warned me, I should not have had
    so much idle time; for we men's-kind in our minority° are like
    women in their uncertainty:° that° they are most forbidden, they
    will soonest attempt; so I now. [*Opens the box*] By my bare honesty,   5
    here's nothing but the bare empty box! Were it not sin against
    secrecy, I would say it were a piece of gentlemanlike knavery. I
    must go to Pedringano, and tell him his pardon is in this box; nay,
    I would have sworn it, had I not seen the contrary. I cannot choose

but smile to think how the villain will flout the gallows, scorn the
audience,° and descant° on the hangman, and all presuming of°
his pardon from hence. Will't not be an odd jest for me to stand
and grace every jest he makes, pointing my finger at this box, as
who would say, 'Mock on, here's thy warrant.'° Is't not a scurvy
jest that a man should jest himself to death? Alas, poor Pedringano,
I am in a sort° sorry for thee; but if I should be hanged with thee,
I cannot weep.
    Exit

[3.6]

    Enter Hieronimo and the Deputy

HIERONIMO Thus must we toil in other men's extremes,°
  That know not how to remedy our own,
  And do them justice when unjustly we
  For all our wrongs can compass no redress.
  But shall I never live to see the day   5
  That I may come, by justice of the heavens,
  To know the cause that may my cares allay?°
  This toils my body, this consumeth age:°
  That only I to all men just must be,
  And neither gods nor men be just to me.   10
DEPUTY Worthy Hieronimo, your office asks
  A care to punish such as do transgress.
HIERONIMO So is't my duty to regard his death
  Who, when he lived, deserved my dearest blood.
  But come: for that we came for, let's begin,   15
  For here lies that which bids me to be gone.°
    Enter Officers,° Page, and Pedringano, with a letter in his
    hand, bound
DEPUTY Bring forth the prisoner, for the court is set.°
PEDRINGANO Gramercy, boy, but it was time to come;
  For I had written to my lord anew
  A nearer matter that concerneth him,°   20
  For fear his lordship had forgotten me.
  But sith he hath remembered me so well—
  Come, come, come on, when shall we to this gear?°
HIERONIMO Stand forth, thou monster, murderer of men,

And here, for satisfaction of the world,   25
Confess thy folly and repent thy fault;
For there's thy place of execution.

PEDRINGANO This is short work. Well, to your marshalship
First I confess—nor fear I death therefore—
I am the man, 'twas I slew Serberine.   30
But, sir, then you think this shall be the place
Where we shall satisfy you for this gear?

DEPUTY Aye, Pedringano.

PEDRINGANO   Now I think not so.

HIERONIMO Peace, impudent, for thou shalt find it so:
For blood with blood shall, while I sit as judge,   35
Be satisfièd, and the law discharged.
And though myself cannot receive the like,
Yet will I see that others have their right.
Dispatch, the fault's approvèd and confessed,°
And by our law he is condemned to die.   40

    [*Enter Hangman*]

HANGMAN Come on, sir, are you ready?

PEDRINGANO To do what, my fine, officious knave?

HANGMAN To go to this gear.

PEDRINGANO O sir, you are too forward: thou wouldst fain furnish me with a halter, to disfurnish me of my habit.° So I should   45
go out of this gear, my raiment, into that gear, the rope. But,
hangman, now I spy your knavery, I'll not change without boot,°
that's flat.°

HANGMAN Come, sir.

PEDRINGANO So, then, I must up?°   50

HANGMAN No remedy.

PEDRINGANO [*mounting the gallows*] Yes, but there shall be for my
coming down.

HANGMAN [*holding up the noose*] Indeed, here's a remedy for that.

PEDRINGANO How? Be turned off?°   55

HANGMAN Aye, truly. Come, are you ready? I pray, sir, dispatch; the
day goes away.

PEDRINGANO What, do you hang by the hour? If you do, I may
chance to break your old custom.

HANGMAN Faith, you have reason; for I am like to break your young   60
neck.

PEDRINGANO Dost thou mock me, hangman? Pray God I be not
preserved to break your knave's pate for this!

HANGMAN Alas, sir, you are a foot too low to reach it, and I hope
  you will never grow so high while I am in the office.   65
PEDRINGANO Sirrah, dost see yonder boy with the box in his hand?
HANGMAN What, he that points to it with his finger?
PEDRINGANO Aye, that companion.°
HANGMAN I know him not; but what of him?
PEDRINGANO Dost thou think to live till his old doublet will make   70
  thee a new truss?°
HANGMAN Aye, and many a fair year after, to truss up many an
  honester man than either thou or he.
PEDRINGANO What hath he in his box, as thou think'st?
HANGMAN Faith, I cannot tell, nor I care not greatly; methinks you   75
  should rather hearken to your soul's health.
PEDRINGANO Why, sirrah hangman, I take it that that is good for
  the body is likewise good for the soul; and it may be, in that box
  is balm for both.
HANGMAN Well, thou art even the merriest piece of man's flesh that   80
  e'er groaned at my office door!
PEDRINGANO Is your roguery become an office° with a knave's name?
HANGMAN Aye, and that shall all they witness that see you seal it°
  with a thief's name.
PEDRINGANO I prithee request this good company to pray with me.   85
HANGMAN Aye, marry, sir, this is a good motion. My masters, you
  see here's a good fellow.
PEDRINGANO Nay, nay, now I remember me, let them alone till
  some other time; for now I have no great need.
HIERONIMO I have not seen a wretch so impudent!   90
  O monstrous times, where murder's set so light,°
  And where the soul that should be shrined in heaven
  Solely delights in interdicted things,
  Still wand'ring in the thorny passages,
  That intercepts itself of happiness.°   95
  Murder! O bloody monster! God forbid
  A fault so foul should 'scape unpunishèd.
  Dispatch, and see this execution done!
  This makes me to remember thee, my son.
    Exit Hieronimo. [Hangman prepares to execute Pedringano]
PEDRINGANO Nay, soft, no haste.°   100
DEPUTY Why, wherefore stay you? Have you hope of life?
PEDRINGANO Why, aye!
HANGMAN   As how?

44

PEDRINGANO Why, rascal, by my pardon from the king.
HANGMAN Stand you on that? Then you shall off with this.°
     He turns him off [the ladder]
DEPUTY So, executioner, convey him hence,   105
  But let his body be unburièd.
  Let not the earth be chokèd or infect
  With that which heaven contemns and men neglect.
     Exeunt

[3.7]

     Enter Hieronimo
HIERONIMO Where shall I run to breathe abroad my woes,°
  My woes whose weight hath wearièd the earth?
  Or mine exclaims that have surcharged the air
  With ceaseless plaints for my deceasèd son?
  The blust'ring winds, conspiring with my words,   5
  At my lament have moved the leafless trees,
  Disrobed the meadows of their flowered green,
  Made mountains marsh with spring-tides of my tears,
  And broken through the brazen gates of hell.
  Yet still tormented is my tortured soul   10
  With broken sighs and restless passions,
  That wingèd mount, and hovering in the air,
  Beat at the windows of the brightest heavens,
  Soliciting for justice and revenge:
  But they are placed in those empyreal heights,   15
  Where, countermured with walls of diamond,
  I find the place impregnable; and they
  Resist my woes and give my words no way.
     Enter Hangman with a letter
HANGMAN O lord, sir, God bless you, sir! The man, sir, Petergade,
  sir—he that was so full of merry conceits—°   20
HIERONIMO Well, what of him?
HANGMAN O lord, sir, he went the wrong way; the fellow had a fair
  commission to the contrary. Sir, here is his passport;° I pray you,
  sir, we have done him wrong.
HIERONIMO I warrant thee; give it me.   25
HANGMAN You will stand between the gallows and me?°

45

HIERONIMO Aye, aye.
HANGMAN I thank your lord worship.
   Exit Hangman
HIERONIMO And yet, though somewhat nearer me concerns,°
  I will, to ease the grief that I sustain,   30
  Take truce with sorrow while I read on this.
  'My lord, I writ, as mine extremes required,
  That you would labour my delivery:°
  If you neglect, my life is desperate,
  And in my death I shall reveal the troth.   35
  You know, my lord, I slew him for your sake,
  And was confederate with the prince and you;
  Won by rewards and hopeful promises,
  I holp to murder Don Horatio too.'
  Holp he to murder mine Horatio?   40
  And actors in th'accursèd tragedy
  Wast thou, Lorenzo, Balthazar and thou,
  Of whom my son, my son deserved so well?
  What have I heard? What have mine eyes beheld?
  O sacred heavens, may it come to pass   45
  That such a monstrous and detested deed,
  So closely smothered and so long concealed,
  Shall thus by this be vengèd or revealed?
  Now see I what I durst not then suspect—
  That Bel-imperia's letter was not feigned,   50
  Nor feignèd she, though falsely they have wronged
  Both her, myself, Horatio, and themselves.
  Now may I make compare 'twixt hers and this,
  Of every accident: I ne'er could find°
  Till now—and now I feelingly perceive—   55
  They did what heaven unpunished would not leave.
  O false Lorenzo, are these thy flattering looks?
  Is this the honour that thou didst my son?
  And Balthazar, bane to thy soul and me,
  Was this the ransom he reserved thee for?   60
  Woe to the cause of these constrainèd wars!
  Woe to thy baseness and captivity!
  Woe to thy birth, thy body, and thy soul,
  Thy cursèd father, and thy conquered self!
  And banned with bitter execrations be°   65
  The day and place where he did pity thee!

But wherefore waste I mine unfruitful words
When naught but blood will satisfy my woes?
I will go plain me to my lord the king,°
And cry aloud for justice through the court,   70
Wearing the flints with these my withered feet,
And either purchase justice by entreats,°
Or tire them all with my revenging threats.
    [*Exit*]

[3.8]

    Enter Isabella and her Maid
ISABELLA So that you say this herb will purge the eye,°
  And this, the head?
  Ah, but none of them will purge the heart.
  No, there's no medicine left for my disease,
  Nor any physic to recure the dead.°   5
    She runs lunatic
  Horatio! O where's Horatio?
MAID Good madam, affright not thus yourself
  With outrage for your son Horatio.
  He sleeps in quiet in the Elysian fields.
ISABELLA Why, did I not give you gowns and goodly things,   10
  Bought you a whistle and a whipstalk too,°
  To be revengèd on their villainies?
MAID Madam, these humours do torment my soul.
ISABELLA My soul? Poor soul, thou talk'st of things
  Thou know'st not what—my soul hath silver wings,   15
  That mounts me up unto the highest heavens.
  To heaven! aye, there sits my Horatio,
  Backed with a troop of fiery cherubims,
  Dancing about his newly healèd wounds,
  Singing sweet hymns and chanting heavenly notes,   20
  Rare harmony to greet his innocence,°
  That died, aye died, a mirror in our days.°
  But say, where shall I find the men, the murderers,
  That slew Horatio? Whither shall I run
  To find them out that murderèd my son?   25
    Exeunt

[3.9]

Bel-imperia at a window [on the upper stage]
BEL-IMPERIA What means this outrage that is offered me?
  Why am I thus sequestered from the court?
  No notice! Shall I not know the cause°
  Of these my secret and suspicious ills?
  Accursèd brother, unkind murderer,   5
  Why bends thou thus thy mind to martyr me?
  Hieronimo, why writ I of thy wrongs,
  Or why art thou so slack in thy revenge?
  Andrea, O Andrea, that thou sawest°
  Me for thy friend Horatio handled thus,   10
  And him for me thus causeless murderèd!
  Well, force perforce, I must constrain myself°
  To patience, and apply me to the time,°
  Till heaven, as I have hoped, shall set me free.
    Enter Christophil
CHRISTOPHIL Come, Madam Bel-imperia, this may not be.   15
    Exeunt

[3.10]

Enter Lorenzo, Balthazar, and the Page
LORENZO Boy, talk no further; thus far things go well.
  Thou art assurèd that thou sawest him dead?
PAGE Or else, my lord, I live not.
LORENZO   That's enough.
  As for his resolution in his end,
  Leave that to Him with whom he sojourns now.   5
  Here, take my ring and give it Christophil,
  And bid him let my sister be enlarged,°
  And bring him hither straight.
    Exit Page
  This that I did was for a policy,
  To smooth and keep the murder secret,   10
  Which, as a nine-day's wonder, being o'erblown,°
  My gentle sister will I now enlarge.

BALTHAZAR And time, Lorenzo, for my lord the duke,°
  You heard, inquired for her yesternight.
LORENZO Why, and my lord, I hope you heard me say   15
  Sufficient reason why she kept away;
  But that's all one. My lord, you love her?
BALTHAZAR   Aye.
LORENZO Then in your love beware; deal cunningly,
  Salve all suspicions, only soothe me up,°
  And if she hap to stand on terms with us—°   20
  As for her sweetheart, and concealment so—
  Jest with her gently: under feignèd jest
  Are things concealed that else would breed unrest.
  But here she comes.
      Enter Bel-imperia
              Now sister—
BEL-IMPERIA   Sister? No!
  Thou art no brother, but an enemy,   25
  Else wouldst thou not have used thy sister so:
  First to affright me with thy weapons drawn
  And with extremes abuse my company;°
  And then to hurry me, like whirlwind's rage,
  Amidst a crew of thy confederates   30
  And clap me up where none might come at me,°
  Nor I at any to reveal my wrongs.
  What madding fury did possess thy wits?
  Or wherein is't that I offended thee?
LORENZO Advise you better, Bel-imperia,   35
  For I have done you no disparagement;
  Unless, by more discretion than deserved,
  I sought to save your honour and mine own.
BEL-IMPERIA Mine honour! Why, Lorenzo, wherein is't
  That I neglect my reputation so,   40
  As you, or any, need to rescue it?
LORENZO His highness and my father were resolved
  To come confer with old Hieronimo
  Concerning certain matters of estate
  That by the viceroy was determinèd.°   45
BEL-IMPERIA And wherein was mine honour touched in that?
BALTHAZAR Have patience, Bel-imperia; hear the rest.
LORENZO Me, next in sight, as messenger they sent°
  To give him notice that they were so nigh:

Now when I came, consorted with the prince,   50
And unexpected in an arbour there
Found Bel-imperia with Horatio—
BEL-IMPERIA   How then?
LORENZO Why then, remembering that old disgrace,
Which you for Don Andrea had endured,
And now were likely longer to sustain   55
By being found so meanly accompanied,°
Thought rather (for I knew no readier mean)
To thrust Horatio forth my father's way.°
BALTHAZAR And carry you obscurely somewhere else,
Lest that his highness should have found you there.   60
BEL-IMPERIA Even so, my lord? And you are witness
That this is true which he entreath of?°
You, gentle brother, forged this for my sake,°
And you, my lord, were made his instrument?
A work of worth, worthy the noting too!   65
But what's the cause that you concealed me since?
LORENZO Your melancholy, sister, since the news
Of your first favourite Don Andrea's death,
My father's old wrath hath exasperate.°
BALTHAZAR And better was't for you, being in disgrace,   70
To absent yourself and give his fury place.°
BEL-IMPERIA But why had I no notice of his ire?
LORENZO That were to add more fuel to your fire,
Who burnt like Aetna for Andrea's loss.°
BEL-IMPERIA Hath not my father then inquired for me?   75
LORENZO Sister, he hath, and thus excused I thee.
      He whispereth in her ear
But Bel-imperia, see the gentle prince,
Look on thy love, behold young Balthazar,
Whose passions by thy presence are increased,
And in whose melancholy thou mayest see   80
Thy hate, his love; thy flight, his following thee.
BEL-IMPERIA Brother, you are become an orator—
I know not, I, by what experience—
Too politic for me, past all compare,°
Since I last saw you; but content yourself,   85
The prince is meditating higher things.
BALTHAZAR 'Tis of thy beauty, then, that conquers kings;
Of those thy tresses, Ariadne's twines,°

Wherewith my liberty thou hast surprised;°
Of that thine ivory front, my sorrow's map,   90
Wherein I see no haven to rest my hope.
BEL-IMPERIA To love and fear, and both at once, my lord,
In my conceit are things of more import
Than women's wits are to be busied with.
BALTHAZAR 'Tis I that love.
BEL-IMPERIA   Whom?
BALTHAZAR   Bel-imperia.   95
BEL-IMPERIA But I that fear.
BALTHAZAR   Whom?
BEL-IMPERIA   Bel-imperia.
LORENZO Fear yourself?
BEL-IMPERIA   Aye, brother.
LORENZO   How?
BEL-IMPERIA   As those
That what they love are loath and fear to lose.
BALTHAZAR Then, fair, let Balthazar your keeper be.
BEL-IMPERIA No, Balthazar doth fear as well as we: 100
Et tremulo metui pavidum iunxere timorem—
Est vanum stolidae proditionis opus.°
          Exit [Bel-imperia]
LORENZO Nay, an you argue things so cunningly,°
We'll go continue this discourse at court.
BALTHAZAR Led by the lodestar of her heavenly looks,°   105
Wends poor, oppressèd Balthazar,
As o'er the mountains walks the wanderer,
Incertain to effect his pilgrimage.°
          Exeunt

[3.11]

          Enter two Portingales, and Hieronimo meets them
FIRST PORTINGALE By your leave, sir.
HIERONIMO Good leave have you; nay, I pray you go,
For I'll leave you, if you can leave me so.
SECOND PORTINGALE Pray you, which is the next way to my lord
the duke's?   5
HIERONIMO The next way from me.

FIRST PORTINGALE To his house, we mean.

HIERONIMO O, hard by; 'tis yon house that you see.

SECOND PORTINGALE You could not tell us if his son were there?

HIERONIMO Who, my Lord Lorenzo?

FIRST PORTINGALE   Aye, sir.

> *Hieronimo goeth in at one door and comes out at another*°

HIERONIMO   O, forbear!   10

For other talk for us far fitter were.
But if you be importunate to know
The way to him, and where to find him out,
Then list to me, and I'll resolve your doubt.°
There is a path upon your left-hand side   15
That leadeth from a guilty conscience
Unto a forest of distrust and fear,
A darksome place, and dangerous to pass.
There shall you meet with melancholy thoughts
Whose baleful humours if you but uphold,°   20
It will conduct you to despair and death;
Whose rocky cliffs when you have once beheld,
Within a hugy dale of lasting night,
That, kindled with the world's iniquities,
Doth cast up filthy and detested fumes.   25
Not far from thence, where murderers have built
A habitation for their cursèd souls,
There, in a brazen cauldron fixed by Jove
In his fell wrath, upon a sulphur flame,
Yourselves shall find Lorenzo bathing him°   30
In boiling lead and blood of innocents.

FIRST PORTINGALE Ha, ha, ha!

HIERONIMO Ha, ha, ha! Why ha, ha, ha! Farewell, good, ha, ha, ha!

> *Exit [Hieronimo]*

SECOND PORTINGALE Doubtless this man is passing lunatic,°
Or imperfection of his age doth make him dote.   35
Come, let's away to seek my lord the duke.

> *[Exeunt]*

[3.12]

Enter Hieronimo, with a poniard in one hand and a rope in the other

HIERONIMO Now, sir, perhaps I come and see the king;
The king sees me and fain would hear my suit.
Why, is not this a strange and seld-seen thing,
That standers-by with toys should strike me mute?°
Go to; I see their shifts and say no more.   5
Hieronimo, 'tis time for thee to trudge.°
Down by the dale that flows with purple gore
Standeth a fiery tower; there sits a judge
Upon a seat of steel and molten brass,
And 'twixt his teeth he holds a firebrand,°   10
That leads unto the lake where hell doth stand.
Away, Hieronimo, to him be gone:
He'll do thee justice for Horatio's death.
Turn down this path, thou shalt be with him straight;
Or this, and then thou need'st not take thy breath: 15
This way, or that way?—Soft and fair, not so!°
For if I hang or kill myself, let's know
Who will revenge Horatio's murder then?
No, no! Fie, no! Pardon me, I'll none of that.
He flings away the dagger and halter
This way I'll take, and this way comes the king: 20
He takes them up again
And here I'll have a fling at him, that's flat;
And Balthazar, I'll be with thee to bring,°
And thee, Lorenzo! Here's the king—nay, stay;
And here, aye here—there goes the hare away.°
Enter King, Ambassador, Castile, and Lorenzo
KING Now show, ambassador, what our viceroy saith.   25
Hath he received the articles we sent?
HIERONIMO Justice! O justice to Hieronimo!
LORENZO Back! Seest thou not the king is busy?
HIERONIMO O, is he so?
KING Who is he that interrupts our business?   30
HIERONIMO Not I. Hieronimo, beware! Go by, go by!°
AMBASSADOR Renownèd king, he hath received and read
Thy kingly proffers, and thy promised league;

And, as a man extremely overjoyed
To hear his son so princely entertained,   35
Whose death he had so solemnly bewailed,
This, for thy further satisfaction
And kingly love, he kindly lets thee know:
First, for the marriage of his princely son
With Bel-imperia, thy belovèd niece,   40
The news are more delightful to his soul
Than myrrh or incense to the offended heavens.°
In person, therefore, will he come himself,
To see the marriage rites solemnised,
And, in the presence of the court of Spain,   45
To knit a sure, inexplicable band°
Of kingly love and everlasting league
Betwixt the crowns of Spain and Portingale.
There will he give his crown to Balthazar
And make a queen of Bel-imperia.   50
KING Brother, how like you this our viceroy's love?
CASTILE No doubt, my lord, it is an argument
Of honourable care to keep his friend,
And wondrous zeal to Balthazar his son;
Nor am I least indebted to his grace,   55
That bends his liking to my daughter thus.
AMBASSADOR Now last, dread lord, here hath his highness sent—
Although he send not that his son return—
His ransom due to Don Horatio.
HIERONIMO Horatio! who calls Horatio?   60
KING And well remembered; thank his majesty.
Here, see it given to Horatio.
HIERONIMO Justice! O justice, justice, gentle king!
KING Who is that? Hieronimo?
HIERONIMO Justice, O justice! O my son, my son!   65
My son, whom naught can ransom or redeem!
LORENZO Hieronimo, you are not well-advised.
HIERONIMO Away, Lorenzo, hinder me no more;
For thou hast made me bankrupt of my bliss.
Give me my son! You shall not ransom him.   70
Away! I'll rip the bowels of the earth,
      He diggeth with his dagger
And ferry over to th'Elysian plains,
And bring my son to show his deadly wounds.

Stand from about me!
I'll make a pickaxe of my poniard,°   75
And here surrender up my marshalship:
For I'll go marshal up the fiends in hell
To be avengèd on you all for this.
KING What means this outrage?°
Will none of you restrain his fury?   80
HIERONIMO Nay, soft and fair! You shall not need to strive:
Needs must he go that the devils drive.°
              Exit [Hieronimo]
KING What accident hath happed Hieronimo?°
I have not seen him to demean him so.°
LORENZO My gracious lord, he is with extreme pride   85
Conceived of young Horatio, his son,
And covetous of having to himself
The ransom of the young prince Balthazar,
Distract, and in a manner lunatic.
KING Believe me, nephew, we are sorry for't;   90
This is the love that fathers bear their sons.
—But, gentle brother, go give to him this gold,
The prince's ransom; let him have his due.
For what he hath Horatio shall not want;
Haply Hieronimo hath need thereof.   95
LORENZO But if he be thus helplessly distract,
'Tis requisite his office be resigned,
And given to one of more discretion.
KING We shall increase his melancholy so.
'Tis best that we see further in it first,   ·100
Till when, ourself will exempt the place.°
And, brother, now bring in the ambassador,
That he may be a witness of the match
'Twixt Balthazar and Bel-imperia,
And that we may prefix a certain time   105
Wherein the marriage shall be solemnised,
That we may have thy lord, the viceroy, here.
AMBASSADOR Therein your highness highly shall content
His majesty, that longs to hear from hence.
KING On then, and hear you, Lord Ambassador.   110
              Exeunt

[3.13]

Enter Hieronimo with a book in his hand
[HIERONIMO *reading*] '*Vindicta mihi!*°
    Aye, heaven will be revenged of every ill,
    Nor will they suffer murder unrepaid.
    Then stay, Hieronimo, attend their will:
    For mortal men may not appoint their time.   5
[*Reading again*] *Per scelus semper tutum est sceleribus iter.*°
    Strike, and strike home, where wrong is offered thee;
    For evils unto ills conductors be,°
    And death's the worst of resolution.°
    For he that thinks with patience to contend°   10
    To quiet life, his life shall easily end.
[*Reading again*] *Fata si miseros iuvant, habes salutem;*
Fata si vitam negant, habes sepulchrum:°
    If destiny thy miseries do ease,
    Then hast thou health, and happy shalt thou be;   15
    If destiny deny thee life, Hieronimo,
    Yet shalt thou be assurèd of a tomb.
    If neither, yet let this thy comfort be:
    Heaven covereth him that hath no burial.
    And, to conclude, I will revenge his death!   20
    But how? Not as the vulgar wits of men,°
    With open, but inevitable ills,
    As by a secret, yet a certain mean,°
    Which under kindship will be cloakèd best.°
    Wise men will take their opportunity,   25
    Closely and safely fitting things to time.°
    But in extremes advantage hath no time,°
    And therefore all times fit not for revenge.
    Thus, therefore, will I rest me in unrest,
    Dissembling quiet in unquietness,   30
    Not seeming that I know their villainies,
    That my simplicity may make them think
    That ignorantly I will let all slip;
    For ignorance, I wot, and well they know,
    Remedium malorum iners est.°   35
    Nor aught avails it me to menace them°
    Who, as a wintry storm upon a plain,

[Handwritten marginal note: Sim. to advice Medea doesn't take in Seneca.]

Will bear me down with their nobility.°
No, no, Hieronimo, thou must enjoin
Thine eyes to observation, and thy tongue   40
To milder speeches than thy spirit affords,
Thy heart to patience, and thy hands to rest,
Thy cap to courtesy, and thy knee to bow,°
Till to revenge thou know when, where, and how.
    A noise within
How now, what noise? what coil is that you keep?° 45
    Enter a Servant
SERVANT Here are a sort of poor petitioners
That are importunate, an it shall please you, sir,
That you should plead their cases to the king.
HIERONIMO That I should plead their several actions?°
Why, let them enter, and let me see them.   50
    Enter Three Citizens and an Old Man
FIRST CITIZEN So, I tell you this: for learning and for law,
There is not any advocate in Spain
That can prevail, or will take half the pain
That he will, in pursuit of equity.
HIERONIMO Come near, you men that thus importune me. 55
[*Aside*] Now must I bear a face of gravity;
For thus I used, before my marshalship,
To plead in causes as corregidor.—
Come on, sirs, what's the matter?
SECOND CITIZEN   Sir, an action.
HIERONIMO Of battery?
FIRST CITIZEN   Mine of debt.
HIERONIMO   Give place.°   60
SECOND CITIZEN No, sir, mine is an action of the case.°
THIRD CITIZEN Mine, an *ejectione firmae* by a lease.°
HIERONIMO Content you, sirs, are you determinèd
That I should plead your several actions?
FIRST CITIZEN Aye, sir, and here's my declaration.   65
SECOND CITIZEN And here is my band.
THIRD CITIZEN   And here is my lease.°
    They give him papers
HIERONIMO But wherefore stands yon silly man so mute,°
With mournful eyes and hands to heaven upreared?
Come hither, father, let me know thy cause.
OLD MAN O worthy sir, my cause, but slightly known, 70

May move the hearts of warlike Myrmidons
And melt the Corsic rocks with ruthful tears.°
HIERONIMO Say, father, tell me what's thy suit?
OLD MAN No, sir, could my woes
 Give way unto my most distressful words,   75
 Then should I not in paper, as you see,
 With ink bewray what blood began in me.°
HIERONIMO What's here? 'The humble supplication
 Of Don Bazulto for his murdered son.'
OLD MAN Aye, sir.
HIERONIMO   No, sir, it was my murdered son: 80
 O my son, my son, O my son Horatio!
 But mine, or thine, Bazulto, be content.
 Here, take my handkercher and wipe thine eyes,
 Whiles wretched I, in thy mishaps, may see
 The lively portrait of my dying self.°   85
   He draweth out a bloody napkin°
 O no, not this! Horatio, this was thine;
 And when I dyed it in thy dearest blood,
 This was a token 'twixt thy soul and me,
 That of thy death revengèd I should be.
 But here, take this, and this—what, my purse? 90
 Aye this, and that, and all of them are thine;°
 For all as one are our extremities.°
FIRST CITIZEN O, see the kindness of Hieronimo!
SECOND CITIZEN This gentleness shows him a gentleman.
HIERONIMO See, see, O see thy shame, Hieronimo, 95
 See here a loving father to his son!
 Behold the sorrows and the sad laments
 That he delivereth for his son's decease!
 If love's effects so strives in lesser things,°
 If love enforce such moods in meaner wits,° 100
 If love express such power in poor estates,
 Hieronimo, whenas a raging sea,
 Tossed with the wind and tide, o'erturneth then
 The upper billows, course of waves to keep,
 Whilst lesser waters labour in the deep,° 105
 Then shamest thou not, Hieronimo, to neglect
 The sweet revenge of thy Horatio?
 Though on this earth justice will not be found,
 I'll down to hell, and in this passion

Knock at the dismal gates of Pluto's court,   110
Getting by force, as once Alcides did,°
A troop of Furies and tormenting hags
To torture Don Lorenzo and the rest.
Yet lest the triple-headed porter should°
Deny my passage to the slimy strand,   115
The Thracian poet thou shalt counterfeit.°
Come on, old father, be my Orpheus,
And if thou canst no notes upon the harp,°
Then sound the burden of thy sore heart's grief,°
Till we do gain that Proserpine may grant   120
Revenge on them that murderèd my son.
Then will I rent and tear them, thus and thus,°
Shivering their limbs in pieces with my teeth.
            Tear[s] the papers
FIRST CITIZEN O sir, my declaration!
            Exit Hieronimo, and the Citizens after
SECOND CITIZEN   Save my bond!
            Enter Hieronimo [pursued by the Citizens]
SECOND CITIZEN Save my bond!   125
THIRD CITIZEN Alas, my lease! It cost me ten pound,
    And you, my lord, have torn the same.
HIERONIMO That cannot be; I gave it never a wound.
    Show me one drop of blood fall from the same!
    How is it possible I should slay it then?   130
    Tush, no; run after, catch me if you can.
            *Exeunt all but the Old Man. He remains till Hieronimo
            enters again, who, staring him in the face, speaks*
HIERONIMO And art thou come, Horatio, from the depth,
    To ask for justice in this upper earth?
    To tell thy father thou art unrevenged?
    To wring more tears from Isabella's eyes,   135
    Whose lights are dimmed with overlong laments?
    Go back, my son, complain to Aeacus,
    For here's no justice; gentle boy, begone,
    For justice is exilèd from the earth:
    Hieronimo will bear thee company.   140
    Thy mother cries on righteous Rhadamanth
    For just revenge against the murderers.
OLD MAN Alas, my lord, whence springs this troubled speech?
HIERONIMO But let me look on my Horatio.

Sweet boy, how art thou changed in death's black shade!   145
Had Proserpine no pity on thy youth,
But suffered thy fair crimson-coloured spring
With withered winter to be blasted thus?
Horatio, thou art older than thy father.
Ah ruthless fate, that favour thus transforms!°   150

OLD MAN Ah, my good lord, I am not your young son.

HIERONIMO What, not my son? Thou then a Fury art,
Sent from the empty kingdom of black night
To summon me to make appearance
Before grim Minos and just Rhadamanth,   155
To plague Hieronimo that is remiss,
And seeks not vengeance for Horatio's death.

OLD MAN I am a grievèd man, and not a ghost,
That came for justice for my murdered son.

HIERONIMO Aye, now I know thee, now thou namest thy son: 160
Thou art the lively image of my grief;
Within thy face my sorrows I may see.
Thy eyes are gummed with tears, thy cheeks are wan,
Thy forehead troubled, and thy mutt'ring lips
Murmur sad words abruptly broken off   165
By force of windy sighs thy spirit breathes;
And all this sorrow riseth for thy son:
And selfsame sorrow feel I for my son.
Come in, old man, thou shalt to Isabel;
Lean on my arm. I thee, thou me shalt stay,°   170
And thou, and I, and she will sing a song,
Three parts in one, but all of discords framed—°
Talk not of chords, but let us now be gone;
For with a cord Horatio was slain.
          Exeunt

[3.14]

*Enter [from one side] King of Spain, Castile, Lorenzo,
Balthazar, and Bel-imperia, [attended]; [from the other side]
Viceroy, Don Pedro, [attended]*

KING Go, brother, it is the Duke of Castile's cause;
Salute the viceroy in our name.

CASTILE   I go.

VICEROY Go forth, Don Pedro, for thy nephew's sake,
　And greet the Duke of Castile.
PEDRO   It shall be so.
KING And now to meet these Portuguese,   5
　For as we now are, so sometimes were these:°
　Kings and commanders of the western Indies.
　Welcome, brave viceroy, to the court of Spain,°
　And welcome, all his honourable train!
　'Tis not unknown to us for why you come,   10
　Or have so kingly crossed the seas.
　Sufficeth it, in this we note the troth
　And more than common love you lend to us.
　So is it that mine honourable niece.
　(For it beseems us now that it be known)   15
　Already is betrothed to Balthazar;
　And by appointment and our condescent
　Tomorrow are they to be marrièd.
　To this intent we entertain thyself,
　Thy followers, their pleasure, and our peace.   20
　Speak, men of Portingale, shall it be so?
　If aye, say so; if not, say flatly no.
VICEROY Renownèd king, I come not, as thou think'st,
　With doubtful followers, unresolvèd men,
　But such as have upon thine articles   25
　Confirmed thy motion and contented me.
　Know, sovereign, I come to solemnize
　The marriage of thy belovèd niece,°
　Fair Bel-imperia, with my Balthazar,
　With thee, my son; whom sith I live to see,   30
　Here take my crown, I give it her and thee;
　And let me live a solitary life
　In ceaseless prayers,
　To think how strangely heaven hath thee preserved.
KING See, brother, see, how nature strives in him!°   35
　Come, worthy viceroy, and accompany
　Thy friend with thine extremities;°
　A place more private fits this princely mood.
VICEROY Or here or where your highness thinks it good.°
　　　Exeunt all but Castile and Lorenzo [and their attendants]
CASTILE Nay, stay, Lorenzo, let me talk with you.   40
　Seest thou this entertainment of these kings?
LORENZO I do, my lord, and joy to see the same.

61

CASTILE And knowest thou why this meeting is?
LORENZO For her, my lord, whom Balthazar doth love,
   And to confirm their promised marriage.   45
CASTILE She is thy sister?
LORENZO   Who, Bel-imperia?
   Aye, my gracious lord, and this is the day,
   That I have longed so happily to see.
CASTILE Thou wouldst be loath that any fault of thine
   Should intercept her in her happiness?°   50
LORENZO Heavens will not let Lorenzo err so much.
CASTILE Why then, Lorenzo, listen to my words.
   It is suspected, and reported too,
   That thou, Lorenzo, wrong'st Hieronimo,
   And in his suits towards his majesty   55
   Still keep'st him back and seeks to cross his suit.
LORENZO That I, my lord—?
CASTILE I tell thee, son, myself have heard it said,
   When to my sorrow I have been ashamed
   To answer for thee, though thou art my son.°   60
   Lorenzo, knowest thou not the common love°
   And kindness that Hieronimo hath won
   By his deserts within the court of Spain?
   Or seest thou not the king my brother's care
   In his behalf, and to procure his health?   65
   Lorenzo, shouldst thou thwart his passions
   And he exclaim against thee to the king,°
   What honour were't in this assembly,
   Or what a scandal were't among the kings
   To hear Hieronimo exclaim on thee?   70
   Tell me—and look thou tell me truly too—
   Whence grows the ground of this report in court?
LORENZO My lord, it lies not in Lorenzo's power
   To stop the vulgar, liberal of their tongues.°
   A small advantage makes a water-breach,°   75
   And no man lives that long contenteth all.
CASTILE Myself have seen thee busy to keep back
   Him and his supplications from the king.
LORENZO Yourself, my lord, hath seen his passions,
   That ill beseemed the presence of a king;°   80
   And for I pitied him in his distress°
   I held him thence with kind and courteous words,

As free from malice to Hieronimo
As to my soul, my lord.

CASTILE Hieronimo, my son, mistakes thee then.   85

LORENZO My gracious father, believe me, so he doth.
But what's a silly man, distract in mind,
To think upon the murder of his son?
Alas, how easy is it for him to err!
But for his satisfaction and the world's   90
'Twere good, my lord, that Hieronimo and I
Were reconciled, if he misconster me.

CASTILE Lorenzo, thou hast said, it shall be so.
Go one of you and call Hieronimo.

[Exit a Servant.] Enter Balthazar and Bel-imperia

BALTHAZAR Come, Bel-imperia, Balthazar's content,   95
My sorrow's ease and sovereign of my bliss,
Sith heaven hath ordained thee to be mine,
Disperse those clouds and melancholy looks,
And clear them up with those thy sun-bright eyes,
Wherein my hope and heaven's fair beauty lies.   100

BEL-IMPERIA My looks, my lord, are fitting for my love,
Which, new begun, can show [no] brighter yet.

BALTHAZAR New-kindled flames should burn as morning sun.

BEL-IMPERIA But not too fast, lest heat and all be done.
I see my lord my father.

BALTHAZAR   Truce, my love;   105
I will go salute him.

CASTILE   Welcome, Balthazar!°
Welcome, brave prince, the pledge of Castile's peace!
And welcome, Bel-imperia! How now, girl?
Why comest thou sadly to salute us thus?
Content thyself, for I am satisfied: 110
It is not now as when Andrea lived;
We have forgotten and forgiven that,
And thou art gracèd with a happier love.
But, Balthazar, here comes Hieronimo;
I'll have a word with him.   115

Enter Hieronimo and a Servant

HIERONIMO And where's the duke?

SERVANT   Yonder.

HIERONIMO   Even so.—
[Aside] What new device have they devisèd, trow?°

Pocas palabras! Mild as the lamb!°
Is't I will be revengèd? No, I am not the man.
CASTILE Welcome, Hieronimo.   120
LORENZO Welcome, Hieronimo.
BALTHAZAR Welcome, Hieronimo.
HIERONIMO My lords, I thank you for Horatio.
CASTILE Hieronimo, the reason that I sent
   To speak with you is this—
HIERONIMO   What, so short?°   125
   Then I'll be gone, I thank you for't.
      [*Starts to leave*]
CASTILE Nay, stay, Hieronimo!—Go call him, son.
[LORENZO] Hieronimo, my father craves a word with you.
HIERONIMO With me, sir?—Why, my lord, I thought you had done.
LORENZO No. [*Aside.*] Would he had!
CASTILE   Hieronimo, I hear   130
   You find yourself aggrievèd at my son,
   Because you have not access unto the king;
   And say 'tis he that intercepts your suits.
HIERONIMO Why, is not this a miserable thing, my lord?
CASTILE Hieronimo, I hope you have no cause,   135
   And would be loath that one of your deserts
   Should once have reason to suspect my son,
   Considering how I think of you myself.
HIERONIMO Your son Lorenzo! Whom, my noble lord?
   The hope of Spain, mine honourable friend?   140
   Grant me the combat of them if they dare,
      Draws out his sword
   I'll meet him face to face, to tell me so!
   These be the scandalous reports of such
   As loves not me, and hate my lord too much.
   Should I suspect Lorenzo would prevent   145
   Or cross my suit, that loved my son so well?
   My lord, I am ashamed it should be said.
LORENZO Hieronimo, I never gave you cause.
HIERONIMO My good lord, I know you did not.
CASTILE   There then pause;°
   And for the satisfaction of the world,   150
   Hieronimo, frequent my homely house,°
   The Duke of Castile, Cyprian's ancient seat;
   And when thou wilt, use me, my son, and it.

But here, before Prince Balthazar and me,
Embrace each other and be perfect friends.   155
HIERONIMO Aye, marry, my lord, and shall.
   Friends, quoth he? See, I'll be friends with you all:
   Specially with you, my lovely lord;°
   For divers causes it is fit for us
   That we be friends—the world is suspicious,   160
   And men may think what we imagine not.
BALTHAZAR Why, this is friendly done, Hieronimo.
LORENZO And that I hope: old grudges are forgot.
HIERONIMO What else? It were a shame it should not be so.
CASTILE Come on, Hieronimo, at my request;   165
   Let us entreat your company today.
HIERONIMO Your lordship's to command.
          Exeunt [all but Hieronimo]
                                  —Pha! keep your way:°

Chi mi fa piu carezze che non suole,
Tradito mi ha, o tradir mi vuole.°
          Exit

[3.15]

          Ghost [of Andrea] and Revenge, [who is asleep]
GHOST Awake, Erichtho! Cerberus, awake!°
   Solicit Pluto, gentle Proserpine!
   To combat, Acheron and Erebus!°
   For ne'er, by Styx and Phlegethon in hell,
   O'er-ferried Charon to the fiery lakes   5
   Such fearful sights, as poor Andrea sees.
   Revenge, awake!
REVENGE   Awake? For why?
GHOST Awake, Revenge; for thou art ill-advised
   To sleep away what thou art warned to watch.
REVENGE Content thyself, and do not trouble me.   10
GHOST Awake, Revenge, if love—as love hath had—
   Have yet the power or prevalence in hell.
   Hieronimo with Lorenzo is joined in league,
   And intercepts our passage to revenge.
   Awake, Revenge, or we are woebegone!   15

65

REVENGE Thus worldlings ground what they have dreamed upon.°
    Content thyself, Andrea; though I sleep,
    Yet is my mood soliciting their souls.°
    Sufficeth thee that poor Hieronimo
    Cannot forget his son Horatio.   20
    Nor dies Revenge, although he sleep awhile;
    For in unquiet, quietness is feigned,
    And slumb'ring is a common worldly wile.
    Behold, Andrea, for an instance, how°
    Revenge hath slept, and then imagine thou   25
    What 'tis to be subject to destiny.
        Enter a dumb show° [which performs as Revenge explains the
        allegory]
GHOST Awake, Revenge, reveal this mystery.
REVENGE The two first, the nuptial torches bore,°
    As brightly burning as the midday's sun;
    But after them doth Hymen hie as fast,   30
    Clothèd in sable, and a saffron robe,°
    And blows them out, and quencheth them with blood,
    As discontent that things continue so.
GHOST Sufficeth me; thy meaning's understood,
    And thanks to thee and those infernal powers   35
    That will not tolerate a lover's woe.
    Rest thee, for I will sit to see the rest.
REVENGE Then argue not, for thou hast thy request.
        Exeunt [Dumb show]

[4.1]

Enter Bel-imperia and Hieronimo

BEL-IMPERIA Is this the love thou bear'st Horatio?
Is this the kindness that thou counterfeits?
Are these the fruits of thine incessant tears?
Hieronimo, are these thy passions,
Thy protestations and thy deep laments,   5
That thou wert wont to weary men withal?
O unkind father! O deceitful world!
With what excuses canst thou show thyself
From this dishonour and the hate of men,
Thus to neglect the loss and life of him   10
Whom both my letters and thine own belief
Assures thee to be causeless slaughterèd?
Hieronimo, for shame, Hieronimo,
Be not a history to aftertimes
Of such ingratitude unto thy son:°   15
Unhappy mothers of such children then—
But monstrous fathers to forget so soon
The death of those whom they with care and cost
Have tendered so, thus careless should be lost.°
Myself, a stranger in respect of thee,°   20
So loved his life, as still I wish their deaths.
Nor shall his death be unrevenged by me,
Although I bear it out for fashion's sake:°
For here I swear, in sight of heaven and earth,
Shouldst thou neglect the love thou shouldst retain,   25
And give it over and devise no more,
Myself should send their hateful souls to hell
That wrought his downfall with extremest death.
HIERONIMO But may it be that Bel-imperia
Vows such revenge as she hath deigned to say?   30
Why, then I see that heaven applies our drift,°
And all the saints do sit soliciting
For vengeance on those cursèd murderers.
Madam, 'tis true, and now I find it so,
I found a letter, written in your name,   35
And in that letter, how Horatio died.
Pardon, O pardon, Bel-imperia,

My fear and care in not believing it;°
Nor think I thoughtless think upon a mean°
To let his death be unrevenged at full.°   40
And here I vow—so you but give consent,
And will conceal my resolution—
I will ere long determine of their deaths
That causeless thus have murderèd my son.

BEL-IMPERIA Hieronimo, I will consent, conceal,   45
And aught that may effect for thine avail,
Join with thee to revenge Horatio's death.

HIERONIMO On then. Whatsoever I devise,
Let me entreat you grace my practices,°
For why the plot's already in mine head.°   50
Here they are.

Enter Balthazar and Lorenzo

BALTHAZAR   How now, Hieronimo?
What, courting Bel-imperia?

HIERONIMO   Aye, my lord;
Such courting as, I promise you,
She hath my heart, but you, my lord, have hers.

LORENZO But now, Hieronimo, or never,   55
We are to entreat your help.

HIERONIMO   My help?
Why, my good lords, assure yourselves of me;°
For you have given me cause—aye, by my faith have you!

BALTHAZAR It pleased you, at the entertainment of the ambassador,
To grace the king so much as with a show.   60
Now, were your study so well furnishèd,°
As for the passing of the first night's sport,°
To entertain my father with the like,
Or any such-like pleasing motion,°
Assure yourself it would content them well.   65

HIERONIMO Is this all?

BALTHAZAR   Aye, this is all.

HIERONIMO Why then, I'll fit you; say no more.°
When I was young, I gave my mind
And plied myself to fruitless poetry,
Which though it profit the professor naught°   70
Yet is it passing pleasing to the world.

LORENZO And how for that?

HIERONIMO   Marry, my good lord, thus—

And yet methinks you are too quick with us—°
When in Toledo there I studièd,
It was my chance to write a tragedy,   75
See here, my lords—
        He shows them a book
Which, long forgot, I found this other day.
Now would your lordships favour me so much
As but to grace me with your acting it—
I mean each one of you to play a part—   80
Assure you it will prove most passing strange,
And wondrous plausible to that assembly.°
BALTHAZAR What, would you have us play a tragedy?°
HIERONIMO Why, Nero thought it no disparagement,°
        And kings and emperors have ta'en delight   85
        To make experience of their wits in plays.°
LORENZO Nay, be not angry, good Hieronimo;
        The prince but asked a question.
BALTHAZAR In faith, Hieronimo, an you be in earnest,
        I'll make one.
LORENZO   And I another.°   90
HIERONIMO Now, my good lord, could you entreat
        Your sister Bel-imperia to make one?
        For what's a play without a woman in it?
BEL-IMPERIA Little entreaty shall serve me, Hieronimo;
        For I must needs be employed in your play.   95
HIERONIMO Why, this is well. I tell you, lordings,
        It was determinèd to have been acted
        By gentlemen and scholars too,
        Such as could tell what to speak.
BALTHAZAR   And now°
        It shall be played by princes and courtiers,   100
        Such as can tell how to speak—
        If, as it is our country manner,°
        You will but let us know the argument.°
HIERONIMO That shall I roundly. The chronicles of Spain°
        Record this written of a knight of Rhodes:°   105
        He was betrothed and wedded at the length
        To one Perseda, an Italian dame,
        Whose beauty ravished all that her beheld,
        Especially the soul of Soliman,°
        Who at the marriage was the chiefest guest.   110

By sundry means sought Soliman to win
Perseda's love, and could not gain the same.
Then 'gan he break his passions to a friend,°
One of his bashaws whom he held full dear.
Her had this bashaw long solicited,   115
And saw she was not otherwise to be won
But by her husband's death, this knight of Rhodes,
Whom presently by treachery he slew.
She, stirred with an exceeding hate therefore,
As cause of this, slew Soliman,   120
And to escape the bashaw's tyranny
Did stab herself, and this the tragedy.

LORENZO O excellent!

BEL-IMPERIA   But say, Hieronimo,
What then became of him that was the bashaw?

HIERONIMO Marry, thus: moved with remorse of his misdeeds,   125
Ran to a mountain top, and hung himself.

BALTHAZAR But which of us is to perform that part?

HIERONIMO O, that will I, my lords, make no doubt of it.
I'll play the murderer, I warrant you,
For I already have conceited that.°   130

BALTHAZAR And what shall I?

HIERONIMO Great Soliman, the Turkish emperor.

LORENZO And I?

HIERONIMO   Erastus, the knight of Rhodes.

BEL-IMPERIA And I?

HIERONIMO   Perseda, chaste and resolute.
And here, my lords, are several abstracts drawn,   135
For each of you to note your parts,
And act it as occasion's offered you.
          Gives a paper to Balthazar
You must provide a Turkish cap,°
A black mustachio and a falchion;
          Gives another to Lorenzo
You with a cross, like to a knight of Rhodes;   140
          He giveth Bel-imperia another
And, madam, you must attire yourself
Like Phoebe, Flora, or the Huntress,°
Which to your discretion shall seem best.
And as for me, my lords, I'll look to one,°
And with the ransom that the viceroy sent   145

So furnish and perform this tragedy
As all the world shall say Hieronimo
Was liberal in gracing of it so.
BALTHAZAR Hieronimo, methinks a comedy were better.
HIERONIMO A comedy?   150
  Fie, comedies are fit for common wits;
  But to present a kingly troop withal,
  Give me a stately-written tragedy;°
  Tragoedia cothurnata, fitting kings,°
  Containing matter, and not common things.°   155
  My lords, all this must be performed
  As fitting for the first night's revelling.
  The Italian tragedians were so sharp of wit,
  That in one hour's meditation
  They would perform anything in action.   160
LORENZO And well it may; for I have seen the like
  In Paris 'mongst the French tragedians.°
HIERONIMO In Paris? mass, and well rememberèd!
  There's one thing more that rests for us to do.°
BALTHAZAR What's that, Hieronimo? Forget not anything.   165
HIERONIMO Each one of us must act his part
  In unknown languages,
  That it may breed the more variety:
  As you, my lord, in Latin, I in Greek,
  You in Italian; and for because I know   170
  That Bel-imperia hath practiced the French,
  In courtly French shall all her phrases be.
BEL-IMPERIA You mean to try my cunning then, Hieronimo?
BALTHAZAR But this will be a mere confusion
  And hardly shall we all be understood.   175
HIERONIMO It must be so; for the conclusion
  Shall prove the invention and all was good;
  And I myself in an oration,
  And with a strange and wondrous show besides,
  That I will have there behind a curtain,   180
  Assure yourself shall make the matter known;
  And all shall be concluded in one scene,
  For there's no pleasure ta'en in tediousness.
BALTHAZAR [*aside to Lorenzo*] How like you this?
LORENZO [*aside to Balthazar*] Why, thus my lord: 185
  We must resolve to soothe his humours up.°

BALTHAZAR On then, Hieronimo; farewell till soon.
HIERONIMO You'll ply this gear?
LORENZO   I warrant you.
            Exeunt all but Hieronimo
HIERONIMO   Why so;°
      Now shall I see the fall of Babylon°
      Wrought by the heavens in this confusion.   190
      And if the world like not this tragedy,
      Hard is the hap of old Hieronimo.
            Exit

[4.2]

            Enter Isabella with a [knife]
ISABELLA Tell me no more! O monstrous homicides!
      Since neither piety nor pity moves
      The king to justice or compassion,
      I will revenge myself upon this place
      Where thus they murdered my belovèd son.   5
            She cuts down the arbour°
      Down with these branches and these loathsome boughs
      Of this unfortunate and fatal pine!
      Down with them, Isabella; rent them up
      And burn the roots from whence the rest is sprung.
      I will not leave a root, a stalk, a tree,   10
      A bough, a branch, a blossom, nor a leaf,
      No, not an herb within this garden plot:
      Accursèd complot of my misery!°
      Fruitless forever may this garden be,
      Barren the earth, and blissless whosoever   15
      Imagines not to keep it unmanured!
      An eastern wind, commixed with noisome airs,°
      Shall blast the plants and the young saplings;
      The earth with serpents shall be pesterèd,
      And passengers, for fear to be infect,°   20
      Shall stand aloof, and looking at it, tell:
      'There, murdered, died the son of Isabel.'
      Aye, here he died, and here I him embrace;
      See where his ghost solicits with his wounds
      Revenge on her that should revenge his death.   25

Hieronimo, make haste to see thy son;
For sorrow and despair hath cited me°
To hear Horatio plead with Rhadamanth.
Make haste, Hieronimo, to hold excused
Thy negligence in pursuit of their deaths°   30
Whose hateful wrath bereaved him of his breath.
Ah, nay, thou dost delay their deaths,
Forgives the murderers of thy noble son,
And none but I bestir me—to no end!
And as I curse this tree from further fruit,   35
So shall my womb be cursèd for his sake;
And with this weapon will I wound the breast,
The hapless breast, that gave Horatio suck.
            She stabs herself [and exits, dying]

[4.3]

            Enter Hieronimo; he knocks up° the curtain, [concealing
            Horatio's corpse behind it.] Enter the Duke of Castile
CASTILE How now, Hieronimo, where's your fellows,°
    That you take all this pain?
HIERONIMO O sir, it is for the author's credit
    To look that all things may go well.
    But, good my lord, let me entreat your grace   5
    To give the king the copy of the play:
            [Gives Castile a book]
    This is the argument of what we show.°
CASTILE I will, Hieronimo.
HIERONIMO   One thing more, my good lord.
CASTILE What's that?
HIERONIMO   Let me entreat your grace
    That, when the train are passed into the gallery,   10
    You would vouchsafe to throw me down the key.
CASTILE I will, Hieronimo.
            Exit Castile
HIERONIMO   What, are you ready, Balthazar?
    Bring a chair and a cushion for the king.
            Enter Balthazar, with a chair
    Well done, Balthazar! hang up the title:°
    Our scene is Rhodes. What, is your beard on?   15

BALTHAZAR Half on; the other is in my hand.
HIERONIMO Dispatch, for shame; are you so long?
        Exit Balthazar
    Bethink thyself, Hieronimo,
    Recall thy wits, recompt thy former wrongs
    Thou hast received by murder of thy son,   20
    And lastly, not least, how Isabel,
    Once his mother and thy dearest wife,
    All woebegone for him hath slain herself.
    Behoves thee then, Hieronimo, to be revenged—
    The plot is laid of dire revenge.   25
    On, then, Hieronimo, pursue revenge,
    For nothing wants but acting of revenge!
        Exit

[4.4]

Enter King of Spain, Viceroy, the Duke of Castile, [Don Pedro] and their train. [They seat themselves to watch the play]

KING Now, viceroy, shall we see the tragedy
    Of Soliman, the Turkish emperor,
    Performed of pleasure by your son the prince,°
    My nephew Don Lorenzo, and my niece.
VICEROY Who? Bel-imperia?
KING   Aye, and Hieronimo, our marshal,   5
    At whose request they deign to do't themselves.
    These be our pastimes in the court of Spain.
    Here, brother, you shall be the bookkeeper:°
    This is the argument of that they show.
        He giveth him a book
        Gentlemen, this play of Hieronimo, in sundry languages, was thought good to be set down in English, more largely,° for the easier understanding to every public reader.
        Enter Balthazar [as Soliman], Bel-imperia [as Perseda], and Hieronimo [as the Bashaw]
    BALTHAZAR Bashaw, that Rhodes is ours, yield heavens the honour,   10
        And holy Mahomet, our sacred prophet!
        And be thou graced with every excellence

74

That Soliman can give, or thou desire.
But thy desert in conquering Rhodes is less
Than in reserving this fair Christian nymph,   15
Perseda, blissful lamp of excellence,
Whose eyes compel, like powerful adamant,
The warlike heart of Soliman to wait.°

KING See, viceroy, that is Balthazar, your son,
  That represents the emperor Soliman: 20
  How well he acts his amorous passion!

VICEROY Aye, Bel-imperia hath taught him that.

CASTILE That's because his mind runs all on Bel-imperia.

HIERONIMO Whatever joy earth yields, betide your majesty.

BALTHAZAR Earth yields no joy without Perseda's love.   25

HIERONIMO Let then Perseda on your grace attend.

BALTHAZAR She shall not wait on me, but I on her:
  Drawn by the influence of her lights, I yield.°
  But let my friend, the Rhodian knight, come forth,
  Erasto, dearer than my life to me,   30
  That he may see Perseda, my beloved.
    Enter [Lorenzo as] Erasto

KING Here comes Lorenzo: look upon the plot,
  And tell me, brother, what part plays he?

BEL-IMPERIA Ah, my Erasto, welcome to Perseda.

LORENZO Thrice happy is Erasto that thou livest;   35
  Rhodes' loss is nothing to Erasto's joy;
  Sith his Perseda lives, his life survives.

BALTHAZAR *[aside to Hieronimo]*
  Ah, bashaw, here is love between Erasto
  And fair Perseda, sovereign of my soul.

HIERONIMO *[aside to Balthazar]* Remove Erasto, mighty Soliman,   40
  And then Perseda will be quickly won.

BALTHAZAR Erasto is my friend; and while he lives,
  Perseda never will remove her love.

HIERONIMO Let not Erasto live to grieve great Soliman.

BALTHAZAR Dear is Erasto in our princely eye.   45

HIERONIMO But if he be your rival, let him die.

BALTHAZAR Why, let him die: so love commandeth me.
  Yet grieve I that Erasto should so die.

HIERONIMO Erasto, Soliman saluteth thee,
  And lets thee wit by me his highness' will,°   50
  Which is, thou shouldst be thus employed.

Stab[s] him

BEL-IMPERIA   Aye me!
　　Erasto! See, Soliman, Erasto's slain!
BALTHAZAR   Yet liveth Soliman to comfort thee.
　　Fair queen of beauty, let not favour die,°
　　But with a gracious eye behold his grief,   55
　　That with Perseda's beauty is increased,
　　If by Perseda his grief be not released.°
BEL-IMPERIA   Tyrant, desist soliciting vain suits;
　　Relentless are mine ears to thy laments,
　　As thy butcher is pitiless and base,   60
　　Which seized on my Erasto, harmless knight.
　　Yet by thy power thou thinkest to command,
　　And to thy power Perseda doth obey;
　　But were she able, thus she would revenge
　　Thy treacheries on thee, ignoble prince!   65

Stab[s] him

　　And on herself she would be thus revenged.

Stab[s] herself

KING   Well said!—Old marshal, this was bravely done.
HIERONIMO   But Bel-imperia plays Perseda well.
VICEROY   Were this in earnest, Bel-imperia,
　　You would be better to my son than so.   70
KING   But now what follows for Hieronimo?
HIERONIMO   Marry, this follows for Hieronimo:
　　Here break we off our sundry languages,
　　And thus conclude I in our vulgar tongue.
　　Haply you think—but bootless are your thoughts—   75
　　That this is fabulously counterfeit,°
　　And that we do as all tragedians do,
　　To die today, for fashioning our scene,
　　The death of Ajax or some Roman peer,
　　And in a minute starting up again,   80
　　Revive to please tomorrow's audience.
　　No, princes, know I am Hieronimo,
　　The hopeless father of a hapless son,
　　Whose tongue is tuned to tell his latest tale,
　　Not to excuse gross errors in the play.   85
　　I see your looks urge instance of these words;°
　　Behold the reason urging me to this!

Shows his dead son

See here my show, look on this spectacle!
Here lay my hope, and here my hope hath end;
Here lay my heart, and here my heart was slain;   90
Here lay my treasure, here my treasure lost;
Here lay my bliss, and here my bliss bereft;
But hope, heart, treasure, joy, and bliss,
All fled, failed, died, yea, all decayed with this.
From forth these wounds came breath that gave me life;   95
They murdered me that made these fatal marks.
The cause was love, whence grew this mortal hate:
The hate, Lorenzo and young Balthazar,
The love, my son to Bel-imperia.
But night, the coverer of accursèd crimes,   100
With pitchy silence hushed these traitors' harms,
And lent them leave, for they had sorted leisure°
To take advantage in my garden plot
Upon my son, my dear Horatio.
There merciless they butchered up my boy,   105
In black, dark night, to pale, dim, cruel death.
He shrieks, I heard—and yet, methinks, I hear—
His dismal outcry echo in the air.
With soonest speed I hasted to the noise,°
Where hanging on a tree I found my son,   110 ·
Through-girt with wounds, and slaughtered as you see.°
And grieved I, think you, at this spectacle?
Speak, Portuguese, whose loss resembles mine:
If thou canst weep upon thy Balthazar,
'Tis like I wailed for my Horatio.   115
And you, my lord, whose reconcilèd son
Marched in a net, and thought himself unseen,°
And rated me for brainsick lunacy,°
With 'God amend that mad Hieronimo!'—
How can you brook our play's catastrophe?   120
And here behold this bloody handkercher,
Which at Horatio's death I weeping dipped
Within the river of his bleeding wounds:
It as propitious, see, I have reserved,
And never hath it left my bloody heart,   125
Soliciting remembrance of my vow
With these, O, these accursèd murderers,
Which now performed, my heart is satisfied.

And to this end the bashaw I became
That might revenge me on Lorenzo's life,   130
Who therefore was appointed to the part
And was to represent the knight of Rhodes,
That I might kill him more conveniently.
So, viceroy, was this Balthazar, thy son,
That Soliman which Bel-imperia,   135
In person of Perseda, murderèd;
Solely appointed to that tragic part
That she might slay him that offended her.
Poor Bel-imperia missed her part in this:
For though the story saith she should have died,   140
Yet I of kindness, and of care to her,
Did otherwise determine of her end;
But love of him whom they did hate too much°
Did urge her resolution to be such.
And, princes, now behold Hieronimo,   145
Author and actor in this tragedy,
Bearing his latest fortune in his fist;°
And will as resolute conclude his part
As any of the actors gone before.
And, gentles, thus I end my play;   150
Urge no more words, I have no more to say.
        He runs to hang himself
KING O hearken, viceroy! Hold, Hieronimo!
   Brother, my nephew and thy son are slain!
VICEROY We are betrayed! My Balthazar is slain!
   Break ope the doors; run, save Hieronimo.°   155
        [*Attendants break in and hold Hieronimo*]
   Hieronimo,
   Do but inform the king of these events;
   Upon mine honour thou shalt have no harm.
HIERONIMO Viceroy, I will not trust thee with my life,
   Which I this day have offered to my son.   160
   [*Struggles with an Attendant*]—Accursèd wretch!
   Why stayest thou him that was resolved to die?
KING Speak, traitor! Damnèd, bloody murderer, speak!
   For now I have thee, I will make thee speak.
   Why hast thou done this undeserving deed?   165
VICEROY Why hast thou murderèd my Balthazar?
CASTILE Why hast thou butchered both my children thus?

HIERONIMO O, good words!
　As dear to me was my Horatio
　As yours, or yours, or yours, my lord, to you.　　　　　170
　My guiltless son was by Lorenzo slain,
　And by Lorenzo and that Balthazar
　Am I at last revengèd thoroughly,
　Upon whose souls may heavens be yet avenged
　With greater far than these afflictions.　　　　　175
CASTILE But who were thy confederates in this?
VICEROY That was thy daughter Bel-imperia,
　For by her hand my Balthazar was slain.
　I saw her stab him.
KING　　　　　　Why speakest thou not?
HIERONIMO What lesser liberty can kings afford　　　180
　Than harmless silence? Then afford it me.
　Sufficeth I may not, nor I will not tell thee.
KING Fetch forth the tortures! Traitor as thou art,
　I'll make thee tell.
HIERONIMO　　　　Indeed,
　Thou mayest torment me as his wretched son　　　185
　Hath done in murd'ring my Horatio;
　But never shalt thou force me to reveal
　The thing which I have vowed inviolate.
　And therefore, in despite of all thy threats,
　Pleased with their deaths, and eased with their revenge,　　190
　First take my tongue, and afterwards my heart.
　　　[*He bites out his tongue*]
KING O monstrous resolution of a wretch!
　See, viceroy, he hath bitten forth his tongue,
　Rather than to reveal what we required.
CASTILE Yet can he write.　　　　　195
KING And if in this he satisfy us not,
　We will devise th'extremest kind of death
　That ever was invented for a wretch.
　　　Then [*Hieronimo*] *makes signs for a knife to mend his pen*
CASTILE O, he would have a knife to mend his pen.
VICEROY Here, and advise thee that thou write the troth.　　200
　　　[*Gives Hieronimo a knife*]
[KING] Look to my brother! Save Hieronimo!
　　　[*Hieronimo*] *with a knife stabs* [*Castile*] *and himself* [*to death*]
KING What age hath ever heard such monstrous deeds?

My brother, and the whole succeeding hope
That Spain expected after my decease!
Go bear his body hence, that we may mourn   205
The loss of our belovèd brother's death,
That he may be entombed whate'er befall.
I am the next, the nearest, last of all.
VICEROY And thou, Don Pedro, do the like for us:
Take up our hapless son, untimely slain;   210
Set me with him and he with woeful me
Upon the mainmast of a ship unmanned,
And let the wind and tide haul me along
To Scylla's barking and untamèd gulf,°
Or to the loathsome pool of Acheron,   215
To weep my want for my sweet Balthazar:
Spain hath no refuge for a Portingale.

> *The trumpets sound a dead march.* [*Exeunt*] *the King of*
> *Spain mourning after his brother's body, and the Viceroy of*
> *Portingale bearing the body of his son*

[4.5]

Ghost of Andrea and Revenge

GHOST Aye, now my hopes have end in their effects,
When blood and sorrow finish my desires:
Horatio murdered in his father's bower;
Vile Serberine by Pedringano slain;
False Pedringano hanged by quaint device;°   5
Fair Isabella by herself misdone;
Prince Balthazar by Bel-imperia stabbed;
The Duke of Castile and his wicked son
Both done to death by old Hieronimo;
My Bel-imperia fall'n as Dido fell,°   10
And good Hieronimo slain by himself:
Aye, these were spectacles to please my soul!
Now will I beg at lovely Proserpine
That by the virtue of her princely doom°
I may consort my friends in pleasing sort,   15
And on my foes work just and sharp revenge.
I'll lead my friend Horatio through those fields

[Handwritten marginal note:] In life, he can't have hoped for all these people dead — but that's the danger of death and revenge. It removes us from the world, therefore our ties / obligations to others in it.

Where never-dying wars are still inured;°
I'll lead fair Isabella to that train
Where pity weeps, but never feeleth pain;   20
I'll lead my Bel-imperia to those joys
That vestal virgins and fair queens possess;°
I'll lead Hieronimo where Orpheus plays,
Adding sweet pleasure to eternal days.
But say, Revenge, for thou must help, or none,   25
Against the rest how shall my hate be shown?
REVENGE This hand shall hale them down to deepest hell,
Where none but Furies, bugs, and tortures dwell.°
GHOST Then, sweet Revenge, do this at my request:
Let me be judge and doom them to unrest.   30
Let loose poor Tityus from the vulture's gripe,°
And let Don Cyprian supply his room;
Place Don Lorenzo on Ixion's wheel,
And let the lover's endless pains surcease
(Juno forgets old wrath, and grants him ease);   35
Hang Balthazar about Chimaera's neck,°
And let him there bewail his bloody love,
Repining at our joys that are above;
Let Serberine go roll the fatal stone,
And take from Sisyphus his endless moan;   40
False Pedringano, for his treachery,
Let him be dragged through boiling Acheron,
And there live, dying still in endless flames,
Blaspheming gods and all their holy names.
REVENGE Then haste we down to meet thy friends and foes: 45
To place thy friends in ease, the rest in woes;
For here though death hath end their misery,
I'll there begin their endless tragedy.
        Exeunt

Additions to *The Spanish Tragedy* in the 1602 edition

Five additional passages first appear in the 1602 edition of *The Spanish Tragedy*. They were probably written in the late 1590s to enhance a revival of a highly popular but perhaps over-familiar play. Their author is unknown, but may have been Ben Jonson. The additions are sometimes meant to supplement the original action, and sometimes to replace Kyd's equivalent scenes.

First Addition, inserted in 2.4 between lines 107 and 108

[For outrage fits our cursèd wretchedness.]
ISABELLA Aye me, Hieronimo, sweet husband, speak!
HIERONIMO He supped with us tonight, frolic and merry,
    And said he would go visit Balthazar
    At the duke's palace: there the prince doth lodge.   5
    He had no custom to stay out so late.
    He may be in his chamber; some go see.
    Roderigo, ho!
        Enter Pedro and Jaques [with torches]
ISABELLA Aye me, he raves! Sweet Hieronimo!
HIERONIMO True, all Spain takes note of it.   10
    Besides, he is so generally beloved;
    His majesty the other day did grace him
    With waiting on his cup. These be favours,
    Which do assure he cannot be short-lived.°
ISABELLA Sweet Hieronimo!   15
HIERONIMO I wonder how this fellow got his clothes!
    Sirrah, sirrah, I'll know the truth of all—
    Jaques, run to the Duke of Castile's presently,°
    And bid my son Horatio to come home:
    I and his mother have had strange dreams tonight.   20
    Do ye hear me, sir?
JAQUES   Aye, sir.
HIERONIMO   Well, sir, be gone.
    Pedro, come hither. Knowest thou who this is?
PEDRO Too well, sir.

HIERONIMO Too well! Who, who is it?—Peace, Isabella!
  Nay, blush not, man.
PEDRO   It is my lord Horatio.   25
HIERONIMO Ha ha, St James! but this doth make me laugh,
  That there are more deluded than myself.
PEDRO Deluded?
HIERONIMO Aye,
  I would have sworn myself, within this hour,   30
  That this had been my son Horatio:
  His garments are so like.
  Ha! Are they not great persuasions?°
ISABELLA O, would to God it were not so!
HIERONIMO Were not, Isabella! Dost thou dream it is?   35
  Can thy soft bosom entertain a thought
  That such a black deed of mischief should be done°
  On one so pure and spotless as our son?
  Away, I am ashamed.
ISABELLA   Dear Hieronimo,
  Cast a more serious eye upon thy grief: 40
  Weak apprehension gives but weak belief.°
HIERONIMO It was a man, sure, that was hanged up here,
  A youth, as I remember: I cut him down.
  If it should prove my son now after all!
  Say you? say you?—Light! Lend me a taper!   45
  Let me look again.—O God!
  Confusion, mischief, torment, death, and hell,
  Drop all your stings at once in my cold bosom,
  That now is stiff with horror; kill me quickly!
  Be gracious to me, thou infective night,   50
  And drop this deed of murder down on me;
  Gird in my waste of grief with thy large darkness,°
  And let me not survive to see the light
  May put me in the mind I had a son.°
ISABELLA O sweet Horatio, O my dearest son!   55
HIERONIMO How strangely had I lost my way to grief.

Second Addition, replacing 3.2.64–65 and part of 66

[LORENZO Why so, Hieronimo? Use me.]
HIERONIMO   Who, you, my lord?

I reserve your favour for a greater honour;
This is a very toy, my lord, a toy.
LORENZO All's one, Hieronimo; acquaint me with it.
HIERONIMO I'faith, my lord, it is an idle thing,   5
I must confess: I ha' been too slack, too tardy,
Too remiss unto your honour.
LORENZO How now, Hieronimo?
HIERONIMO In troth, my lord, it is a thing of nothing,°
The murder of a son, or so—   10
A thing of nothing, my lord!

Third Addition, inserted between 3.11.1 and 2

[FIRST PORTINGALE By your leave, sir.]
HIERONIMO 'Tis neither as you think, nor as you think,
Nor as you think; you're wide all:°
These slippers are not mine, they were my son Horatio's.
My son! and what's a son? A thing begot   5
Within a pair of minutes, thereabout;
A lump bred up in darkness, and doth serve°
To ballace these light creatures we call women;
And, at nine months' end, creeps forth to light.
What is there yet in a son   10
To make a father dote, rave, or run mad?
Being born, it pouts, cries, and breeds teeth.°
What is there yet in a son? He must be fed,
Be taught to go, and speak. Aye, or yet°
Why might not a man love a calf as well?   15
Or melt in passion o'er a frisking kid,
As for a son? Methinks, a young bacon°
Or a fine little smooth horse-colt
Should move a man as much as doth a son.
For one of these, in very little time,   20
Will grow to some good use; whereas a son,
The more he grows in stature and in years,
The more unsquared, unbevelled, he appears,°
Reckons his parents among the rank of fools,
Strikes care upon their heads with his mad riots,°   25
Makes them look old before they meet with age.
This is a son! And what a loss were this,

Considered truly?—O, but my Horatio
Grew out of reach of these insatiate humours:
He loved his loving parents,   30
He was my comfort, and his mother's joy,
The very arm that did hold up our house:
Our hopes were stored up in him,
None but a damnèd murderer could hate him.
He had not seen the back of nineteen year,°   35
When his strong arm unhorsed
The proud Prince Balthazar, and his great mind,
Too full of honour, took him unto mercy,
That valiant but ignoble Portingale.
Well, heaven is heaven still.   40
And there is Nemesis, and Furies,
And things called whips,°
And they sometimes do meet with murderers;
They do not always 'scape, that's some comfort.
Aye, aye, aye, and then time steals on,   45
And steals, and steals, till violence leaps forth
Like thunder wrapped in a ball of fire,
And so doth bring confusion to them all.°

Fourth Addition, inserted between 3.12 and 3.13

Enter Jaques and Pedro [with torches]

JAQUES I wonder, Pedro, why our master thus
    At midnight sends us with our torches' light,
    When man and bird and beast are all at rest,
    Save those that watch for rape and bloody murder?
PEDRO O Jaques, know thou that our master's mind   5
    Is much distraught since his Horatio died,
    And—now his agèd years should sleep in rest,
    His heart in quiet—like a desperate man,
    Grows lunatic and childish for his son.
    Sometimes, as he doth at his table sit,   10
    He speaks as if Horatio stood by him;
    Then starting in a rage, falls on the earth,
    Cries out, 'Horatio? Where is my Horatio?'
    So that with extreme grief and cutting sorrow
    There is not left in him one inch of man.   15
    See where he comes.

Enter Hieronimo

HIERONIMO I pry through every crevice of each wall,
  Look on each tree, and search through every brake,
  Beat at the bushes, stamp our grandam earth,
  Dive in the water, and stare up to heaven,   20
  Yet cannot I behold my son Horatio.—
  How now, who's there? Sprites? Sprites?

PEDRO We are your servants that attend you, sir,

HIERONIMO What make you with your torches in the dark?

PEDRO You bid us light them, and attend you here.   25

HIERONIMO No, no, you are deceived, not I—you are deceived!
  Was I so mad to bid you light your torches now?
  Light me your torches at the mid of noon,
  Whenas the sun-god rides in all his glory;
  Light me your torches then.

PEDRO   Then we burn daylight.°   30

HIERONIMO Let it be burnt; night is a murderous slut
  That would not have her treasons to be seen;
  And yonder pale-faced Hecate there, the moon,
  Doth give consent to that is done in darkness;
  And all those stars that gaze upon her face,   35
  Are aglets on her sleeve, pins on her train;
  And those that should be powerful and divine
  Do sleep in darkness when they most should shine.

PEDRO Provoke them not, fair sir, with tempting words;
  The heavens are gracious, and your miseries   40
  And sorrow makes you speak you know not what.

HIERONIMO Villain, thou liest! And thou doest naught
  But tell me I am mad: thou liest, I am not mad.
  I know thee to be Pedro, and he Jaques.
  I'll prove it to thee; and were I mad, how could I?   45
  Where was she that same night when my Horatio°
  Was murdered? She should have shone; search thou the book.°
  Had the moon shone, in my boy's face there was a kind of
    grace,
  That I know—nay, I do know—had the murderer seen him,
  His weapon would have fall'n and cut the earth,   50
  Had he been framed of naught but blood and death.
  Alack, when mischief doth it knows not what,
  What shall we say to mischief?°

    Enter Isabella

ISABELLA Dear Hieronimo, come in a-doors;
    O, seek not means so to increase thy sorrow.   55
HIERONIMO Indeed, Isabella, we do nothing here;
    I do not cry—ask Pedro, and ask Jaques—
    Not I, indeed; we are very merry, very merry.
ISABELLA How? Be merry here, be merry here?
    Is not this the place, and this the very tree,   60
    Where my Horatio died, where he was murdered?
HIERONIMO Was—do not say what: let her weep it out.
    This was the tree; I set it of a kernel;°
    And when our hot Spain could not let it grow,
    But that the infant and the human sap°   65
    Began to wither, duly twice a morning
    Would I be sprinkling it with fountain water.
    At last it grew and grew, and bore and bore,
    Till at the length
    It grew a gallows, and did bear our son;   70
    It bore thy fruit and mine—O wicked, wicked plant!
            One knocks within at the door
    See who knock there.
PEDRO   It is a painter, sir.
HIERONIMO Bid him come in and paint some comfort,
    For surely there's none lives but painted comfort.°
    Let him come in. One knows not what may chance: 75
    God's will that I should set this tree! But even so
    Masters ungrateful servants rear from naught,
    And then they hate them that did bring them up.
            Enter the Painter
PAINTER God bless you, sir.
HIERONIMO Wherefore? Why, thou scornful villain?   80
    How, where, or by what means should I be blessed?
ISABELLA What wouldst thou have, good fellow?
PAINTER   Justice, madam.
HIERONIMO O ambitious beggar!
    Wouldest thou have that that lives not in the world?
    Why, all the undelved mines cannot buy   85
    An ounce of justice, 'tis a jewel so inestimable.
    I tell thee,
    God hath engrossed all justice in his hands,
    And there is none but what comes from him.
PAINTER O, then I see   90

That God must right me for my murdered son.

HIERONIMO How, was thy son murdered?

PAINTER Aye, sir; no man did hold a son so dear.

HIERONIMO What, not as thine? That's a lie
As massy as the earth. I had a son   95
Whose least unvalued hair did weigh°
A thousand of thy sons; and he was murdered.

PAINTER Alas, sir, I had no more but he.

HIERONIMO Nor I, nor I; but this same one of mine
Was worth a legion. But all is one.   100
Pedro, Jaques, go in a-doors; Isabella, go,
And this good fellow here and I
Will range this hideous orchard up and down,
Like to two lions reavèd of their young.
Go in a-doors, I say.   105
         *Exeunt [Isabella, Pedro, Jaques]. The Painter and he sits
         down*
Come, let's talk wisely now. Was thy son murdered?

PAINTER Aye, sir.

HIERONIMO So was mine. How dost take it? Art thou not sometimes
mad?
Is there no tricks that comes before thine eyes?°   110

PAINTER O Lord, yes, sir.

HIERONIMO Art a painter? Canst paint me a tear, or a wound, a
groan, or a sigh? Canst paint me such a tree as this?

PAINTER Sir, I am sure you have heard of my painting; my name's
Bazardo.   115

HIERONIMO Bazardo! Afore God, an excellent fellow! Look you, sir,
do you see? I'd have you paint me [in] my gallery, in your oil
colours matted,° and draw me five years younger than I am—do
you see, sir, let five years go; let them go like the Marshal of
Spain—my wife Isabella standing by me, with a speaking° look to   120
my son Horatio, which should intend to this or some such like
purpose: 'God bless thee, my sweet son,' and my hand leaning
upon his head, thus, sir; do you see? May it be done?

PAINTER Very well, sir.

HIERONIMO Nay, I pray mark me, sir. Then, sir, would I have you   125
paint me this tree, this very tree. Canst paint a doleful cry?

PAINTER Seemingly,° sir.

HIERONIMO Nay, it should cry; but all is one. Well, sir, paint me a
youth run through and through with villains' swords, hanging
upon this tree. Canst thou draw a murderer?   130

88

PAINTER I'll warrant you, sir; I have the pattern of the most notorious villains that ever lived in all Spain.

HIERONIMO O, let them be worse, worse; stretch thine art, and let their beards be of Judas his own colour;° and let their eyebrows jutty over: in any case observe that. Then, sir, after some violent 135 noise, bring me forth in my shirt, and my gown under mine arm, with my torch in my hand, and my sword reared up, thus—and with these words:
'What noise is this? Who calls Hieronimo?'
May it be done? 140

PAINTER Yea, sir.

HIERONIMO Well, sir, then bring me forth; bring me through alley° and alley, still with a distracted countenance going along, and let my hair heave up my nightcap. Let the clouds scowl, make the moon dark, the stars extinct, the winds blowing, the bells 145 tolling, the owl shrieking, the toads croaking, the minutes jarring,° and the clock striking twelve. And then at last, sir, starting, behold a man hanging, and tottering° and tottering, as you know the wind will weave° a man, and I with a trice° to cut him down. And looking upon him by the advantage of my torch, find it to be my 150 son Horatio. There you may [show] a passion; there you may show a passion. Draw me like old Priam° of Troy, crying, 'The house is afire, the house is afire, as the torch over my head!' Make me curse, make me rave, make me cry, make me mad, make me well again, make me curse hell, invocate heaven, and in the end, leave 155 me in a trance—and so forth.

PAINTER And is this the end?

HIERONIMO O no, there is no end, the end is death and madness. As I am never better than when I am mad, then methinks I am a brave° fellow, then I do wonders; but reason abuseth° me, and 160 there's the torment, there's the hell. At the last, sir, bring me to one of the murderers: were he as strong as Hector, thus would I tear and drag him up and down.

He beats the Painter in, then comes out again, with a book in his hand

Fifth Addition, replacing 4.4.170–194, and incorporating some of Kyd's original material

[CASTILE Why hast thou butchered both my children thus?]
HIERONIMO But are you sure they are dead?
CASTILE   Aye, slave, too sure.

HIERONIMO What, and yours too?

VICEROY Aye, all are dead; not one of them survive.

HIERONIMO Nay, then I care not; come, and we shall be friends.   5
    Let us lay our heads together:
    See, here's a goodly noose will hold them all.

VICEROY O damnèd devil, how secure he is!°

HIERONIMO Secure? Why, dost thou wonder at it?
    I tell thee, viceroy, this day I have seen revenge,   10
    And in that sight am grown a prouder monarch,
    Than ever sat under the crown of Spain.
    Had I as many lives as there be stars,
    As many heavens to go to, as those lives,
    I'd give them all, aye, and my soul to boot,   15
    But I would see thee ride in this red pool.°

CASTILE Speak, who were thy confederates in this?

VICEROY That was thy daughter, Bel-imperia;
    For by her hand my Balthazar was slain:
    I saw her stab him.

HIERONIMO   O, good words!   20
    As dear to me was my Horatio,
    As yours, or yours, or yours, my lord, to you.
    My guiltless son was by Lorenzo slain,
    And by Lorenzo and that Balthazar
    Am I at last revengèd thoroughly,   25
    Upon whose souls may heavens be yet revenged
    With greater far than these afflictions.
    Methinks since I grew inward with revenge°
    I cannot look with scorn enough on death.

KING What, dost thou mock us, slave? Bring tortures forth!   30

HIERONIMO Do, do, do; and meantime I'll torture you.
    [To the Viceroy] You had a son, as I take it; and your son
    Should ha' been married to [to Castile] your daughter.
    Ha, was't not so? You had a son too;
    He was my liege's nephew. He was proud   35
    And politic; had he lived, he might 'a' come
    To wear the crown of Spain, I think 'twas so.
    'Twas I that killed him; look you, this same hand.
    'Twas I that stabbed his heart—do you see? this hand—
    For one Horatio, if you ever knew him, a youth,   40
    One that they hanged up in his father's garden;
    One that did force your valiant son to yield,

While your more valiant son did take him prisoner.
VICEROY Be deaf, my senses; I can hear no more.
KING Fall, heaven, and cover us with thy sad ruins.   45
CASTILE Roll all the world within thy pitchy cloud.
HIERONIMO Now do I applaud what I have acted.
  Nunc iners cadat manus!°
  Now to express the rupture of my part:°
  First take my tongue, and afterward my heart.   50

THE REVENGER'S TRAGEDY

[DRAMATIS PERSONAE°

The Duke

Lecherous Lussurioso, the Duke's son by an earlier marriage, and heir

Bastard Spurio, his bastard son

Ambitious Ambitioso, the Duchess's eldest son

super- *Fluous* Supervacuo, the Duchess's second son

Junior Brother, the youngest son of the Duchess

Antonio and Piero, noblemen of the Duke's court

Revenger Vindice, the revenger, sometimes disguised as Piato *Hidden*

Hippolito, his brother, also called Carlo

Idiot Dondolo, servant to Gratiana and Castiza

Dolt Nencio and Sordido, servants of Lussurioso

Judges, Nobles, Gentlemen, Officers, a Prison-keeper, Guards, and
  Servants

The Duchess

Grace Gratiana, mother of Vindice, Hippolito, and Castiza

Chastity Castiza, sister of Vindice and Hippolito]

The servants of
both Grace/Chastity
and Lecherousness are
Idiots and Dolts?

94

[1.1]

Enter Vindice, [holding a skull °; then] the Duke, Duchess,
Lussurioso, Spurio, with a train, pass over the stage with
torchlight

VINDICE Duke—royal lecher! Go, grey-haired adultery;
And thou his son, as impious steeped as he;
And thou his bastard true-begot in evil;
And thou his duchess that will do with devil,°
Four ex'lent characters.—O, that marrowless age°   5
Would stuff the hollow bones with damned desires,
And 'stead of heat kindle infernal fires°
Within the spendthrift veins of a dry duke,
A parched and juiceless luxur. O God! one
That has scarce blood enough to live upon,   10
And he to riot it like a son and heir?
O, the thought of that
Turns my abusèd heartstrings into fret.°
[*To the skull*] Thou sallow picture of my poisoned love,
My study's ornament, thou shell of death,°   15
Once the bright face of my betrothèd lady,
When life and beauty naturally filled out
These ragged imperfections,
When two heaven-pointed diamonds were set
In those unsightly rings—then 'twas a face°   20
So far beyond the artificial shine
Of any woman's bought complexion
That the uprightest man (if such there be,
That sin but seven times a day) broke custom
And made up eight with looking after her.   25
O she was able to ha' made a usurer's son
Melt all his patrimony in a kiss,
And what his father fifty years told°
To have consumed, and yet his suit been cold.
But O, accursèd palace!
Thee when thou wert appareled in thy flesh   30
The old duke poisoned,
Because thy purer part would not consent
Unto his palsy-lust; for old men lustful

95

Do show like young men angry, eager, violent,
Outbid like their limited performances.
O 'ware an old man hot and vicious:
'Age, as in gold, in lust is covetous.'°
Vengeance, thou murder's quit-rent, and whereby°   35
Thou show'st thyself tenant to Tragedy,
O keep thy day, hour, minute, I beseech,   40
For those thou hast determined. Hum, who e'er knew°
Murder unpaid? Faith, give Revenge her due,
Sh'as kept touch hitherto. Be merry, merry;°
Advance thee, O thou terror to fat folks,   45
To have their costly three-piled flesh worn off °
As bare as this—for banquets, ease, and laughter
Can make great men, as greatness goes by clay,°
But wise men little are more great than they.
    Enter Hippolito
HIPPOLITO Still sighing o'er death's vizard?
VINDICE   Brother, welcome;   50
  What comfort bring'st thou? how go things at court?
HIPPOLITO In silk and silver, brother; never braver.°
VINDICE Puh,
  Thou play'st upon my meaning. Prithee say,
  Has that bald madam, Opportunity,°   55
  Yet thought upon's? Speak, are we happy yet?
  Thy wrongs and mine are for one scabbard fit.
HIPPOLITO It may prove happiness.
VINDICE   What is't may prove?
  Give me to taste.
HIPPOLITO   Give me your hearing then.°
  You know my place at court.
VINDICE   Aye, the duke's chamber;   60
  But 'tis a marvel thou'rt not turned out yet!°
HIPPOLITO Faith, I have been shoved at, but 'twas still my hap
  To hold by th'duchess' skirt—you guess at that;°
  Whom such a coat keeps up can ne'er fall flat.
  But to the purpose: 65
  Last evening, predecessor unto this,
  The duke's son warily inquired for me,
  Whose pleasure I attended. He began
  By policy to open and unhusk me
  About the time and common rumour;   70

But I had so much wit to keep my thoughts
Up in their built houses, yet afforded him°
An idle satisfaction without danger.
But the whole aim and scope of his intent°
Ended in this: conjuring me in private°   75
To seek some strange-digested fellow forth,°
Of ill-contented nature, either disgraced
In former times, or by new grooms displaced°
Since his stepmother's nuptials; such a blood,°
A man that were for evil only good—   80
To give you the true word, some base-coined pander.°

VINDICE I reach you, for I know his heat is such,°
Were there as many concubines as ladies
He would not be contained, he must fly out.
I wonder how ill-featured, vile-proportioned   85
That one should be, if she were made for woman,
Whom at the insurrection of his lust
He would refuse for once; heart, I think none,
Next to a skull, though more unsound than one.°
Each face he meets he strongly dotes upon.   90

HIPPOLITO Brother, y'ave truly spoke him.
He knows not you, but I'll swear you know him.

VINDICE And therefore I'll put on that knave for once,°
And be a right man then, a man o' th' time;°
For to be honest is not to be i' th' world.   95
Brother, I'll be that strange-composèd fellow.

HIPPOLITO And I'll prefer you, brother.

VINDICE   Go to, then;°
The small'st advantage fattens wrongèd men.
It may point out Occasion; if I meet her,
I'll hold her by the foretop fast enough,°   100
Or like the French mole heave up hair and all.°
I have a habit that will fit it quaintly.°
Here comes our mother.

HIPPOLITO   And sister.

VINDICE   We must coin.°
Women are apt, you know, to take false money,
But I dare stake my soul for these two creatures—   105
Only excuse excepted, that they'll swallow
Because their sex is easy in belief.°

   [*Enter Gratiana and Castiza*]

GRATIANA What news from court, son Carlo?
HIPPOLITO   Faith, mother,
   'Tis whispered there the duchess' youngest son
   Has played a rape on Lord Antonio's wife.   110
GRATIANA On that religious lady!
CASTIZA Royal blood! Monster, he deserves to die,
   If Italy had no more hopes but he.
VINDICE Sister, y'ave sentenced most direct and true;
   The law's a woman, and would she were you.°   115
   Mother, I must take leave of you.
GRATIANA   Leave for what?
VINDICE I intend speedy travel.
HIPPOLITO That he does, madam.
GRATIANA   Speedy indeed!
VINDICE For since my worthy father's funeral,
   My life's unnatural to me, e'en compelled,   120
   As if I lived now when I should be dead.
GRATIANA Indeed, he was a worthy gentleman,
   Had his estate been fellow to his mind.
VINDICE The duke did much deject him.
GRATIANA   Much!
VINDICE   Too much,°
   And through disgrace oft smothered in his spirit°   125
   When it would mount. Surely I think he died
   Of discontent, the nobleman's consumption.
GRATIANA Most sure he did.
VINDICE   Did he? 'lack—you know all,
   You were his midnight secretary.
GRATIANA   No.°
   He was too wise to trust me with his thoughts.   130
VINDICE I'faith then, father, thou wast wise indeed:
   'Wives are but made to go to bed and feed.'
   Come mother, sister. You'll bring me onward, brother?
HIPPOLITO I will.
VINDICE [aside] I'll quickly turn into another.
   Exeunt

[1.2]

*Enter the Duke, Lussurioso, the Duchess, Spurio, Ambitioso
and Supervacuo; Junior Brother brought out with Officers
[to stand trial] for the rape; two judges*

DUKE Duchess, it is your youngest son, we're sorry,
His violent act has e'en drawn blood of honour
And stained our honours;
Thrown ink upon the forehead of our state
Which envious spirits will dip their pens into   5
After our death, and blot us in our tombs.°
For that which would seem treason in our lives°
Is laughter when we're dead; who dares now whisper
That dares not then speak out, and e'en proclaim
With loud words and broad pens our closest shame.°   10
[FIRST] JUDGE Your grace hath spoke like to your silver years,°
Full of confirmèd gravity; for what is it to have
A flattering false insculption on a tomb,
And in men's hearts reproach? The bowelled corpse°
May be cered in, but, with free tongue I speak,°   15
'The faults of great men through their cerecloths break.'
DUKE They do; we're sorry for't. It is our fate
To live in fear and die to live in hate.
I leave him to your sentence; doom him, lords—
The fact is great—whilst I sit by and sigh.°   20
DUCHESS [*kneels*] My gracious lord, I pray be merciful.
Although his trespass far exceed his years,
Think him to be your own, as I am yours;
Call him not son-in-law. The law, I fear,°
Will fall too soon upon his name and him;   25
Temper his fault with pity!
LUSSURIOSO   Good my lord,
Then 'twill not taste so bitter and unpleasant
Upon the judges' palate; for offenses
Gilt o'er with mercy show like fairest women,
Good only for their beauties, which washed off,   30
No sin is uglier.
AMBITIOSO   I beseech your grace,
Be soft and mild; let not relentless Law
Look with an iron forehead on our brother.°

[handwritten margin notes:]
Applicable to writers for the stage as well?
The viceroy of Portugal says a similar thing of the notable person's life in The Spanish Tragedy.
As the Duke clearly does in not sticking up for Little / Junior Brother.
Food

SPURIO [aside] He yields small comfort yet; hope he shall die.
   And if a bastard's wish might stand in force,   35
   Would all the court were turned into a corse.°
DUCHESS No pity yet? Must I rise fruitless then,°
   A wonder in a woman? Are my knees
   Of such low metal that without respect—°
FIRST JUDGE Let the offender stand forth.   40
   'Tis the duke's pleasure that impartial doom
   Shall take fast hold of his unclean attempt.°
   A rape! why, 'tis the very core of lust,
   Double adultery.
JUNIOR BROTHER   So, sir.
SECOND JUDGE   And which was worse,
   Committed on the Lord Antonio's wife,   45
   That general-honest lady. Confess, my lord,°
   What moved you to't?
JUNIOR BROTHER   Why, flesh and blood, my lord.
   What should move men unto a woman else?
LUSSURIOSO O do not jest thy·doom; trust not an axe°
   Or sword too far. The law is a wise serpent   50
   And quickly can beguile thee of thy life.
   Though marriage only has made thee my brother,
   I love thee so far, play not with thy death.
JUNIOR BROTHER I thank you, troth; good admonitions, faith,
   If I'd the grace now to make use of them.   55
FIRST JUDGE That lady's name has spread such a fair wing
   Over all Italy, that if our tongues
   Were sparing toward the fact, judgement itself
   Would be condemned and suffer in men's thoughts.
JUNIOR BROTHER Well then, 'tis done, and it would please me well   60
   Were it to do again: sure she's a goddess,
   For I'd no power to see her, and to live.
   It falls out true in this, for I must die;
   Her beauty was ordained to be my scaffold.
   And yet, methinks I might be easier 'sessed—°   65
   My fault being sport, let me but die in jest.
FIRST JUDGE This be the sentence—
DUCHESS O keep't upon your tongue, let it not slip.
   Death too soon steals out of a lawyer's lip.
   Be not so cruel-wise!
FIRST JUDGE   Your grace must pardon us,   70

'Tis but the justice of the law.
DUCHESS   The law
Is grown more subtle than a woman should be.
SPURIO [*aside*] Now, now he dies; rid 'em away!
DUCHESS [*aside*] O what it is to have an old-cool duke,
To be as slack in tongue as in performance!°   75
FIRST JUDGE Confirmed, this be the doom irrevocable—
DUCHESS O!
FIRST JUDGE Tomorrow early—
DUCHESS   Pray be abed, my lord.
FIRST JUDGE Your grace much wrongs yourself.
AMBITIOSO   No, 'tis that tongue,
Your too much right, does do us too much wrong.
FIRST JUDGE Let that offender—
DUCHESS   Live, and be in health.   80
FIRST JUDGE Be on a scaffold—
DUKE   Hold, hold, my lord!
SPURIO   Pox on 't,°
What makes my dad speak now?°
DUKE We will defer the judgement till next sitting.°
In the meantime let him be kept close prisoner.
Guard, bear him hence.
AMBITIOSO [*to Junior Brother*] Brother, this makes for thee;°   85
Fear not, we'll have a trick to set thee free.
JUNIOR BROTHER [*to Ambitioso and Supervacuo*]
Brother, I will expect it from you both,
And in that hope I rest.
SUPERVACUO   Farewell, be merry.
      Exit [Junior Brother] with a Guard
SPURIO [*aside*] Delayed, deferred—nay then, if judgement have
Cold blood, flattery and bribes will kill it.°   90
DUKE About it then, my lords, with your best powers;
More serious business calls upon our hours.
      Exeunt [all except] Duchess
DUCHESS Was't ever known step-duchess was so mild
And calm as I? Some now would plot his death
With easy doctors, those loose-living men,°   95
And make his withered grace fall to his grave,
And keep church better.°
Some second wife would do this, and dispatch
Her double-loathèd lord at meat and sleep.

Indeed 'tis true an old man's twice a child—   100
Mine cannot speak. One of his single words
Would quite have freed my youngest, dearest son
From death or durance, and have made him walk
With a bold foot upon the thorny law,
Whose prickles should bow under him. But 'tis not,   105 .
And therefore wedlock faith shall be forgot.
I'll kill him in his forehead; hate, there feed;°
That wound is deepest, though it never bleed.
      [*Enter Spurio*]
And here comes he whom my heart points unto,
His bastard son, but my love's true-begot;   110
Many a wealthy letter have I sent him,
Swelled up with jewels, and the timorous man
Is yet but coldly kind.
That jewel's mine that quivers in his ear,
Mocking his master's chillness and vain fear.   115
H'as spied me now.
SPURIO   Madam, your grace so private?
      My duty on your hand.°
DUCHESS Upon my hand, sir! Troth, I think you'd fear
      To kiss my hand too if my lip stood there.
SPURIO Witness I would not, madam.
      [*He kisses her*]
DUCHESS   'Tis a wonder,   120
      For ceremony has made many fools.
      It is as easy way unto a duchess
      As to a hatted dame (if her love answer),°
      But that by timorous honours, pale respects,
      Idle degrees of fear, men make their ways   125
      Hard of themselves. What have you thought of me?
SPURIO Madam, I ever think of you in duty,
      Regard, and—
DUCHESS   Puh, upon my love, I mean.
SPURIO I would 'twere love, but 'tis a fouler name
      Than lust. You are my father's wife,   130
      Your grace may guess now what I could call it.
DUCHESS Why, th'art his son but falsely;
      'Tis a hard question whether he begot thee.
SPURIO I'faith, 'tis true too; I'm an uncertain man, of more uncertain
      woman. Maybe his groom o' th'. stable begot me—you know I   135

know not. He could ride a horse well,° a shrewd° suspicion, marry!
He was wondrous tall, he had his length, i' faith, for peeping over
half-shut holiday windows.° Men would desire him 'light° when
he was afoot, he made a goodly show under a penthouse,° and
when he rid,° his hat would check the signs, and clatter barbers'   140
basins.°

DUCHESS Nay, set you a-horseback once, you'll ne'er 'light off.

SPURIO Indeed, I am a beggar.°

DUCHESS That's more the sign th'art great. But to our love:
Let it stand firm both in thought and mind   145
That the duke was thy father, as no doubt then
He bid fair for't; thy injury is the more.°
For had he cut thee a right diamond,
Thou hadst been next set in the dukedom's ring,
When his worn self, like age's easy slave,   150
Had dropped out of the collet into th' grave.°
What wrong can equal this? Canst thou be tame
And think upon't?

SPURIO   No, mad and think upon't.

DUCHESS Who would not be revenged of such a father,
E'en in the worst way? I would thank that sin   155
That could most injury him, and be in league with it.°
O what a grief 'tis, that a man should live
But once i' th' world, and then to live a bastard,
The curse o' the womb, the thief of nature,
Begot against the seventh commandment,°   160
Half damned in the conception, by the justice
Of that unbribèd, everlasting law.

SPURIO O, I'd a hot-backed devil to my father.°

DUCHESS Would not this mad e'en patience, make blood rough?°
Who but an eunuch would not sin, his bed   165
By one false minute disinherited?

SPURIO [aside]
Aye, there's the vengeance that my birth was wrapped in.
I'll be revenged for all. Now hate begin;
I'll call foul incest but a venial sin.

DUCHESS Cold still! In vain then must a duchess woo?   170

SPURIO Madam, I blush to say what I will do.

DUCHESS Thence flew sweet comfort.
    [Kisses him]
                    Earnest and farewell.°

SPURIO O, one incestuous kiss picks open hell.°
DUCHESS Faith, now, old duke, my vengeance shall reach high:
 I'll arm thy brow with woman's heraldry.°   175
  Exit [Duchess]
SPURIO Duke, thou didst do me wrong, and by thy act
 Adultery is my nature.
 Faith, if the truth were known, I was begot
 After some gluttonous dinner; some stirring dish°
 Was my first father, when deep healths went round,° 180
 And ladies' cheeks were painted red with wine,
 Their tongues, as short and nimble as their heels,°
 Uttering words sweet and thick; and when they rose,°
 Were merrily disposed to fall again.
 In such a whisp'ring and withdrawing hour,   185
 When base male-bawds kept sentinel at stair-head,
 Was I stol'n softly. O, damnation met
 The sin of feasts, drunken adultery.
 I feel it swell me. My revenge is just;
 I was begot in impudent wine and lust.   190
 Stepmother, I consent to thy desires;
 I love thy mischief well, but I hate thee,
 And those three cubs, thy sons, wishing confusion,
 Death, and disgrace may be their epitaphs.
 As for my brother, the duke's only son,   195
 Whose birth is more beholding to report
 Than mine, and yet perhaps as falsely sown°
 (Women must not be trusted with their own),
 I'll loose my days upon him, hate all I.°
 Duke, on thy brow I'll draw my bastardy.°   200
 For indeed a bastard by nature should make cuckolds,
 Because he is the son of a cuckold-maker.
  Exit

[1.3]

Enter Vindice and Hippolito, Vindice in disguise [as Piato] to
attend Lussurioso
VINDICE What, brother? Am I far enough from myself?°
HIPPOLITO As if another man had been sent whole
 Into the world, and none wist how he came.

VINDICE It will confirm me bold, the child o' th' court.
   Let blushes dwell i' th' country. Impudence,   5
   Thou goddess of the palace, mistress of mistresses,
   To whom the costly perfumed people pray,
   Strike thou my forehead into dauntless marble,
   Mine eyes to steady sapphires; turn my visage,
   And if I must needs glow, let me blush inward,   10
   That this immodest season may not spy
   That scholar in my cheeks, fool-bashfulness,°
   That maid in the old time, whose flush of grace°
   Would never suffer her to get good clothes.°
   Our maids are wiser, and are less ashamed;   15
   Save Grace the bawd, I seldom hear grace named!
HIPPOLITO Nay, brother, you reach out o' th' verge° now. 'Sfoot,
   the duke's son; settle your looks.
       [Enter Lussurioso]
VINDICE Pray let me not be doubted.
HIPPOLITO My lord—
LUSSURIOSO   Hippolito? [To Vindice] Be absent, leave us.   20
       [Vindice withdraws to one side]
HIPPOLITO My lord, after long search, wary inquiries,
   And politic siftings, I made choice of yon fellow,°
   Whom I guess rare for many deep employments.°
   This our age swims within him—and if Time°
   Had so much hair, I should take him for Time,   25
   He is so near kin to this present minute.
LUSSURIOSO 'Tis enough.
   We thank thee; yet words are but great men's blanks.°
   Gold, though it be dumb, does utter the best thanks.
       [Gives Hippolito money]
HIPPOLITO Your plenteous honour! An ex'lent fellow, my lord.   30
LUSSURIOSO So, give us leave.
       [Exit Hippolito]
   [To Vindice] Welcome, be not far off, we must be better acquainted.
   Push,° be bold with us; thy hand.
VINDICE With all my heart, i' faith.
       [Embraces Lussurioso]
                How dost, sweet muskcat?°
   When shall we lie together?
LUSSURIOSO [aside]   Wondrous knave!
   Gather him into boldness? 'Sfoot, the slave's°
   Already as familiar as an ague,°

And shakes me at his pleasure. [*To Vindice*] Friend, I can
Forget myself in private, but elsewhere
I pray do you remember me.°   40
VINDICE O very well, sir—I conster myself saucy.
LUSSURIOSO What hast been, of what profession?
VINDICE A bone-setter.
LUSSURIOSO A bone-setter?
VINDICE A bawd, my lord; one that sets bones together.   45
LUSSURIOSO Notable bluntness!
   Fit, fit for me, e'en trained up to my hand.°
   Thou hast been scrivener to much knavery, then?°
VINDICE Fool° to abundance, sir; I have been witness to the surren-
   ders of a thousand virgins, and not so little. I have seen patri-   50
   monies washed a-pieces,° fruit fields turned into bastards, and, in
   a world of acres, not so much dust due to the heir 'twas left to, as
   would well gravel a petition.°
LUSSURIOSO [*aside*] Fine villain! troth, I like him wondrously,
   He's e'en shaped for my purpose. [*To Vindice*] Then thou   55
      know'st
   I' th' world strange lust.
VINDICE   O Dutch lust! fulsome lust!°
   Drunken procreation, which begets so many drunkards.
   Some father dreads not (gone to bed in wine)
   To slide from the mother, and cling the daughter-in-law;°
   Some uncles are adulterous with their nieces,   60
   Brothers with brothers' wives. O hour of incest!
   Any kin now, next to the rim o' th' sister,°
   Is man's meat in these days; and in the morning,
   When they are up and dressed and their mask on,
   Who can perceive this, save that eternal eye   65
   That sees through flesh and all? Well, if any thing
   Be damned, it will be twelve o'clock at night;
   That twelve will never 'scape:
   It is the Judas of the hours, wherein
   Honest salvation is betrayed to sin.   70
LUSSURIOSO In troth, it is, too. But let this talk glide.
   It is our blood to err, though hell gaped loud;
   Ladies know Lucifer fell, yet still are proud.
   Now, sir, wert thou as secret as thou'rt subtle
   And deeply fathomed into all estates,°   75
   I would embrace thee for a near employment,°

And thou shouldst swell in money, and be able
To make lame beggars crouch to thee.
VINDICE   My lord,
Secret? I ne'er had that disease o' th' mother,°
I praise my father. Why are men made close,°   80
But to keep thoughts in best? I grant you this,
Tell but some woman a secret over night,
Your doctor may find it in the urinal i' th' morning.
But, my lord—
LUSSURIOSO   So, thou'rt confirmed in me,°
And thus I enter thee.
        [*Gives money*]
VINDICE   This Indian devil°   85
Will quickly enter any man but a usurer:
He prevents that by ent'ring the devil first.
LUSSURIOSO Attend me: I am past my depth in lust,
And I must swim or drown. All my desires
Are levelled at a virgin not far from court,   90
To whom I have conveyed by messenger
Many waxed lines, full of my neatest spirit,°
And jewels that were able to ravish her
Without the help of man; all which and more
She, foolish chaste, sent back, the messengers   95
Receiving frowns for answers.
VINDICE   Possible?
'Tis a rare phoenix, whoe'er she be.
If your desires be such, she so repugnant,°
In troth, my lord, I'd be revenged and marry her.
LUSSURIOSO Push, the dowry of her blood and of her fortunes°   100
Are both too mean—good enough to be bad withal.
I'm one of that number can defend
Marriage is good, yet rather keep a friend.°
Give me my bed by stealth—there's true delight;
What breeds a loathing in't, but night by night?°   105
VINDICE A very fine religion.
LUSSURIOSO   Therefore, thus,
I'll trust thee in the business of my heart,
Because I see thee well experienced
In this luxurious day wherein we breathe.
Go thou, and with a smooth enchanting tongue   110
Bewitch her ears, and cozen her of all grace,

Enter upon the portion of her soul,°
Her honour, which she calls her chastity,
And bring it into expense; for honesty°
Is like a stock of money laid to sleep,   115
Which, ne'er so little broke, does never keep.

VINDICE You have gi'en 't the tang, i'faith, my lord.°
Make known the lady to me, and my brain
Shall swell with strange invention; I will move it
Till I expire with speaking, and drop down   120
Without a word to save me, but I'll work—

LUSSURIOSO We thank thee, and will raise° thee. Receive her name:
it is the only daughter to Madam Gratiana, the late° widow.

VINDICE [aside] O, my sister, my sister!

LUSSURIOSO   Why dost walk aside?

VINDICE My lord, I was thinking how I might begin,   125
As thus, 'O lady'—or twenty hundred devices;
Her very bodkin will put a man in.°

LUSSURIOSO Aye, or the wagging of her hair.°

VINDICE No, that shall put you in, my lord.

LUSSURIOSO Shall't? Why, content. Dost know the daughter then?   130

VINDICE O, ex'lent well by sight.

LUSSURIOSO   That was her brother
That did prefer thee to us.

VINDICE   My lord, I think so;
I knew I had seen him somewhere—

LUSSURIOSO And therefore prithee let thy heart to him
Be as a virgin, close.

VINDICE   O me, good lord.   135

LUSSURIOSO We may laugh at that simple age within him.°

VINDICE Ha, ha, ha!

LUSSURIOSO Himself being made the subtle instrument,
To wind up a good fellow—

VINDICE   That's I, my lord.°

LUSSURIOSO That's thou—to entice and work his sister.°   140

VINDICE A pure novice!

LUSSURIOSO   'Twas finely managed.

VINDICE Gallantly carried; [aside] a pretty perfumed villain.°

LUSSURIOSO I've bethought me:
If she prove chaste still and immovable,
Venture upon the mother, and with gifts   145

As I will furnish thee, begin with her.

VINDICE O fie, fie! that's the wrong end, my lord. 'Tis mere
impossible that a mother by any gifts should become a bawd to her
own daughter!

LUSSURIOSO Nay then, I see thou'rt but a puny in the subtle mystery   150
of a woman.
Why, 'tis held now no dainty dish: the name°
Is so in league with age, that nowadays°
It does eclipse three quarters of a mother.°

VINDICE Does't so, my lord?   155
Let me alone then to eclipse the fourth.

LUSSURIOSO Why, well said. Come, I'll furnish thee, but first°
Swear to be true in all.

VINDICE   True?

LUSSURIOSO   Nay, but swear.

VINDICE Swear? I hope your honour little doubts my faith.

LUSSURIOSO Yet for my humour's sake, 'cause I love swearing.   160

VINDICE 'Cause you love swearing, 'slud, I will.

LUSSURIOSO   Why, enough.
Ere long look to be made of better stuff.

VINDICE That will do well indeed, my lord.

LUSSURIOSO   Attend me!
        [*Exit Lussurioso*]

VINDICE O!
Now let me burst, I've eaten noble poison.
We are made strange fellows, brother: innocent villains.   165
Wilt not be angry when thou hear'st on't, think'st thou?
I'faith, thou shalt. Swear me to foul my sister!
        [*Unsheathes his sword*]
Sword, I durst make a promise of him to thee:
Thou shalt disheir him; it shall be thine honour.°
And yet, now angry froth is down in me,°   170
It would not prove the meanest policy°
In this disguise to try the faith of both.
Another might have had the selfsame office—
Some slave, that would have wrought effectually,
Aye, and perhaps o'erwrought 'em. Therefore I,°   175
Being thought travelled, will apply myself
Unto the selfsame form, forget my nature,
As if no part about me were kin to 'em;

So touch 'em—though I durst, almost for good,°
Venture my lands in heaven upon their blood.°   180
   Exit

[1.4]

*Enter the discontented Lord Antonio, whose wife the Duchess's
youngest son ravished; he discovering° the body of her dead to
certain lords [including Piero,] and Hippolito*

ANTONIO Draw nearer, lords, and be sad witnesses
  Of a fair, comely building newly fall'n,
  Being falsely undermined. Violent rape
  Has played a glorious act. Behold, my lords,°
  A sight that strikes man out of me.°   5
PIERO That virtuous lady!
ANTONIO   Precedent for wives!
HIPPOLITO The blush of many women, whose chaste presence
  Would e'en call shame up to their cheeks, and make
  Pale wanton sinners have good colours.
ANTONIO   Dead!
  Her honour first drunk poison, and her life,   10
  Being fellows in one house, did pledge her honour.°
PIERO O grief of many!
ANTONIO   I marked not this before—
  A prayer-book the pillow to her cheek;
  This was her rich confection, and another°
  Placed in her right hand, with a leaf tucked up,°   15
  Pointing to these words:
  '*Melius virtute mori, quam per dedecus vivere.*'°
  True and effectual it is indeed.°
HIPPOLITO My lord, since you invite us to your sorrows,
  Let's truly taste 'em, that with equal comfort,   20
  As to ourselves, we may relieve your wrongs;°
  We have grief too, that yet walks without tongue—
  Curae leves loquuntur, majores stupent.°
ANTONIO You deal with truth, my lord.
  Lend me but your attentions, and I'll cut   25
  Long grief into short words. Last revelling night,
  When torchlight made an artificial noon

About the court, some courtiers in the masque,
Putting on better faces than their own
(Being full of fraud and flattery), amongst whom   30
The duchess' youngest son (that moth to honour)°
Filled up a room; and with long lust to eat°
Into my wearing, amongst all the ladies°
Singled out that dear form, who ever lived
As cold in lust as she is now in death   35
(Which that step-duchess' monster knew too well);
And therefore in the height of all the revels,
When music was heard loudest, courtiers busiest,
And ladies great with laughter—O vicious minute,
Unfit but for relation to be spoke of!—°   40
Then, with a face more impudent than his vizard,
He harried her amidst a throng of panders
That live upon damnation of both kinds,°
And fed the ravenous vulture of his lust.
O death to think on't! She, her honour forced,   45
Deemed it a nobler dowry for her name°
To die with poison than to live with shame.

HIPPOLITO A wondrous lady, of rare fire compact;
  Sh'as made her name an empress by that act.

PIERO My lord, what judgement follows the offender?   50

ANTONIO Faith, none, my lord; it cools and is deferred.

PIERO Delay the doom for rape?

ANTONIO O, you must note who 'tis should die,
  The duchess' son. She'll look to be a saver:
  'Judgement in this age is near kin to favour.'   55

HIPPOLITO Nay then, step forth, thou bribeless officer.
      [*He draws his sword*]
  I bind you all in steel to bind you surely;
  Here let your oaths meet, to be kept and paid,
  Which else will stick like rust, and shame the blade.
  Strengthen my vow, that if at the next sitting°   60
  Judgement speak all in gold, and spare the blood°
  Of such a serpent, e'en before their seats
  To let his soul out, which long since was found
  Guilty in heaven.

ALL   We swear it and will act it.°

ANTONIO Kind gentlemen, I thank you in mine ire.   65

HIPPOLITO 'Twere pity

The ruins of so fair a monument
Should not be dipped in the defacer's blood.
PIERO Her funeral shall be wealthy, for her name
Merits a tomb of pearl. My Lord Antonio,   70
For this time wipe your lady from your eyes;
No doubt our grief and yours may one day court it,°
When we are more familiar with revenge.
ANTONIO That is my comfort, gentlemen, and I joy
In this one happiness above the rest,   75
Which will be called a miracle at last:
That being an old man, I'd a wife so chaste.
    Exeunt

[2.1]

Enter Castiza

CASTIZA How hardly shall that maiden be beset,°
Whose only fortunes are her constant thoughts,°
That has no other child's-part but her honour
That keeps her low and empty in estate.
Maids and their honours are like poor beginners;   5
Were not sin rich, there would be fewer sinners.
Why had not virtue a revenue? Well,°
I know the cause, 'twould have impoverished hell.
        [*Enter Dondolo*]
How now, Dondolo?

DONDOLO Madonna, there is one, as they say, a thing of flesh and   10
    blood, a man I take him by his beard, that would very desirously
    mouth to mouth with you.

CASTIZA What's that?

DONDOLO Show his teeth in your company.

CASTIZA I understand thee not.   15

DONDOLO Why, speak with you, madonna!

CASTIZA Why, say so, madman, and cut off a great deal of dirty way;°
    had it not been better spoke in ordinary words, that one would
    speak with me?

DONDOLO Ha, ha, that's as ordinary as two shillings. I would strive 20
    a little to show myself in my place; a gentleman-usher° scorns to
    use the phrase and fancy of a servingman.

CASTIZA Yours be your own,° sir; go direct him hither.
        [*Exit Dondolo*]
I hope some happy tidings from my brother
That lately travelled, whom my soul affects.°   25
Here he comes.
        Enter Vindice, disguised

VINDICE Lady, the best of wishes to your sex—
Fair skins and new gowns.
        [*Gives her a letter*]

CASTIZA   O, they shall thank you, sir.
Whence this?

VINDICE   O, from a dear and worthy friend,
Mighty!

CASTIZA   From whom?

VINDICE   The duke's son!
CASTIZA   Receive that!   30
        Gives a box o' th' ear to Vindice
    I swore I'd put anger in my hand,
    And pass the virgin limits of my self,
    To him that next appeared in that base office,
    To be his sin's attorney. Bear to him°
    That figure of my hate upon thy cheek   35
    Whilst 'tis yet hot, and I'll reward thee for't;
    Tell him my honour shall have a rich name,
    When several harlots shall share his with shame.
    Farewell! Commend me to him in my hate.
        Exit [Castiza]
VINDICE It is the sweetest box that e'er my nose came nigh,°   40
    The finest drawn-work cuff that e'er was worn;°
    I'll love this blow forever, and this cheek
    Shall still henceforward take the wall of this.°
    O, I'm above my tongue! Most constant sister,°
    In this thou hast right honourable shown;°   45
    Many are called by their honour that have none.
    Thou art approved forever in my thoughts.°
    It is not in the power of words to taint thee;
    And yet for the salvation of my oath,
    As my resolve in that point, I will lay°   50
    Hard siege unto my mother, though I know
    A siren's tongue could not bewitch her so.°
        [Enter Gratiana]
    Mass, fitly here she comes; thanks, my disguise.
    —Madam, good afternoon.
GRATIANA   Y'are welcome, sir!
VINDICE The next of Italy commends him to you,   55
    Our mighty expectation, the duke's son.
GRATIANA I think myself much honoured that he pleases
    To rank me in his thoughts.
VINDICE   So may you, lady:
    One that is like to be our sudden duke;°
    The crown gapes for him every tide, and then°   60
    Commander o'er us all. Do but think on him;
    How blest were they now that could pleasure him,
    E'en with anything almost.
GRATIANA   Aye, save their honour.
VINDICE Tut, one would let a little of that go, too,

And ne'er be seen in't: ne'er be seen in't, mark you.°   65
I'd wink and let it go—

GRATIANA   Marry, but I would not.

VINDICE Marry, but I would, I hope; I know you would too,
If you'd that blood now which you gave your daughter.°
To her indeed 'tis, this wheel comes about;°
That man that must be all this, perhaps ere morning   70
(For his white father does but mould away),°
Has long desired your daughter.

GRATIANA   Desired?

VINDICE Nay, but hear me:
He desires now that will command hereafter.
Therefore be wise—I speak as more a friend   75
To you than him. Madam, I know y'are poor,
And, 'lack the day, there are too many poor ladies already.
Why should you vex the number? 'tis despised!°
Live wealthy, rightly understand the world,
And chide away that foolish country girl°   80
Keeps company with your daughter, Chastity.

GRATIANA O fie, fie, the riches of the world cannot hire
A mother to such a most unnatural task.

VINDICE No, but a thousand angels can;°
Men have no power, angels must work you to 't.   85
The world descends into such base-born evils
That forty angels can make fourscore devils.
There will be fools still, I perceive, still fools.
Would I be poor, dejected, scorned of greatness,°
Swept from the palace, and see other daughters   90
Spring with the dew o' th' court, having mine own°
So much desired and loved—by the duke's son?
No, I would raise my state upon her breast,°
And call her eyes my tenants; I would count
My yearly maintenance upon her cheeks,   95
Take coach upon her lip; and all her parts
Should keep men after men, and I would ride°
In pleasure upon pleasure.
You took great pains for her, once when it was;
Let her requite it now, though it be but some.°   100
You brought her forth; she may well bring you home.°

GRATIANA O heavens! this overcomes me.

VINDICE [aside] Not, I hope, already!

GRATIANA [aside] It is too strong for me, men know that know us,

We are so weak their words can overthrow us.   105
He touched me nearly, made my virtues bate,°
When his tongue struck upon my poor estate.
VINDICE [*aside*] I e'en quake to proceed, my spirit turns edge!°
   I fear me she's unmothered, yet I'll venture:
   'That woman is all male, whom none can enter.'—   110
   What think you now, lady? Speak, are you wiser?
   What said advancement to you? Thus it said:
   The daughter's fall lifts up the mother's head.
   Did it not, madam? But I'll swear it does
   In many places; tut, this age fears no man.   115
   ' 'Tis no shame to be bad, because 'tis common.'
GRATIANA Aye, that's the comfort on't.
VINDICE   The comfort on't!
   I keep the best for last; can these persuade you
   To forget heaven, and—
        [*Gives her money*]
GRATIANA   Aye, these are they—
VINDICE [*aside*] O!
GRATIANA   —that enchant our sex; these are the means   120
   That govern our affections. That woman
   Will not be troubled with the mother long,°
   That sees the comfortable shine of you:
   I blush to think what for your sakes I'll do.
VINDICE [*aside*] O suff'ring heaven, with thy invisible finger   125
   E'en at this instant turn the precious side°
   Of both mine eyeballs inward, not to see myself.
GRATIANA Look you, sir.
VINDICE   Holla.
GRATIANA   Let this thank your pains.
        [*Tips him*]
VINDICE O, y'are a kind madam.
GRATIANA I'll see how I can move.
VINDICE   Your words will sting.   130
GRATIANA If she be still chaste, I'll ne'er call her mine.
VINDICE [*aside*] Spoke truer than you meant it.
GRATIANA Daughter Castiza!
        [*Enter Castiza*]
CASTIZA   Madam?
VINDICE O, she's yonder; meet her.—
        [*Aside*] Troops of celestial soldiers guard her heart;   135

116

[Handwritten marginalia:] → occasional couplet rhyme echoes the epigrammatic wisdom sayings here.

[Handwritten marginalia:] Like the duchess's interjections w/ junior Brother. A "stop, let it not be so" moment.

[Handwritten marginalia, left:] Aristotle, the old as calculating.

Yon dam has devils enough to take her part.
CASTIZA Madam, what makes yon evil-officed man
  In presence of you?
GRATIANA   Why?
CASTIZA   He lately brought
  Immodest writing sent from the duke's son
  To tempt me to dishonourable act.   140
GRATIANA Dishonourable act? Good honourable fool,
  That wouldst be honest 'cause thou wouldst be so,
  Producing no one reason but thy will.
  And 't'as good report, prettily commended,
  But pray, by whom?—mean people, ignorant people;   145
  The better sort, I'm sure, cannot abide it.
  And by what rule should we square out our lives,°
  But by our betters' actions? O, if thou knew'st
  What 'twere to lose it, thou would never keep it.
  But there's a cold curse laid upon all maids,   150
  Whilst others clip the sun they clasp the shades.°
  Virginity is paradise, locked up.
  You cannot come by your selves without fee,°
  And 'twas decreed that man should keep the key.
  Deny advancement, treasure, the duke's son?   155
CASTIZA I cry you mercy, lady, I mistook you;
  Pray, did you see my mother? Which way went you?
  Pray God I have not lost her.
VINDICE [aside]   Prettily put by.
GRATIANA Are you as proud to me as coy to him?
  Do you not know me now?
CASTIZA   Why, are you she?   160
  The world's so changed, one shape into another,
  It is a wise child now that knows her mother!°
VINDICE [aside] Most right, i' faith.
GRATIANA   I owe your cheek my hand°
  For that presumption now, but I'll forget it.
  Come, you shall leave those childish 'haviours,°   165
  And understand your time. Fortune's flow to you;°
  What, will you be a girl?
  If all feared drowning that spy waves ashore,
  Gold would grow rich, and all the merchants poor.°
CASTIZA It is a pretty saying of a wicked one;   170
  But methinks now

[handwritten margin note:] Aristotle: the young as obsessed with honor, but also lust/desires of the body.

It does not show so well out of your mouth;
Better in his.
VINDICE [*aside*] Faith, bad enough in both,
  Were I in earnest, as I'll seem no less.
  [*To Castiza*] I wonder, lady, your own mother's words   175
  Cannot be taken, nor stand in full force.
  'Tis honesty you urge; what's honesty?
  'Tis but heaven's beggar;
  And what woman is so foolish to keep honesty,°
  And be not able to keep herself? No,   180
  Times are grown wiser and will keep less charge.°
  A maid that has small portion now intends
  To break up house and live upon her friends.°
  How blest are you! You have happiness alone.
  Others must fall to thousands, you to one,°   185
  Sufficient in himself to make your forehead
  Dazzle the world with jewels, and petitionary people°
  Start at your presence.
GRATIANA   O, if I were young,
  I should be ravished.
CASTIZA   Aye, to lose your honour.°
VINDICE 'Slid, how can you lose your honour   190
  To deal with my lord's grace?
  He'll add more honour to it by his title—
  Your mother will tell you how.
GRATIANA   That I will.
VINDICE O, think upon the pleasure of the palace:
  Securèd ease and state; the stirring meats°   195
  Ready to move out of the dishes,
  That e'en now quicken when they're eaten;°
  Banquets abroad by torchlight, musics, sports;
  Bareheaded vassals, that had ne'er the fortune
  To keep on their own hats, but let horns wear 'em;°   200
  Nine coaches waiting—hurry, hurry, hurry!
CASTIZA Aye, to the devil.
VINDICE [*aside*] Aye, to the devil.—[*Aloud*] To th' duke, by my faith.
GRATIANA Aye, to the duke! Daughter, you'd scorn to think o' th'
  devil, an you were there once.   205
VINDICE [*aside*] True, for most there are as proud as he for his heart,
  i'faith.—
  [*Aloud*] Who'd sit at home in a neglected room,

Dealing her short-lived beauty to the pictures
That are as useless as old men, when those° 210
Poorer in face and fortune than herself
Walk with a hundred acres on their backs,
Fair meadows cut into green foreparts?—O,°
It was the greatest blessing ever happened to women,
When farmers' sons agreed, and met again° 215
To wash their hands, and come up gentlemen;°
The commonwealth has flourished ever since.
Lands that were mete by the rod, that labour's spared;°
Tailors ride down, and measure 'em by the yard.
Fair trees, those comely foretops of the field,° 220
Are cut to maintain head-tires—much untold;°
All thrives but chastity; she lies a-cold.
Nay, shall I come nearer to you? Mark but this:
Why are there so few honest women, but because 'tis the poorer
profession? That's accounted best, that's best followed—least in 225
trade, least in fashion—and that's not honesty, believe it.
And do but note the low and dejected price of it:
'Lose but a pearl, we search and cannot brook it;
But that once gone, who is so mad to look it?'
GRATIANA Troth, he says true.
CASTIZA   False! I defy you both. 230
I have endured you with an ear of fire;
Your tongues have struck hot irons on my face.°
Mother, come from that poisonous woman there!°
GRATIANA Where?
CASTIZA   Do you not see her? She's too inward then.°
[*To Vindice*] Slave, perish in thy office! You heavens, please 235
Henceforth to make the mother a disease,°
Which first begins with me; yet I've outgone you.°
        Exit [Castiza]
VINDICE [*aside*] O angels, clap your wings upon the skies,
And give this virgin crystal plaudities!°
GRATIANA Peevish, coy, foolish!—but return this answer: 240
My lord shall be most welcome, when his pleasure
Conducts him this way. I will sway mine own.
Women with women can work best alone.
VINDICE Indeed, I'll tell him so.
        Exit [Gratiana]
O, more uncivil, more unnatural 245

Than those base-titled creatures that look downward!°
Why does not heaven turn black, or with a frown
Undo the world? Why does not earth start up
And strike the sins that tread upon't? O,
Were't not for gold and women, there would be no damnation;   250
Hell would look like a lord's great kitchen without fire in't.°
But 'twas decreed before the world began,
That they should be the hooks to catch at man.
    Exit

[2.2]

    Enter Lussurioso with Hippolito

LUSSURIOSO I much applaud thy judgement.
  Thou art well read in a fellow,°
  And 'tis the deepest art to study man.
  I know this, which I never learnt in schools:
  The world's divided into knaves and fools.   5
HIPPOLITO [*aside*] Knave in your face, my lord—behind your back.°
LUSSURIOSO And I much thank thee that thou hast preferred
  A fellow of discourse, well mingled,
  And whose brain time hath seasoned.
HIPPOLITO   True, my lord.
  [*Aside*] We shall find season once, I hope. O villain,°   10
  To make such an unnatural slave of me! but—
    [*Enter Vindice, disguised*]
LUSSURIOSO Mass, here he comes.
HIPPOLITO [*aside*] And now shall I have free leave to depart.
LUSSURIOSO Your absence, leave us.
HIPPOLITO [*aside*]   Are not my thoughts true?
  I must remove, but brother, you may stay.   15
  Heart, we are both made bawds a new-found way!
    Exit [*Hippolito*]
LUSSURIOSO Now we're an even number. A third man's dangerous,
  Especially her brother; say, be free,
  Have I a pleasure toward?
VINDICE   O my lord!°
LUSSURIOSO Ravish me in thine answer; art thou rare?°   20
  Hast thou beguiled her of salvation,

And rubbed hell o'er with honey? Is she a woman?°
VINDICE In all but in desire.
LUSSURIOSO   Then she's in nothing—
   I bate in courage now.
VINDICE   The words I brought°
   Might well have made indifferent-honest naught.°   25
   A right good woman in these days is changed
   Into white money with less labour far.°
   Many a maid has turned to Mahomet°
   With easier working; I durst undertake,
   Upon the pawn and forfeit of my life,   30
   With half those words to flat a Puritan's wife.°
   But she is close and good—yet 'tis a doubt°
   By this time. O, the mother, the mother!
LUSSURIOSO I never thought their sex had been a wonder
   Until this minute. What fruit from the mother?   35
VINDICE [aside] Now must I blister my soul, be forsworn,
   Or shame the woman that received me first.
   I will be true, thou liv'st not to proclaim:°
   Spoke to a dying man, shame has no shame.—
   My lord.
LUSSURIOSO Who's that?
VINDICE   Here's none but I, my lord.   40
LUSSURIOSO What would thy haste utter?
VINDICE   Comfort.
LUSSURIOSO   Welcome.
VINDICE The maid being dull, having no mind to travel
   Into unknown lands, what did me I straight,°
   But set spurs to the mother? Golden spurs°
   Will put her to a false gallop in a trice.   45
LUSSURIOSO Is't possible that in this
   The mother should be damned before the daughter?
VINDICE O, that's good manners, my lord; the mother for her age°
   must go foremost, you know.
LUSSURIOSO
   Thou'st spoke that true! but where comes in this comfort?   50
VINDICE In a fine place, my lord. The unnatural mother
   Did with her tongue so hard beset her honour,
   That the poor fool was struck to silent wonder.°
   Yet still the maid, like an unlighted taper,
   Was cold and chaste, save that her mother's breath   55

Did blow fire on her cheeks. The girl departed,
But the good ancient madam, half mad, threw me
These promising words, which I took deeply note of:
'My lord shall be most welcome—'
LUSSURIOSO   Faith, I thank her.
VINDICE 'When his pleasure conducts him this way—'   60
LUSSURIOSO That shall be soon, i' faith.
VINDICE   'I will sway mine own—'
LUSSURIOSO She does the wiser; I commend her for't.
VINDICE 'Women with women can work best alone.'
LUSSURIOSO By this light, and so they can. Give 'em their due, men
   are not comparable to 'em.   65
VINDICE No, that's true; for you shall have one woman knit more in
   a hour than any man can ravel again in seven-and-twenty year.
LUSSURIOSO Now my desires are happy; I'll make 'em freemen now.
   Thou art a precious fellow; faith, I love thee.
   Be wise and make it thy revenue: beg, leg!°   70
   What office couldst thou be ambitious for?
VINDICE Office, my lord? Marry, if I might have my wish, I would
   have one that was never begged yet.
LUSSURIOSO Nay, then thou canst have none.
VINDICE Yes, my lord, I could pick out another office yet; nay, and   75
   keep a horse and drab upon 't.
LUSSURIOSO Prithee, good bluntness, tell me.
VINDICE Why, I would desire but this, my lord: to have all the fees
   behind the arras,° and all the farthingales° that fall plump° about
   twelve o'clock at night upon the rushes.°   80
LUSSURIOSO Thou'rt a mad, apprehensive knave. Dost think to
   make any great purchase of that?
VINDICE O, 'tis an unknown thing, my lord; I wonder 't 'as been
   missed° so long!
LUSSURIOSO Well, this night I'll visit her, and 'tis till then   85
   A year in my desires. Farewell. Attend;
   Trust me with thy preferment.
VINDICE   My loved lord.
      Exit [Lussurioso. Vindice puts his hand to his sword]
   O, shall I kill him o' th' wrong side now? No!°
   Sword, thou wast never a backbiter yet.
   I'll pierce him to his face; he shall die looking upon me. 90,
   Thy veins are swelled with lust, this shall unfill 'em:
   Great men were gods, if beggars could not kill 'em.

Forgive me, heaven, to call my mother wicked.
O, lessen not my days upon the earth;°
I cannot honour her. By this, I fear me, 95
Her tongue has turned my sister into use.°
I was a villain not to be forsworn
To this our lecherous hope, the duke's son;
For lawyers, merchants, some divines, and all
Count beneficial perjury a sin small. 100
It shall go hard yet, but I'll guard her honour,°
And keep the ports sure.°
        Enter Hippolito
HIPPOLITO Brother, how goes the world? I would know news
    Of you, but I have news to tell you.
VINDICE What, in the name of knavery?
HIPPOLITO   Knavery, faith: 105
    This vicious old duke's worthily abused.
    The pen of his bastard writes him cuckold!
VINDICE His bastard?
HIPPOLITO   Pray believe it; he and the duchess
    By night meet in their linen; they have been seen°
    By stair-foot panders.
VINDICE   O sin foul and deep! 110
    Great faults are winked at when the duke's asleep.
        [*Enter Spurio with two Servants*]
    See, see, here comes the Spurio.
HIPPOLITO   Monstrous luxur!
VINDICE Unbraced, two of his valiant bawds with him.
        [*Spurio and his servants talk apart*]
    O, there's a wicked whisper; hell is in his ear.
    Stay, let's observe his passage. 115
        [*Vindice and Hippolito withdraw to one side*]
SPURIO O, but are you sure on't?
SERVANT My lord, most sure on't, for 'twas spoke by one
    That is most inward with the duke's son's lust:°
    That he intends within this hour to steal
    Unto Hippolito's sister, whose chaste life 120
    The mother has corrupted for his use.
SPURIO Sweet word, sweeter occasion! Faith then, brother,
    I'll disinherit you in as short time
    As I was when I was begot in haste;
    I'll damn you at your pleasure. Precious deed! 125

After your lust, O, 'twill be fine to bleed.
Come, let our passing out be soft and wary.
            Exeunt [Spurio and Servants]
VINDICE Mark! there, there, that step, now to the duchess.
   This, their second meeting, writes the duke cuckold
   With new additions, his horns newly revived.°   130
   Night, thou that look'st like funeral herald's fees°
   Torn down betimes i' th' morning, thou hang'st fitly
   To grace those sins that have no grace at all.
   Now 'tis full sea abed over the world,°
   There's juggling of all sides; some that were maids°   135
   E'en at sunset are now perhaps i' th' toll-book.°
   This woman in immodest thin apparel
   Lets in her friend by water; here a dame,°
   Cunning, nails leather hinges to a door
   To avoid proclamation. Now cuckolds are°   140
   A-coining, apace, apace, apace, apace!
   And careful sisters spin that thread i' th' night°
   That does maintain them and their bawds i' th' day.
HIPPOLITO You flow well, brother.
VINDICE   Puh, I'm shallow yet,
   Too sparing and too modest. Shall I tell thee?   145
   If every trick were told that's dealt by night,
   There are few here that would not blush outright.
HIPPOLITO I am of that belief, too.
VINDICE   Who's this comes?
            [Enter Lussurioso]
   The duke's son up so late? Brother, fall back,
   And you shall learn some mischief.
            [Hippolito withdraws to one side]
                              —My good lord.   150
LUSSURIOSO Piato! why, the man I wished for! Come,
   I do embrace this season for the fittest°
   To taste of that young lady.
VINDICE *[aside]*   Heart and hell!
HIPPOLITO *[aside]* Damned villain.
VINDICE *[aside]* I ha' no way now to cross it but to kill him.   155
LUSSURIOSO Come, only thou and I.
VINDICE   My lord, my lord!
LUSSURIOSO Why dost thou start us?°
VINDICE I'd almost forgot—the bastard!

LUSSURIOSO   What of him?
VINDICE This night, this hour—this minute, now—
LUSSURIOSO What, what?
VINDICE   Shadows the duchess—°   160
LUSSURIOSO Horrible word!
VINDICE   And, like strong poison, eats
  Into the duke your father's forehead.
LUSSURIOSO   O!
VINDICE He makes horn royal.
LUSSURIOSO   Most ignoble slave!°
VINDICE This is the fruit of two beds.
LUSSURIOSO   I am mad.°
VINDICE That passage he trod warily—
LUSSURIOSO   He did!   165
VINDICE And hushed his villains every step he took.
LUSSURIOSO His villains? I'll confound them.
VINDICE Take 'em finely, finely now.
LUSSURIOSO The duchess' chamber-door shall not control me.
       Exeunt [Lussurioso and Vindice]
HIPPOLITO Good, happy, swift! There's gunpowder i' th' court,   170
  Wildfire at midnight. In this heedless fury°
  He may show violence to cross himself.
  I'll follow the event.°
       Exit

[2.3]

    *Enter again [Lussurioso and Vindice; the Duke and the
    Duchess in bed]°*
LUSSURIOSO Where is that villain?
VINDICE Softly, my lord, and you may take 'em twisted.°
LUSSURIOSO I care not how!
VINDICE   O, 'twill be glorious
  To kill 'em doubled, when they're heaped. Be soft, my lord.°
LUSSURIOSO Away, my spleen is not so lazy; thus, and thus,°   5
  I'll shake their eyelids ope, and with my sword
  Shut 'em again forever.
       [Lussurioso draws his sword]
                    —Villain! strumpet!

DUKE You upper guard, defend us!
DUCHESS   Treason, treason!°
DUKE O, take me not in sleep; I have great sins.
 I must have days—   10
 Nay, months, dear son, with penitential heaves,°
 To lift 'em out, and not to die unclear.
 O, thou wilt kill me both in heaven and here.
LUSSURIOSO I am amazed to death.
DUKE   Nay, villain, traitor,
 Worse than the foulest epithet, now I'll gripe thee   15
 E'en with the nerves of wrath, and throw thy head°
 Amongst the lawyers. Guard!°
   [Guards enter and seize Lussurioso.] Enter Nobles,
   [Hippolito,] Ambitioso, and Supervacuo
FIRST NOBLE How comes the quiet of your grace disturbed?
DUKE This boy, that should be myself after me,°
 Would be myself before me, and in heat   20
 Of that ambition bloodily rushed in,
 Intending to depose me in my bed.
SECOND NOBLE Duty and natural loyalty forfend!
DUCHESS He called his father villain, and me strumpet,
 A word that I abhor to file my lips with.°   25
AMBITIOSO That was not so well done, brother.
LUSSURIOSO   I am abused—°
 I know there's no excuse can do me good.
VINDICE [aside to Hippolito]
 'Tis now good policy to be from sight.°
 His vicious purpose to our sister's honour
 Is crossed, beyond our thought.
HIPPOLITO [aside to Vindice]   You little dreamt   30
 His father slept here.
VINDICE [aside to Hippolito] O, 'twas far beyond me.
 But since it fell so—without frightful words,°
 Would he had killed him; 'twould have eased our swords.
   [Exeunt Vindice and Hippolito furtively]
DUKE Be comforted, our duchess, he shall die.
   [Exit Duchess]
LUSSURIOSO Where's this slave-pander now? Out of mine eye,   35
 Guilty of this abuse.
   Enter Spurio with his two Servants
SPURIO   Y'are villains, fablers!

You have knaves' chins and harlots' tongues; you lie,°
And I will damn you with one meal a day.°
FIRST SERVANT O good my lord!
SPURIO   'Sblood, you shall never sup.
SECOND SERVANT O, I beseech you, sir!
SPURIO   To let my sword   40
Catch cold so long, and miss him.
FIRST SERVANT   Troth, my lord,
'Twas his intent to meet there.
SPURIO   Heart, he's yonder!
Ha, what news here? Is the day out o' th' socket,°
That it is noon at midnight? the court up?
How comes the guard so saucy with his elbows?°   45
LUSSURIOSO [aside] The bastard here?
Nay, then the truth of my intent shall out.—
My lord and father, hear me.
DUKE   Bear him hence.
LUSSURIOSO I can with loyalty excuse—
DUKE Excuse? To prison with the villain!   50
Death shall not long lag after him.
SPURIO [aside] Good, i' faith; then 'tis not much amiss.
LUSSURIOSO Brothers, my best release lies on your tongues;°
I pray persuade for me.
AMBITIOSO   It is our duties;
Make yourself sure of us.
SUPERVACUO   We'll sweat in pleading.   55
LUSSURIOSO And I may live to thank you.
          Exeunt [Lussurioso and Guards]
AMBITIOSO [aside]   No, thy death
Shall thank me better.
SPURIO [aside]   He's gone; I'll after him,
And know his trespass, seem to bear a part
In all his ills, but with a Puritan heart.°
          Exit [Spurio]
AMBITIOSO [aside to Supervacuo]
Now, brother, let our hate and love be woven   60
So subtly together, that in speaking
One word for his life, we may make three for his death.
The craftiest pleader gets most gold for breath.°
SUPERVACUO [aside to Ambitioso]
Set on; I'll not be far behind you, brother.°

DUKE
    Is't possible a son should be disobedient as far as the sword?   65
    It is the highest; he can go no farther.
AMBITIOSO My gracious lord, take pity—
DUKE   Pity, boys?
AMBITIOSO Nay, we'd be loath to move your grace too much.
    We know the trespass is unpardonable,   70
    Black, wicked, and unnatural.
SUPERVACUO In a son, O monstrous!
AMBITIOSO   Yet, my lord,
    A duke's soft hand strokes the rough head of law,
    And makes it lie smooth.
DUKE   But my hand shall ne'er do 't.
AMBITIOSO That as you please, my lord.
SUPERVACUO   We must needs confess   75
    Some father would have entered into hate
    So deadly pointed, that before his eyes
    He would ha' seen the execution sound,°
    Without corrupted favor.
AMBITIOSO   But my lord,°
    Your grace may live the wonder of all times,   80
    In pard'ning that offence which never yet
    Had face to beg a pardon.
DUKE [aside]   Honey? How's this?°
AMBITIOSO Forgive him, good my lord; he's your own son,
    And I must needs say, 'twas the vilelier done.
SUPERVACUO He's the next heir; yet this true reason gathers:°   85
    None can possess that dispossess their fathers.
    Be merciful—
DUKE [aside]   Here's no stepmother's wit;°
    I'll try 'em both upon their love and hate.
AMBITIOSO Be merciful—although—
DUKE   You have prevailed.
    My wrath, like flaming wax, hath spent itself.   90
    I know 'twas but some peevish moon in him;°
    Go, let him be released.
SUPERVACUO [aside to Ambitioso] 'Sfoot, how now, brother?
AMBITIOSO Your grace doth please to speak beside your spleen;°
    I would it were so happy.
DUKE   Why, go release him.

SUPERVACUO O, my good lord, I know the fault's too weighty   95
   And full of general loathing; too inhuman,
   Rather by all men's voices worthy death.
DUKE 'Tis true too.
   Here then, receive this signet: doom shall pass.°
   Direct it to the judges; he shall die   100
   Ere many days. Make haste.
AMBITIOSO   All speed that may be.°
   We could have wished his burden not so sore;
   We knew your grace did but delay before.
      Exeunt [Ambitioso and Supervacuo]
DUKE Here's envy with a poor thin cover o'er't,
   Like scarlet hid in lawn, easily spied through.°   105
   This their ambition by the mother's side
   Is dangerous, and for safety must be purged.
   I will prevent their envies; sure it was°
   But some mistaken fury in our son,
   Which these aspiring boys would climb upon.   110
   He shall be released suddenly.°
      Enter Nobles
FIRST NOBLE Good morning to your grace.
DUKE   Welcome, my lords.
      [Nobles kneel]
SECOND NOBLE Our knees shall take away
   The office of our feet forever,
   Unless your grace bestow a father's eye   115
   Upon the clouded fortunes of your son,
   And in compassionate virtue grant him that
   Which makes e'en mean men happy: liberty.
DUKE *[aside]* How seriously their loves and honours woo
   For that which I am about to pray them do: 120
   Which—*[to the Nobles]* rise, my lords; your knees sign his release.
   We freely pardon him.
FIRST NOBLE We owe your grace much thanks, and he much duty.
      Exeunt [Nobles]
DUKE It well becomes that judge to nod at crimes°
   That does commit greater himself, and lives.   125
   I may forgive a disobedient error
   That expect pardon for adultery
   And in my old days am a youth in lust.

Many a beauty have I turned to poison
In the denial, covetous of all.°   130
Age hot is like a monster to be seen:°
My hairs are white, and yet my sins are green.
        [*Exit*]

[3.1]

Enter Ambitioso and Supervacuo

SUPERVACUO Brother, let my opinion sway you once;
   I speak it for the best, to have him die°
   Surest and soonest. If the signet come
   Unto the judges' hands, why then his doom
   Will be deferred till sittings and court-days,   5
   Juries, and further. Faiths are bought and sold;°
   Oaths in these days are but the skin of gold.°

AMBITIOSO In troth, 'tis true too!

SUPERVACUO   Then let's set by the judges°
   And fall to the officers. 'Tis but mistaking
   The duke our father's meaning, and where he named   10
   'Ere many days', 'tis but forgetting that,
   And have him die i' th' morning.

AMBITIOSO   Excellent!
   Then am I heir—duke in a minute.

SUPERVACUO [*aside, grasping his sword*] Nay,
   An he were once puffed out, here is a pin°
   Should quickly prick your bladder.

AMBITIOSO   Blest occasion!   15
   He being packed, we'll have some trick and wile°
   To wind our younger brother out of prison,°
   That lies in for the rape: the lady's dead,°
   And people's thought will soon be buried.

SUPERVACUO We may with safety do't, and live and feed;   20
   The duchess' sons are too proud to bleed.

AMBITIOSO We are i'faith, to say true. Come, let's not linger.
   I'll to the officers; go you before,
   And set an edge upon the executioner.°

SUPERVACUO Let me alone to grind him.

AMBITIOSO   Meet; farewell.—°   25
   Exit [Supervacuo]
   I am next now; I rise just in that place
   Where thou'rt cut off—upon thy neck, kind brother.°
   The falling of one head lifts up another.
      Exit

[3.2]

Enter, with the Nobles, Lussurioso from prison

LUSSURIOSO My lords,
  I am so much indebted to your loves
  For this, O this delivery.
FIRST NOBLE   But our duties,°
  My lord, unto the hopes that grow in you.
LUSSURIOSO If e'er I live to be myself, I'll thank you.°   5
  O liberty, thou sweet and heavenly dame!
  But hell for prison is too mild a name.
    Exeunt

[3.3]

Enter Ambitioso and Supervacuo, with Officers

AMBITIOSO Officers, here's the duke's signet, your firm warrant,
  Brings the command of present death along with it
  Unto our brother, the duke's son. We are sorry
  That we are so unnaturally employed
  In such an unkind office, fitter far   5
  For enemies than brothers.
SUPERVACUO   But you know
  The duke's command must be obeyed.
FIRST OFFICER It must and shall, my lord. This morning then,
  So suddenly?
AMBITIOSO   Aye, alas. Poor, good soul,
  He must breakfast betimes; the executioner   10
  Stands ready to put forth his cowardly valour.
SECOND OFFICER Already?
SUPERVACUO Already, i'faith. O sir, destruction hies,
  And that is least impudent, soonest dies.°
FIRST OFFICER Troth, you say true, my lord; we take our leaves.   15
  Our office shall be sound; we'll not delay°
  The third part of a minute.
AMBITIOSO   Therein you show
  Yourselves good men, and upright officers.
  Pray let him die as private as he may;
  Do him that favour, for the gaping people°   20

Will but trouble him at his prayers
And make him curse and swear, and so die black.°
Will you be so far kind?
FIRST OFFICER   It shall be done, my lord.
AMBITIOSO Why, we do thank you; if we live to be,°
    You shall have a better office.
SECOND OFFICER   Your good lordship.   25
SUPERVACUO Commend us to the scaffold in our tears.
FIRST OFFICER We'll weep, and do your commendations.
        Exeunt [Officers]
AMBITIOSO Fine fools in office!
SUPERVACUO   Things fall out so fit!
AMBITIOSO So happily! Come, brother, ere next clock
    His head will be made serve a bigger block.°   30
        Exeunt

[3.4]

Enter in prison Junior Brother
JUNIOR BROTHER Keeper!
        [*Enter Keeper*]
KEEPER My lord.
JUNIOR BROTHER No news lately from our brothers? Are they
    unmindful of us?
KEEPER My lord, a messenger came newly in and brought this from   5
    'em.
        [*Gives him a letter*]
JUNIOR BROTHER Nothing but paper comforts? I looked for my
    delivery before this, had they been worth their oaths. Prithee,
    be from° us.
        [*Exit Keeper*]
    Now, what say you, forsooth? Speak out, I pray. ([*Reading the*]   10
    letter) 'Brother, be of good cheer.'° 'Slud, it begins like a whore,
    with good cheer. 'Thou shalt not be long a prisoner.' Not
    five-and-thirty year, like a bankrupt,° I think so. 'We have thought
    upon a device to get thee out by a trick.' By a trick! Pox o' your
    trick,° an it be so long a-playing. 'And so rest comforted, be merry   15
    and expect it suddenly.' Be merry! Hang merry! Draw and quarter
    merry! I'll be mad. [*Tears up the letter*] Is't not strange that a man
    should lie in° a whole month for a woman? Well, we shall see how

sudden our brothers will be in their promise. I must expect still a
trick. I shall not be long a prisoner.   20
   [*Enter Keeper*]
How now, what news?

KEEPER Bad news, my lord, I am discharged of° you.

JUNIOR BROTHER Slave, call'st thou that bad news? I thank you,
brothers.

KEEPER My lord, 'twill prove so: here come the officers into whose   25
hands I must commit you.
   [*Enter four Officers*]

JUNIOR BROTHER Ha? Officers! what? why?

FIRST OFFICER You must pardon us, my lord, our office
Must be sound. Here is our warrant, the signet
From the duke; you must straight suffer.

JUNIOR BROTHER   Suffer?°   30
I'll suffer you to be gone; I'll suffer you
To come no more. What would you have me suffer?

SECOND OFFICER
My lord, those words were better changed to prayers.
The time's but brief with you; prepare to die.

JUNIOR BROTHER Sure 'tis not so.

THIRD OFFICER   It is too true, my lord.   35

JUNIOR BROTHER I tell you 'tis not, for the duke my father
Deferred me till next sitting, and I look
E'en every minute, threescore times an hour,
For a release, a trick wrought by my brothers.

FIRST OFFICER A trick, my lord? If you expect such comfort,   40
Your hope's as fruitless as a barren woman.
Your brothers were the unhappy messengers
That brought this powerful token for your death.°

JUNIOR BROTHER My brothers? No, no!

SECOND OFFICER   'Tis most true, my lord.

JUNIOR BROTHER My brothers to bring a warrant for my death?   45
How strange this shows!

THIRD OFFICER   There's no delaying time.

JUNIOR BROTHER Desire 'em hither, call 'em up. My brothers?
They shall deny it to your faces.

FIRST OFFICER   My lord,
They're far enough by this, at least at court,
And this most strict command they left behind 'em.   50
When grief swum in their eyes, they showed like brothers,

Brimful of heavy sorrow; but the duke
Must have his pleasure.
JUNIOR BROTHER   His pleasure!
FIRST OFFICER
   These were their last words which my memory bears:
   'Commend us to the scaffold in our tears.'   55
JUNIOR BROTHER Pox dry their tears! What should I do with tears?
   I hate 'em worse than any citizen's son°
   Can hate salt water. Here came a letter now,
   New-bleeding from their pens, scarce stinted yet—°
   Would I'd been torn in pieces when I tore it.   60
        [*He picks up the pieces*]
   Look, you officious whoresons, words of comfort:
   'Not long a prisoner.'
FIRST OFFICER It says true in that, sir, for you must suffer presently.
JUNIOR BROTHER A villainous duns° upon the letter, knavish expo-
   sition! Look you then here, sir: 'We'll get thee out by a trick,' says   65
   he.
SECOND OFFICER That may hold too, sir, for you know a trick° is
   commonly four cards, which was meant by us four officers.
JUNIOR BROTHER Worse and worse dealing.
FIRST OFFICER   The hour beckons us,
   The headsman waits; lift up your eyes to heaven.   70
JUNIOR BROTHER
   I thank you, faith; good, pretty, wholesome counsel!
   I should look up to heaven as you said,
   Whilst he behind me cozens me of my head.
   Aye, that's the trick.
THIRD OFFICER   You delay too long, my lord.   75
JUNIOR BROTHER Stay, good authority's bastards; since I must
   Through brothers' perjury die, O let me venom
   Their souls with curses.
FIRST OFFICER   Come, 'tis no time to curse.
JUNIOR BROTHER Must I bleed then, without respect of sign?°
   Well—   80
   My fault was sweet sport, which the world approves;
   I die for that which every woman loves.
       Exeunt

[3.5]

*Enter Vindice [disguised] with Hippolito, [who holds a torch
and an incense-burner]*

VINDICE O sweet, delectable, rare, happy, ravishing!

HIPPOLITO Why, what's the matter, brother?

VINDICE   O, 'tis able
  To make a man spring up, and knock his forehead
  Against yon silver ceiling.

HIPPOLITO   Prithee tell me,°
  Why may not I partake with you? You vowed once°   5
  To give me share to every tragic thought.

VINDICE By th' mass, I think I did too;
  Then I'll divide it to thee. The old duke,
  Thinking my outward shape and inward heart
  Are cut out of one piece (for he that prates his secrets,°   10
  His heart stands o' th' outside), hires me by price°
  To greet him with a lady   .
  In some fit place veiled from the eyes o' th' court,
  Some darkened, blushless angle, that is guilty°
  Of his forefathers' lusts and great folks' riots;   15
  To which I easily (to maintain my shape)
  Consented, and did wish his impudent grace
  To meet her here in this unsunnèd lodge,
  Wherein 'tis night at noon; and here the rather
  Because, unto the torturing of his soul,   20
  The bastard and the duchess have appointed
  Their meeting too in this luxurious circle,°
  Which most afflicting sight will kill his eyes
  Before we kill the rest of him.

HIPPOLITO 'Twill, i'faith; most dreadfully digested.°   25
  I see not how you could have missed me, brother.°

VINDICE True, but the violence of my joy forgot it.

HIPPOLITO Aye, but where's that lady now?

VINDICE   O, at that word
  I'm lost again: you cannot find me yet.°
  I'm in a throng of happy apprehensions.°   30
  He's suited for a lady; I have took care
  For a delicious lip, a sparkling eye.
  You shall be witness, brother.
  Be ready; stand with your hat off.

136

Exit [Vindice]

HIPPOLITO Troth, I wonder what lady it should be?   35
  Yet 'tis no wonder, now I think again,
  To have a lady stoop to a duke, that stoops unto his men.°
  'Tis common to be common, through the world:°
  And there's more private-common shadowing vices°
  Than those who are known both by their names and prices.   40
  'Tis part of my allegiance to stand bare°
  To the duke's concubine—and here she comes.
    Enter Vindice, with the skull of his love dressed up in tires°
    [and masked]
VINDICE [*to the skull*] Madam, his grace will not be absent long.—
  Secret? ne'er doubt us, madam. 'Twill be worth
  Three velvet gowns to your ladyship.—Known?   45
  Few ladies respect that!—Disgrace? A poor thin shell;°
  'Tis the best grace you have to do it well.°
  I'll save your hand that labour; I'll unmask you!
    [Vindice unmasks the skull]
HIPPOLITO Why, brother, brother!   •
VINDICE Art thou beguiled now? Tut, a lady can,   50
  At such all-hid, beguile a wiser man.°
  Have I not fitted the old surfeiter
  With a quaint piece of beauty? Age and bare bone°
  Are e'er allied in action. Here's an eye°
  Able to tempt a great man—to serve God;   55
  A pretty hanging lip, that has forgot now to dissemble;
  Methinks this mouth should make a swearer tremble,
  A drunkard clasp his teeth, and not undo 'em
  To suffer wet damnation to run through 'em.
  Here's a cheek keeps her colour, let the wind go whistle.°   60
  Spout, rain, we fear thee not; be hot or cold,
  All's one with us. And is not he absurd,
  Whose fortunes are upon their faces set,
  That fear no other god but wind and wet?
HIPPOLITO Brother, y'ave spoke that right.   65
  Is this the form that, living, shone so bright?
VINDICE The very same.
  And now methinks I could e'en chide myself
  For doting on her beauty, though her death
  Shall be revenged after no common action.   70
  Does the silkworm expend her yellow labours°
  For thee? for thee does she undo herself?

Are lordships sold to maintain ladyships°
For the poor benefit of a bewitching minute?
Why does yon fellow falsify highways,°   75
And put his life between the judge's lips,°
To refine such a thing, keeps horse and men
To beat their valours for her?°
Surely we are all mad people, and they
Whom we think are, are not; we mistake those: 80
'Tis we are mad in sense, they but in clothes.

HIPPOLITO Faith, and in clothes too we, give us our due.

VINDICE Does every proud and self-affecting dame
Camphor her face for this? and grieve her Maker
In sinful baths of milk, when many an infant starves,   85
For her superfluous outside—all for this?
Who now bids twenty pound a night, prepares
Music, perfumes, and sweetmeats? All are hushed;
Thou may'st lie chaste now! It were fine, methinks,
To have thee seen at revels, forgetful feasts,°   90
And unclean brothels; sure, 'twould fright the sinner
And make him a good coward, put a reveller
Out of his antic amble,°
And cloy an epicure with empty dishes.
Here might a scornful and ambitious woman   95
Look through and through herself. See, ladies, with false forms
You deceive men, but cannot deceive worms.
Now to my tragic business. Look you, brother,
I have not fashioned this only for show
And useless property; no, it shall bear a part°   100
E'en in it own revenge. This very skull,°
Whose mistress the duke poisoned with this drug,
The mortal curse of the earth, shall be revenged
In the like strain, and kiss his lips to death.°
As much as the dumb thing can, he shall feel;   105
What fails in poison, we'll supply in steel.

HIPPOLITO Brother, I do applaud thy constant vengeance,
The quaintness of thy malice, above thought.°

VINDICE [putting poison on the skull's mouth]
So, 'tis laid on: now come and welcome, duke;
I have her for thee. I protest it, brother,   110
Methinks she makes almost as fair a sign°
As some old gentlewoman in a periwig.°

[*To the skull*] Hide thy face now for shame; thou hadst need have
   a mask now.
     [*Vindice puts the mask back on the skull*]
   'Tis vain when beauty flows, but when it fleets,   115
   This would become graves better than the streets.°
HIPPOLITO You have my voice in that.
     [*Noises within*]
                          Hark, the duke's come.°
VINDICE Peace, let's observe what company he brings,
   And how he does absent 'em; for you know°
   He'll wish all private. Brother, fall you back a little   120
   With the bony lady.
HIPPOLITO   That I will.
     [*Hippolito retires with the skull and the torch*]
VINDICE   So, so—
   Now nine years' vengeance crowd into a minute!
     [*Enter the Duke and Gentlemen; Vindice is unobserved*]
DUKE You shall have leave to leave us, with this charge,
   Upon your lives: if we be missed by th' duchess
   Or any of the nobles, to give out   125
   We're privately rid forth.
VINDICE [*aside*]   O happiness!°
DUKE With some few honourable gentlemen, you may say;
   You may name those that are away from court.
[FIRST] GENTLEMAN Your will and pleasure shall be done, my lord.
     [*Exeunt Gentlemen*]
VINDICE [*aside*] 'Privately rid forth!'   130
   He strives to make sure work on 't.
     [*Steps forward*]
                      Your good grace.
DUKE Piato, well done. Hast brought her? What lady is't?
VINDICE Faith, my lord, a country lady, a little bashful at first, as
   most of them are, but after the first kiss, my lord, the worst is past
   with them. Your grace knows now what you have to do. Sh'as 135
   somewhat a grave look with her, but—
DUKE I love that best. Conduct her.
VINDICE [*aside*]   Have at all!°
DUKE In gravest looks the greatest faults seem less;
   Give me that sin that's robed in holiness.
VINDICE [*aside to Hippolito*]
   Back with the torch, brother; raise the perfumes.   140

[*Hippolito retires with the torch and lights the incense-burner.*
Vindice advances with the skull]

DUKE How sweet can a duke breathe? Age has no fault;
   Pleasure should meet in a perfumèd mist.—
   Lady, sweetly encountered. I came from court,
   I must be bold with you.
      [*Kisses the skull*]
                          O, what's this! O!
VINDICE Royal villain! white devil!
DUKE   O!
VINDICE   Brother,°   145
   Place the torch here, that his affrighted eyeballs
   May start into those hollows. Duke, dost know
   Yon dreadful vizard? View it well; 'tis the skull
   Of Gloriana, whom thou poisonedst last.°
DUKE O, 't'as poisoned me.
VINDICE   Didst not know that till now?   150
DUKE What are you two?
VINDICE .   Villains all three.
   The very ragged bone has been sufficiently revenged.
DUKE O Hippolito, call treason!
HIPPOLITO Yes, my good lord: treason, treason, treason!
      Stamping on him
DUKE Then I'm betrayed.   155
VINDICE Alas, poor lecher, in the hands of knaves,
   A slavish duke is baser than his slaves.
DUKE My teeth are eaten out.
VINDICE   Hadst any left?
HIPPOLITO I think but few.
VINDICE   Then those that did eat are eaten.
DUKE O, my tongue!   160
VINDICE Your tongue? 'twill teach you to kiss closer,°
   Not like a slobbering Dutchman. You have eyes still:
   Look, monster, what a lady hast thou made me
   My once-betrothèd wife.
DUKE   Is it thou, villain?
   Nay, then—
VINDICE   'Tis I, 'tis Vindice, 'tis I.   165
HIPPOLITO And let this comfort thee: our lord and father
   Fell sick upon the infection of thy frowns°
   And died in sadness; be that thy hope of life.
DUKE   O!

VINDICE He had his tongue, yet grief made him die speechless.
Puh, 'tis but early yet; now I'll begin 170
To stick thy soul with ulcers. I will make°
Thy spirit grievous sore; it shall not rest,
But like some pestilent man toss in thy breast.
Mark me, duke:
Thou'rt a renownèd, high, and mighty cuckold.

DUKE   O! 175

VINDICE Thy bastard, thy bastard rides a-hunting in thy brow.

DUKE Millions of deaths!

VINDICE   Nay, to afflict thee more,
Here in this lodge they meet for damnèd clips;
Those eyes shall see the incest of their lips. 180

DUKE Is there a hell besides this, villains?

VINDICE   Villain!
Nay, heaven is just, scorns are the hires of scorns;
I ne'er knew yet adulterer without horns.

HIPPOLITO Once ere they die 'tis quitted.
        [Music within]

VINDICE   Hark, the music;
Their banquet is prepared, they're coming— 185

DUKE O, kill me not with that sight.

VINDICE Thou shalt not lose that sight for all thy dukedom.

DUKE Traitors, murderers!

VINDICE What, is not thy tongue eaten out yet?
Then we'll invent a silence. Brother, stifle the torch. 190
        [Hippolito puts out the torch]

DUKE Treason, murder!

VINDICE Nay, faith, we'll have you hushed.—Now with thy dagger
Nail down his tongue, and mine shall keep possession
About his heart; if he but gasp, he dies.
We dread not death to quittance injuries. Brother, 195
If he but wink, not brooking the foul object,°
Let our two other hands tear up his lids
And make his eyes like comets shine through blood:°
When the bad bleeds, then is the tragedy good.

HIPPOLITO Whist, brother, music's at our ear; they come.° 200
        Enter Spurio meeting the Duchess [and Attendants with
        torches. Spurio and the Duchess kiss]

SPURIO Had not that kiss a taste of sin, 'twere sweet.

DUCHESS Why, there's no pleasure sweet but it is sinful.

SPURIO True, such a bitter sweetness fate hath given,

141

Best side to us is the worst side to heaven.

DUCHESS Push, come; 'tis the old duke thy doubtful father,   205
The thought of him rubs heaven in thy way.°
But I protest, by yonder waxen fire,°
Forget him, or I'll poison him.

SPURIO Madam, you urge a thought which ne'er had life.
So deadly do I loathe him for my birth,   210
That if he took me hasped within his bed,°
I would add murder to adultery,
And with my sword give up his years to death.

DUCHESS Why, now thou'rt sociable; let's in and feast.
Loud'st music sound! Pleasure is banquet's guest.   215
    Exeunt [Spurio and Duchess, with Attendants, as offstage
    music plays]

DUKE I cannot brook—
    [Vindice stabs the Duke to death]

VINDICE   The brook is turned to blood.°

HIPPOLITO Thanks to loud music.

VINDICE   'Twas our friend indeed.
'Tis state in music for a duke to bleed.°
The dukedom wants a head, though yet unknown:°
As fast as they peep up, let's cut 'em down.°   220
    Exeunt

[3.6]

    Enter Ambitioso and Supervacuo

AMBITIOSO Was not his execution rarely plotted?
We are the duke's sons now.

SUPERVACUO Aye, you may thank my policy for that.

AMBITIOSO Your policy? For what?

SUPERVACUO Why, was 't not my invention, brother,   5
To slip the judges? And, in lesser compass,°
Did not I draw the model of his death,
Advising you to sudden officers,
And e'en extemporal execution?

AMBITIOSO Heart, 'twas a thing I thought on too.   10

SUPERVACUO You thought on 't too! 'Sfoot, slander not your thoughts
With glorious untruth; I know 'twas from you.°

AMBITIOSO Sir, I say 'twas in my head.
SUPERVACUO   Aye, like your brains then:
    Ne'er to come out as long as you lived.
AMBITIOSO You'd have the honour on't, forsooth, that your wit   15
    Led him to the scaffold.
SUPERVACUO   Since it is my due,
    I'll publish 't, but I'll ha't in spite of you.°
AMBITIOSO Methinks y'are much too bold; you should a little
    Remember us, brother, next to be honest duke.°
SUPERVACUO [aside] Aye, it shall be as easy for you to be duke   20
    As to be honest, and that's never, i'faith.
AMBITIOSO Well, cold he is by this time; and because
    We're both ambitious, be it our amity,
    And let the glory be shared equally.
SUPERVACUO I am content to that.   25
AMBITIOSO This night our younger brother shall out of prison;
    I have a trick.
SUPERVACUO   A trick, prithee, what is't?
AMBITIOSO We'll get him out by a wile.
SUPERVACUO   Prithee, what wile?
AMBITIOSO No, sir, you shall not know it till't be done;
    For then you'd swear 'twere yours.   30
        [Enter an Officer, with a head covered in a cloth]
SUPERVACUO How now! what's he?
AMBITIOSO   One of the officers.
SUPERVACUO Desired news.
AMBITIOSO   How now, my friend?
OFFICER My lords, under your pardon, I am allotted
    To that desertless office to present you°
    With the yet bleeding head.
        [Gives the covered head to Supervacuo]
SUPERVACUO [aside to Ambitioso] Ha, ha, excellent.   35
AMBITIOSO [aside to Supervacuo]
    All's sure our own. Brother, canst weep, think'st thou?
    'Twould grace our flattery much. Think of some dame;°
    'Twill teach thee to dissemble.
SUPERVACUO [aside to Ambitioso] I have thought;
    Now for yourself.
AMBITIOSO [aloud] Our sorrows are so fluent,°
    Our eyes o'erflow our tongues; words spoke in tears   40
    Are like the murmurs of the waters; the sound

143

Is loudly heard, but cannot be distinguished.
SUPERVACUO How died he, pray?
OFFICER   O, full of rage and spleen.
SUPERVACUO He died most valiantly then; we're glad
  To hear it.
OFFICER   We could not woo him once to pray.   45
AMBITIOSO He showed himself a gentleman in that,
  Give him his due.
OFFICER   But in the stead of prayer,
  He drew forth oaths.
SUPERVACUO   Then did he pray, dear heart,
  Although you understood him not.
OFFICER   My lords,
  E'en at his last, with pardon be it spoke,   50
  He cursed you both.
SUPERVACUO   He cursed us? 'las, good soul.
AMBITIOSO It was not in our powers, but the duke's pleasure.—
  [Aside] Finely dissembled o' both sides, sweet fate,
  O happy opportunity!
          Enter Lussurioso
LUSSURIOSO Now, my lords—
BOTH   O!
LUSSURIOSO   Why do you shun me, brothers?   55
  You may come nearer now;
  The savour of the prison has forsook me.
  I thank such kind lords as yourselves, I'm free.
AMBITIOSO Alive!
SUPERVACUO   In health!
AMBITIOSO   Released?
  We were both e'en amazed with joy to see it.   60
LUSSURIOSO I am much to thank you.
SUPERVACUO Faith, we spared no tongue unto my lord the duke.°
AMBITIOSO I know your delivery, brother,
  Had not been half so sudden but for us.
SUPERVACUO O how we pleaded!
LUSSURIOSO   Most deserving brothers,   65
  In my best studies I will think of it.
        Exit Lussurioso
AMBITIOSO O death and vengeance!
SUPERVACUO   Hell and torments!
AMBITIOSO Slave, cam'st thou to delude us?
OFFICER   Delude you, my lords?

SUPERVACUO Aye, villain, where's this head now?

OFFICER   Why, here, my lord.
  Just after his delivery, you both came   70
  With warrant from the duke to behead your brother.

AMBITIOSO Aye, our brother, the duke's son.

OFFICER   The duke's son,
  My lord, had his release before you came.

AMBITIOSO Whose head's that then?

OFFICER   His whom you left command for,
  Your own brother's.

AMBITIOSO   Our brother's? O furies!   75

SUPERVACUO Plagues!

AMBITIOSO   Confusions!

SUPERVACUO   Darkness!

AMBITIOSO   Devils!

SUPERVACUO Fell it out so accursèdly?

AMBITIOSO   So damnedly?

SUPERVACUO [brandishing the head]
  Villain, I'll brain thee with it.

OFFICER   O my good lord!

SUPERVACUO The devil overtake thee!
    [Exit Officer]

AMBITIOSO   O, fatal!

SUPERVACUO O prodigious to our bloods.

AMBITIOSO   Did we dissemble?   80

SUPERVACUO Did we make our tears women for thee?°

AMBITIOSO Laugh and rejoice for thee?

SUPERVACUO Bring warrant for thy death?

AMBITIOSO   Mock off thy head?

SUPERVACUO You had a trick, you had a wile, forsooth.

AMBITIOSO A murrain meet 'em! There's none of these wiles that   85
  ever come to good. I see now there is nothing sure in mortality,
  but mortality.
  Well, no more words; shalt be revenged, i' faith.
  Come, throw off clouds now, brother; think of vengeance
  And deeper-settled hate. Sirrah, sit fast,°   90
  We'll pull down all, but thou shalt down at last.
    Exeunt, [carrying the head]

[handwritten margin note: Realization from reversal + recognition of their miscalc. Leads only to more desire for revenge bk that's the only sure thing in the world of revenge plays.]

[4.1]

Enter Lussurioso with Hippolito

LUSSURIOSO Hippolito.

HIPPOLITO   My lord, has your good lordship
  Aught to command me in?

LUSSURIOSO   I prithee leave us.

HIPPOLITO [*aside*] How's this? Come and leave us?

LUSSURIOSO   Hippolito.

HIPPOLITO
  Your honour, I stand ready for any duteous employment.

LUSSURIOSO Heart, what mak'st thou here?

HIPPOLITO [*aside*]   A pretty lordly humour: 5
  He bids me to be present, to depart; something
  Has stung his honour.

LUSSURIOSO   Be nearer, draw nearer.
  Y'are not so good, methinks; I'm angry with you.

HIPPOLITO With me, my lord? I'm angry with myself for't.

LUSSURIOSO You did prefer a goodly fellow to me;   10
  'Twas wittily elected, 'twas. I thought°
  H'ad been a villain, and he proves a knave,
  To me a knave.

HIPPOLITO   I chose him for the best, my lord.
  'Tis much my sorrow, if neglect in him
  Breed discontent in you.

LUSSURIOSO   Neglect! 'Twas will.°   15
  Judge of it:
  Firmly to tell of an incredible act,
  Not to be thought, less to be spoken of,
  'Twixt my stepmother and the bastard, O,
  Incestuous sweets between 'em.

HIPPOLITO   Fie, my lord.   20

LUSSURIOSO I in kind loyalty to my father's forehead
  Made this a desperate arm, and in that fury
  Committed treason on the lawful bed,
  And with my sword e'en rased my father's bosom,
  For which I was within a stroke of death.   25

HIPPOLITO Alack, I'm sorry.

      Enter Vindice

[*Aside*]   'Sfoot, just upon the stroke
Jars in my brother: 'twill be villainous music.°
VINDICE My honoured lord.
LUSSURIOSO Away, prithee forsake us; hereafter we'll not know thee.
VINDICE Not know me, my lord? Your lordship cannot choose.   30
LUSSURIOSO Begone, I say; thou art a false knave.
VINDICE Why, the easier to be known, my lord.
LUSSURIOSO Push, I shall prove too bitter with a word,
   Make thee a perpetual prisoner,
   And lay this iron-age upon thee.
VINDICE [*aside*]   Mum!°   35
   For there's a doom would make a woman dumb.°
   Missing the bastard, next him, the wind's come about;°
   Now 'tis my brother's turn to stay, mine to go out.
        Exit Vindice
LUSSURIOSO H'as greatly moved me.
HIPPOLITO   Much to blame, i' faith.
LUSSURIOSO But I'll recover, to his ruin. 'Twas told me lately,   40
   I know not whether falsely, that you'd a brother.
HIPPOLITO Who, I? Yes, my good lord, I have a brother.
LUSSURIOSO How chance the court ne'er saw him? Of what nature?
   How does he apply his hours?
HIPPOLITO   Faith, to curse fates°
   Who, as he thinks, ordained him to be poor;   45
   Keeps at home, full of want and discontent.
LUSSURIOSO There's hope in him, for discontent and want
   Is the best clay to mould a villain of.
   Hippolito, wish him repair to us.
   If there be aught in him to please our blood,°   50
   For thy sake we'll advance him, and build fair
   His meanest fortunes; for it is in us°
   To rear up towers from cottages.
HIPPOLITO It is so, my lord. He will attend your honour;
   But he's a man in whom much melancholy dwells.   55
LUSSURIOSO Why, the better; bring him to court.
HIPPOLITO With willingness and speed.
   [*Aside*] Whom he cast off e'en now, must now succeed.°
   Brother, disguise must off;
   In thine own shape now I'll prefer thee to him: 60
   How strangely does himself work to undo him.°
        Exit [Hippolito]

LUSSURIOSO This fellow will come fitly; he shall kill
That other slave, that did abuse my spleen°
And made it swell to treason. I have put
Much of my heart into him; he must die.°   65
He that knows great men's secrets and proves slight,°
That man ne'er lives to see his beard turn white.
Aye, he shall speed him. I'll employ thee, brother:°
Slaves are but nails to drive out one another.
He being of black condition, suitable°   70
To want and ill content, hope of preferment
Will grind him to an edge.°
    The Nobles enter
FIRST NOBLE Good days unto your honour.
LUSSURIOSO My kind lords, I do return the like.
SECOND NOBLE Saw you my lord the duke?
LUSSURIOSO   My lord and father,   75
Is he from court?
FIRST NOBLE   He's sure from court,
But where, which way, his pleasure took we know not,
Nor can we hear on 't.
    [*Enter the Duke's Gentlemen*]
LUSSURIOSO   Here come those should tell.
Saw you my lord and father?
[FIRST] GENTLEMAN Not since two hours before noon, my lord.   80
And then he privately rid forth.
LUSSURIOSO O, he's rode forth.
FIRST NOBLE   'Twas wondrous privately.
SECOND NOBLE There's none i' th' court had any knowledge on 't.
LUSSURIOSO His grace is old and sudden; 'tis no treason°
To say, the duke my father has a humour,   85
Or such a toy about him; what in us
Would appear light, in him seems virtuous.°
[FIRST] GENTLEMAN 'Tis oracle, my lord.
    Exeunt

148

[4.2]

Enter Vindice and Hippolito, Vindice out of his disguise

HIPPOLITO So, so, all's as it should be; y'are yourself.

VINDICE How that great villain puts me to my shifts.°

HIPPOLITO He that did lately in disguise reject thee
Shall, now thou art thyself, as much respect thee.

VINDICE 'Twill be the quainter fallacy. But brother,°   5
'Sfoot, what use will he put me to now, think'st thou?

HIPPOLITO Nay, you must pardon me in that, I know not.
H'as some employment for you, but what 'tis
He and his secretary the devil knows best.

VINDICE Well, I must suit my tongue to his desires,   10
What colour soe'er they be, hoping at last
To pile up all my wishes on his breast.°

HIPPOLITO Faith, brother, he himself shows the way.

VINDICE Now the duke is dead, the realm is clad in clay.°
His death being not yet known, under his name   15
The people still are governed. Well, thou his son
Art not long-lived; thou shalt not joy his death.°
To kill thee, then, I should most honour thee:
For 'twould stand firm in every man's belief,
Thou'st a kind child, and only died'st with grief.   20

HIPPOLITO You fetch about well, but let's talk in present.°
How will you appear in fashion different,
As well as in apparel, to make all things possible?
If you be but once tripped, we fall forever.
It is not the least policy to be doubtful;°   25
You must change tongue—familiar was your first.°

VINDICE Why, I'll bear me in some strain of melancholy,
And string myself with heavy-sounding wire,°
Like such an instrument that speaks merry things sadly.

HIPPOLITO Then 'tis as I meant;   30
I gave you out at first in discontent.°

VINDICE I'll turn myself, and then—
          [*Enter Lussurioso*]

HIPPOLITO   'Sfoot, here he comes;
Hast thought upon't?

VINDICE   Salute him, fear not me.

LUSSURIOSO Hippolito.

HIPPOLITO   Your lordship.

LUSSURIOSO   What's he yonder?

HIPPOLITO 'Tis Vindice, my discontented brother,   35
  Whom, 'cording to your will, I've brought to court.

LUSSURIOSO Is that thy brother? Beshrew me, a good presence.°
  I wonder h'as been from the court so long!
  Come nearer.

HIPPOLITO Brother, Lord Lussurioso, the duke's son.   40

LUSSURIOSO Be more near to us. Welcome; nearer yet.
      [*Vindice*] *snatches off his hat and makes legs to him.*
      [*Hippolito stands apart*]

VINDICE How don you? God you god den.

LUSSURIOSO   We thank thee.°
  How strangely such a coarse, homely salute
  Shows in the palace, where we greet in fire:°
  Nimble and desperate tongues, should we name   45
  God in a salutation, 'twould ne'er be stood on't—heaven!°
  Tell me, what has made thee so melancholy?

VINDICE Why, going to law.

LUSSURIOSO Why, will that make a man melancholy?

VINDICE Yes, to look long upon ink and black buckram.° I went me   50
  to law in *anno quadragesimo secundo*, and I waded out of it in *anno*
  sextagesimo tertio.°

LUSSURIOSO What, three and twenty° years in law?

VINDICE I have known those that have been five and fifty, and all
  about pullen and pigs.   55

LUSSURIOSO May it be possible such men should breathe,
  To vex the terms so much?

VINDICE   'Tis food to some, my lord.°
  There are old men at the present, that are so poisoned with the
  affectation of law words (having had many suits canvassed),° that
  their common talk is nothing but Barbary° Latin. They cannot so   60
  much as pray but in law,° that their sins may be removed with a
  writ of error,° and their souls fetched up to heaven with a
  sasarara.°

[LUSSURIOSO] It seems most strange to me;
  Yet all the world meets round in the same bent:°   65
  Where the heart's set, there goes the tongue's consent.
  How dost apply thy studies, fellow?

VINDICE Study? Why, to think how a great rich man lies a-dying,
  and a poor cobbler tolls the bell° for him; how he cannot depart

the world and see the great chest stand before him; when he lies ⁣70
speechless, how he will point you readily to all the boxes; and when
he is past all memory, as the gossips guess, then thinks he of
forfeitures and obligations.° Nay, when to all men's hearings he
whurls and rattles in the throat, he's busy threatening his poor
tenants. And this would last me now some seven years' thinking ⁣75
or thereabouts. But I have a conceit a–coming in picture° upon
this: I draw it myself, which, i' faith la,° I'll present to your
honour. You shall not choose but like it, for your lordship shall
give me nothing for it.

LUSSURIOSO Nay, you mistake me then, ⁣80
For I am published bountiful enough.°
Let's taste of your conceit.

VINDICE In picture, my lord?

LUSSURIOSO   Aye, in picture.

VINDICE Marry, this it is—*A usuring father, to be boiling in hell, and*
his son and heir with a whore dancing over him. ⁣85

HIPPOLITO [*aside*] H'as pared° him to the quick.

LUSSURIOSO The conceit's pretty, i' faith. But take't upon my life,
'twill ne'er be liked.

VINDICE No? Why, I'm sure the whore will be liked well enough.

HIPPOLITO [*aside*] Aye, if she were out o' th' picture, he'd like her ⁣90
then himself.

VINDICE And as for the son and heir, he shall be an eyesore to no
young revellers, for he shall be drawn in cloth-of-gold°
breeches.

LUSSURIOSO And thou hast put my meaning in the pockets,° ⁣95
And canst not draw that out. My thought was this:°
To see the picture of a usuring father
Boiling in hell, our rich men would ne'er like it.

VINDICE O true, I cry you heartily mercy.° I know the reason, for
some of 'em had rather be damned indeed than damned in ⁣100
colours.°

LUSSURIOSO [*aside*] A parlous melancholy! H'as wit enough
To murder any man, and I'll give him means.
[*To Vindice*] I think thou art ill-monied?

VINDICE   Money! ho, ho,
'T'as been my want so long, 'tis now my scoff; ⁣105
I've e'en forgot what colour silver's of.

LUSSURIOSO [*aside*] It hits as I could wish.

VINDICE   I get good clothes°

Of those that dread my humour, and for table-room
I feed on those that cannot be rid of me.°

LUSSURIOSO Somewhat to set thee up withal.   110
    [*He gives him gold*]

VINDICE O, mine eyes!

LUSSURIOSO   How now, man?

VINDICE   Almost struck blind:
This bright unusual shine to me seems proud;
I dare not look till the sun be in a cloud.

LUSSURIOSO [*aside*] I think I shall affect his melancholy.—°
How are they now?

VINDICE   The better for your asking.   115

LUSSURIOSO You shall be better yet if you but fasten
Truly on my intent. Now y'are both present,
I will unbrace such a close, private villain
Unto your vengeful swords, the like ne'er heard of,
Who hath disgraced you much and injured us.   120

HIPPOLITO Disgraced us, my lord?

LUSSURIOSO   Aye, Hippolito.
I kept it here till now, that both your angers°
Might meet him at once.

VINDICE   I'm covetous
To know the villain.

LUSSURIOSO [*to Hippolito*] You know him—that slave pander
Piato, whom we threatened last   125
With irons in perpetual prisonment.

VINDICE [*aside*] All this is I.

HIPPOLITO   Is 't he, my lord?

LUSSURIOSO   I'll tell you;
You first preferred him to me.

VINDICE   Did you, brother?

HIPPOLITO I did indeed.

LUSSURIOSO   And the ingrateful villain,
To quit that kindness, strongly wrought with me,°   130
Being, as you see, a likely man for pleasure,
With jewels to corrupt your virgin sister.

HIPPOLITO O villain!

VINDICE   He shall surely die that did it.°

LUSSURIOSO I, far from thinking any virgin harm,
Especially knowing her to be as chaste   135
As that part which scarce suffers to be touched,

The eye, would not endure him.

VINDICE   Would you not, my lord?°
'Twas wondrous honourably done.

LUSSURIOSO But with some fine frowns kept him out.

VINDICE   Out, slave!°

LUSSURIOSO What did me he but, in revenge of that,   140
Went of his own free will to make infirm
Your sister's honour, whom I honour with my soul
For chaste respect; and not prevailing there
(As 'twas but desperate folly to attempt it),
In mere spleen, by the way, waylays your mother,   145
Whose honour being a coward, as it seems,
Yielded by little force.

VINDICE   Coward indeed.

LUSSURIOSO He, proud of their advantage (as he thought),
Brought me these news for happy; but I, heaven°
Forgive me for't—

VINDICE   What did your honour?   150

LUSSURIOSO In rage pushed him from me,
Trampled beneath his throat, spurned him, and bruised.
Indeed, I was too cruel, to say troth.

HIPPOLITO Most nobly managed!

VINDICE [aside] Has not heaven an ear? Is all the lightning wasted?   155

LUSSURIOSO If I now were so impatient in a modest cause,
What should you be?

VINDICE Full mad; he shall not live to see the moon change.

LUSSURIOSO He's about the palace. Hippolito, entice him this way,
that thy brother may take full mark of° him.   160

HIPPOLITO Heart! that shall not need, my lord; I can direct him so
far.

LUSSURIOSO Yet for my hate's sake, go, wind° him this way; I'll see
him bleed myself.

HIPPOLITO [aside to Vindice] What now, brother?   165

VINDICE [aside to Hippolito] Nay, e'en what you will; y'are put to 't,
brother!

HIPPOLITO [aside] An impossible task, I'll swear,
To bring him hither that's already here.
        Exit Hippolito

LUSSURIOSO Thy name? I have forgot it.

VINDICE   Vindice, my lord.   170

LUSSURIOSO 'Tis a good name that.

> Speaking
> of generic
> char.
> imperatives

VINDICE   Aye, a revenger.

LUSSURIOSO It does betoken courage; thou shouldst be valiant
  And kill thine enemies.

VINDICE   That's my hope, my lord.

LUSSURIOSO This slave is one.

VINDICE   I'll doom him.

LUSSURIOSO   Then I'll praise thee.
  Do thou observe me best, and I'll best raise thee.°   175
      Enter Hippolito

VINDICE Indeed, I thank you.

LUSSURIOSO Now, Hippolito, where's the slave pander?

HIPPOLITO Your good lordship
  Would have a loathsome sight of him, much offensive.
  He's not in case now to be seen, my lord;°   180
  The worst of all the deadly sins is in him—
  That beggarly damnation, drunkenness.

LUSSURIOSO Then he's a double slave.

VINDICE [*aside*]   'Twas well conveyed,°
  Upon a sudden wit.

LUSSURIOSO   What, are you both
  Firmly resolved? I'll see him dead myself.   185

> By
> definition
> in vis case.

VINDICE Or else let not us live.

LUSSURIOSO   You may direct
  Your brother to take note of him.

HIPPOLITO   I shall.

LUSSURIOSO Rise but in this, and you shall never fall.

VINDICE Your honour's vassals.

> Many
> examples
> of one

LUSSURIOSO [*aside*]   This was wisely carried.°
  Deep policy in us makes fools of such: 190
  Then must a slave die when he knows too much.

> bead
> falling raise up
> another:
> Gratiana
> Castiza, etc.

      Exit Lussurioso

VINDICE O, thou almighty patience! 'Tis my wonder
  That such a fellow, impudent and wicked,
  Should not be cloven as he stood,
  Or with a secret wind burst open!   195
  Is there no thunder left, or is't kept up
  In stock for heavier vengeance?
      [*Thunder*]
                              There it goes!°

HIPPOLITO Brother, we lose ourselves.

VINDICE   But I have found it.°
  'Twill hold, 'tis sure; thanks, thanks to any spirit

That mingled it 'mongst my inventions.   200
HIPPOLITO What is 't?
VINDICE   'Tis sound, and good; thou shalt partake it.
  I'm hired to kill myself.
HIPPOLITO   True.
VINDICE   Prithee mark it.
  And the old duke being dead, but not conveyed;°
  For he's already missed too, and you know
  Murder will peep out of the closest husk—°   205
HIPPOLITO Most true.
VINDICE   What say you then to this device?
  If we dressed up the body of the duke—
HIPPOLITO In that disguise of yours.
VINDICE   Y'are quick, y'ave reached it.
HIPPOLITO I like it wondrously.
VINDICE And being in drink, as you have published him,°   210
  To lean him on his elbow, as if sleep had caught him,
  Which claims most interest in such sluggy men.
HIPPOLITO Good yet, but here's a doubt:
  We—thought by th'duke's son to kill that pander—
  Shall, when he is known, be thought to kill the duke.   215
VINDICE Neither—O thanks—it is substantial:°
  For that disguise being on him which I wore, it will be thought I,
  which he calls the pander, did kill the duke and fled away in his
  apparel, leaving him so disguised to avoid swift pursuit.
HIPPOLITO Firmer and firmer.
VINDICE   Nay, doubt not 'tis in grain;°   220
  I warrant it hold colour.
HIPPOLITO   Let's about it.°
VINDICE But by the way too, now I think on 't, brother,
  Let's conjure that base devil out of our mother.
     Exeunt

[4.3]

Enter the Duchess arm in arm with Spurio; he seemeth°
lasciviously to her. After them, enter Supervacuo, running
with a rapier; Ambitioso stops him
SPURIO Madam, unlock yourself; should it be seen,°
  Your arm would be suspected.

DUCHESS Who is't that dares suspect or this or these?°
  May not we deal our favours where we please?°
SPURIO I'm confident you may.
      Exeunt [Spurio and Duchess]
AMBITIOSO   'Sfoot, brother, hold.   5
SUPERVACUO Wouldst let the bastard shame us?
AMBITIOSO   Hold, hold, brother!
  There's fitter time than now.
SUPERVACUO   Now, when I see it.
AMBITIOSO 'Tis too much seen already.
SUPERVACUO   Seen and known.
  The nobler she's, the baser is she grown.
AMBITIOSO If she were bent lasciviously, the fault°   10
  Of mighty women that sleep soft—O death!°
  Must she needs choose such an unequal sinner,°
  To make all worse?
SUPERVACUO   A bastard, the duke's bastard!
  Shame heaped on shame!
AMBITIOSO   O our disgrace!
  Most women have small waist the world throughout;°   15
  But their desires are thousand miles about.°
SUPERVACUO Come, stay not here; let's after and prevent;
  Or else they'll sin faster than we'll repent.
      Exeunt

[4.4]

*Enter Vindice and Hippolito bringing out Gratiana, one by
one shoulder, and the other by the other, with daggers in their
hands*

VINDICE O thou, for whom no name is bad enough!
GRATIANA What means my sons? What, will you murder me?
VINDICE Wicked, unnatural parent!
HIPPOLITO   Fiend of women!
GRATIANA O, are sons turned monsters? Help!
VINDICE   In vain.
GRATIANA Are you so barbarous to set iron nipples°   5
  Upon the breast that gave you suck?
VINDICE   That breast

Is turned to quarled poison.

GRATIANA Cut not your days for 't; am not I your mother?°

VINDICE Thou dost usurp that title now by fraud,
For in that shell of mother breeds a bawd.   10

GRATIANA A bawd! O name far loathsomer than hell!

HIPPOLITO It should be so, knew'st thou thy office well.

GRATIANA I hate it.

VINDICE Ah, is 't possible, you powers on high,°
That women should dissemble when they die?   15

GRATIANA Dissemble?

VINDICE   Did not the duke's son direct
A fellow of the world's condition hither°
That did corrupt all that was good in thee?
Made thee uncivilly forget thyself,°
And work our sister to his lust?

GRATIANA   Who, I?   20
That had been monstrous! I defy that man
For any such intent. None lives so pure,
But shall be soiled with slander.
Good son, believe it not.

VINDICE   O I'm in doubt
Whether I'm myself or no.   25
Stay, let me look again upon this face.
Who shall be saved when mothers have no grace?

HIPPOLITO 'Twould make one half despair.

VINDICE   I was the man.
Defy me now! Let's see; do 't modestly.

GRATIANA O hell unto my soul!   30

VINDICE In that disguise, I, sent from the duke's son,
Tried you, and found you base metal,°
As any villain might have done.

GRATIANA   O no,
No tongue but yours could have bewitched me so.

VINDICE O nimble in damnation, quick in tune,°   35
There is no devil could strike fire so soon.
I am confuted in a word.

GRATIANA O sons, forgive me! To myself I'll prove more true;
You that should honour me, I kneel to you.
    [*Gratiana kneels, weeping*]

VINDICE A mother to give aim to her own daughter!°   40

HIPPOLITO True, brother; how far beyond nature 'tis,

*can't be so far, if
it's not so unusual.*

Though many mothers do't.

VINDICE Nay, an you draw tears once, go you to bed.°
   [*Sheaths his dagger*]
   Wet will make iron blush and change to red.°
   Brother, it rains; 'twill spoil your dagger; house it.   45

HIPPOLITO [*puts away his dagger*] 'Tis done.

VINDICE I'faith, 'tis a sweet shower; it does much good:
   The fruitful grounds and meadows of her soul
   Has been long dry. Pour down, thou blessèd dew.
   Rise, mother. Troth, this shower has made you higher.   50

GRATIANA O you heavens,
   Take this infectious spot out of my soul;
   I'll rinse it in seven waters of mine eyes.°
   Make my tears salt enough to taste of grace!°
   To weep is to our sex naturally given;   55
   But to weep truly, that's a gift from heaven.

VINDICE Nay, I'll kiss you now. Kiss her, brother!
   Let's marry her to our souls, wherein's no lust,
   And honourably love her.

HIPPOLITO   Let it be.

VINDICE For honest women are so seld and rare,   60
   'Tis good to cherish those poor few that are.
   O you of easy wax, do but imagine,°
   Now the disease has left you, how leprously
   That office would have clinged unto your forehead.°
   All mothers that had any graceful hue   65
   Would have worn masks to hide their face at you.
   It would have grown to this: at your foul name
   Green-coloured maids would have turned red with shame.°

HIPPOLITO And then our sister, full of hire and baseness.°

VINDICE There had been boiling lead again.°   70
   The duke's son's great concubine!
   A drab of state, a cloth-o'-silver slut,°
   To have her train borne up, and her soul trail i' th' dirt.
   Great—

HIPPOLITO To be miserably great; rich, to be
   Eternally wretched.

VINDICE   O common madness!   75
   Ask but the thriving'st harlot in cold blood:
   She'd give the world to make her honour good.
   Perhaps you'll say, 'But only to th' duke's son,

In private'. Why, she first begins with one,
Who afterward to thousand proves a whore: 80
'Break ice in one place, it will crack in more.'°
GRATIANA Most certainly applied!°
HIPPOLITO O brother, you forget our business.
VINDICE And well remembered. Joy's a subtle elf;
   I think man's happiest when he forgets himself.   85
   Farewell, once dried, now holy-watered mead;°
   Our hearts wear feathers that before wore lead.°
GRATIANA I'll give you this: that one I never knew
   Plead better for, and 'gainst, the devil than you.
VINDICE You make me proud on 't.   90
HIPPOLITO Commend us in all virtue to our sister.
VINDICE Aye, for the love of heaven, to that true maid.
GRATIANA With my best words.
VINDICE   Why, that was motherly said.
     Exeunt [Vindice and Hippolito]
GRATIANA I wonder now what fury did transport me!
   I feel good thoughts begin to settle in me.   95
   O, with what forehead can I look on her,°
   Whose honour I've so impiously beset!
    [Enter Castiza]
   And here she comes.
CASTIZA Now, mother, you have wrought with me so strongly,
   That what for my advancement, as to calm°   100
   The trouble of your tongue, I am content.
GRATIANA Content, to what?
CASTIZA   To do as you have wished me:
   To prostitute my breast to the duke's son,
   And put myself to common usury.°
GRATIANA I hope you will not so.
CASTIZA   Hope you I will not?   105
   That's not the hope you look to be saved in.°
GRATIANA Truth, but it is.
CASTIZA   Do not deceive yourself;
   I am as you e'en out of marble wrought.°
   What would you now? Are ye not pleased yet with me?
   You shall not wish me to be more lascivious   110
   Than I intend to be.
GRATIANA   Strike not me cold.
CASTIZA How often have you charged me on your blessing

(marginal note: As actor or spectator in the theatre.)

To be a cursèd woman? When you knew
Your blessing had no force to make me lewd,
You laid your curse upon me; that did more.°   115
The mother's curse is heavy: where that fights,
Sons set in storm, and daughters lose their lights.°
GRATIANA Good child, dear maid, if there be any spark
Of heavenly intellectual fire within thee,
O, let my breath revive it to a flame.   120
Put not all out with woman's wilful follies.
I am recovered of that foul disease
That haunts too many mothers; kind, forgive me,°
Make me not sick in health. If then°
My words prevailed when they were wickedness,   125
How much more now when they are just and good!
CASTIZA I wonder what you mean. Are not you she
For whose infect persuasions I could scarce
Kneel out my prayers, and had much ado,
In three hours' reading, to untwist so much°   130
Of the black serpent as you wound about me?
GRATIANA 'Tis unfruitful, held tedious, to repeat what's past.
I'm now your present mother.
CASTIZA   Push, now 'tis too late.
GRATIANA Bethink again, thou know'st not what thou say'st.
CASTIZA No? 'Deny advancement, treasure, the duke's son?'   135
GRATIANA O see, I spoke those words, and now they poison me.
What will the deed do then?
Advancement? True, as high as shame can pitch.°
For treasure—who e'er knew a harlot rich,
Or could build by the purchase of her sin°   140
An hospital to keep their bastards in?
The duke's son? O, when women are young courtiers,
They are sure to be old beggars.
To know the miseries most harlots taste,
Thou'dst wish thyself unborn, when thou'rt unchaste.   145
CASTIZA O mother, let me twine about your neck,
And kiss you till my soul melt on your lips.
I did but this to try you.
GRATIANA   O speak truth!
CASTIZA Indeed, I did not;
For no tongue has force to alter me from honest.   150
If maidens would, men's words could have no power;

A virgin honour is a crystal tower,
Which, being weak, is guarded with good spirits;
Until she basely yields, no ill inherits.°
GRATIANA O happy child! Faith and thy birth hath saved me.   155
'Mongst thousand daughters, happiest of all others,
Be thou a glass for maids, and I for mothers.°
    Exeunt

> They are their ideal types after all, despite the paces the play puts them through.

[5.1]

Enter Vindice and Hippolito [with the Duke's body dressed in Vindice's disguise. They arrange the body to look like a sleeping man]

VINDICE So, so, he leans well; take heed you wake him not, brother.

HIPPOLITO I warrant you, my life for yours.

VINDICE That's a good lay,° for I must kill myself. Brother, that's I; that sits for me; do you mark it? And I must stand ready here to make away myself yonder. I must sit to be killed, and stand to kill myself. I could vary it not so little as thrice over again; 't'as some eight returns,° like Michaelmas term.

HIPPOLITO That's enow, o' conscience.

VINDICE But, sirrah, does the duke's son come single?

HIPPOLITO No, there's the hell on 't. His faith's too feeble to go alone. He brings flesh-flies° after him that will buzz against° supper-time, and hum for his coming out.

VINDICE Ah, the fly-flop of vengeance beat 'em to pieces! Here was the sweetest occasion, the fittest hour, to have made my revenge familiar° with him, show him the body of the duke his father, and how quaintly he died, like a politician,° in hugger-mugger, made no man acquainted with it, and in catastrophe,° slain him over his father's breast, and—O I'm mad to lose such a sweet opportunity.

HIPPOLITO Nay, push, prithee be content; there's no remedy present. May not hereafter times open in as fair faces° as this?

VINDICE They may, if they can paint° so well.

HIPPOLITO Come, now to avoid all suspicion, let's forsake this room, and be going to meet the duke's son.

VINDICE Content, I'm for any weather.° Heart, step close; here he comes.

Enter Lussurioso

HIPPOLITO My honoured lord!

LUSSURIOSO O me! you both present!

VINDICE E'en newly, my lord, just as your lordship entered now. About this place we had notice given he should be, but in some loathsome plight or other.

HIPPOLITO Came your honour private?

162

LUSSURIOSO Private enough for this; only a few attend my coming out.

HIPPOLITO [*aside*] Death rot those few. 35

LUSSURIOSO Stay, yonder's the slave.

VINDICE Mass, there's the slave indeed, my lord. [*Aside*] 'Tis a good child; he calls his father slave.

LUSSURIOSO Aye, that's the villain, the damned villain. Softly, tread easy. 40

VINDICE Puh, I warrant you, my lord, we'll stifle in° our breaths.

LUSSURIOSO That will do well.—Base rogue, thou sleepest thy last.—[*Aside*] 'Tis policy to have him killed in's sleep, for if he waked, he would betray all to them.

VINDICE But, my lord— 45

LUSSURIOSO Ha, what say'st?

VINDICE Shall we kill him now he's drunk?

LUSSURIOSO Aye, best of all.

VINDICE Why, then he will ne'er live to be sober.

LUSSURIOSO No matter, let him reel to hell. 50

VINDICE But being so full of liquor, I fear he will put out all the fire.

LUSSURIOSO Thou art a mad beast.

VINDICE [*aside*] And leave none to warm your lordship's golls withal, for he that dies drunk falls into hellfire like a bucket o' water, qush, qush.° 55

LUSSURIOSO Come, be ready! Nake your swords, think of your wrongs. This slave has injured you.

VINDICE Troth, so he has!—[*aside*] and he has paid well for 't.

LUSSURIOSO Meet with him now.

VINDICE You'll bear us out,° my lord? 60

LUSSURIOSO Puh, am I a lord for nothing, think you? Quickly now.

VINDICE Sa, sa, sa!
  [*Vindice and Hippolito stab the corpse, which falls forward*]
     Thump, there he lies.°

LUSSURIOSO Nimbly done.
  [*Approaches the corpse*]
      Ha! O, villains, murderers,
'Tis the old duke my father!

VINDICE   That's a jest. 65

LUSSURIOSO What, stiff and cold already?
O pardon me to call you from your names;°

'Tis none of your deed. That villain Piato,
Whom you thought now to kill, has murdered him
And left him thus disguised.

HIPPOLITO   And not unlikely.   70

VINDICE O rascal! Was he not ashamed
To put the duke into a greasy doublet?

LUSSURIOSO He has been cold and stiff, who knows how long?

VINDICE [aside] Marry, that do I.

LUSSURIOSO No words, I pray, of anything intended.°   75

VINDICE O, my lord.

HIPPOLITO I would fain have your lordship think that we have small
reason to prate.

LUSSURIOSO Faith, thou say'st true. I'll forthwith send to court
For all the nobles, bastard, duchess, all,   80
How here by miracle we found him dead,
And in his raiment that foul villain fled.

VINDICE That will be the best way, my lord, to clear us all; let's cast
about to be clear.°

LUSSURIOSO Ho, Nencio, Sordido, and the rest!   85

        Enter [Nencio, Sordido, and] all [his servants]

FIRST SERVANT My lord.

SECOND SERVANT My lord.

LUSSURIOSO Be witnesses of a strange spectacle.
Choosing for private conference that sad room,
We found the duke my father gealed in blood.   90

FIRST SERVANT My lord the duke!—Run, hie thee, Nencio,
Startle the court by signifying so much.

        [Exit Nencio]

VINDICE [aside] Thus much by wit a deep revenger can:°
When murder's known, to be the clearest man.
We're furthest off, and with as bold an eye   95
Survey his body as the standers-by.

LUSSURIOSO My royal father, too basely let blood°
By a malevolent slave.

HIPPOLITO [aside to Vindice] Hark,
He calls thee slave again.

VINDICE [aside to Hippolito] H'as lost; he may.°

LUSSURIOSO O sight!   100
Look hither, see, his lips are gnawn with poison.

VINDICE How, his lips? By th' mass, they be.

LUSSURIOSO O villain! O rogue! O slave! O rascal!

HIPPOLITO [*aside*] O good deceit; he quits him with like terms.
    [*Enter two Nobles, Guards, Gentlemen, Ambitioso and*
      Supervacuo]
FIRST NOBLE Where? 105
SECOND NOBLE Which way?
AMBITIOSO Over what roof hangs this prodigious comet
    In deadly fire?
LUSSURIOSO   Behold, behold, my lords:
    The duke my father's murdered by a vassal
    That owes this habit, and here left disguised.° 110
    [*Enter Duchess and Spurio*]
DUCHESS My lord and husband!
SECOND NOBLE   Reverend majesty!
FIRST NOBLE I have seen these clothes° often attending on him.
VINDICE [*aside*] That nobleman has been i' th' country,° for he does
    not lie!
SUPERVACUO [*aside to Ambitioso*]
    Learn of our mother; let's dissemble too. 115
    I'm glad he's vanished; so, I hope, are you?
AMBITIOSO [*aside to Supervacuo*] Aye, you may take my word for 't.
SPURIO [*aside*]   Old dad, dead?
    I, one of his cast sins, will send the fates°
    Most hearty commendations by his own son.
    I'll tug in the new stream till strength be done.° 120
LUSSURIOSO Where be those two that did affirm to us
    My lord the duke was privately rid forth?
FIRST GENTLEMAN O, pardon us, my lords; he gave that charge
    Upon our lives, if he were missed at court,°
    To answer so. He rode not anywhere; 125
    We left him private with that fellow here.°
VINDICE [*aside*] Confirmed.
LUSSURIOSO   O heavens, that false charge was his death.
    Impudent beggars! durst you to our face
    Maintain such a false answer? Bear him straight
    To execution.
FIRST GENTLEMAN My lord!
LUSSURIOSO   Urge me no more. 130
    In this, the excuse may be called half the murder!
VINDICE [*aside*] You've sentenced well.
LUSSURIOSO   Away, see it be done.
    [*Exit First Gentleman, guarded*]

VINDICE [*aside*] Could you not stick? See what confession doth!°
  Who would not lie when men are hanged for truth?
HIPPOLITO [*aside to Vindice*] Brother, how happy is our vengeance.
VINDICE [*aside to Hippolito*]   Why, it hits 135
  Past the apprehension of indifferent wits.°
LUSSURIOSO My lord, let post-horse be sent
  Into all places to entrap the villain.
VINDICE [*aside*] Post-horse! ha, ha.
[FIRST] NOBLE My lord, we're something bold to know our duty.° 140
  Your father's accidentally departed;
  The titles that were due to him meet you.
LUSSURIOSO Meet me? I'm not at leisure, my good lord;
  I've many griefs to dispatch out o' th' way.—
  [*Aside*] Welcome, sweet titles!—Talk to me, my lords, 145
  Of sepulchres and mighty emperors' bones;
  That's thought for me.
VINDICE [*aside*]   So one may see by this
  How foreign markets go:°
  Courtiers have feet o' th' nines, and tongues o' th' twelves;°
  They flatter dukes, and dukes flatter themselves. 150
[SECOND] NOBLE My lord, it is your shine must comfort us.
LUSSURIOSO Alas, I shine in tears, like the sun in April.
[FIRST] NOBLE Y'are now my lord's grace.
LUSSURIOSO   My lord's grace!
  I perceive you'll have it so.
[FIRST] NOBLE   'Tis but your own.°
LUSSURIOSO Then heavens give me grace to be so. 155
VINDICE [*aside*] He prays well for himself.
[SECOND] NOBLE [*to the Duchess*]   Madam,
  All sorrows must run their circles into joys.
  No doubt but time will make the murderer
  Bring forth himself.
VINDICE [*aside*]   He were an ass then, i' faith.
[FIRST] NOBLE In the mean season, 160
  Let us bethink the latest funeral honours
  Due to the duke's cold body—and, withal,
  Calling to memory our new happiness,
  Spread in his royal son. Lords, gentlemen,°
  Prepare for revels.
VINDICE [*aside*]   Revels!
[SECOND] NOBLE   Time hath several falls;° 165

Griefs lift up joys, feasts put down funerals.°
LUSSURIOSO Come then, my lords, my favours to you all.
[*Aside*] The duchess is suspected foully bent;°
I'll begin dukedom with her banishment.
        Exeunt Lussurioso, Nobles, Duchess, [Sordido, and Servants]
HIPPOLITO [*aside to Vindice*] Revels!   170
VINDICE [*aside to Hippolito*] Aye, that's the word; we are firm yet;°
Strike one strain more, and then we crown our wit.
        Exeunt [Vindice and Hippolito]
SPURIO [*aside*] Well, have [at] the fairest mark!°
So said the duke when he begot me;
And if I miss his heart or near about,   175
Then have at any; a bastard scorns to be out.°
        [Exit Spurio]
SUPERVACUO Note'st thou that Spurio, brother?
AMBITIOSO Yes, I note him to our shame.
SUPERVACUO He shall not live, his hair shall not grow much longer.
In this time of revels, tricks may be set afoot. Seest thou yon new   180
moon? It shall outlive the new duke by much; this hand shall
dispossess him, then we're mighty.
A mask is treason's license—that build upon;
'Tis murder's best face when a vizard's on.
        Exit Supervacuo
AMBITIOSO Is't so? 'tis very good;   185
And do you think to be duke then, kind brother?
I'll see fair play: drop one, and there lies t'other.°
        Exit

[5.2]

        Enter Vindice and Hippolito, with Piero and other Lords
VINDICE My lords, be all of music;°
Strike old griefs into other countries
That flow in too much milk and have faint livers,°
Not daring to stab home their discontents.°
Let our hid flames break out, as fire, as lightning,   5
To blast this villainous dukedom vexed with sin;
Wind up your souls to their full height again.°
PIERO How?

FIRST LORD   Which way?

THIRD LORD   Any way; our wrongs are such,
We cannot justly be revenged too much.

VINDICE You shall have all enough. Revels are toward,°   10
And those few nobles that have long suppressed you
Are busied to the furnishing of a masque,
And do affect to make a pleasant tale on't;°   *acting apparel*
The masquing suits are fashioning—now comes in
That which must glad us all: we to take pattern°   15
Of all those suits, the colour, trimming, fashion,
E'en to an undistinguished hair almost.
Then, ent'ring first, observing the true form,
Within a strain or two we shall find leisure°
To steal our swords out handsomely,   20
And when they think their pleasure sweet and good,
In midst of all their joys, they shall sigh blood.

PIERO Weightily, effectually!

THIRD LORD Before the t'other masquers come—

VINDICE We're gone, all done and past.   25

PIERO But how for the duke's guard?

VINDICE   Let that alone;°
By one and one their strengths shall be drunk down.°

HIPPOLITO There are five hundred gentlemen in the action,°
That will apply themselves, and not stand idle.

PIERO O, let us hug your bosoms!

VINDICE   Come, my lords,   30
Prepare for deeds; let other times have words.
          Exeunt

[5.3]

In a dumb show, the possessing° of Lussurioso, with [three]
Nobles; then sounding music. A furnished table is brought
forth; then enters [again] Lussurioso and his Nobles to the
banquet. A blazing star° appeareth   *comet of bad omen*

[FIRST] NOBLE Many harmonious hours and choicest pleasures
Fill up the royal numbers of your years.

LUSSURIOSO
My lords, we're pleased to thank you—though we know

'Tis but your duty now to wish it so.

[SECOND] NOBLE That shine makes us all happy.

THIRD NOBLE [*aside*]   His grace frowns.   5

SECOND NOBLE [*aside*] Yet we must say he smiles.

FIRST NOBLE [*aside*]   I think we must.

LUSSURIOSO [*aside*]
    That foul, incontinent duchess we have banished;
    The bastard shall not live. After these revels,
    I'll begin strange ones; he and the stepsons
    Shall pay their lives for the first subsidies.°   10
    We must not frown so soon, else 't had been now.°

FIRST NOBLE My gracious lord, please you prepare for pleasure;
    The masque is not far off.

LUSSURIOSO   We are for pleasure.
    [*To the star*] Beshrew thee! what art thou, mad'st me start?
    Thou hast committed treason. [*To the Nobles*] A blazing star!   15

FIRST NOBLE A blazing star? O where, my lord?

LUSSURIOSO   Spy out.

SECOND NOBLE See, see, my lords, a wondrous dreadful one!

LUSSURIOSO I am not pleased at that ill-knotted fire,
    That bushing, flaring star. Am not I duke?°
    It should not quake me now; had it appeared°   20
    Before it, I might then have justly feared.°
    But yet they say, whom art and learning weds,
    When stars wear locks they threaten great men's heads.
    Is it so? You are read, my lords.

FIRST NOBLE   May it please your grace,°
    It shows great anger.

LUSSURIOSO   That does not please our grace.   25

SECOND NOBLE Yet here's the comfort, my lord: many times,
    When it seems most, it threatens farthest off.

LUSSURIOSO Faith, and I think so too.

FIRST NOBLE   Beside, my lord,
    You're gracefully established with the loves
    Of all your subjects; and for natural death,   30
    I hope it will be threescore years a-coming.

LUSSURIOSO True. No more but threescore years?

FIRST NOBLE Fourscore, I hope, my lord.

SECOND NOBLE   And fivescore, I.°

THIRD NOBLE But 'tis my hope, my lord, you shall ne'er die.

LUSSURIOSO Give me thy hand, these others I rebuke;   35

He that hopes so is fittest for a duke.
Thou shalt sit next me. Take your places, lords;
We're ready now for sports; let 'em set on.
[*To the star*] You thing, we shall forget you quite anon!°
THIRD NOBLE I hear 'em coming, my lord.
>   *Enter the masque of revengers: Vindice, Hippolito, and two*
>   *lords more*

LUSSURIOSO   Ah, 'tis well.—   40
[*Aside*] Brothers, and bastard, you dance next in hell.
>   *The revengers dance; at the end, steal out their swords, and*
>   *these four kill the four at the table, in their chairs. It thunders*

VINDICE Mark, thunder!
Dost know thy cue, thou big-voiced crier?
Dukes' groans are thunder's watchwords.
HIPPOLITO So, my lords, you have enough.   45
VINDICE Come, let's away, no ling'ring.
HIPPOLITO   Follow! Go!
>   *Exeunt [revengers except Vindice]*
VINDICE No power is angry when the lustful die;
When thunder claps, heaven likes the tragedy.
>   *Exit Vindice*
LUSSURIOSO O, O.
>   *Enter the other masque of intended murderers: Ambitioso,*
>   *Supervacuo, Spurio, and a Fourth Man, coming in dancing.*
>   *Lussurioso recovers a little in voice, and groans—calls 'A*
>   *guard, treason.' At which they all start out of their*
>   *measure,° and turning towards the table, they find them all to*
>   *be murdered*

SPURIO Whose groan was that?
LUSSURIOSO   Treason, a guard.   50
AMBITIOSO How now? All murdered!
SUPERVACUO   Murdered!
FOURTH MAN And those his nobles!
AMBITIOSO   Here's a labour saved;
I thought to have sped him.° 'Sblood, how came this?
[SUPERVACUO] Then I proclaim myself; now I am duke.
AMBITIOSO Thou duke! brother, thou liest.
>   [*Stabs Supervacuo*]
SPURIO   Slave, so dost thou!   55
>   [*Stabs Ambitioso*]
FOURTH MAN Base villain, hast thou slain my lord and master?
>   [*Stabs Spurio.*] *Enter Vindice, Hippolito, and the two Lords*

VINDICE Pistols! treason! murder! help! Guard my lord
  The duke!
      [*Enter Antonio and Guards*]
HIPPOLITO Lay hold upon this traitor.
      [*They seize the Fourth Man*]
LUSSURIOSO   O.
VINDICE Alas, the duke is murdered.
HIPPOLITO   And the nobles.
VINDICE Surgeons, surgeons! [*Aside*] Heart! does he breathe so long? 60
ANTONIO A piteous tragedy! able to wake
  An old man's eyes bloodshot.
LUSSURIOSO   O.°
VINDICE
  Look to my lord the duke! [*Aside*] A vengeance throttle him.
  [*To Fourth Man*] Confess, thou murd'rous and unhallowed man,
  Didst thou kill all these?
FOURTH MAN   None but the bastard, I. 65
VINDICE How came the duke slain, then?
FOURTH MAN   We found him so.
LUSSURIOSO O villain.
VINDICE   Hark.
LUSSURIOSO   Those in the masque did murder us.
VINDICE Law you now, sir.°
  O marble impudence! will you confess now?
FOURTH MAN 'Slud, 'tis all false!
ANTONIO   Away with that foul monster, 70
  Dipped in a prince's blood.
FOURTH MAN   Heart, 'tis a lie!
ANTONIO Let him have bitter execution.
      [*Exit Fourth Man, guarded*]
VINDICE [*aside*] New marrow! No, I cannot be expressed.—°
  How fares my lord the duke?
LUSSURIOSO   Farewell to all;
  He that climbs highest has the greatest fall. 75
  My tongue is out of office.
VINDICE   Air, gentlemen, air!°
      [*The others step back. Vindice whispers to Lussurioso*]
  Now thou'lt not prate on't, 'twas Vindice murdered thee—°
LUSSURIOSO O.
VINDICE [*whispers*] Murdered thy father—
LUSSURIOSO   O.
VINDICE [*whispers*]   —And I am he.

Tell nobody.
>   [*Lussurioso dies*]
>   [*Aloud*]   So, so, the duke's departed.
ANTONIO   It was a deadly hand that wounded him;   80
  The rest, ambitious who should rule and sway
  After his death, were so made all away.
VINDICE   My lord was unlikely.
HIPPOLITO [*to Antonio*]   Now the hope°
  Of Italy lies in your reverend years.
VINDICE   Your hair will make the silver age again,°   85
  When there was fewer but more honest men.
ANTONIO   The burden's weighty and will press age down.
  May I so rule that heaven may keep the crown.
VINDICE   The rape of your good lady has been quited
  With death on death.
ANTONIO   Just is the law above.   90
  But of all things it puts me most to wonder
  How the old duke came murdered.
VINDICE   .   O, my lord.
ANTONIO   It was the strangeliest carried; I not heard of the like.°
HIPPOLITO   'Twas all done for the best, my lord.
VINDICE   All for your grace's good. We may be bold   95
  To speak it now. 'Twas somewhat witty carried,
  Though we say it; 'twas we two murdered him.
ANTONIO   You two?
VINDICE   None else, i' faith, my lord; nay, 'twas well managed.
ANTONIO   Lay hands upon those villains.
        [*Guards seize them*]
VINDICE   How! on us?   100
ANTONIO   Bear 'em to speedy execution.
VINDICE   Heart! was 't not for your good, my lord?
ANTONIO   My good? Away with 'em. Such an old man as he!
  You that would murder him would murder me.
VINDICE   Is 't come about?
HIPPOLITO   'Sfoot, brother, you begun.°   105
VINDICE   May not we set as well as the duke's son?°
  Thou hast no conscience: are we not revenged?
  Is there one enemy left alive amongst those?
  'Tis time to die, when we are ourselves our foes.
  When murd'rers shut deeds close, this curse does seal 'em: 110
  If none disclose 'em, they themselves reveal 'em.

This murder might have slept in tongueless brass,°
But for ourselves, and the world died an ass.
Now I remember too, here was Piato
Brought forth a knavish sentence once:°
No doubt, said he, but time   115
Will make the murderer bring forth himself.
'Tis well he died; he was a witch.—°
And now, my lord, since we are in forever:°
This work was ours, which else might have been slipped;
And if we list, we could have nobles clipped°   120
And go for less than beggars; but we hate
To bleed so cowardly. We have enough,
I' faith, we're well: our mother turned, our sister true,°
We die after a nest of dukes—adieu.   125
    Exeunt [*Vindice and Hippolito, guarded*]
ANTONIO How subtly was that murder closed! Bear up°
Those tragic bodies; 'tis a heavy season.
Pray heaven their blood may wash away all treason.
    [*Exeunt*]

(handwritten marginal note): → I said it. It must be carried forth, for convention to be upheld.

THE REVENGE OF BUSSY D'AMBOIS

GEORGE CHAPMAN

To the right virtuous and truly noble knight, Sir Thomas Howard,° etc.

Sir,
Since works of this kind have been lately esteemed worthy the patronage of some of our worthiest nobles, I have made no doubt to prefer° this of mine to your undoubted virtue and exceeding true noblesse: as containing matter no less deserving your reading, and excitation° to heroical life, than any such late dedication. Nor have the greatest princes of Italy and other countries conceived it any least diminution to their greatness, to have their names winged with these tragic plumes, and dispersed by way of patronage through the most noble notices of Europe.

Howsoever therefore in the scenical presentation it might meet with some maligners, yet considering even therein it passed with approbation of more worthy judgements, the balance of their side (especially being held by your impartial hand) I hope will to no grain abide the outweighing.° And for the authentical truth of either person or action, who (worth the respecting) will expect it in a poem, whose subject is not truth, but things like truth? Poor envious souls they are that cavil at truth's want in these natural fictions: material° instruction, elegant and sententious° excitation to virtue, and deflection from her contrary being the soul, limbs, and limits° of an authentical tragedy. But whatsoever merit of your full countenance and favour suffers defect in this, I shall soon supply with some other of more general account:° wherein your right virtuous name made famous and preserved to posterity, your future comfort and honour in your present acceptation,° and love of all virtuous and divine expression, may be so much past others of your rank increased, as they are short of your judicial ingenuity° in their due estimation.

For howsoever those ignoble and sour-browed worldlings are careless of whatsoever future or present opinion spreads of them, yet (with the most divine philosopher,° if scripture did not confirm it) I make it matter of my faith, that we truly retain an intellectual feeling of good or bad after this life, proportionably answerable to the love or neglect we bear here to all virtue and truly humane instruction: in whose favour and honour I wish you most eminent; and rest ever,

> Your true virtue's most true observer,
> George Chapman

[DRAMATIS PERSONAE]°

Henry,° the king
Monsieur,° his brother
Guise,° a duke
Renel, a marquess
Montsurry, an earl
Baligny, Lord Lieutenant [of
   Cambrai]
Clermont D'Ambois
Maillard, Chalon, Aumale,
   captains
Espernon, Soisson, courtiers
Perricot, [an usher to Guise]
[An usher to the Countess]
The Guard

Soldiers
Servants
[A Messenger]
The ghosts of Bussy,
   Monsieur, Guise, Cardinal
   Guise, Chatillon°
Countess of Cambrai
Tamyra, wife to Montsurry
Charlotte, wife to Baligny
Riova, a servant [to the
   Countess]

[1.1]

Enter Baligny, Renel

BALIGNY To what will this declining kingdom turn,
Swingeing in every license, as in this°
Stupid permission of brave D'Ambois' murder?°
Murder made parallel with law! Murder used°
To serve the kingdom, given by suit to men   5
For their advancement, suffered scarecrow-like°
To fright adultery! What will policy°
At length bring under his capacity?°
RENEL All things: for as, when the high births of kings,
Deliverances, and coronations,°   10
We celebrate with all the cities' bells
Jangling together in untuned confusion,
All ordered clocks are tied up: so when glory,°
Flattery, and smooth applauses of things ill°
Uphold th' inordinate swinge of downright power,   15
Justice and truth—that tell the bounded use,°
Virtuous and well-distinguished forms of time—°
Are gagged and tongue-tied. But we have observed
Rule in more regular motion: things most lawful°
Were once most royal; kings sought common good,   20
Men's manly liberties, though ne'er so mean,°
And had their own swinge so more free, and more.
But when pride entered them, and rule by power,
All brows that smiled beneath them frowned, hearts grieved
By imitation, virtue quite was vanished,°   25
And all men studied self-love, fraud, and vice;
Then no man could be good but he was punished:
Tyrants, being still more fearful of the good
Than of the bad, their subjects' virtues ever
Managed with curbs and dangers, and esteemed°   30
As shadows and detractions to their own.°
BALIGNY Now all is peace, no danger: now what follows?
Idleness rusts us, since no virtuous labour
Ends aught rewarded: ease, security°
Now all the palm wears. We made war before°   35
So to prevent war; men with giving gifts

More than receiving made our country strong;
Our matchless race of soldiers then would spend
In public wars, not private brawls, their spirits,
In daring enemies, armed with meanest arms,   40
Not courting strumpets, and consuming birthrights
In apishness and envy of attire.
No labour then was harsh, no way so deep,
No rock so steep, but if a bird could scale it
Up would our youth fly too. A foe in arms   45
Stirred up a much more lust of his encounter
Than of a mistress never so be-painted.°
Ambition, then, was only scaling walls
And overtopping turrets; fame was wealth;
Best parts, best deeds, were best nobility;   50
Honour with worth, and wealth well got or none.°
Countries we won with as few men as countries;
Virtue subdued all.
RENEL   Just: and then our nobles
Loved virtue so, they praised and used it too;°
Had rather do than say, their own deeds hearing   55
By others glorified, than be so barren
That their parts only stood in praising others.°
BALIGNY Who could not do, yet praised and envied not;°
Civil behaviour flourished; bounty flowed;°
Avarice to upland boors, slaves, hangmen, banished.°   60
RENEL 'Tis now quite otherwise; but to note the cause
Of all these foul digressions and revolts
From our first natures, this 'tis in a word:°
Since good arts fail, crafts and deceits are used.°
Men ignorant are idle; idle men   65
Most practice what they most may do with ease,
Fashion and favour; all their studies aiming°
At getting money, which no wise man ever
Fed his desires with.
BALIGNY   Yet now none are wise
That think not heaven's true foolish, weighed with that.°   70
Well, thou most worthy to be greatest Guise,°
Make with thy greatness a new world arise.
Such depressed nobles, followers of his,°
As you yourself, my lord, will find a time
When to revenge your wrongs.

RENEL   I make no doubt;   75
  In meantime I could wish the wrong were righted
  Of your slain brother-in-law, brave Bussy D'Ambois.
BALIGNY That one accident was made my charge.°
  My brother Bussy's sister, now my wife,°
  By no suit would consent to satisfy°   80
  My love of her with marriage, till I vowed
  To use my utmost to revenge my brother:
  But Clermont D'Ambois, Bussy's second brother,°
  Had (since his apparition and excitement)°
  To suffer none but his hand in his wreak,   85
  Which he hath vowed, and so will needs acquit
  Me of my vow made to my wife, his sister,°
  And undertake himself Bussy's revenge;
  Yet loathing any way to give it act
  But in the noblest and most manly course,   90
  If th' earl dares take it, he resolves to send
  A challenge to him, and myself must bear it;°
  To which delivery I can use no means,
  He is so barricadoed in his house°
  And armed with guard still.
RENEL   That means lay on me,   95
  Which I can strangely make. My last lands' sale,°
  By his great suit, stands now on price with him,°
  And he, as you know, passing covetous
  (With that blind greediness that follows gain),
  Will cast no danger where her sweet feet tread.°   100
  Besides, you know, his lady by his suit
  (Wooing as freshly as when first love shot
  His faultless arrows from her rosy eyes)°
  Now lives with him again, and she, I know,
  Will join with all helps in her friend's revenge.°   105
BALIGNY No doubt, my lord, and therefore let me pray you
  To use all speed; for so on needles' points°
  My wife's heart stands with haste of the revenge—°
  Being, as you know, full of her brother's fire—°
  That she imagines I neglect my vow,   110
  Keeps off her kind embraces, and still asks,
  'When, when, will this revenge come? When performed
  Will this dull vow be?' And, I vow to heaven,
  So sternly and so past her sex she urges°

My vow's performance, that I almost fear   115
To see her when I have a while been absent,
Not showing her before I speak the blood
She so much thirsts for, freckling hands and face.
RENEL Get you the challenge writ, and look from me
To hear your passage cleared no long time after.°   120
BALIGNY All restitution to your worthiest lordship.°
        Exit Renel
—Whose errand I must carry to the king,
As having sworn my service in the search
Of all such malcontents and their designs,
By seeming one affected with their faction°   125
And discontented humours 'gainst the state.
Nor doth my brother Clermont 'scape my counsel
Given to the king about his Guisean greatness,
Which, as I spice it, hath possessed the king°
(Knowing his daring spirit) of much danger   130
Charged in it to his person: though my conscience°
Dare swear him clear of any power to be
Infected with the least dishonesty.
Yet that sincerity, we politicians°
Must say, grows out of envy, since it cannot   135
Aspire to policy's greatness; and the more
We work on all respects of kind and virtue,°
The more our service to the king seems great
In sparing no good that seems bad to him;
And the more bad we make the most of good,   140
The more our policy searcheth, and our service°
Is wondered at for wisdom and sincereness.
'Tis easy to make good suspected still,
Where good, and God, are made but cloaks for ill.
        Enter [King] Henry, Monsieur, Guise, Clermont, Espernon,
        Soisson. Monsieur taking leave of the King
See Monsieur taking now his leave for Brabant,°   145
        [Exit Henry]
The Guise and his dear minion, Clermont D'Ambois,
Whispering together, not of state affairs
I durst lay wagers (though the Guise be now
In chief heat of his faction), but of something°
Savouring of that which all men else despise,   150
How to be truly noble, truly wise.

MONSIEUR [*to Espernon and Soisson*]
                              See how he hangs upon the ear of Guise
    Like to his jewel.
ESPERNON   He's now whisp'ring in
    Some doctrine of stability and freedom,°
    Contempt of outward greatness, and the guises
    That vulgar great ones make their pride and zeal,°   155
    Being only servile trains and sumptuous houses,
    High places, offices.
MONSIEUR   Contempt of these
    Does he read to the Guise? 'Tis passing needful,°
    And he, I think, makes show t'affect his doctrine.
ESPERNON Commends, admires it.
MONSIEUR   And pursues another.   160
    'Tis fine hypocrisy, and cheap, and vulgar,
    Known for a covert practice, yet believed°
    (By those abused souls that they teach and govern)°
    No more than wives' adulteries by their husbands,
    They bearing it with so unmoved aspects,   165
    Hot coming from it, as 'twere not [at] all,
    Or made by custom nothing. This same D'Ambois°
    Hath gotten such opinion of his virtues
    (Holding all learning but an art to live well,°
    And showing he hath learned it in his life,   170
    Being thereby strong in his persuading others)
    That this ambitious Guise, embracing him,°
    Is thought t' embrace his virtues.
ESPERNON   Yet in some°
    His virtues are held false for th' other's vices:°
    For 'tis more cunning held, and much more common,°   175
    To suspect truth than falsehood: and of both
    Truth still fares worse, as hardly being believed,°
    As 'tis unusual and rarely known.
MONSIEUR I'll part engend'ring virtue. Men affirm°
    Though this same Clermont hath a D'Ambois spirit   180
    And breathes his brother's valour, yet his temper°
    Is so much past his that you cannot move him:
    I'll try that temper in him.
    [*To Guise and Clermont*]   Come, you two
    Devour each other with your virtue's zeal
    And leave for other friends no fragment of ye: 185

I wonder, Guise, you will thus ravish him°
Out of my bosom that first gave the life
His manhood breathes, spirit, and means, and lustre.
What do men think of me, I pray thee, Clermont?
Once give me leave (for trial of that love   190
That from thy brother Bussy thou inherit'st)
T'unclasp thy bosom.°

CLERMONT   As how, sir?

MONSIEUR Be a true glass to me, in which I may°
  Behold what thoughts the many-headed beast,°
  And thou thyself, breathes out concerning me,   195
  My ends, and new-upstarted state in Brabant°
  (For which I now am bound), my higher aims°
  Imagined here in France: speak, man, and let
  Thy words be born as naked as thy thoughts.
  O, were brave Bussy living!

CLERMONT   Living, my lord?   200

MONSIEUR 'Tis true thou art his brother, but durst thou
  Have braved the Guise? Maugre his presence courted°
  His wedded lady? Emptied even the dregs
  Of his worst thoughts of me even to my teeth?°
  Discerned not me, his rising sovereign,°   205
  From any common groom, but let me hear
  My grossest faults as gross-full as they were?°
  Durst thou do this?

CLERMONT   I cannot tell: a man
  Does never know the goodness of his stomach
  Till he sees meat before him. Were I dared,   210
  Perhaps, as he was, I durst do like him.

MONSIEUR Dare then to pour out here thy freest soul
  Of what I am.

CLERMONT   'Tis stale; he told you it.

MONSIEUR He only jested, spake of spleen and envy;°
  Thy soul, more learn'd, is more ingenuous,°   215
  Searching, judicial; let me then from thee
  Hear what I am.

CLERMONT   What but the sole support
  And most expectant hope of all our France,
  The toward victor of the whole Low Countries?°

MONSIEUR Tush, thou wilt sing encomiums of my praise.   220
  Is this like D'Ambois? I must vex the Guise

Or never look to hear free truth. Tell me,
For Bussy lives not: he durst anger me,
Yet, for my love, would not have feared to anger
The king himself. Thou understand'st me, dost not?   225
CLERMONT I shall, my lord, with study.
MONSIEUR Dost understand thyself? I pray thee tell me,
  Dost never search thy thoughts what my design
  Might be to entertain thee and thy brother,°
  What turn I meant to serve with you?°   230
CLERMONT Even what you please to think.
MONSIEUR   But what think'st thou?
  Had I no end in't, think'st?
CLERMONT   I think you had.°
MONSIEUR When I took in such two as you two were,
  A ragged couple of decayed commanders,°
  When a French crown would plentifully serve°   235
  To buy you both to anything i' th' earth?°
CLERMONT So it would you.
MONSIEUR   Nay, bought you both outright,
  You, and your trunks. I fear me, I offend thee.°
CLERMONT No, not a jot.
MONSIEUR   The most renownèd soldier
  Epaminondas (as good authors say)°   240
  Had no more suits than backs, but you two shared
  But one suit 'twixt you both, when both your studies°
  Were not what meat to dine with, if your partridge,
  Your snipe, your woodcock, lark, or your red herring,
  But where to beg it—whether at my house   245
  Or at the Guise's (for you know you were
  Ambitious beggars), or at some cook's shop,
  T'eternize the cook's trust, and score it up.°
  Does 't not offend thee?
CLERMONT   No, sir. Pray proceed.
MONSIEUR As for thy gentry, I dare boldly take°   250
  Thy honourable oath: and yet some say
  Thou and thy most renownèd noble brother
  Came to the court first in a keel of sea-coal;°
  Does 't not offend thee?
CLERMONT   Never doubt it, sir.
MONSIEUR Why do I love thee then? Why have I raked thee   255
  Out of the dunghill, cast my cast wardrobe on thee?°

Brought thee to court too, as I did thy brother?
Made ye my saucy boon companions?
Taught ye to call our greatest noblemen
By the corruption of their names, Jack, Tom?°   260
Have I blown both for nothing to this bubble?°
Though thou art learn'd, th'ast no enchanting wit;
Or were thy wit good, am I therefore bound
To keep thee for my table?
CLERMONT   Well, sir, 'twere°
    A good knight's place. Many a proud dubbed gallant   265
    Seeks out a poor knight's living from such emrods.°
[MONSIEUR] Or what use else should I design thee to?
    Perhaps you'll answer me, to be my pander.°
CLERMONT Perhaps I shall.
MONSIEUR   Or did the sly Guise put thee
    Into my bosom t'undermine my projects?   270
    I fear thee not; for though I be not sure
    I have thy heart, I know thy brainpan yet
    To be as empty a dull piece of wainscot
    As ever armed the scalp of any courtier,
    A fellow only that consists of sinews,   275
    Mere Swisser, apt for any execution.°
CLERMONT But killing of the king.
MONSIEUR   Right. Now I see°
    Thou understand'st thyself.
CLERMONT   Aye, and you better:
    You are a king's son born—
MONSIEUR   Right.
CLERMONT   And a king's brother—
MONSIEUR True.   280
CLERMONT And might not any fool have been so too,
    As well as you?
MONSIEUR   A pox upon you!
CLERMONT   You did no princely deeds
    Ere you're born, I take it, to deserve it;°
    Nor did you any since that I have heard,
    Nor will do ever any, as all think.   285
MONSIEUR The devil take him! I'll no more of him.
GUISE Nay, stay, my lord, and hear him answer you.
MONSIEUR No more, I swear. Farewell.
        Exeunt Monsieur, Espernon, Soisson.

GUISE   No more? Ill fortune!
  I would have given a million to have heard
  His scoffs retorted, and the insolence°   290
  Of his high birth and greatness (which were never
  Effects of his deserts, but of his fortune)
  Made show to his dull eyes beneath the worth
  That men aspire to by their knowing virtues,°
  Without which greatness is a shade, a bubble.°   295
CLERMONT But what one great man dreams of that but you?
  All take their births and birthrights left to them
  (Acquired by others) for their own worth's purchase,°
  When many a fool in both is great as they:°
  And who would think they could win with their worths   300
  Wealthy possessions, when, won to their hands,°
  They neither can judge justly of their value,
  Nor know their use? And therefore they are puffed
  With such proud tumours as this Monsieur is,°
  Enabled only by the goods they have   305
  To scorn all goodness: none great fill their fortunes,
  But as those men that make their houses greater,
  Their households being less, so fortune raises°
  Huge heaps of outside in these mighty men,°
  And gives them nothing in them.
GUISE   True as truth:°   310
  And therefore they had rather drown their substance°
  In superfluities of bricks and stones
  (Like Sisyphus, advancing of them ever°
  And ever pulling down) than lay the cost
  Of any sluttish corner on a man,   315
  Built with God's finger and enstyled His temple.°
BALIGNY 'Tis nobly said, my lord.
GUISE   I would have these things
  Brought upon stages, to let mighty misers°
  See all their grave and serious miseries played
  As once they were in Athens and old Rome.   320
CLERMONT Nay, we must now have nothing brought on stages
  But puppetry and pied ridiculous antics:°
  Men thither come to laugh and feed fool-fat,
  Check at all goodness there as being profaned;°
  When wheresoever goodness comes she makes   325
  The place still sacred, though with other feet

Never so much 'tis scandaled and polluted.
Let me learn anything that fits a man,°
In any stables shown, as well as stages.
BALIGNY Why, is not all the world esteemed a stage?   330
CLERMONT Yes, and right worthily: and stages too
  Have a respect due to them, if but only
  For what the good Greek moralist says of them:°
  'Is a man proud of greatness, or of riches?
  Give me an expert actor, I'll show all   335
  That can within his greatest glory fall.
  Is a man frayed with poverty and lowness?
  Give me an actor, I'll show every eye
  What he laments so and so much doth fly,
  The best and worst of both.' If but for this then,   340
  To make the proudest outside, that most swells
  With things without him and above his worth,°
  See how small cause he has to be so blown up,
  And the most poor man to be grieved with poorness,
  Both being so easily borne by expert actors.°   345
  The stage and actors are not so contemptful
  As every innovating Puritan,°
  And ignorant sweater-out of zealous envy,°
  Would have the world imagine. And besides
  That, all things have been likened to the mirth   350
  Used upon stages, and for stages fitted.°
  The splenative philosopher, that ever°
  Laughed at them all, were worthy the enstaging:
  All objects, were they ne'er so full of tears,
  He so conceited that he could distil thence   355
  Matter that still fed his ridiculous humour.°
  Heard he a lawyer never so vehement pleading,
  He stood and laughed. Heard he a tradesman swearing
  Never so thriftily, selling of his wares,°
  He stood and laughed. Heard he an holy brother,   360
  For hollow ostentation at his prayers
  Ne'er so impetuously, he stood and laughed.°
  Saw he a great man never so insulting,°
  Severely inflicting, gravely giving laws,
  Not for their good, but his, he stood and laughed.°   365
  Saw he a youthful widow
  Never so weeping, wringing of her hands

For her lost lord, still the philosopher laughed.
Now whether he supposed all these presentments
Were only maskeries and wore false faces,   370
Or else were simply vain, I take no care;
But still he laughed, how grave soe'er they were.
GUISE And might right well, my Clermont, and for this
    Virtuous digression we will thank the scoffs
    Of vicious Monsieur. But now for the main point   375
    Of your late resolution for revenge
    Of your slain friend.
CLERMONT   I have here my challenge,°
    Which I will pray my brother Baligny
    To bear the murderous earl.
BALIGNY   I have prepared
    Means for access to him through all his guard.   380
GUISE About it then, my worthy Baligny,
    And bring us the success.
BALIGNY   I will, my lord.°
        Exeunt

[1.2]

    [*Enter*] *Tamyra*
TAMYRA Revenge, that ever red sitt'st in the eyes°
    Of injured ladies, till we crown thy brows
    With bloody laurel, and receive from thee°
    Justice for all our honour's injury;
    Whose wings none fly that wrath or tyranny°   5
    Have ruthless made and bloody, enter here,
    Enter, O enter! and, though length of time
    Never lets any 'scape thy constant justice,°
    Yet now prevent that length. Fly, fly, and here°
    Fix thy steel footsteps: here, O here, where still°   10
    Earth, moved with pity, yielded and embraced
    My love's fair figure, drawn in his dear blood,°
    And marked the place to show thee where was done
    The cruell'st murder that e'er fled the sun.
    O Earth, why keep'st thou not as well his spirit   15
    To give his form life? No, that was not earthly;

That (rarefying the thin and yielding air)°
Flew sparkling up into the sphere of fire,°
Whence endless flames it sheds in my desire.
Here be my daily pallet; here all nights   20
That can be wrested from thy rival's arms,°
O my dear Bussy, I will lie and kiss
Spirit into thy blood, or breathe out mine
In sighs and kisses and sad tunes to thine.
     [*Lying down,*] *she sings. Enter Montsurry*

MONTSURRY Still on this haunt? Still shall adulterous blood°   25
Affect thy spirits? Think, for shame, but this:
This blood that cockatrice-like thus thou brood'st°
Too dry is to breed any quench to thine.°
And therefore now (if only for thy lust°
A little covered with a veil of shame)   30
Look out for fresh life, rather than witchlike°
Learn to kiss horror and with death engender.
Strange cross in nature, purest virgin shame
Lies in the blood as lust lies; and together
Many times mix too, and in none more shameful   35
Than in the shamefaced. Who can then distinguish°
'Twixt their affections, or tell when he meets
With one not common? Yet, as worthiest poets°
Shun common and plebeian forms of speech,
Every illiberal and affected phrase,°   40
To clothe their matter, and together tie
Matter and form with art and decency;
So worthiest women should shun vulgar guises,°
And though they cannot but fly out for change,°
Yet modesty, the matter of their lives,°   45
Be it adulterate, should be painted true°
With modest out-parts; what they should do still
Graced with good show, though deeds be ne'er so ill.°

TAMYRA That is so far from all ye seek of us°
That (though yourselves be common as the air)°   50
We must not take the air, we must not fit
Our actions to our own affections:
But as geometricians (you still say)
Teach that no lines nor superficies
Do move themselves but still accompany   55
The motions of their bodies, so poor wives

Must not pursue nor have their own affections—
But to their husbands' earnests and their jests,°
To their austerities of looks and laughters
(Though ne'er so foolish and injurious)   60
Like parasites and slaves, fit their disposures.
MONTSURRY I used thee as my soul, to move and rule me.
TAMYRA So said you when you wooed. So soldiers, tortured
With tedious sieges of some well-walled town,
Propound conditions of most large contents—°   65
Freedom of laws, all former government.
But having once set foot within the walls
And got the reins of power into their hands,
Then do they tyrannize at their own rude swinges,
Seize all their goods, their liberties, and lives,°   70
And make advantage and their lusts their laws.°
MONTSURRY But love me and perform a wife's part yet:
With all my love before, I swear forgiveness.°
TAMYRA Forgiveness! That grace you should seek of me:
These tortured fingers and these stabbed-through arms°   75
Keep that law in their wounds yet, unobserved,°
And ever shall.
MONTSURRY   Remember their deserts.
TAMYRA Those with fair warnings might have been reformed,
Not these unmanly rages. You have heard
The fiction of the north wind and the sun,   80
Both working on a traveller and contending
Which had most power to take his cloak from him:
Which when the wind attempted, he roared out
Outrageous blasts at him to force it off,°
That wrapped it closer on; when the calm sun   85
(The wind once leaving) charged him with still beams,°
Quiet and fervent, and therein was constant,
Which made him cast off both his cloak and coat:
Like whom should men do. If ye wish your wives
Should leave disliked things, seek it not with rage,   90
For that enrages: what ye give, ye have.°
But use calm warnings and kind manly means,
And that in wives most prostitute will win°
Not only sure amends, but make us wives
Better than those that ne'er led faulty lives.   95
        Enter a Soldier

SOLDIER My lord.
MONTSURRY   How now, would any speak with me?
SOLDIER Aye, sir.
MONTSURRY   Perverse and traitorous miscreant,
  Where are your other fellows of my guard?
  Have I not told you I will speak with none
  But Lord Renel?
SOLDIER   And 'tis he that stays you.°   100
MONTSURRY O, is it he? 'Tis well, attend him in.
        [*Exit Soldier*]
  I must be vigilant: the Furies haunt me.
  Do you hear, dame?°
        Enter Renel with the Soldier
RENEL [*aside to the Soldier*] Be true now for your lady's injured sake,
  Whose bounty you have so much cause to honour: 105
  For her respect is chief in this design,°
  And therefore serve it; call out of the way
  All your confederate fellows of his guard
  Till Monsieur Baligny be entered here.
SOLDIER Upon your honour, my lord shall be free   110
  From any hurt, you say?
RENEL Free as myself. Watch then, and clear his entry.
SOLDIER I will not fail, my lord.
        Exit Soldier
RENEL   God save your lordship!
MONTSURRY My noblest Lord Renel, past all men welcome!
  Wife, welcome his lordship.
        Renel kisses Tamyra
RENEL [*to Tamyra*]   I much joy   115
  In your return here.
TAMYRA   You do more than I.
MONTSURRY She's passionate still to think we ever parted°
  By my too stern injurious jealousy.
RENEL 'Tis well your lordship will confess your error
  In so good time yet.
        Enter Baligny with a challenge
MONTSURRY   Death! Who have we here?   120
  Ho! Guard! Villains!
BALIGNY   Why exclaim you so?
MONTSURRY Negligent traitors! Murder, murder, murder!
BALIGNY Y'are mad. Had mine intent been so, like yours,°

It had been done ere this.
RENEL   Sir, your intent,
  And action too, was rude to enter thus.°   125
BALIGNY Y'are a decayed lord to tell me of rudeness,
  As much decayed in manners as in means.
RENEL You talk of manners, that thus rudely thrust
  Upon a man that's busy with his wife.
BALIGNY And kept your lordship then the door?
RENEL   The door?   130
      [*Draws his sword*]°
MONTSURRY [*to Renel*] Sweet lord, forbear. [*To Baligny*] Show,
  show your purpose, sir,
  To move such bold feet into others' roofs.
BALIGNY This is my purpose, sir: from Clermont D'Ambois
  I bring this challenge.
MONTSURRY   Challenge! I'll touch none.°
BALIGNY I'll leave it here then.
RENEL   Thou shalt leave thy life first.   135
MONTSURRY Murder, murder!
RENEL [*to Montsurry*]   Retire, my lord; get off.
  [*To Baligny*] Hold, or thy death shall hold thee.—Hence, my lord!
BALIGNY There lie the challenge.
        [*Baligny throws down the challenge.*] *They all fight and*
        Baligny drives in Montsurry. Exit Montsurry
RENEL Was not this well handled?
BALIGNY Nobly, my lord. All thanks.
        Exit Baligny
TAMYRA   I'll make him read it.
        Exit Tamyra
RENEL This was a sleight well masked. O, what is man,   140
  Unless he be a politician!°
        Exit

[2.1]

[Enter] Henry, Baligny

HENRY Come, Baligny, we now are private. Say,
What service bring'st thou? Make it short; the Guise
(Whose friend thou seem'st) is now in court, and near,
And may observe us.

BALIGNY   This, sir, then, in short.
The faction of the Guise (with which my policy   5
For service to your Highness seems to join)
Grows ripe and must be gathered into hold:°
Of which my brother Clermont, being a part
Exceeding capital, deserves to have°
A capital eye on him. And as you may,   10
With best advantage and your speediest charge
Command his apprehension: which (because
The court, you know, is strong in his defense)
We must ask country swinge and open fields.°
And therefore I have wrought him to go down°   15
To Cambrai with me (of which government°
Your Highness' bounty made me your lieutenant),
Where when I have him I will leave my house
And feign some service out about the confines;°
When in the meantime, if you please to give   20
Command to my lieutenant, by your letters,
To train him to some muster, where he may°
(Much to his honour) see for him your forces°
Put into battle, when he comes, he may°
With some close stratagem be apprehended: 25
For otherwise your whole powers there will fail°
To work his apprehension: and with that°
My hand needs never be discerned therein.

HENRY Thanks, honest Baligny.

BALIGNY   Your Highness knows°
I will be honest, and betray for you   30
Brother and father; for I know, my lord,
Treachery for kings is truest loyalty,°
Nor is to bear the name of treachery,
But grave, deep policy. All acts that seem

Ill in particular respects are good°   35
As they respect your universal rule:°
As, in the main sway of the universe,°
The supreme Rector's general decrees°
To guard the mighty globes of earth and heaven,°
Since they make good that guard to preservation   40
Of both those in their order and first end,
No man's particular (as he thinks) wrong
Must hold him wronged: no, not though all men's reasons,°
All law, all conscience, concludes it wrong.
Nor is comparison a flatterer   45
To liken you here to the King of kings,
Nor any man's particular offence
Against the world's sway to offence at yours
In any subject; who as little may°
Grudge at their particular wrong, if so it seem,°   50
For th' universal right of your estate,
As (being a subject of the world's whole sway
As well as yours, and being a righteous man
To whom heaven promises defense and blessing,
Brought to decay, disgrace, and quite defenseless)   55
He may complain of heaven for wrong to him.°
HENRY 'Tis true: the simile at all parts holds,
As all good subjects hold that love our favour.
BALIGNY Which is our heaven here; and a misery
Incomparable, and most truly hellish,   60
To live deprived of our king's grace and countenance,
Without which best conditions are most cursed.
Life of that nature, howsoever short,
Is a most lingering and tedious life,
Or rather no life, but a languishing   65
And an abuse of life.
HENRY   'Tis well conceited.
BALIGNY I thought it not amiss to yield your Highness
A reason of my speeches, lest perhaps
You might conceive I flattered: which, I know,
Of all ills under heaven you most abhor.   70
HENRY Still thou art right, my virtuous Baligny,
For which I thank and love thee. Thy advice
I'll not forget. Haste to thy government,°
And carry D'Ambois with thee. So farewell.

BALIGNY Your Majesty fare ever like itself.   75
    Exit [Henry]. Enter Guise
GUISE My sure friend Baligny!
BALIGNY   Noblest of princes!
GUISE How stands the state of Cambrai?
BALIGNY   Strong, my lord,
    And fit for service: for whose readiness
    Your creature, Clermont D'Ambois, and myself °
    Ride shortly down.
GUISE   That Clermont is my love;   80
    France never bred a nobler gentleman
    For all parts; he exceeds his brother Bussy.
BALIGNY Aye, my lord?
GUISE   Far: because, besides his valour,
    He hath the crown of man, and all his parts,°
    Which learning is, and that so true and virtuous   85
    That it gives power to do as well as say
    Whatever fits a most accomplished man:
    Which Bussy, for his valour's season, lacked,°
    And so was rapt with outrage oftentimes°
    Beyond decorum; where this absolute Clermont,   90
    Though (only for his natural zeal to right)
    He will be fiery when he sees it crossed
    And in defense of it, yet when he lists
    He can contain that fire, as hid in embers.
BALIGNY No question, he's a true, learn'd gentleman.   95
GUISE He is as true as tides or any star
    Is in his motion; and for his rare learning,°
    He is not (as all else are that seek knowledge)
    Of taste so much depraved that they had rather
    Delight and satisfy themselves to drink   100
    Of the stream troubled, wand'ring ne'er so far
    From the clear fount, than of the fount itself.°
    In all, Rome's Brutus is revived in him,°
    Whom he of industry doth imitate.°
    Or rather, as great Troy's Euphorbus was°   105
    After Pythagoras; so is Brutus, Clermont.
    And, were not Brutus a conspirator—
BALIGNY Conspirator, my lord? Doth that impair him?
    Caesar began to tyrannize; and when virtue
    Nor the religion of the gods could serve   110

To curb the insolence of his proud laws,
Brutus would be the gods' just instrument.
What said the princess, sweet Antigone,
In the grave Greek tragedian, when the question°
'Twixt her and Creon is for laws of kings?°   115
Which when he urges, she replies on him:°
Though his laws were a king's, they were not God's;
Nor would she value Creon's written laws
With God's unwrit edicts, since they last not°
This day and the next, but every day and ever,   120
Where king's laws alter every day and hour,
And in that change imply a bounded power.°
GUISE Well, let us leave these vain disputings what
   Is to be done, and fall to doing something.
   When are you for your government in Cambrai?   125
BALIGNY When you command, my lord.
GUISE   Nay, that's not fit.°
   Continue your designments with the king
   With all your service; only, if I send,
   Respect me as your friend and love my Clermont.
BALIGNY Your Highness knows my vows.
GUISE   Aye, 'tis enough.   130
      Exit Guise
BALIGNY Thus must we play on both sides, and thus hearten
   In any ill those men whose good we hate.
   Kings may do what they list, and for kings, subjects,°
   Either exempt from censure or exception:°
   For, as no man's worth can be justly judged   135
   But when he shines in some authority,°
   So no authority should suffer censure
   But by a man of more authority.
   Great vessels into less are emptied never;
   There's a redundance past their continent ever.°   140
   These *virtuosi* are the poorest creatures;°
   For look how spinners weave out of themselves°
   Webs, whose strange matter none before can see;
   So these, out of an unseen good in virtue,°
   Make arguments of right and comfort in her°   145
   That clothe them like the poor web of a spinner.
      Enter Clermont
CLERMONT Now, to my challenge. What's the place, the weapon?°

BALIGNY Soft, sir; let first your challenge be received.°
    He would not touch nor see it.
CLERMONT   Possible?
    How did you then?
BALIGNY   Left it in his despite.°   150
    But when he saw me enter so expectless,
    To hear his base exclaims of 'murder, murder!'
    Made me think noblesse lost, in him quick buried.°
CLERMONT They are the breathing sepulchres of noblesse:°
    No trulier noble men, than lions' pictures   155
    Hung up for signs are lions. Who knows not
    That lions the more soft kept are more servile?°
    And look how lions close kept, fed by hand,°
    Lose quite th' innative fire of spirit and greatness°
    That lions free breathe, foraging for prey,   160
    And grow so gross that mastiffs, curs, and mongrels°
    Have spirit to cow them: so our soft French nobles,
    Chained up in ease and numbed security
    (Their spirits shrunk up like their covetous fists,
    And never opened but Domitian-like,°   165
    And all his base obsequious minions
    When they were catching, though it were but flies),
    Besotted with their peasants' love of gain,°
    Rusting at home and on each other preying,
    Are for their greatness but the greater slaves,   170
    And none is noble but who scrapes and saves.
BALIGNY 'Tis base, 'tis base, and yet they think them high.
CLERMONT So children mounted on their hobby-horse
    Think they are riding when with wanton toil°
    They bear what should bear them. A man may well   175
    Compare them to those foolish great-spleened camels
    That, to their high heads, begged of Jove horns higher;
    Whose most uncomely and ridiculous pride
    When he had satisfied, they could not use,
    But where they went upright before, they stooped,   180
    And bore their heads much lower for their horns;
    As these high men do, low in all true grace,
    Their height being privilege to all things base.°
    And as the foolish poet that still writ°
    All his most self-loved verse in paper royal°   185
    Or parchment ruled with lead, smoothed with the pumice,°

Bound richly up, and strung with crimson strings;°
Never so blest as when he writ and read°
The ape-loved issue of his brain, and never°
But joying in himself, admiring ever,   190
Yet in his works behold him, and he showed
Like to a ditcher: so these painted men°
All set on outside, look upon within
And not a peasant's entrails you shall find
More foul and measled, nor more starved of mind.   195

BALIGNY That makes their bodies fat. I fain would know°
How many millions of our other nobles
Would make one Guise. There is a true tenth Worthy°
Who, did not one act only blemish him—

CLERMONT One act? What one?

BALIGNY   One that, though years past done,   200
Sticks by him still and will distain him ever.

CLERMONT Good heaven! wherein? What one act can you name
Supposed his stain, that I'll not prove his lustre?

BALIGNY To satisfy you, 'twas the Massacre.°

CLERMONT The Massacre? I thought 'twas some such blemish.   205

BALIGNY O, it was heinous.

CLERMONT   To a brutish sense,°
But not a manly reason. We so tender
The vile part in us, that the part divine°
We see in hell and shrink not. Who was first
Head of that Massacre?

BALIGNY   The Guise.

CLERMONT   'Tis nothing so.   210
Who was in fault for all the slaughters made
In Ilion and about it? Were the Greeks?
Was it not Paris ravishing the Queen
Of Lacedaemon? Breach of shame and faith°
And all the laws of hospitality?°   215
This is the beastly slaughter made of men
When truth is overthrown, his laws corrupted;°
When souls are smothered in the flattered flesh,°
Slain bodies are no more than oxen slain.

BALIGNY Differ not men from oxen?

CLERMONT   Who says so?   220
But see wherein: in the understanding rules°
Of their opinions, lives, and actions,

In their communities of faith and reason.
Was not the wolf that nourished Romulus°
More human than the men that did expose him?   225
BALIGNY That makes against you.
CLERMONT   Not, sir, if you note
    That, by that deed, the actions difference make
    'Twixt men and beasts, and not their names nor forms.°
    Had faith, nor shame, all hospitable rights
    Been broke by Troy, Greece had not made that slaughter.   230
    Had that been saved (says a philosopher)°
    The *Iliads* and *Odysseys* had been lost;°
    Had faith and true religion been preferred,°
    Religious Guise had never massacred.
BALIGNY Well, sir, I cannot when I meet with you   235
    But thus digress a little, for my learning,°
    From any other business I intend.
    But now the voyage we resolved for Cambrai,
    I told the Guise, begins, and we must haste.
    And till the Lord Renel hath found some mean,   240
    Conspiring with the countess, to make sure°
    Your sworn wreak on her husband (though this failed),°
    In my so brave command we'll spend the time,°
    Sometimes in training out in skirmishes°
    And battles all our troops and companies;   245
    And sometimes breathe your brave Scotch running horse°
    That great Guise gave you, that all th' horse in France
    Far overruns at every race and hunting
    Both of the hare and deer. You shall be honoured
    Like the great Guise himself, above the king.   250
    And (can you but appease your great-spleened sister
    For our delayed wreak of your brother's slaughter)
    At all parts you'll be welcomed to your wonder.°
CLERMONT I'll see my lord the Guise again before
    We take our journey.
BALIGNY   O, sir, by all means;   255
    You cannot be too careful of his love
    That ever takes occasion to be raising
    Your virtues past the reaches of this age°
    And ranks you with the best of th' ancient Romans.
CLERMONT That praise at no part moves me, but the worth°   260
    Of all he can give others sphered in him.°

BALIGNY He yet is thought to entertain strange aims.
CLERMONT He may be well, yet not (as you think) strange.°
　　His strange aims are to cross the common custom°
　　Of servile nobles, in which he's so ravished°   265
　　That quite the earth he leaves, and up he leaps
　　On Atlas' shoulders, and from thence looks down,°
　　Viewing how far off other high ones creep:
　　Rich, poor of reason, wander; all pale-looking°
　　And trembling but to think of their sure deaths,   270
　　Their lives so base are and so rank their breaths:°
　　Which I teach Guise to heighten and make sweet
　　With life's dear odours, a good mind and name;°
　　For which he only loves me and deserves°
　　My love and life, which through all deaths I vow,   275
　　Resolving this (whatever change can be):°
　　Thou hast created, thou hast ruined me.°
　　　　Exeunt

[3.1]

A march of Captains over the stage. Maillard, Chalon,
Aumale, following with Soldiers

MAILLARD These troops and companies come in with wings:°
  So many men, so armed, so gallant horse,
  I think no other government in France
  So soon could bring together. With such men
  Methinks a man might pass th' insulting pillars   5
  Of Bacchus and Alcides.

CHALON   I much wonder°
  Our Lord Lieutenant brought his brother down
  To feast and honour him, and yet now leaves him
  At such an instance.

MAILLARD   'Twas the king's command,°
  For whom he must leave brother, wife, friend, all things.   10

AUMALE The confines of his government, whose view
  Is the pretext of his command, hath need
  Of no such sudden expedition.

MAILLARD We must not argue that. The king's command
  Is need and right enough; and that he serves   15
  (As all true subjects should) without disputing.

CHALON But knows not he of your command to take
  His brother Clermont?

MAILLARD   No, the king's will is
  Expressly to conceal his apprehension
  From my Lord Governor. Observed ye not?   20
  Again peruse the letters. Both you are
  Made my assistants, and have right and trust
  In all the weighty secrets like myself.

AUMALE 'Tis strange a man that had, through his life past,
  So sure a foot in virtue and true knowledge   25
  As Clermont D'Ambois, should be now found tripping,
  And taken up thus, so to make his fall°
  More steep and headlong.

MAILLARD   It is Virtue's fortune
  To keep her low and in her proper place.°
  Height hath no room for her. But as a man   30
  That hath a fruitful wife, and every year

A child by her, hath every year a month
To breathe himself, where he that gets no child°
Hath not a night's rest (if he will do well);
So, let one marry this same barren Virtue,   35
She never lets him rest; where fruitful Vice
Spares her rich drudge, gives him in labour breath,
Feeds him with bane, and makes him fat with death.
CHALON I see that good lives never can secure
  Men from bad livers. Worst men will have best°   40
  As ill as they, or heaven to hell they'll wrest.
AUMALE There was a merit for this in the fault°
  That Bussy made, for which he (doing penance)°
  Proves that these foul adulterous guilts will run
  Through the whole blood, which not the clear can shun.°   45
MAILLARD I'll therefore take heed of the bastarding°
  Whole innocent races; 'tis a fearful thing.
  And as I am true bachelor, I swear
  To touch no woman to the coupling ends°
  Unless it be mine own wife, or my friend's:°   50
  I may make bold with him.
AUMALE   'Tis safe and common:°
  The more your friend dares trust, the more deceive him.
  And as through dewy vapours the sun's form
  Makes the gay rainbow girdle to a storm,
  So in hearts hollow, friendship (even the sun   55
  To all good growing in society)°
  Makes his so glorious and divine name hold
  Colours for all the ill that can be told.°
        Trumpets [sound] within
MAILLARD Hark, our last troops are come.
        Drums beat [within]
CHALON   Hark, our last foot.
MAILLARD Come, let us put all quickly into battle   60
  And send for Clermont, in whose honour all
  This martial preparation we pretend.°
CHALON We must bethink us, ere we apprehend him,°
  (Besides our main strength) of some stratagem°
  To make good our severe command on him,   65
  As well to save blood as to make him sure:°
  For if he come on his Scotch horse, all France
  Put at the heels of him will fail to take him.

MAILLARD What think you if we should disguise a brace
   Of our best soldiers in fair lackeys' coats,°   70
   And send them for him, running by his side,
   Till they have brought him in some ambuscado
   We close may lodge for him, and suddenly°
   Lay sure hand on him, plucking him from horse.°
AUMALE It must be sure and strong hand: for if once   75
   He feels the touch of such a stratagem,
   'Tis not the choicest brace of all our bands°
   Can manacle or quench his fiery hands.
MAILLARD When they have seized him, the ambush shall make in.°
AUMALE Do as you please; his blameless spirit deserves   80
   (I dare engage my life) of all this nothing.°
CHALON Why should all this stir be, then?
AUMALE   Who knows not
   The bombast Polity thrusts into his giant°
   To make his wisdom seem of size as huge,
   And all for slight encounter of a shade,   85
   So he be touched, he would have heinous made?°
MAILLARD It may be once so, but so ever, never.°
   Ambition is abroad, on foot, on horse;
   Faction chokes every corner, street, the court;
   Whose faction 'tis you know, and who is held   90
   The fautor's right hand; how high his aims reach°
   Naught but a crown can measure. This must fall
   Past shadows' weights, and is most capital.°
CHALON No question; for since he is come to Cambrai,
   The malcontent, decayed Marquess Renel,   95
   Is come, and new arrived, and made partaker
   Of all the entertaining shows and feasts
   That welcomed Clermont to the brave virago,
   His manly sister. Such we are esteemed
   As are our consorts. Marquess Malcontent°   100
   Comes where he knows his vein hath safest vent.°
MAILLARD Let him come at his will, and go as free;
   Let us ply Clermont, our whole charge is he.°
     Exeunt

[3.2]

Enter a Gentleman Usher° before Clermont, Renel, Charlotte
with two women attendants, with others: shows° having passed
within

CHARLOTTE This for your lordship's welcome into Cambrai.°
RENEL Noblest of ladies, 'tis beyond all power
  (Were my estate at first full) in my means°
  To quit or merit.
CLERMONT   You come something later°
  From court, my lord, than I: and since news there   5
  Is every day increasing with th' affairs,°
  Must I not ask now what the news is there?
  Where the court lies? what stir, change, what advice°
  From England, Italy?
RENEL   You must do so,
  If you'll be called a gentleman well qualified,°   10
  And wear your time and wits in those discourses.
CLERMONT The Locrian princes therefore were brave rulers:°
  For whosoever there came new from country
  And in the city asked 'What news?' was punished,
  Since commonly such brains are most delighted   15
  With innovations, gossips' tales, and mischiefs.°
  But as of lions it is said, and eagles,
  That when they go they draw their seres and talons°
  Close up, to shun rebating of their sharpness:°
  So our wit's sharpness, which we should employ   20
  In noblest knowledge, we should never waste
  In vile and vulgar admirations.°
RENEL 'Tis right—but who, save only you, performs it,
  And your great brother? Madam, where is he?
CHARLOTTE Gone a day since into the country's confines,   25
  To see their strength and readiness for service.
RENEL 'Tis well. His favour with the king hath made him
  Most worthily great, and live right royally.
CLERMONT Aye, would he would not do so. Honour never
  Should be esteemed with wise men as the price   30
  And value of their virtuous services,
  But as their sign or badge; for that bewrays
  More glory in the outward grace of goodness°

Than in the good itself, and then 'tis said:
'Who more joy takes that men his good advance   35
Than in the good itself does it by chance.'
CHARLOTTE My brother speaks all principle. What man
  Is moved with your soul, or hath such a thought
  In any rate of goodness?
CLERMONT   'Tis their fault.°
  We have examples of it, clear and many.   40
  Demetrius Phalerius, an orator°
  And (which not oft meet) a philosopher,
  So great in Athens grew that she erected
  Three hundred statues of him; of all which
  No rust nor length of time corrupted one,   45
  But in his lifetime all were overthrown.
  And Demades, that passed Demosthenes°
  For all extemporal orations,
  Erected many statues, which (he living)
  Were broke and melted into chamber pots.   50
  Many such ends have fallen on such proud honours,
  No more because the men on whom they fell
  Grew insolent and left their virtue's state
  Than for their hugeness that procured their hate;°
  And therefore little pomp in men most great   55
  Makes mightily and strongly to the guard°
  Of what they win by chance or just reward.
  Great and immodest braveries again,°
  Like statues much too high made for their bases,
  Are overturned as soon as given their places.°   60
        Enter a Messenger with a letter
MESSENGER Here is a letter, sir, delivered me
  Now at the foregate by a gentleman.°
CLERMONT What gentleman?
MESSENGER   He would not tell his name.
  He said he had not time enough to tell it
  And say the little rest he had to say.   65
CLERMONT That was a merry saying; he took measure
  Of his dear time like a most thrifty husband.°
        [*Reads the letter silently*]
CHARLOTTE What news?
CLERMONT   Strange ones, and fit for a novation,°
  Weighty, unheard of, mischievous enough.

RENEL Heaven shield! What are they?

CLERMONT   Read them, good my lord.°   70
  [*Gives the letter to Renel, who reads from it*]

RENEL 'You are betrayed into this country.' Monstrous!

CHARLOTTE How's that?

CLERMONT Read on.

RENEL 'Maillard, your brother's lieutenant, that yesterday invited
    you to see his musters, hath letters and strict charge from the king   75
    to apprehend you.'

CHARLOTTE To apprehend him?

RENEL 'Your brother absents himself of purpose.'

CLERMONT That's a sound one!°

CHARLOTTE That's a lie!   80

RENEL 'Get on your Scotch horse and retire to your strength;° you
    know where it is, and there it expects you. Believe this as° your
    best friend had sworn it. Fare well, if you will.° Anonymous.'
    What's that?

CLERMONT Without a name.   85

CHARLOTTE And all his notice, too, without all truth.°

CLERMONT So I conceive it, sister: I'll not wrong
    My well-known brother for Anonymous.

CHARLOTTE Some fool hath put this trick on you, yet more
    T' uncover your defect of spirit and valour,   90
    First shown in ling'ring my dear brother's wreak.°
    See what it is to give the envious world
    Advantage to diminish eminent virtue.
    Send him a challenge? Take a noble course
    To wreak a murder done so like a villain?   95

CLERMONT Shall we revenge a villainy with villainy?

CHARLOTTE Is it not equal?

CLERMONT   Shall we equal be°
    With villains? Is that your reason?

CHARLOTTE   Cowardice evermore°
    Flies to the shield of reason.

CLERMONT   Naught that is
    Approved by reason can be cowardice.   100

CHARLOTTE
    Dispute, when you should fight! Wrong, wreakless sleeping,
    Makes men die honourless: one borne, another°
    Leaps on our shoulders.

CLERMONT   We must wreak our wrongs

So as we take not more.
CHARLOTTE   One wreaked in time
     Prevents all other. Then shines virtue most   105
     When time is found for facts—and found, not lost.°
CLERMONT No time occurs to kings, much less to virtue;°
     Nor can we call it virtue that proceeds
     From vicious fury. I repent that ever
     (By any instigation in th' appearance   110
     My brother's spirit made, as I imagined)
     That e'er I yielded to revenge his murder.
     All worthy men should ever bring their blood
     To bear all ill, not to be wreaked with good.°
     Do ill for no ill: never private cause°   115
     Should take on it the part of public laws.
CHARLOTTE A D'Ambois bear in wrong so tame a spirit!
RENEL Madam, be sure there will be time enough
     For all the vengeance your great spirit can wish.
     The course yet taken is allowed by all,°   120
     Which being noble, and refused by th' earl,
     Now makes him worthy of your worst advantage;°
     And I have cast a project with the countess°
     To watch a time when all his wariest guards
     Shall not exempt him. Therefore give him breath;   125
     Sure death delayed is a redoubled death.
CLERMONT Good sister, trouble not yourself with this.
     Take other ladies' care; practice your face.°
     There's the chaste matron, Madam Perigot,
     Dwells not far hence; I'll ride and send her to you.   130
     She did live by retailing maidenheads°
     In her minority, but now she deals
     In wholesale altogether for the court.
     I tell you, she's the only fashionmonger
     For your complexion, powd'ring of your hair,   .   135
     Shadows, rebatoes, wires, tires, and such tricks,
     That Cambrai or, I think, the court affords.
     She shall attend you, sister, and with these
     Womanly practices employ your spirit;
     This other suits you not, nor fits the fashion.   140
     Though she be dear, lay't on, spare for no cost;°
     Ladies in these have all their bounties lost.°
RENEL Madam, you see his spirit will not check°

At any single danger, when it stands
Thus merrily firm against an host of men   145
Threatened to be [in] arms for his surprise.°
CHARLOTTE That's a mere bugbear, an impossible mock.°
If he, and him I bound by nuptial faith,
Had not been dull and drossy in performing
Wreak of the dear blood of my matchless brother,   150
What prince, what king, which of the desperat'st ruffians,
Outlaws in Arden, durst have tempted thus°
One of our blood and name, be 't true or false?
CLERMONT This is not caused by that: 'twill be as sure
As yet it is not, though this should be true.°   155
CHARLOTTE True? 'Tis past thought false!
CLERMONT   I suppose the worst,
Which far I am from thinking, and despise
The army now in battle that should act it.
CHARLOTTE I would not let my blood up to that thought°
But it should cost the dearest blood in France.   160
CLERMONT (kissing her) Sweet sister, far be both off as the fact
Of my feigned apprehension.
CHARLOTTE   I would once
Strip off my shame with my attire and try
If a poor woman, votist of revenge,°
Would not perform it with a precedent°   165
To all you bungling, foggy-spirited men.
But, for our birthright's honour, do not mention
One syllable of any word may go
To the begetting of an act so tender
And full of sulphur as this letter's truth.°   170
It comprehends so black a circumstance,°
Not to be named, that but to form one thought
It is, or can be so, would make me mad.
Come, my lord, you and I will fight this dream
Out at the chess.
RENEL   Most gladly, worthiest lady.   175
        Exeunt Charlotte and Renel. Enter a Messenger
MESSENGER Sir, my Lord Governor's lieutenant prays
Access to you.
CLERMONT   Himself alone?
MESSENGER   Alone, sir.
CLERMONT Attend him in.

Exit Messenger
                              Now comes this plot to trial.
I shall discern (if it be true as rare)°
Some sparks will fly from his dissembling eyes.   180
I'll sound his depth.
     Enter Maillard with the Messenger
MAILLARD   Honour, and all things noble.
CLERMONT As much to you, good captain. What's th'affair?°
MAILLARD Sir, the poor honour we can add to all
    Your studied welcome to this martial place°
    In presentation of what strength consists°   185
    My lord your brother's government is ready.
    I have made all his troops and companies
    Advance and put themselves ranged in battalia
    That you may see both how well armed they are,
    How strong is every troop and company,   190
    How ready, and how well prepared for service.
CLERMONT And must they take me?
MAILLARD [*averts his face*]   Take you, sir? O, heaven!°
MESSENGER [*aside to Clermont*]
    Believe it, sir; his count'nance changed in turning.
MAILLARD What do you mean, sir?
CLERMONT   If you have charged them,
    You being charged yourself, to apprehend me,   195
    Turn not your face: throw not your looks about so.
MAILLARD Pardon me, sir. You amaze me to conceive
    From whence our wills to honour you should turn
    To such dishonour of my lord your brother.
    Dare I, without him, undertake your taking?   200
CLERMONT Why not? by your direct charge from the king?
MAILLARD By my charge from the king? Would he so much
    Disgrace my lord, his own lieutenant here,
    To give me his command without his forfeit?°
CLERMONT Acts that are done by kings are not asked why.   205
    I'll not dispute the case, but I will search you.
MAILLARD Search me? for what?
CLERMONT   For letters.
MAILLARD   I beseech you,
    Do not admit one thought of such a shame
    To a commander.
CLERMONT   Go to, I must do't.

CLERMONT   Stand and be searched; you know me.
MAILLARD [*avoiding him*]   You forget   210
    What 'tis to be a captain, and yourself.
CLERMONT   Stand, or I vow to heaven I'll make you lie
    Never to rise more.
MAILLARD   If a man be mad,
    Reason must bear him.
CLERMONT   So coy to be searched?°
MAILLARD   'Sdeath, sir, use a captain like a carrier!   215
CLERMONT   Come, be not furious; when I have done
    You shall make such a carrier of me
    If 't be your pleasure: you're my friend, I know,
    And so am bold with you.
MAILLARD   You'll nothing find
    Where nothing is.
CLERMONT   Swear you have nothing.   220
MAILLARD   Nothing you seek, I swear. I beseech you,
    Know I desired this out of great affection,
    To th' end my lord may know out of your witness°
    His forces are not in so bad estate
    As he esteemed them lately in your hearing: 225
    For which he would not trust me with the confines,
    But went himself to witness their estate.
CLERMONT   I heard him make that reason, and am sorry
    I had no thought of it before I made
    Thus bold with you, since 'tis such rhubarb to you.°   230
    I'll therefore search no more. If you are charged
    (By letters from the king, or otherwise)
    To apprehend me, never spice it more°
    With forced terms of your love, but say. I yield;
    Hold, take my sword, here; I forgive thee freely;   235
    Take, do thine office.
MAILLARD   'Sfoot, you make m' a hangman:°
    By all my faith to you, there's no such thing.
CLERMONT   Your faith to me?
MAILLARD   My faith to God; all's one:°
    Who hath no faith to men to God hath none.
CLERMONT   In that sense I accept your oath, and thank you.   240
    I gave my word to go, and I will go.
        Exit Clermont
MAILLARD   I'll watch you whither. .

Exit Maillard

MESSENGER   If he goes, he proves
  How vain are men's foreknowledges of things,
  When heaven strikes blind their powers of note and use,°
  And makes their way to ruin seem more right°   245
  Than that which safety opens to their sight.
  Cassandra's prophecy had no more profit
  With Troy's blind citizens when she foretold
  Troy's ruin: which, succeeding, made her use°
  This sacred inclamation: 'God', said she,   250
  'Would have me utter things uncredited,°
  For which now they approve what I presaged;°
  They count me wise that said before I raged.'°
     [*Exit*]

[3.3]

Enter Chalon with two Soldiers

CHALON Come, soldiers, you are downwards fit for lackeys.°
  Give me your pieces, and take you these coats°
  To make you complete footmen, in whose forms°
  You must be complete soldiers: you two only
  Stand for our army.
FIRST SOLDIER   That were much.
CHALON   'Tis true: 5
  You two must do, or enter, what our army°
  Is now in field for.
SECOND SOLDIER   I see then our guerdon
  Must be the deed itself, 'twill be such honour.
CHALON What fight soldiers most for?
FIRST SOLDIER   Honour only.
CHALON Yet here are crowns beside.
    [*Chalon gives the soldiers money*]
BOTH   We thank you, captain.   10
    [*The soldiers change into the lackeys' coats*]
SECOND SOLDIER Now, sir, how show we?
CHALON   As you should at all parts.°
  Go now to Clermont D'Ambois and inform him
  Two battles are set ready in his honour,°

And stay his presence only for their signal
When they shall join; and that, t'attend him hither°   15
Like one we so much honour, we have sent him—
FIRST SOLDIER Us two in person.
CHALON   Well, sir, say it so.
And having brought him to the field, when I
Fall in with him, saluting, get you both
Of one side of his horse and pluck him down,   20
And I with th' ambush laid will second you.
FIRST SOLDIER Nay, we shall lay on hands of too much strength
To need your secondings.
SECOND SOLDIER   I hope we shall.
Two are enough to encounter Hercules.°
CHALON 'Tis well said, worthy soldiers; haste, and haste him.°   25
    [*Exeunt*]

[3.4]

Enter Clermont, Maillard close following him
CLERMONT [*to himself*] My Scotch horse to their army—
MAILLARD   Please you, sir?
CLERMONT 'Sdeath, you're passing diligent.
MAILLARD   Of my soul,
'Tis only in my love to honour you
With what would grace the king; but since I see
You still sustain a jealous eye on me,°   5
I'll go before.
CLERMONT   'Tis well; I'll come; my hand.
MAILLARD Your hand, sir! Come, your word, your choice be used.°
    Exit [*Maillard*]
CLERMONT I had an aversation to this voyage
When first my brother moved it, and have found
That native power in me was never vain,°   10
Yet now neglected it. I wonder much
At my inconstancy in these decrees
I every hour set down to guide my life.
When Homer made Achilles passionate,°
Wrathful, revengeful, and insatiate   15
In his affections, what man will deny

He did compose it all of industry°
To let men see that men of most renown,
Strong'st, noblest, fairest, if they set not down
Decrees within them for disposing these—°   20
Of judgement, resolution, uprightness,
And certain knowledge of their use and ends—
Mishap and misery no less extends
To their destruction, with all that they prized,°
Than to the poorest and the most despised?   25
    Enter Renel
RENEL Why, how now, friend? Retired? Take heed you prove not
Dismayed with this strange fortune: all observe you.
Your government's as much marked as the king's.°
What said a friend to Pompey?
CLERMONT   What?
RENEL   'The people°
Will never know, unless in death thou try,   30
That thou know'st how to bear adversity.'
CLERMONT I shall approve how vile I value fear°
Of death at all times; but to be too rash,
Without both will and care to shun the worst
(It being in power to do, well and with cheer),   35
Is stupid negligence and worse than fear.
RENEL Suppose this true now.
CLERMONT   No, I cannot do't.
My sister truly said there hung a tale
Of circumstance so black on that supposure
That to sustain it thus abhorred our mettle.°   40
And I can shun it too, in spite of all,
Not going to field; and there, too, being so mounted
As I will, since I go.
RENEL   You will then go?
CLERMONT I am engaged both in my word and hand.
But this is it that makes me thus retired   45
To call myself t'account how this affair
Is to be managed if the worst should chance,°
With which I note how dangerous it is
For any man to press beyond the place
To which his birth, or means, or knowledge ties him;   50
For my part, though of noble birth, my birthright°
Had little left it, and I know 'tis better

To live with little, and to keep within
A man's own strength still, and in man's true end,
Than run a mixed course. Good and bad hold never°   55
Anything common: you can never find°
Things' outward care, but you neglect your mind.°
God hath the whole world perfect made and free,
His parts to th' use of th' All; men then that [be]°
Parts of that All must, as the general sway   60
Of that importeth, willingly obey°
In everything without their power to change.°
He that, unpleased to hold his place, will range°
Can in no other be contained that's fit,
And so resisting th' All, is crushed with it.   65
But he that knowing how divine a frame°
The whole world is, and of it all can name
(Without self-flattery) no part so divine
As he himself, and therefore will confine
Freely his whole powers in his proper part,°   70
Goes on most god-like. He that strives t'invert°
The Universal's course with his poor way,
Not only dust-like shivers with the sway,°
But, crossing God in his great work, all earth°
Bears not so cursèd and so damned a birth.°   75

RENEL Go, on, I'll take no care what comes of you;
Heaven will not see it ill, howe'er it show:
But the pretext to see these battles ranged°
Is much your honour.

CLERMONT   As the world esteems it.
But to decide that, you make me remember   80
An accident of high and noble note,
And fits the subject of my late discourse
Of holding on our free and proper way.
I overtook, coming from Italy,
In Germany, a great and famous earl°   85
Of England, the most goodly-fashioned man
I ever saw, from head to foot in form
Rare and most absolute. He had a face
Like one of the most ancient honoured Romans,
From whence his noblest family was derived;°   90
He was beside of spirit passing great,°
Valiant, and learn'd, and liberal as the sun,

Spoke and writ sweetly, or of learnèd subjects,°
Or of the discipline of public weals;°
And 'twas the Earl of Oxford; and being offered   95
At that time by Duke Casimir the view°
Of his right royal army then in field,
Refused it, and no foot was moved to stir
Out of his own free fore-determined course.
I, wond'ring at it, asked for it his reason,   100
It being an offer so much for his honour.
He, all acknowledging, said 'twas not fit
To take those honours that one cannot quit.
RENEL 'Twas answered like the man you have described.
CLERMONT And yet he cast it only in the way,   105
To stay and serve the world. Nor did it fit°
His own true estimate how much it weighed,
For he despised it, and esteemed it freer
To keep his own way straight, and swore that he
Had rather make away his whole estate   110
In things that crossed the vulgar, than he would°
Be frozen up, stiff (like a Sir John Smith,°
His countryman) in common nobles' fashions,
Affecting, as the end of noblesse were
Those servile observations.
RENEL   It was strange.°   115
CLERMONT O, 'tis a vexing sight to see a man,
Out of his way, stalk proud, as he were in:°
Out of his way to be officious,
Observant, wary, serious, and grave,
Fearful, and passionate, insulting, raging,   120
Labour with iron flails to thresh down feathers
Flitting in air.
RENEL   What one considers this,
Of all that are thus out? or once endeavours,°
Erring, to enter on man's right-hand path?°
CLERMONT These are too grave for brave wits: give them toys;°   125
Labour bestowed on these is harsh and thriftless.
'If you would consul be', says one, 'of Rome,
You must be watching, starting out of sleeps,
Every way whisking, glorifying plebeians,
Kissing patricians' hands; rot at their doors;°   130
Speak and do basely; every day bestow

Gifts and observance upon one or other:
And what's th' event of all? Twelve rods before thee;°
Three or four times sit 'fore the whole tribunal;°
Exhibit Circene games; make public feasts:°   135
And for these idle outward things,' says he,
'Wouldst thou lay on such cost, toil, spend thy spirits?
And, to be void of perturbation,°
For constancy (sleep when thou wouldst have sleep,°
Wake when thou wouldst wake, fear naught, vex for naught),°   140
No pains wilt thou bestow? no cost? no thought?'
RENEL What should I say? As good consort with you
As with an angel; I could hear you ever.
CLERMONT Well, in, my lord, and spend time with my sister,
And keep her from the field with all endeavour;°   145
The soldiers love her so, and she so madly
Would take my apprehension, if it chance,°
That blood would flow in rivers.
RENEL   Heaven forbid,
And all with honour your arrival speed.°
        Exit [Renel]. Enter Messenger with two Soldiers like° Lackeys
MESSENGER Here are two lackeys, sir, have message to you.   150
CLERMONT What is your message? and from whom, my friends?
FIRST SOLDIER From the lieutenant colonel and the captains,
Who sent us to inform you that the battles
Stand ready ranged, expecting but your presence°
To be their honoured signal when to join,   155
And we are charged to run by and attend you.
CLERMONT I come. I pray you see my running horse
Brought to the back gate to me.
MESSENGER   Instantly.
        Exit Messenger
CLERMONT Chance what can chance me, well or ill is equal
In my acceptance since I joy in neither,°   160
But go with sway of all the world together.
In all successes Fortune and the day
To me alike are: I am fixed, be she
Never so fickle, and will there repose
Far past the reach of any die she throws.°   165
        Exit [Clermont] with the soldiers

[4.1]

*Alarm° within. Excursions over the stage,° the [Soldiers
disguised like] Lackeys running, Maillard following them*

MAILLARD Villains, not hold him when ye had him down?

FIRST SOLDIER Who can hold lightning? 'Sdeath, a man as well
  Might catch a cannon bullet in his mouth
  And spit it in your hands as take and hold him.

MAILLARD Pursue, enclose him! stand or fall on him,   5
  And ye may take him. 'Sdeath, they make him guards!°

      *Exit [Maillard with the soldiers]. Alarm still, and enter [two
      more Soldiers, followed by] Chalon*

CHALON Stand, cowards, stand! Strike! Send your bullets at him!

FIRST SOLDIER We came to entertain him, sir, for honour.°

SECOND SOLDIER Did ye not say so?

CHALON   Slaves, he is a traitor.
  Command the horse troops to overrun the traitor!   10

      *Exeunt [Chalon and the Soldiers]. Shouts within. Alarm still,
      and chambers° shot off. Then enter Aumale*

AUMALE What spirit breathes thus in this more than man,
  Turns flesh to air possessed, and in a storm°
  Tears men about the field like autumn leaves?
  He turned wild lightning in the lackey's hands,
  Who, though their sudden violent twitch unhorsed him,   15
  Yet when he bore himself, their saucy fingers°
  Flew as too hot off, as he had been fire.
  The ambush then made in, through all whose force
  He drave as if a fierce and fire-given cannon
  Had spit his iron vomit out amongst them.   20
  The battles then in two half-moons enclosed him—
  In which he showed as if he were the light°
  And they but earth—who, wond'ring what he was,
  Shrunk their steel horns and gave him glorious pass.°
  And as a great shot from a town besieged   25
  At foes before it flies forth black and roaring,
  But they too far, and that with weight oppressed,°
  As if disdaining earth, doth only graze,
  Strike earth, and up again into the air,
  Again sinks to it, and again doth rise,   30

And keeps such strength that when it softliest moves,°
It piecemeal shivers any let it proves:°
So flew brave Clermont forth till breath forsook him,
Then fell to earth, and yet (sweet man) even then
His spirit's convulsions made him bound again   35
Past all their reaches, till, all motion spent,°
His fixed eyes cast a blaze of such disdain
All stood and stared and untouched let him lie,
As something sacred fallen out of the sky.°
        A cry within
O, now some rude hand hath laid hold on him.   40
        Enter Maillard, Chalon leading Clermont, Captains and
        Soldiers following
See, prisoner led, with his bands honoured more°
Than all the freedom he enjoyed before.
MAILLARD At length we have you, sir.
CLERMONT   You have much joy, too,
    I made you sport yet; but I pray you tell me,
    Are not you perjured?
MAILLARD   No: I swore for the king.   45
CLERMONT Yet perjury, I hope, is perjury.
MAILLARD But thus forswearing is not perjury.
    You are no politician: not a fault,
    How foul soever done for private ends,
    Is fault in us sworn to the public good.   50
    We never can be of the damnèd crew;°
    We may impolitic ourselves (as 'twere)°
    Into the kingdom's body politic,
    Whereof indeed we're members: you misterm 's.
CLERMONT The things are yet the same.   55
MAILLARD 'Tis nothing so, the property is altered;°
    Y'are no lawyer. Or say that oath and oath
    Are still the same in number, yet their species
    Differ extremely, as, for flat example,°
    When politic widows try men for their turn°   60
    Before they wed them, they are harlots then,
    But when they wed them, they are honest women:
    So private men, when they forswear, betray,
    Are perjured treachers, but being public once,°
    That is, sworn, married, to the public good—   65

CLERMONT Are married women public?
MAILLARD   Public good;°
  For marriage makes them, being the public good,°
  And could not be without them. So I say
  Men public, that is, being sworn or married
  To the public good, being one body made   70
  With the realm's body politic, are no more
  Private, nor can be perjured, though forsworn,
  More than a widow, married for the act
  Of generation, is for that an harlot,°
  Because for that she was so, being unmarried: 75
  An argument *a paribus*.
CHALON   'Tis a shrewd one.°
CLERMONT 'Who hath no faith to men to God hath none':
  Retain you that, sir? who said so?
MAILLARD   'Twas I.°
CLERMONT Thy own tongue damn thy infidelity.
  But, captains all, you know me nobly born: 80
  Use ye t'assault such men as I with lackeys?°
CHALON They are no lackeys, sir, but soldiers
  Disguised in lackeys' coats.
FIRST SOLDIER   Sir, we have seen
  The enemy.
CLERMONT   Avaunt, ye rascals, hence!
MAILLARD Now leave your coats.
CLERMONT   Let me not see them more.°   85
     [Exeunt Soldiers]
AUMALE I grieve that virtue lives so undistinguished
  From vice in any ill; and though the crown°
  Of sovereign law, she should be yet her footstool,
  Subject to censure, all the shame and pain
  Of all her rigour.
CLERMONT   Yet false policy   90
  Would cover all, being like offenders hid
  That (after notice taken where they hide)
  The more they crouch and stir, the more are spied.
AUMALE I wonder how this chanced you.
CLERMONT   Some informer,
  Bloodhound to mischief, usher to the hangman,   95
  Thirsty of honour for some huge state act,°

Perceiving me great with the worthy Guise°
(And he, I know not why, held dangerous),°
Made me the desperate organ of his danger—°
Only with that poor colour. 'Tis the common   100
And more than whore-like trick of treachery
And vermin bred to rapine and to ruin,
For which this fault is still to be accused:
Since good arts fail, crafts and deceits are used.°
If it be other, never pity me.°   105
AUMALE Sir, we are glad, believe it, and have hope
    The king will so conceit it.
CLERMONT   At his pleasure.
    In meantime, what's your will, Lord Lieutenant?
MAILLARD To leave your own horse and to mount the trumpet's.°
CLERMONT It shall be done. This heavily prevents°   110
    My purposed recreation in these parts;
    Which now I think on, let me beg you, sir,
    To lend me some one captain of your troops
    To bear the message of my hapless service°
    And misery to my most noble mistress,   115
    Countess of Cambrai, to whose house this night
    I promised my repair, and know most truly,
    With all the ceremonies of her favour,
    She sure expects me.
MAILLARD   Think you now on that?
CLERMONT On that, sir? Aye, and that so worthily   120
    That if the king, in spite of your great service,
    Would send me instant promise of enlargement,
    Condition I would set this message by,°
    I would not take it, but had rather die.
AUMALE Your message shall be done, sir: I myself   125
    Will be for you a messenger of ill.
CLERMONT I thank you, sir, and doubt not yet to live
    To quite your kindness.
AUMALE   Mean space, use your spirit°
    And knowledge for the cheerful patience°
    Of this so strange and sudden consequence.°   130
CLERMONT Good sir, believe that no particular torture
    Can force me from my glad obedience
    To anything the high and general Cause,°
    To match with His whole fabric, hath ordained;°

And know ye all (though far from all your aims,   135
Yet worth them all and all men's endless studies)
That in this one thing all the discipline
Of manners and of manhood is contained:°
A man to join himself with th' Universe°
In his main sway, and make (in all things fit)   140
One with that All, and go on round as it,
Not plucking from the whole his wretched part,
And into straits, or into naught revert,°
Wishing the complete Universe might be
Subject to such a rag of it as he;   145
But to consider great Necessity
All things, as well refract as voluntary,°
Reduceth to the prime celestial Cause,°
Which he that yields to with a man's applause,°
And cheek by cheek goes, crossing it no breath,°   150
But, like God's image, follows to the death:
That man is truly wise, and everything
(Each cause, and every part distinguishing)
In nature with enough art understands;°
And that full glory merits at all hands   155
That doth the whole world at all parts adorn,
And appertains to one celestial born.°
        Exeunt

[4.2]

        Enter Baligny, Renel
BALIGNY So foul a scandal never man sustained,°
    Which, caused by th' king, is rude and tyrannous:
    Give me a place, and my lieutenant make
    The filler of it!
RENEL   I should never look
    For better of him; never trust a man   5
    For any justice that is rapt with pleasure,
    To order arms well that makes smocks his ensigns°
    And his whole government's sails: you heard of late°
    He had the four-and-twenty ways of venery°
    Done all before him.

BALIGNY   'Twas abhorred and beastly.   10
RENEL 'Tis more than Nature's mighty hand can do
    To make one human and a lecher too.
    Look how a wolf doth like a dog appear,
    So like a friend is an adulterer:
    Voluptuaries and these belly-gods°   15
    No more true men are than so many toads.
    A good man happy is a common good;
    Vile men advanced live of the common blood.°
BALIGNY Give and then take, like children!
RENEL   Bounties are°
    As soon repented as they happen rare.   20
BALIGNY What should kings do, and men of eminent places,°
    But, as they gather, sow gifts to the graces?°
    And where they have given, rather give again
    (Being given for virtue) than like babes and fools
    Take and repent gifts? Why are wealth and power?°   25
RENEL Power and wealth move to tyranny, not bounty;
    The merchant for his wealth is swoll'n in mind°
    When yet the chief lord of it is the wind.°
BALIGNY That may so chance to our state-merchants too:
    Something performed that hath not far to go.°   30
RENEL That's the main point, my lord; insist on that.
BALIGNY But doth this fire rage further? hath it taken
    The tender tinder of my wife's sere blood?°
    Is she so passionate?
RENEL   So wild, so mad
    She cannot live and this unwreaked sustain.   35
    The woes are bloody that in women reign:
    The Sicile gulf keeps fear in less degree,°
    There is no tiger not more tame than she.
BALIGNY There is no looking home, then?
RENEL   Home! Medea°
    With all her herbs, charms, thunders, lightnings,   40
    Made not her presence and black haunts more dreadful.
BALIGNY Come, to the king; if he reform not all,°
    Mark the event: none stand where that must fall.
            Exeunt

[4.3]

Enter Countess, Riova, and an Usher
USHER Madam, a captain come from Clermont D'Ambois
  Desires access to you.
COUNTESS   And not himself?
USHER No, madam.
COUNTESS   That's not well. Attend him in.
    Exit Usher
  The last hour of his promise now run out,
  And he break? Some brack's in the frame of nature°   5
  That forceth his breach.
    Enter Usher and Aumale
AUMALE   Save your ladyship.
COUNTESS All welcome! Come you from my worthy servant?
AUMALE Aye, madam, and confer such news from him—°
COUNTESS Such news? What news?
AUMALE News that I wish some other had the charge of.°   10
COUNTESS O, what charge? What news?
AUMALE Your ladyship must use some patience
  Or else I cannot do him that desire°
  He urged with such affection to your graces.
COUNTESS Do it, for heaven's love do it! If you serve   15
  His kind desires I will have patience.
  Is he in health?
AUMALE   He is.
COUNTESS   Why, that's the ground°
  Of all the good estate we hold in earth;
  All our ill built upon that is no more
  Than we may bear, and should; express it all.   20
AUMALE Madam, 'tis only this: his liberty—
COUNTESS His liberty! Without that, health is nothing.
  Why live I but to ask, in doubt of that,
  Is that bereft him?
AUMALE   You'll again prevent me.
COUNTESS No more, I swear; I must hear, and together   25
  Come all my misery! I'll hold though I burst.°
AUMALE Then, madam, thus it fares: he was invited
  By way of honour to him, to take view
  Of all the powers his brother Baligny

Hath in his government; which ranged in battles,   30
Maillard, lieutenant to the Governor,
Having received strict letters from the king
To train him to the musters and betray him°
To their surprise, which, with Chalon in chief
And other captains (all the field put hard   35
By his incredible valour for his 'scape),
They haplessly and guiltlessly performed,°
And to Bastille he's now led prisoner.
COUNTESS What change is here? How are my hopes prevented!
O my most faithful servant, thou betrayed!   40
Will kings make treason lawful? Is society
(To keep which only kings were first ordained)°
Less broke in breaking faith 'twixt friend and friend
Than 'twixt the king and subject? Let them fear:
Kings' precedents in license lack no danger.°   45
Kings are compared to gods and should be like them,
Full in all right, in naught superfluous,
Nor nothing straining past right for their right:°
Reign justly and reign safely. Policy
Is but a guard corrupted, and a way   50
Ventured in deserts without guide or path.
Kings punish subjects' errors with their own.
Kings are like archers, and their subjects, shafts;
For as when archers let their arrows fly,
They call to them and bid them fly or fall,   55
As if 'twere in the free power of the shaft
To fly or fall, when only 'tis the strength,
Straight shooting, compass, given it by the archer,°
That makes it hit or miss; and doing either,
He's to be praised or blamed, and not the shaft: 60
So kings to subjects crying, 'Do, do not this,'
Must to them by their own example's strength,
The straightness of their acts, and equal compass
Give subjects power t'obey them in the like;°
Not shoot them forth with faulty aim and strength   65
And lay the fault in them for flying amiss.
AUMALE But, for your servant, I dare swear him guiltless.°
COUNTESS He would not for his kingdom traitor be:
His laws are not so true to him as he.°
O knew I how to free him, by way forced   70

Through all their army, I would fly and do it.
And had I of my courage and resolve
But ten such more, they should not all retain him.
But I will never die before I give
Maillard an hundred slashes with a sword,   75
Chalon an hundred breaches with a pistol.
They could not all have taken Clermont D'Ambois
Without their treachery; he had bought his bands out°
With their slave bloods. But he was credulous;
He would believe since he would be believed: 80
Your noblest natures are most credulous.
Who gives no trust, all trust is apt to break;
Hate like hell-mouth who think not what they speak.°

AUMALE Well, madam, I must tender my attendance
On him again. Will 't please you to return   85
No service to him by me?

COUNTESS   Fetch me straight°
My little cabinet.

    Exit Riova
              'Tis little, tell him,°
And much too little for his matchless love:
But as in him the worths of many men
Are close contracted,

    Enter Riova [with the cabinet]
              so in this are jewels°   90
Worth many cabinets. Here, with this, good sir,
Commend my kindest service to my servant.

    [Gives the cabinet to Aumale]
Thank him with all my comforts, and, in them,°
With all my life for them—all sent from him
In his remembrance of me, and true love;   95
And look you tell him, tell him how I lie

    She kneels down at his feet
Prostrate at feet of his accursed misfortune,
Pouring my tears out, which shall ever fall
Till I have poured for him out eyes and all.

AUMALE O, madam, this will kill him. Comfort you   100
With full assurance of his quick acquittal;
Be not so passionate: rise, cease your tears.

COUNTESS Then must my life cease. Tears are all the vent
My life hath to 'scape death; tears please me better

Than all life's comforts, being the natural seed   105
Of hearty sorrow. As a tree fruit bears,
So doth an undissembled sorrow tears.
  He raises her and leads her out.
USHER This might have been before and saved much charge.°
  Exit

[4.4]

  Enter Henry, Guise, Baligny, Espernon, Soisson, Pericot with
  pen, ink, and paper
GUISE Now, sir, I hope your much abused eyes see,
 In my word for my Clermont, what a villain
 He was that whispered in your jealous ear
 His own black treason in suggesting Clermont's,
 Coloured with nothing but being great with me.°   5
 Sign then this writ for his delivery;
 Your hand was never urged with worthier boldness.
 Come, pray, sir, sign it: why should kings be prayed
 To acts of justice? 'Tis a reverence°
 Makes them despised and shows they stick and tire   10
 In what their free powers should be hot as fire.°
HENRY Well, take your will, sir; [*aside*] I'll have mine ere long.—
 But wherein is this Clermont such a rare one?
GUISE In his most gentle and unwearied mind
 Rightly to virtue framed; in very nature;   15
 In his most firm inexorable spirit
 To be removed from anything he chooseth
 For worthiness, or bear the least persuasion
 To what is base, or fitteth not his object;°
 In his contempt of riches and of greatness,   20
 In estimation of th' idolatrous vulgar;°
 His scorn of all things servile and ignoble,
 Though they could gain him never such advancement;
 His liberal kind of speaking what is truth°
 In spite of temporizing; the great rising°   25
 And learning of his soul, so much the more
 Against ill Fortune (as she set herself
 Sharp against him, or would present most hard)°

To shun the malice of her deadliest charge;°
His detestation of his special friends   30
When he perceived their tyrannous will to do,°
Or their abjection basely to sustain°
Any injustice that they could revenge;
The flexibility of his most anger,°
Even in the main career and fury of it,   35
When any object of desertful pity
Offers itself to him; his sweet disposure,
As much abhorring to behold as do
Any unnatural and bloody action;
His just contempt of jesters, parasites,   40
Servile observers, and polluted tongues.°
In short, this Senecal man is found in him:°
He may with heaven's immortal powers compare,
To whom the day and fortune equal are.°
Come fair or foul, whatever chance can fall,   45
Fixed in himself, he still is one to all.°
HENRY Shows he to others thus?
ALL   To all that know him.
HENRY And apprehend I this man for a traitor?
GUISE These are your Machiavellian villains,°
     Your bastard Teucers that, their mischiefs done,°   50
     Run to your shield for shelter, Cacusses°
     That cut their too large murderous thieveries
     To their dens' length still. Woe be to that state
     Where treachery guards, and ruin makes men great.
HENRY Go, take my letters for him and release him.   55
ALL Thanks to your Highness! Ever live your Highness!
          Exeunt [all except Baligny]
BALIGNY Better a man were buried quick than live°
     A property for state, and spoil to thrive.°
          Exit

[4.5]

Enter Clermont, Maillard, Chalon, with Soldiers
MAILLARD We joy you take a chance so ill, so well.°
CLERMONT Who ever saw me differ in acceptance

Of either fortune?
CHALON   What, love bad like good?
  How should one learn that?
CLERMONT   To love nothing outward
  Or not within our own powers to command,   5
  And so being sure of everything we love,
  Who cares to lose the rest? If any man
  Would neither live nor die in his free choice,
  But as he sees Necessity will have it
  (Which if he would resist, he strives in vain),   10
  What can come near him, that he doth not well?°
  And if in worst events his will be done,
  How can the best be better? all is one.
MAILLARD Methinks 'tis pretty.
CLERMONT   Put no difference°
  If you have this, or not this; but as children   15
  Playing at quoits ever regard their game
  And care not for their quoits, so let a man
  The things themselves that touch him not esteem,
  But his free power in well disposing them.
CHALON Pretty, from toys!
CLERMONT   Methinks this double distich   20
  Seems prettily too to stay superfluous longings:°
  'Not to have want, what riches doth exceed?
  Not to be subject, what superior thing?
  He that to naught aspires doth nothing need;
  Who breaks no law is subject to no king.'   25
MAILLARD This goes to mine ear well, I promise you.
CHALON O, but 'tis passing hard to stay one thus.°
CLERMONT 'Tis so, rank custom raps men so beyond it.°
  And as 'tis hard so well men's doors to bar
  To keep the cat out, and th' adulterer;°   30
  So 'tis as hard to curb affections so
  We let in naught to make them overflow.°
  And as of Homer's verses many critics°
  On those stand of which Time's old moth hath eaten°
  The first or last feet, and the perfect parts°   35
  Of his unmatchèd poem sink beneath,°
  With upright gasping and sloth dull as death:°
  So the unprofitable things of life,
  And those we cannot compass, we affect;

All that doth profit, and we have, neglect;   40
Like covetous and basely getting men°
That, gathering much, use never what they keep,
But for the least they lose, extremely weep.

MAILLARD This pretty talking and our horses walking
Down this steep hill spends time with equal profit.   45

CLERMONT 'Tis well bestowed on ye! meat and men sick
Agree like this and you: and yet even this°
Is th' end of all skill, power, wealth, all that is.

CHALON I long to hear, sir, how your mistress takes this.

Enter Aumale with a cabinet

MAILLARD We soon shall know it; see Aumale returned.   50

AUMALE Ease to your bands, sir.

CLERMONT   Welcome, worthy friend.°

CHALON How took his noblest mistress your sad message?

AUMALE As great rich men take sudden poverty.
I never witnessed a more noble love,
Nor a more ruthful sorrow: I well wished   55
Some other had been master of my message.

MAILLARD Y'are happy, sir, in all things, but this one
Of your unhappy apprehension.

CLERMONT This is to me, compared with her much moan,°
As one tear is to her whole passion.   60

AUMALE Sir, she commends her kindest service to you,
And this rich cabinet.

CHALON   O happy man,
This may enough hold to redeem your bands.°

CLERMONT These clouds, I doubt not, will be soon blown over.

Enter Baligny with Clermont's discharge; Renel, and others

AUMALE Your hope is just and happy; see, sir, both   65
In both the looks of these.

BALIGNY   Here's a discharge
For this your prisoner, my good Lord Lieutenant.°

MAILLARD Alas, sir, I usurp that style enforced,°
And hope you know it was not my aspiring.

BALIGNY Well, sir, my wrong aspired past all men's hopes.   70

MAILLARD I sorrow for it, sir.

RENEL   You see, sir, there
Your prisoner's discharge authentical.

MAILLARD It is, sir, and I yield it him with gladness.

BALIGNY Brother, I brought you down to much good purpose.°

CLERMONT Repeat not that, sir; the amends makes all.   75
RENEL I joy in it, my best and worthiest friend.
    O, y'ave a princely fautor of the Guise.
BALIGNY I think I did my part too.
RENEL   Well, sir, all
    Is in the issue well—and, worthiest friend,°
       [*Giving Clermont letters*]
    Here's from your friend, the Guise; here from the countess,°   80
    Your brother's mistress, the contents whereof
    I know, and must prepare you now to please°
    Th' unrested spirit of your slaughtered brother,
    If it be true (as you imagined once)
    His apparition showed it. The complot°   85
    Is now laid sure betwixt us; therefore haste
    Both to your great friend (who hath some use weighty°
    For your repair to him) and to the countess,
    Whose satisfaction is no less important.
CLERMONT I see all and will haste as it importeth.   90
    [*To Aumale*] And, good friend, since I must delay a little
    My wished attendance on my noblest mistress,
    Excuse me to her, with return of this°
    And endless protestation of my service;
    And now become as glad a messenger   95
    As you were late a woeful.
AUMALE   Happy change!
    I ever will salute thee with my service.
       Exit [*Aumale*]
BALIGNY Yet more news, brother. The late jesting Monsieur
    Makes now your brother's dying prophecy equal°
    At all parts, being dead as he presaged.   100
RENEL Heaven shield the Guise from seconding that truth°
    With what he likewise prophesied on him.
CLERMONT It hath enough. 'Twas graced with truth in one;°
    To th' other, falsehood and confusion!
    Lead to th' court, sir.
BALIGNY   You I'll lead no more;   105
    It was too ominous and foul before.
       Exeunt

[5.1]

The Ghost of Bussy ascends°

GHOST Up from the chaos of eternal night
　　(To which the whole digestion of the world°
　　Is now returning), once more I ascend
　　And bide the cold damp of this piercing air°
　　To urge the justice whose almighty word　　　　　5
　　Measures the bloody acts of impious men
　　With equal penance, who in th' act itself
　　Includes th' infliction, which like chainèd shot°
　　Batter together still; though as the thunder°
　　Seems, by men's duller hearing than their sight,　　10
　　To break a great time after lightning forth,
　　Yet both at one time tear the labouring cloud,
　　So men think penance of their ills is slow,
　　Though th' ill and penance still together go.
　　Reform, ye ignorant men, your manless lives,　　　15
　　Whose laws, ye think, are nothing but your lusts;
　　When leaving, but for supposition sake,°
　　The body of felicity, religion°
　　(Set in the midst of Christendom, and her head
　　Cleft to her bosom, one half one way swaying,°　　20
　　Another th' other), all the Christian world
　　And all her laws, whose observation°
　　Stands upon faith, above the power of reason—
　　Leaving (I say) all these, this might suffice
　　To fray ye from your vicious swinge in ill　　　　25
　　And set you more on fire to do more good:
　　That since the world (as which of you denies?)
　　Stands by proportion, all may thence conclude°
　　That all the joints and nerves sustaining nature
　　As well may break, and yet the world abide,　　　30
　　As any one good unrewarded die,
　　Or any one ill 'scape his penalty.°
　　　　The Ghost stands close.° *Enter Guise, Clermont*

GUISE Thus, friend, thou seest how all good men would thrive,
　　Did not the good thou prompt'st me with prevent°
　　The jealous ill pursuing them in others.　　　　　35

But now thy dangers are dispatched, note mine:°
Hast thou not heard of that admirèd voice°
That at the barricadoes spake to me°
(No person seen), 'Let's lead my lord to Rheims'?°
CLERMONT Nor could you learn the person?
GUISE   By no means.   40
CLERMONT 'Twas but your fancy, then, a waking dream.
　　For as in sleep, which binds both th' outward senses
　　And the sense common too, th' imagining power°
　　(Stirred up by forms hid in the memory's store,
　　Or by the vapours of o'erflowing humours°   45
　　In bodies full and foul, and mixed with spirits)°
　　Feigns many strange, miraculous images,
　　In which act it so painfully applies°
　　Itself to those forms that the common sense
　　It actuates with his motion, and thereby°   50
　　Those fictions true seem and have real act:
　　So, in the strength of our conceits, awake,°
　　The cause alike doth oft like fictions make.°
GUISE Be what it will, 'twas a presage of something
　　Weighty and secret, which th' advertisements°   55
　　I have received from all parts, both without
　　And in this kingdom, as from Rome and Spain,
　　Lorraine and Savoy, gives me cause to think,°
　　All writing that our plot's catastrophe°
　　For propagation of the Catholic cause   60
　　Will bloody prove, dissolving all our counsels.°
CLERMONT Retire, then, from them all.
GUISE   I must not do so.
　　The Archbishop of Lyons tells me plain°
　　I shall be said then to abandon France
　　In so important an occasion,°   65
　　And that mine enemies (their profit making
　　Of my faint absence) soon would let that fall°
　　That all my pains did to this height exhale.°
CLERMONT Let all fall that would rise unlawfully.
　　Make not your forward spirit in virtue's right   70
　　A property for vice, by thrusting on
　　Further than all your powers can fetch you off.°
　　It is enough your will is infinite
　　To all things virtuous and religious,
　　Which, within limits kept, may without danger   75

Let virtue some good from your graces gather:
Avarice of all is ever nothing's father.°
GHOST [*advances and addresses Clermont*]
    Danger, the spur of all great minds, is ever°
    The curb to your tame spirits; you respect not—°
    With all your holiness of life and learning—   80
    More than the present, like illiterate vulgars.°
    Your mind, you say, kept in your flesh's bounds,
    Shows that man's will must ruled be by his power;
    When by true doctrine you are taught to live°
    Rather without the body than within,   85
    And rather to your God still than yourself.
    To live to Him is to do all things fitting
    His image, in which, like Himself, we live;
    To be His image is to do those things
    That make us deathless, which, by death, is only°   90
    Doing those deeds that fit eternity;°
    And those deeds are the perfecting that justice°
    That makes the world last, which proportion is
    Of punishment and wreak for every wrong,
    As well as for right a reward as strong.   95
    Away then, use the means thou hast to right
    The wrong I suffered. What corrupted law
    Leaves unperformed in kings do thou supply,
    And be above them all in dignity.
        Exit [*Ghost*]
GUISE Why stand'st thou still thus, and apply'st thine ears   100
    And eyes to nothing?
CLERMONT   Saw you nothing here?
GUISE Thou dream'st awake now; what was here to see?
CLERMONT My brother's spirit urging his revenge.
GUISE Thy brother's spirit! Pray thee mock me not.
CLERMONT No, by my love and service.
GUISE   Would he rise   105
    And not be thund'ring threats against the Guise?
CLERMONT You make amends for enmity to him
    With ten parts more love and desert of me;°
    And as you make your hate to him no let°
    Of any love to me, no more bears he   110
    (Since you to me supply it) hate to you:°
    Which reason and which justice is performed
    In spirits ten parts more than fleshy men,°

To whose foresights our acts and thoughts lie open.
And therefore, since he saw the treachery   115
Late practiced by my brother Baligny,
He would not honour his hand with the justice,
As he esteems it, of his blood's revenge—
To which my sister needs would have him sworn
Before she would consent to marry him.   120
GUISE O, Baligny, who would believe there were
   A man that (only since his looks are raised°
   Upwards and have but sacred heaven in sight)
   Could bear a mind so more than devilish
   As (for the painted glory of the countenance,   125
   Flitting in kings) doth good for naught esteem,°
   And the more ill he does, the better seem?
CLERMONT We easily may believe it, since we see
   In this world's practice few men better be.
   Justice to live doth naught but justice need,   130
   But policy must still on mischief feed.
   Untruth, for all his ends, truth's name doth sue in;°
   None safely live but those that study ruin.°
   A good man happy is a common good;
   Ill men advanced live of the common blood.   135
GUISE But this thy brother's spirit startles me,
   These spirits seld or never haunting men
   But some mishap ensues.
CLERMONT   Ensue what can;
   Tyrants may kill, but never hurt a man;°
   All to his good makes, spite of death and hell.°   140
        Enter Aumale
AUMALE All the desert of good renown, your Highness.
GUISE Welcome, Aumale.
CLERMONT   My good friend, friendly welcome.
   How took my noblest mistress the changed news?
AUMALE It came too late, sir; for those loveliest eyes
   (Through which a soul looked so divinely loving,   145
   Tears nothing uttering her distress enough)°
   She wept quite out, and like two falling stars
   Their dearest sights quite vanished with her tears.
CLERMONT All good forbid it!
GUISE   What events are these!
CLERMONT All must be borne, my lord, and yet this chance°   150

234

Would willingly enforce a man to cast off
All power to bear with comfort, since he sees
In this our comforts made our miseries.

GUISE How strangely thou art loved of both the sexes;
Yet thou lov'st neither, but the good of both.   155

CLERMONT In love of women, my affection first
Takes fire out of the frail parts of my blood,°
Which, till I have enjoyed, is passionate°
Like other lovers; but fruition past,
I then love out of judgement; the desert   160
Of her I love still sticking in my heart,°
Though the desire and the delight be gone,°
Which must chance still, since the comparison
Made upon trial 'twixt what reason loves,
And what affection, makes in me the best   165
Ever preferred; what most love, valuing least.°

GUISE Thy love being judgement then, and of the mind,
Marry thy worthiest mistress now being blind.

CLERMONT If there were love in marriage, so I would.
But I deny that any man doth love,   170
Affecting wives, maids, widows, any women:
For neither flies love milk, although they drown
In greedy search thereof; nor doth the bee
Love honey, though the labour of her life
Is spent in gathering it; nor those that fat°   175
On beasts or fowls do anything therein
For any love: for as when only nature
Moves men to meat, as far as her power rules,
She doth it with a temperate appetite
(The too much men devour, abhorring nature;°   180
And in our most health is our most disease),°
So, when humanity rules men and women,
'Tis for society confined in reason.°
But what excites the bed's desire in blood
By no means justly can be construed love;   185
For when love kindles any knowing spirit,
It ends in virtue and effects divine,
And is in friendship chaste and masculine.°

GUISE Thou shalt my mistress be; methinks my blood
Is taken up to all love with thy virtues.   190
And howsoever other men despise

These paradoxes strange and too precise,°
Since they hold on the right way of our reason,
I could attend them ever. Come, away;
Perform thy brother's thus importuned wreak,   195
And I will see what great affairs the king
Hath to employ my counsel, which he seems
Much to desire, and more and more esteems.
    Exeunt

[5.2]

Enter Henry, Baligny, with six of the Guard

HENRY Saw you his saucy forcing of my hand
  To D'Ambois' freedom?
BALIGNY   Saw, and through mine eyes
  Let fire into my heart that burned to bear°
  An insolence so giantly austere.°
HENRY The more kings bear at subjects' hands, the more   5
  Their ling'ring justice gathers, that resembles
  The weighty and the goodly-bodied eagle,
  Who (being on earth) before her shady wings°
  Can raise her into air, a mighty way
  Close by the ground she runs; but being aloft,   10
  All she commands she flies at, and the more°
  Death in her seres bears, the more time she stays°
  Her thund'ry stoop from that on which she preys.
BALIGNY You must be then more secret in the weight
  Of these your shady counsels, who will else°   15
  Bear (where such sparks fly as the Guise and D'Ambois)
  Powder about them. Counsels (as your entrails)°
  Should be unpierced and sound kept; for not those
  Whom you discover you neglect, but ope
  A ruinous passage to your own best hope.°   20
HENRY We have spies set on us, as we on others,
  And therefore they that serve us must excuse us,
  If what we most hold in our hearts take wind:°
  Deceit hath eyes that see into the mind.
  But this plot shall be quicker than their twinkling,°   25
  On whose lids Fate with her dead weight shall lie,

And Confidence that lightens ere she die.°
Friends of my guard, as ye gave oath to be
True to your sovereign, keep it manfully.
Your eyes have witnessed oft th' ambition   30
That never made access to me in Guise°
But treason ever sparkled in his eyes:
Which if you free us of, our safety shall
You not our subjects but our patrons call.°
GUARDS Our duties bind us; he is now but dead.   35
HENRY We trust in it, and thank ye. Baligny,
  Go lodge their ambush; and thou God that art°
  Fautor of princes, thunder from the skies°
  Beneath his hill of pride this giant Guise.
      Exeunt

[5.3]

  Enter Tamyra with a letter, Charlotte in man's attire
TAMYRA I see y' are servant, sir, to my dear sister,°
  The lady of her loved Baligny.
CHARLOTTE Madam, I am bound to her virtuous bounties
  For that life which I offer in her service
  To the revenge of her renownèd brother.   5
TAMYRA She writes to me as much, and much desires
  That you may be the man, whose spirit she knows
  Will cut short off these long and dull delays
  Hitherto bribing the eternal justice:°
  Which I believe, since her unmatchèd spirit   10
  Can judge of spirits that have her sulphur in them;
  But I must tell you that I make no doubt
  Her living brother will revenge her dead,
  On whom the dead imposed the task; and he,
  I know, will come t'effect it instantly.   15
CHARLOTTE They are but words in him; believe them not.
TAMYRA See, this is the vault where he must enter,°
  Where now I think he is.
      Enter Renel at the vault, with the Countess being blind
RENEL   God save you, lady.
  What gentleman is this, with whom you trust

The deadly weighty secret of this hour?   20
TAMYRA One that yourself will say I well may trust.
RENEL Then come up, madam.
          He helps the Countess up
                                        See here, honoured lady,
A countess that in love's mishap doth equal
At all parts your wronged self, and is the mistress°
Of your slain servant's brother, in whose love,   25
For his late treach'rous apprehension,
She wept her fair eyes from her ivory brows,
And would have wept her soul out, had not I
Promised to bring her to this mortal quarry,°
That, by her lost eyes for her servant's love,   30
She might conjure him from this stern attempt,
In which (by a most ominous dream she had)
She knows his death fixed and that never more
Out of this place the sun shall see him live.
CHARLOTTE I am provided, then, to take his place   35
And undertaking on me.
RENEL   You, sir, why?
CHARLOTTE Since I am charged so by my mistress,
His mournful sister.
TAMYRA   See her letter, sir.
          Renel reads [the letter]
[*To the Countess*] Good madam, I rue your fate more than mine,
And know not how to order these affairs,   40
They stand on such occurrents.
RENEL   This indeed°
I know to be your lady mistress' hand°
And know, besides, his brother will and must
Endure no hand in this revenge but his.
          Enter the Ghost of Bussy
GHOST Away, dispute no more! get up and see—   45
Clermont must author this just tragedy.
COUNTESS Who's that?
RENEL   The spirit of Bussy.
TAMYRA   O my servant!
Let us embrace.
GHOST   Forbear! The air, in which
My figure's likeness is impressed, will blast.
Let my revenge for all loves satisfy,   50

[*To the Countess*] In which, dame, fear not, Clermont shall not die.
No word dispute more. Up, and see th' event.°
      Exeunt [*Tamyra, Countess, Charlotte*]
Make the guard sure, Renel, and then the doors
Command to make fast when the earl is in.
      Exit Renel
The black soft-footed hour is now on wing,   55
Which, for my just wreak, ghosts shall celebrate
With dances dire and of infernal state.°
      Exit

[5.4]

      Enter Guise

GUISE Who says that death is natural, when nature
Is with the only thought of it dismayed?°
I have had lotteries set up for my death,°
And I have drawn beneath my trencher one,
Knit in my handkerchief another lot,°   5
The word being, 'Y'are a dead man if you enter';°
And these words this imperfect blood and flesh
Shrink at in spite of me, their solid'st part
Melting like snow within me with cold fire.
I hate myself, that, seeking to rule kings,   10
I cannot curb my slave. Would any spirit,°
Free, manly, princely, wish to live to be
Commanded by this mass of slavery,
Since reason, judgement, resolution,
And scorn of what we fear will yield to fear?   15
While this same sink of sensuality swells,°
Who would live sinking in it, and not spring
Up to the stars and leave this carrion here
For wolves and vultures and for dogs to tear?
O Clermont D'Ambois, wert thou here to chide   20
This softness from my flesh, far as my reason,°
Far as my resolution not to stir
One foot out of the way for death and hell.
Let my false man by falsehood perish here;°
There's no way else to set my true man clear.°   25

Enter Messenger

MESSENGER The king desires your grace to come to Council.

GUISE I come.

        [Exit Messenger]

                It cannot be: he will not dare

To touch me with a treachery so profane.

Would Clermont now were here, to try how he°

Would lay about him if this plot should be:°   30

Here would be tossing souls into the sky.

Who ever knew blood saved by treachery?°

Well, I must on, and will; what should I fear?

Not against two, Alcides? Against two,°

And Hercules to friend, the Guise will go.°   35

        He takes up the arras, and the Guard enters° upon him:
        he draws

Hold, murderers!

        The Guard strike him down

               So then, this is confidence°

In greatness, not in goodness. Where is the king?

        Henry comes in sight with Espernon, Soisson, [Aumale,]
        and others

Let him appear to justify his deed,

In spite of my betrayed wounds, ere my soul

Take her flight through them and my tongue hath strength   40

To urge his tyranny.

HENRY   See, sir, I am come°

To justify it before men, and God,

Who knows with what wounds in my heart for woe

Of your so wounded faith I made these wounds,°

Forced to it by an insolence of force°   45

To stir a stone; nor is a rock, opposed

To all the billows of the churlish sea,

More beat and eaten with them than was I

With your ambitious mad idolatry;°

And this blood I shed is to save the blood   50

Of many thousands.

GUISE   That's your white pretext,

But you will find one drop of blood shed lawless

Will be the fountain to a purple sea:°

The present lust and shift made for kings' lives

Against the pure form and just power of law   55

Will thrive like shifters' purchases; there hangs°

A black star in the skies, to which the sun
Gives yet no light, will rain a poisoned shower°
Into your entrails that will make you feel
How little safety lies in treacherous steel. 60
HENRY Well, sir, I'll bear it. Y'ave a brother too,
Bursts with like threats, the scarlet Cardinal:°
[*To the Guard*] Seek, and lay hands on him; and take this hence.
Their bloods, for all you, on my conscience.
    [*Exeunt Henry, Espernon, Soisson, and other courtiers;*
    Aumale remains]
GUISE So, sir, your full swinge take; mine, death hath curbed. 65
Clermont, farewell. O, didst thou see but this!
But it is better; see by this the ice .
Broke to thine own blood, which thou wilt despise
When thou hear'st mine shed. Is there no friend here
Will bear my love to him?
AUMALE   I will, my lord. 70
GUISE Thanks with my last breath: recommend me, then,
To the most worthy of the race of men.
    Dies. Exeunt, [the Guard bearing off Guise's body]

[5.5]

Enter Montsurry and Tamyra
MONTSURRY Who have you let into my house?
TAMYRA   I? None.
MONTSURRY 'Tis false. I savour the rank blood of foes
In every corner.
TAMYRA   That you may do well;
It is the blood you lately shed you smell.
MONTSURRY 'Sdeath, the vault opes.
    The gulf° opens
TAMYRA   What vault? Hold your sword! 5
    Clermont ascends
CLERMONT No, let him use it.
MONTSURRY   Treason! Murder, murder!
CLERMONT Exclaim not; 'tis in vain, and base in you,
Being one to only one.
MONTSURRY   O, bloody strumpet!
CLERMONT With what blood charge you her? It may be mine

241

As well as yours; there shall not any else   10
Enter or touch you. I confer no guards,°
Nor imitate the murderous course you took,
But, single here, will have my former challenge
Now answered single; not a minute more
My brother's blood shall stay for his revenge   15
If I can act it; if not, mine shall add
A double conquest to you that alone
Put it to fortune now and use no odds.
Storm not, nor beat yourself thus 'gainst the doors,
Like to a savage vermin in a trap: 20
All doors are sure made, and you cannot 'scape
But by your valour.
MONTSURRY   No, no, come and kill me!
     [*Lies down*]
CLERMONT If you will die so like a beast, you shall;
But when the spirit of a man may save you,
Do not so shame man, and a nobleman.   25
MONTSURRY I do not show this baseness, that I fear thee,°
But to prevent and shame thy victory,°
Which of one base is base, and so I'll die.°
CLERMONT Here, then.
     [*Offers to kill Montsurry*]
MONTSURRY   Stay, hold! One thought hath hardened me,
     He starts up
And since I must afford thee victory,   30
It shall be great and brave, if one request
Thou wilt admit me.
CLERMONT   What's that?
MONTSURRY   Give me leave
To fetch and use the sword thy brother gave me°
When he was bravely giving up his life.
CLERMONT No, I'll not fight against my brother's sword,   35
Not that I fear it, but since 'tis a trick
For you to show your back.
MONTSURRY   By all truth, no.°
Take but my honourable oath, I will not.
CLERMONT Your honourable oath! Plain truth no place has
Where oaths are honourable.
TAMYRA   Trust not his oath.   40
He will lie like a lapwing: when she flies°

Far from her sought nest, still 'Here 'tis', she cries.

MONTSURRY Out on thee, dam of devils! I will quite
Disgrace thy brave's conquest—die, not fight.
   Lies down

TAMYRA Out on my fortune to wed such an abject!°   45
Now is the people's voice the voice of God:°
He that to wound a woman vaunts so much
(As he did me) a man dares never touch.

CLERMONT Revenge your wounds now, madam; I resign him
Up to your full will, since he will not fight.   50
First you shall torture him (as he did you,
And justice wills), and then pay I my vow.
Here, take this poniard.

MONTSURRY   Sink earth, open heaven,
And let fall vengeance!

TAMYRA   Come sir; good sir, hold him.

MONTSURRY O, shame of women, whither art thou fled? 55

CLERMONT Why, good my lord, is it a greater shame
For her than you? Come, I will be the bands°
You used to her, profaning her fair hands.

MONTSURRY No, sir. [*Rises*] I'll fight now, and the terror be
Of all you champions to such as she.   60
I did but thus far dally: now observe,
O all you aching foreheads that have robbed°
Your hands of weapons and your hearts of valour;
Join in me all your rages and rebutters
And into dust ram this same race of Furies: 65
In this one relic of the D'Ambois gall,°
In his one purple soul shed, drown it all.°
   [*Clermont and Montsurry*] *fight*
Now give me breath a while.

CLERMONT   Receive it freely.

MONTSURRY What think y' o' this now?

CLERMONT   It is very noble,
Had it been free, at least, and of yourself;°   70
And thus we see (where valour most doth vaunt)
What 'tis to make a coward valiant.

MONTSURRY Now I shall grace your conquest.

CLERMONT   That you shall.

MONTSURRY If you obtain it.

CLERMONT   True, sir, 'tis in fortune.

MONTSURRY If you were not a D'Ambois, I would scarce   75
    Change lives with you, I feel so great a change°
    In my tall spirits breathed, I think, with the breath
    A D'Ambois breathes here; and Necessity
    (With whose point now pricked on, and so, whose help°
    My hands may challenge), that doth all men conquer,°   80
    If she except not you of all men only,
    May change the case here.
CLERMONT   True, as you are changed,
    Her power, in me urged, makes y'another man°
    Than yet you ever were.
MONTSURRY   Well, I must on.
CLERMONT Your lordship must by all means.
MONTSURRY   Then at all.°   85
    [Montsurry] fights, and Clermont hurts him. Charlotte
    [appears] above [with Renel and the Countess]
CHARLOTTE Death of my father, what a shame is this.
    Stick in his hands thus?
RENEL *[trying to stop her]* Gentle sir, forbear.°
    Charlotte gets down°
COUNTESS Is he not slain yet?
RENEL   No, madam, but hurt
    In divers parts of him.
MONTSURRY   Y'ave given it me.°
    And yet I feel life for another veny.   90
    Enter Charlotte below
CLERMONT What would you, sir?
CHARLOTTE   I would perform this combat.
CLERMONT Against which of us?
CHARLOTTE   I care not much if 'twere
    Against thyself: thy sister would have shamed
    To have thy brother's wreak with any man
    In single combat stick so in her fingers.   95
CLERMONT My sister? Know you her?
TAMYRA   Aye, sir, she sent him
    With this kind letter to perform the wreak
    Of my dear servant.
CLERMONT   Now, alas, good sir,
    Think you you could do more?
CHARLOTTE   Alas, I do.
    And wer't not I, fresh, sound, should charge a man°   100

Weary and wounded, I would long ere this
Have proved what I presume on.
CLERMONT   Y'ave a mind°
Like to my sister, but have patience now;
If next charge speed not, I'll resign to you.°
MONTSURRY [to Clermont] Pray thee let him decide it.
CLERMONT   No, my lord,   105
I am the man in fate; and since so bravely°
Your lordship stands me, 'scape but one more charge,
And on my life, I'll set your life at large.
MONTSURRY Said like a D'Ambois, and if now I die,
Sit joy and all good on thy victory.   110

      [Montsurry] fights and [mortally wounded by Clermont], falls
      down. He gives his hand to Clermont and Tamyra

Farewell, I heartily forgive thee—wife,
And thee; let penitence spend thy rest of life.
CLERMONT Noble and Christian.
TAMYRA   O, it breaks my heart.
CLERMONT And should; for all faults found in him before,
These words, this end, makes full amends and more.   115
Rest, worthy soul, and with it the dear spirit
Of my loved brother rest in endless peace.
Soft lie thy bones, heaven be your soul's abode,
And to your ashes be the earth no load.

      [Montsurry dies.] Music, and the Ghost of Bussy enters,
      leading the Ghost[s] of the Guise, Monsieur, Cardinal Guise,
      and Chatillon; they dance about the dead body, and exeunt

CLERMONT How strange is this! The Guise amongst these spirits,   120
And his great brother Cardinal, both yet living,
And that the rest with them with joy thus celebrate
This our revenge! This certainly presages
Some instant death both to the Guise and Cardinal.°
That the Chatillon's ghost too should thus join   125
In celebration of this just revenge
With Guise that bore a chief stroke in his death,
It seems that now he doth approve the act;°
And these true shadows of the Guise and Cardinal,
Forerunning thus their bodies, may approve°   130
That all things to be done, as here we live,°
Are done before all times in th' other life.
That spirits should rise in these times yet are fables,°

Though learned'st men hold that our sensive spirits
A little time abide about the graves   135
Of their deceasèd bodies, and can take
In cold condensed air the same forms they had
When they were shut up in this body's shade.
        Enter Aumale
AUMALE O sir, the Guise is slain.
CLERMONT   Avert it, heaven!
AUMALE Sent for to Council by the king, an ambush,   140
    Lodged for the purpose, rushed on him and took
    His princely life; who sent (in dying then)
    His love to you as to the best of men.
CLERMONT The worst and most accursed of things creeping
    On earth's sad bosom! Let me pray ye all   145
    A little to forbear, and let me use
    Freely mine own mind in lamenting him.
    I'll call ye straight again.
AUMALE   We will forbear
    And leave you free, sir.
        Exeunt [Aumale, Tamyra, Charlotte]
CLERMONT   Shall I live, and he
    Dead that alone gave means of life to me?   150
    There's no disputing with the acts of kings:
    Revenge is impious on their sacred persons;
    And could I play the worldling (no man loving
    Longer than gain is reaped, or grace, from him),
    I should survive; and shall be wondered at   155
    Though (in mine own hands being) I end with him.°
    But friendship is the cement of two minds,
    As of one man the soul and body is,
    Of which one cannot sever but the other
    Suffers a needful separation.°   160
RENEL I fear your servant, madam: let's descend.°   .
        Descend Renel and Countess
CLERMONT Since I could skill of man, I never lived°
    To please men worldly; and shall I in death
    Respect their pleasures, making such a jar°
    Betwixt my death and life, when death should make   165
    The consort sweetest, th' end being proof and crown
    To all the skill and worth we truly own?
    Guise, O my lord, how shall I cast from me

The bands and coverts hind'ring me from thee?°
The garment or the cover of the mind   170
The human soul is; of the soul, the spirit
The proper robe is; of the spirit, the blood;
And of the blood, the body is the shroud:
With that must I begin then to unclothe,
And come at th' other. Now, then, as a ship,°   175
Touching at strange and far-removèd shores,
Her men ashore go for their several ends,
Fresh water, victuals, precious stones, and pearl,
All yet intentive (when the master calls,
The ship to put off ready) to leave all   180
Their greediest labours, lest they there be left
To thieves or beasts, or be the country's slaves:
So now my master calls, my ship, my venture
All in one bottom put, all quite put off,°
Gone under sail, and I left negligent   185
To all the horrors of the vicious time,
The far-removed shores to all virtuous aims,°
None favouring goodness, none but he respecting°
Piety or manhood. Shall I here survive,
Not cast me after him into the sea,   190
Rather than here live, ready every hour
To feed thieves, beasts, and be the slave of power?
I come, my lord; Clermont, thy creature, comes!
        He kills himself. Enter Aumale, Tamyra, Charlotte
AUMALE What? lie and languish, Clermont?
        [*Examines the body*]
                                                Cursèd man,
To leave him here thus; he hath slain himself.   195
TAMYRA Misery on misery! O me, wretched dame
  Of all that breathe! All heaven turn all his eyes°
  In hearty envy thus on one poor dame!
CHARLOTTE Well done, my brother. I did love thee ever,
  But now adore thee: loss of such a friend   200
  None should survive, [or] of such a brother;
  With my false husband live, and both these slain?
  Ere I return to him, I'll turn to earth.
        Enter Renel, leading the Countess
RENEL Horror of human eyes! O, Clermont D'Ambois!
  Madam, we stayed too long; your servant's slain.   205

COUNTESS It must be so: he lived but in the Guise,
  As I in him. O follow, life, mine eyes!
TAMYRA Hide, hide thy snaky head! To cloisters fly,°
  In penance pine! Too easy 'tis to die.
CHARLOTTE It is. In cloisters, then, let's all survive.   210
  Madam, since wrath nor grief can help these fortunes,
  Let us forsake the world in which they reign,
  And for their wished amends to God complain.°
COUNTESS 'Tis fit and only needful: lead me on.
  In heaven's course comfort seek, in earth is none.   215
      Exeunt [Aumale, Tamyra, Charlotte, Renel, Countess.] Enter
      Henry, Espernon, Soisson, and others
HENRY We came indeed too late, which much I rue,
  And would have kept this Clermont as my crown.
  Take in the dead and make this fatal room
  (The house shut up) the famous D'Ambois tomb.
      Exeunt, [bearing the bodies of Clermont and Montsurry]

THE ATHEIST'S TRAGEDY;

Or, The Honest Man's Revenge

CYRIL TOURNEUR

[DRAMATIS PERSONAE]

Montferrers, a baron
Belforest, a baron
D'Amville,° brother to
    Montferrers
Levidulcia,° lady to Belforest
Castabella,° daughter to
    Belforest
Charlemont, son to Montferrers
Rousard, elder son to D'Amville
Sebastian, younger son to
    D'Amville
Languebeau Snuffe,° a Puritan;
    chaplain to Belforest
Borachio,° D'Amville's
    instrument°

Cataplasma,° a maker of
    periwigs and attires
Soquette, a seeming
    gentlewoman to Cataplasma
Fresco,° servant to Cataplasma
Other servants
Sergeant in war
Soldiers
Watchmen
Officers
Judges
[Musketeer
Doctor
Keeper of the Prison
Executioner]

250

[1.1]

Enter D'Amville, Borachio, attended [by a servant]

D'AMVILLE I saw my nephew Charlemont but now
　Part from his father. Tell him I desire
　To speak with him.
　　　Exit Servant
　　　　　　　Borachio, thou art read°
　In Nature and her large philosophy.°
　Observ'st thou not the very selfsame course　　　　　　5
　Of revolution both in man and beast?°
BORACHIO The same—for birth, growth, state, decay, and death:°
　Only a man's beholding to his Nature
　For th'better composition o' the two.°
D'AMVILLE But where that favour of his Nature is　　　10
　Not full and free, you see a man becomes
　A fool, as little-knowing as a beast.
BORACHIO That shows there's nothing in a man above
　His Nature; if there were, consid'ring 'tis
　His being's excellency, 'twould not yield　　　　　　15
　To Nature's weakness.
D'AMVILLE　　　　　　　Then if death casts up°
　Our total sum of joy and happiness,
　Let me have all my senses feasted in
　Th'abundant fullness of delight at once,
　And with a sweet insensible increase°　　　　　　20
　Of pleasing surfeit melt into my dust.
BORACHIO That revolution is too short methinks.
　If this life comprehends our happiness,°
　How foolish to desire to die so soon!
　And if our time runs home unto the length　　　25
　Of Nature, how improvident it were°
　To spend our substance on a minute's pleasure
　And after live an age in misery!
D'AMVILLE So thou conclud'st that pleasure only flows
　Upon the stream of riches.
BORACHIO　　　　　　　　Wealth is lord　　　30
　Of all felicity.
D'AMVILLE　　　'Tis oracle,
　For what's a man that's honest without wealth?

251

BORACHIO Both miserable and contemptible.
D'AMVILLE He's worse, Borachio. For if charity
  Be an essential part of honesty   35
  And should be practised first upon ourselves—
  Which must be granted—then your honest man
  That's poor is most dishonest, for he is
  Uncharitable to the man whom he
  Should most respect. But what doth this touch me°   40
  That seem to have enough? Thanks industry,°
  'Tis true. Had not my body spread itself
  Into posterity, perhaps I should
  Desire no more increase of substance than
  Would hold proportion with mine own dimensions.   45
  Yet even in that sufficiency of state
  A man has reason to provide and add.
  For what is he hath such a present eye°
  And so prepared a strength, that can foresee
  And fortify his substance and himself   50
  Against those accidents, the least whereof
  May rob him of an age's husbandry?°
  And for my children, they are as near to me
  As branches to the tree whereon they grow,
  And may as numerously be multiplied.   55
  As they increase, so should my providence,°
  For from my substance they receive the sap
  Whereby they live and flourish.
BORACHIO   Sir, enough,
  I understand the mark whereat you aim.
      Enter Charlemont [with the servant]
D'AMVILLE Silence. W'are interrupted.—Charlemont!   60
CHARLEMONT Good morrow, uncle.
D'AMVILLE   Noble Charlemont,
  Good morrow. Is not this the honoured day
  You purposed to set forward to the war?
CHARLEMONT My inclination did intend it so.
D'AMVILLE And not your resolution?
CHARLEMONT   Yes, my lord,   65
  Had not my father contradicted it.
D'AMVILLE O noble war, thou first original°
  Of all man's honour! How dejectedly
  The baser spirit of our present time

Hath cast itself below the ancient worth   70
Of our forefathers! from whose noble deeds
Ignobly we derive our pedigrees.
CHARLEMONT Sir, tax not me for his unwillingness.
By the command of his authority
My disposition's forced against itself.   75
D'AMVILLE Nephew, you are the honour of our blood.
The troop of gentry, whose inferior worth°
Should second your example, are become
Your leaders; and the scorn of their discourse
Turns smiling back upon your backwardness.   80
CHARLEMONT You need not urge my spirit by disgrace;
'Tis free enough. My father hinders it.°
To curb me, he denies me maintenance°
To put me in the habit of my rank.°
Unbind me from that strong necessity,°   85
And call me coward if I stay behind.
D'AMVILLE For want of means? Borachio, where's the gold?
    [*Exit Borachio*]
I'd disinherit my posterity
To purchase honour. 'Tis an interest
I prize above the principal of wealth.°   90
I'm glad I had th'occasion to make known
How readily my substance shall unlock
Itself to serve you.
    [*Enter Borachio with the money*]
                    Here's a thousand crowns.
CHARLEMONT My worthy uncle, in exchange for this
I leave my bond. So I am doubly bound:°   95
By that for the repayment of this gold,
And by this gold to satisfy your love.
D'AMVILLE Sir, 'tis a witness, only, of my love,
And love doth always satisfy itself.°
Now to your father; labour his consent.°   100
My importunity shall second yours.
We will obtain it.
CHARLEMONT   If entreaty fail,
The force of reputation shall prevail.
    Exit [*Charlemont*]
D'AMVILLE [*to Servant*]
Go call my sons, that they may take their leaves

Of noble Charlemont.
          [*Exit Servant*]
                              Now, my Borachio!   105
BORACHIO The substance of our former argument
    Was wealth.
D'AMVILLE   The question how to compass it.
BORACHIO Young Charlemont is going to the war.
D'AMVILLE O, thou begin'st to take me.
BORACHIO   Mark me then.°
    Methinks the pregnant wit of man might make°   110
    The happy absence of this Charlemont
    A subject for commodious providence.°
    He has a wealthy father, ready ev'n
    To drop into his grave, and no man's power
    When Charlemont is gone can interpose   115
    'Twixt you and him.
D'AMVILLE   Th'ast apprehended—both
    My meaning and my love. Now let thy trust,
    For undertaking and for secrecy,°
    Hold measure with thy amplitude of wit,
    And thy reward shall parallel thy worth.   120
BORACHIO My resolution has already bound
    Me to your service.
D'AMVILLE   And my heart to thee.
          Enter Rousard and Sebastian
    Here are my sons—
    There's my eternity. My life in them
    And their succession shall forever live,   125
    And in my reason dwells the providence
    To add to life as much of happiness.
    Let all men lose, so I increase my gain:
    I have no feeling of another's pain.
          Exeunt

[1.2]

          Enter Montferrers and Charlemont
MONTFERRERS I prithee let this current of my tears
    Divert thy inclination from the war,

For of my children thou art only left
To promise a succession to my house,
And all the honour thou canst get by arms   5
Will give but vain addition to thy name,°
Since from thy ancestors thou dost derive
A dignity sufficient, and as great
As thou hast substance to maintain and bear.
I prithee stay at home.
CHARLEMONT   My noble father,   10
The weakest sigh you breathe hath power to turn
My strongest purpose, and your softest tear
To melt my resolution to as soft
Obedience. But my affection to the war
Is as hereditary as my blood   15
To ev'ry life of all my ancestry.°
Your predecessors were your precedents,
And you are my example. Shall I serve
For nothing but a vain parenthesis
I' th'honoured story of your family,   20
Or hang but like an empty scutcheon
Between the trophies of my predecessors
And the rich arms of my posterity?
There's not a Frenchman of good blood and youth
But either out of spirit or example   25
Is turned a soldier. Only Charlemont
Must be reputed that same heartless thing
That cowards will be bold to play upon.°
          Enter D'Amville, Rousard, and Sebastian
D'AMVILLE Good morrow, my lord.
MONTFERRERS Morrow, good brother.   30
CHARLEMONT Good morrow, uncle.
D'AMVILLE Morrow, kind nephew.
     What, ha' you washed your eyes wi' tears this morning?
     [*To Montferrers*] Come, by my soul, his purpose does deserve
     Your free consent. Your tenderness dissuades him.°   35
     What to the father of a gentleman
     Should be more tender than the maintenance
     And the increase of honour to his house?
     My lord, here are my boys. I should be proud
     That either this were able, or that inclined°   40
     To be my nephew's brave competitor.°

MONTFERRERS Your importunities have overcome.
  Pray God my forced grant prove not ominous.
D'AMVILLE [aside to Charlemont] We have obtained it. [To Montfer-
    rers] Ominous? In what?
  It cannot be in anything but death.   45
  And I am of a confident belief
  That ev'n the time, place, manner of our deaths
  Do follow fate with that necessity
  That makes us sure to die. And in a thing
  Ordained so certainly unalterable   50
  What can the use of providence prevail?
      [Enter] Belforest, Levidulcia, Castabella, attended [by servants]
BELFOREST Morrow, my Lord Montferrers, Lord D'Amville.
  Good morrow, gentlemen. Cousin Charlemont,
  Kindly good morrow! Troth, I was afeared
  I should ha' come too late to tell you that   55
  I wish your undertakings a success
  That may deserve the measure of their worth.°
CHARLEMONT My lord, my duty would not let me go
  Without receiving your commandments.
BELFOREST Accompliments are more for ornament   60
  Than use. We should employ no time in them
  But what our serious business will admit.
MONTFERRERS Your favour had by his duty been prevented,°
  If we had not withheld him in the way.°
D'AMVILLE He was a-coming to present his service.   65
  But now no more. The cook invites to breakfast.
  Will't please your lordship enter? Noble lady!
      [Exeunt all except] Charlemont and Castabella
CHARLEMONT My noble mistress, this accompliment
  Is like an elegant and moving speech
  Composed of many sweet persuasive points   70
  Which second one another with a fluent
  Increase and confirmation of their force,
  Reserving still the best until the last,
  To crown the strong impulsion of the rest
  With a full conquest of the hearer's sense;   75
  Because th'impression of the last we speak
  Doth always longest and most constantly
  Possess the entertainment of remembrance.°
  So all that now salute my taking leave

Have added numerously to the love   80
Wherewith I did receive their courtesy.
But you, dear mistress, being the last and best
That speaks my farewell, like th'imperious close
Of a most sweet oration, wholly have
Possessed my liking, and shall ever live   85
Within the soul of my true memory.
So, mistress, with this kiss I take my leave.
     [They kiss]
CASTABELLA My worthy servant, you mistake th' intent
Of kissing. 'Twas not meant to separate
A pair of lovers, but to be the seal   90
Of love, importing by the joining of
Our mutual and incorporated breaths°
That we should breathe but one contracted life.°
Or stay at home, or let me go with you.°
CHARLEMONT My Castabella, for myself to stay   95
Or you to go would either tax my youth
With a dishonourable weakness, or
Your loving purpose with immodesty.
     Enter Languebeau Snuffe
And for the satisfaction of your love,
Here comes a man whose knowledge I have made   100.
A witness to the contract of our vows,
Which my return by marriage shall confirm.
LANGUEBEAU I salute you both with the spirit of copulation.° I am
already informed of your matrimonial purposes, and will be a
testimony to the integrity of your promises.   105
CASTABELLA O the sad trouble of my fearful soul!
My faithful servant, did you never hear
That when a certain great man went to th'war
The lovely face of Heav'n was masked with sorrow,
The sighing winds did move the breast of earth,   110
The heavy clouds hung down their mourning heads
And wept sad showers the day that he went hence,
As if that day presaged some ill success
That fatally should kill his happiness;°
And so it came to pass. Methinks my eyes,   115
Sweet Heav'n forbid, are like those weeping clouds,
And as their showers presaged, so do my tears;
Some sad event will follow my sad fears.°

CHARLEMONT Fie, superstitious! Is it bad to kiss?
CASTABELLA May all my fears hurt me no more than this.   120
        [*They kiss*]
LANGUEBEAU Fie, fie, fie, these carnal kisses do stir up the con-
    cupiscences° of the flesh.
        Enter Belforest and Levidulcia
LEVIDULCIA O, here's your daughter under her servant's lips.
CHARLEMONT Madam, there is no cause you should mistrust
    The kiss I gave; 'twas but a parting one.   125
LEVIDULCIA A lusty blood! Now, by the lip of Love,
    Were I to choose, your joining one for me.°
BELFOREST Your father stays to bring you on the way.
    Farewell. The great commander of the war
    Prosper the course you undertake. Farewell.   130
CHARLEMONT My lord, I humbly take my leave.
                        [*To Levidulcia*] Madam,
    I kiss your hand. [*To Castabella*] And your sweet lip. Farewell.
        [*Exeunt all but*] *Charlemont and Languebeau Snuffe*
    Her power to speak is perished in her tears.
    Something within me would persuade my stay,
    But reputation will not yield unto 't.   135
    Dear sir, you are the man whose honest trust
    My confidence hath chosen for my friend.
    I fear my absence will discomfort her.
    You have the power and opportunity
    To moderate her passion. Let her grief   140
    · Receive that friendship from you, and your love
    Shall not repent itself of courtesy.
LANGUEBEAU Sir, I want words and protestations to insinuate into
    your credit, but in plainness and truth, I will qualify her grief with
    the spirit of consolation.   145
CHARLEMONT Sir, I will take your friendship up at use.
    And fear not that your profit shall be small;
    Your interest shall exceed your principal.°
        Exit Charlemont. Enter D'Amville and Borachio
D'AMVILLE Monsieur Languebeau, happily encountered! The hon-
    esty of your conversation makes me request more interest in your   150
    familiarity.°
LANGUEBEAU If your lordship will be pleased to salute me without
    ceremony, I shall be willing to exchange my service for your

favour, but this worshipping kind of entertainment° is a superstitious vanity; in plainness and truth I love it not.   155
D'AMVILLE I embrace your disposition, and desire to give you as
liberal assurance of my love as my Lord Belforest, your deserved
favourer.
LANGUEBEAU His lordship is pleased with my plainness and truth of
conversation.   160
D'AMVILLE It cannot displease him. In the behaviour of his noble
daughter Castabella a man may read her worth and your instruc-
tion.
LANGUEBEAU That gentlewoman is most sweetly modest, fair,
honest, handsome, wise, well-born, and rich.   165
D'AMVILLE You have given me her picture in small.°
LANGUEBEAU She's like your diamond, a temptation in every man's
eye, yet not yielding to any light° impression herself.
D'AMVILLE The praise is hers, but the comparison your own.
    Gives him the ring
LANGUEBEAU You shall forgive me that, sir.   170
D'AMVILLE I will not do so much at your request as forgive you it.
 I will only give you it, sir. By—you will make me swear.
LANGUEBEAU O, by no means! Profane not your lips with the
foulness of that sin. I will rather take it. To save your oath, you
shall lose your ring. Verily, my lord, my praise came short of her   175
worth. She exceeds a jewel. This is but only for ornament, she
both for ornament and use.
D'AMVILLE Yet unprofitably kept without use. She deserves a
worthy husband, sir. I have often wished a match between my
elder son and her. The marriage would join the houses of Belforest 180
and D'Amville into a noble alliance.
LANGUEBEAU And the unity of families is a work of love and charity.
D'AMVILLE And that work an employment well becoming the goodness of your disposition.
LANGUEBEAU If your lordship please to impose it upon me, I will   185
carry it without any second end,° the surest way to satisfy your
wish.
D'AMVILLE Most joyfully accepted. [*Calls offstage*] Rousard!—Here
are letters to my Lord Belforest touching my desire to that
purpose.   190
    Enter Rousard, sickly
Rousard, I send you a suitor to Castabella. To this gentleman's

discretion I commit the managing of your suit. His good success
shall be most thankful to your trust.° Follow his instructions; he
will be your leader.

LANGUEBEAU In plainness and truth.   195

ROUSARD My leader? Does your lordship think me too weak to give
the onset° myself?

LANGUEBEAU I will only assist your proceedings.

ROUSARD To say true, so I think you had need, for a sick man can
hardly get a woman's good will° without help.   200

LANGUEBEAU [aside] Charlemont, thy gratuity° and my promises
were both but words, and both like words shall vanish into air.
For thy poor empty hand I must be mute;
This gives me feeling of a better suit.°

        Exeunt Languebeau [Snuffe] and Rousard

D'AMVILLE Borachio, didst precisely note this man?°   205

BORACHIO His own profession would report him pure.°

D'AMVILLE And seems to know if any benefit
Arises of religion after death;
Yet but compare 's profession with his life;°
They so directly contradict themselves   210
As if the end of his instructions were
But to divert the world from sin, that he
More easily might engross it to himself.°
By that I am confirmed an atheist.
Well! Charlemont is gone, and here thou seest   215
His absence the foundation of my plot.

BORACHIO He is the man whom Castabella loves.

D'AMVILLE That was the reason I propounded him
Employment fixed upon a foreign place,
To draw his inclination out o'th' way.   220

BORACHIO 'T has left the passage of our practice free.

D'AMVILLE This Castabella is a wealthy heir,
And by her marriage with my elder son
My house is honoured and my state increased.°
This work alone deserves my industry;   225
But if it prosper, thou shalt see my brain
Make this but an induction to a point°
So full of profitable policy°
That it would make the soul of honesty
Ambitious to turn villain.

BORACHIO   I bespeak   230
Employment in't. I'll be an instrument

To grace performance with dexterity.
D'AMVILLE Thou shalt. No man shall rob thee of the honour.
Go presently and buy a crimson scarf
Like Charlemont's. Prepare thee a disguise   235
I' th'habit of a soldier, hurt and lame,
And then be ready at the wedding feast,
Where thou shalt have employment in a work
Will please thy disposition.
BORACHIO   As I vowed,
Your instrument shall make your project proud.   240
D'AMVILLE This marriage will bring wealth. If that succeed,
I will increase it though my brother bleed.
      Exeunt

[1.3]

Enter Castabella, avoiding the importunity of Rousard

CASTABELLA Nay, good sir; in troth if you knew how little it pleases
me, you would forbear it.
ROUSARD I will not leave thee till th'ast entertained me for thy
servant.°
CASTABELLA My servant? You are sick, you say. You would tax me   5
of indiscretion to entertain one that is not able to do me service.
ROUSARD The service of a gentlewoman consists most in chamber
work, and sick men are fittest for the chamber. I prithee give me
a favour.
CASTABELLA Methinks you have a very sweet favour° of your own.   10
ROUSARD I lack but your black eye.°
CASTABELLA If you go to buffets° among the boys, they'll give you
one.
ROUSARD Nay, if you grow bitter,° I'll dispraise your black eye. The
gray-eyed° morning makes the fairest day.   15
CASTABELLA Now that you dissemble not, I could be willing to give
you a favour. What favour would you have?
ROUSARD Any toy, any light° thing.
CASTABELLA Fie! Will you be so uncivil to ask a light thing at a
gentlewoman's hand?   20
ROUSARD Wilt give me a bracelet o' thy hair° then?
CASTABELLA Do you want hair,° sir?
ROUSARD No, faith, I'll want no hair so long as I can have it for
money.

CASTABELLA What would you do with my hair then?   25
ROUSARD Wear it for thy sake, sweetheart.
CASTABELLA Do you think I love to have my hair worn off?°
ROUSARD Come, you are so witty now and so sensible.°
        Kisses her
CASTABELLA Tush, I would I wanted one o' my senses now.
ROUSARD Bitter again! What's that? Smelling?°   30
CASTABELLA No, no, no. Why, now y'are satisfied, I hope. I have
    given you a favour.
ROUSARD What favour? A kiss? I prithee give me another.
CASTABELLA Show me that I gave you then.
ROUSARD How should I show it?   35
CASTABELLA You are unworthy of a favour if you will not bestow
    the keeping of it° one minute.
ROUSARD Well, in plain terms, dost love me? That's the purpose of
    my coming.
CASTABELLA Love you? Yes. Very well.   40
ROUSARD Give me thy hand upon't.
CASTABELLA Nay, you mistake me. If I love you very well, I must
    not love you now. For now you are not very well; y'are sick.
ROUSARD This equivocation° is for the jest now.
CASTABELLA I speak't as 'tis now in fashion, in earnest. But I shall 45
    not be in quiet for° you, I perceive, till I have given you a favour.
    Do you love me?
ROUSARD With all my heart.
CASTABELLA Then with all my heart I'll give you a jewel to hang in
    your ear. Hark ye—I can never love you.   50
        Exit [Castabella]
ROUSARD Call you this a jewel to hang in mine ear? 'Tis no light
    favour, for I'll be sworn it comes somewhat heavily to me. Well, I 55
    will not leave her for all this. Methinks it animates a man to stand
    to't° when a woman desires to be rid of him at the first sight.
        Exit

[1.4]

Enter Belforest and Languebeau Snuffe

BELFOREST I entertain the offer of this match
  With purpose to confirm it presently.
  I have already moved it to my daughter.°
  Her soft excuses savoured at the first,°
  Methought, but of a modest innocence   5
  Of blood, whose unmoved stream was never drawn
  Into the current of affection. But when I°
  Replied with more familiar arguments,°
  Thinking to make her apprehension bold,°
  Her modest blush fell to a pale dislike,   10
  And she refused it with such confidence
  As if she had been prompted by a love
  Inclining firmly to some other man,
  And in that obstinacy she remains.

LANGUEBEAU Verily, that disobedience doth not become a child. It   15
  proceedeth from an unsanctified liberty. You will be accessory to
  your own dishonour if you suffer it.

BELFOREST Your honest wisdom has advised me well.
  Once more I'll move her by persuasive means;
  If she resist, all mildness set apart,   20
  I will make use of my authority.

LANGUEBEAU And instantly, lest, fearing your constraint, her
  contrary° affection teach her some device that may prevent
  you.

BELFOREST To cut off ev'ry opportunity   25
  Procrastination may assist her with,
  This instant night she shall be married.

LANGUEBEAU   Best.°

Enter Castabella

CASTABELLA Please it your lordship, my mother attends
  I' th'gallery, and desires your conference.°

Exit Belforest

  This means I used to bring me to your ear.   30
  Time cuts off circumstance; I must be brief.°
  To your integrity did Charlemont
  Commit the contract of his love and mine,
  Which now so strong a hand seeks to divide

That if your grave advice assist me not   35
I shall be forced to violate my faith.

LANGUEBEAU Since Charlemont's absence, I have weighed his love
with the spirit of consideration, and in sincerity I find it to be
frivolous and vain. Withdraw your respect; his affection deserveth
it not.   40

CASTABELLA Good sir, I know your heart cannot profane
The holiness you make profession of
With such a vicious purpose as to break
The vow your own consent did help to make.

LANGUEBEAU Can he deserve your love who in neglect of your   45
delightful conversation, and in obstinate contempt of all your
prayers and tears, absents himself so far from your sweet fellow-
ship, and with a purpose so contracted to° that absence that you
see he purchases your separation with the hazard of his blood and
life, fearing to want pretence° to part your companies?   50
'Tis rather hate that doth division move;
Love still desires the presence of his love.
Verily, he is not of the Family of Love.°

CASTABELLA O do not wrong him. 'Tis a generous mind°
That led his disposition to the war,   55
For gentle love and noble courage are
So near allied that one begets another,
Or love is sister, and courage is the brother.
Could I affect him better than before,
His soldier's heart would make me love him more.   60

LANGUEBEAU But, Castabella—
          Enter Levidulcia

LEVIDULCIA Tush, you mistake the way into a woman;°
The passage lies not through her reason but her blood.°
          Exit Languebeau Snuffe; Castabella about to follow
Nay, stay! How wouldst thou call the child
That, being raised with cost and tenderness   65
To full ability of body and means,
Denies relief unto the parents who
Bestowed that bringing up?

CASTABELLA   Unnatural.

LEVIDULCIA Then Castabella is unnatural.
Nature, the loving mother of us all,   70
Brought forth a woman for her own relief,
By generation to revive her age,

264

Which, now thou hast ability and means
Presented, most unkindly dost deny.°
CASTABELLA Believe me, mother, I do love a man.   75
LEVIDULCIA Prefer'st th'affection of an absent love
  Before the sweet possession of a man,
  The barren mind before the fruitful body,
  Where our creation has no reference°
  To man but in his body, being made   80
  Only for generation, which (unless
  Our children can be gotten by conceit)
  Must from the body come. If reason were
  Our counsellor, we would neglect the work
  Of generation for the prodigal   85
  Expense it draws us to of that which is°
  The wealth of life. Wise Nature, therefore, hath
  Reserved for an inducement to our sense
  Our greatest pleasure in that greatest work,
  Which, being offered thee, thy ignorance   90
  Refuses for th'imaginary joy
  Of an unsatisfied affection to
  An absent man—whose blood once spent i'th'war,
  Then he'll come home sick, lame, and impotent,
  And wed thee to a torment, like the pain   95
  Of Tantalus, continuing thy desire
  With fruitless presentation of the thing
  It loves, still moved and still unsatisfied.
     Enter Belforest, D'Amville, Rousard, Sebastian, Languebeau
     Snuffe, [and Servants]
BELFOREST Now, Levidulcia, hast thou yet prepared
  My daughter's love to entertain this man,   100
  Her husband here?
LEVIDULCIA   I'm but her mother i'law;°
  Yet if she were my very flesh and blood,
  I could advise no better for [her] good.
ROUSARD Sweet wife! Thy joyful husband thus salutes
  Thy cheek.
     [Rousard kisses Castabella]
CASTABELLA   My husband? O, I am betrayed!   105
  [To Languebeau Snuffe] Dear friend of Charlemont, your purity
  Professes a divine contempt o' th' world;
  O be not bribed by that you so neglect,

In being the world's hated instrument,
To bring a just neglect upon yourself.°   110
    Kneel [*s*] *from one to another*
[*To Belforest*] Dear father, let me but examine my
Affection. [*To D'Amville*] Sir, your prudent judgement can
Persuade your son that 'tis improvident
To marry one whose disposition he
Did ne'er observe. [*To Rousard*] Good sir, I may be of   115
A nature so unpleasing to your mind,
Perhaps you'll curse the fatal hour wherein
You rashly married me.
D'AMVILLE   My Lord Belforest,
I would not have her forced against her choice.
BELFOREST Passion o' me, thou peevish girl! I charge   120
Thee by my blessing and th'authority
I have to claim th'obedience: marry him.
CASTABELLA Now Charlemont! O my presaging tears;
This sad event hath followed my sad fears.
SEBASTIAN A rape, a rape, a rape!
BELFOREST   How now?
D'AMVILLE   What's that?   125
SEBASTIAN Why, what is't but a rape to force a wench to marry,
since it forces her to lie with him she would not?
LANGUEBEAU Verily, his tongue is an unsanctified member.°
SEBASTIAN Verily, your gravity becomes your perished soul as hoary
mouldiness does rotten fruit.   130
BELFOREST Cousin, y' are both uncivil and profane.
D'AMVILLE Thou disobedient villain, get thee out of my sight!
Now, by my soul, I'll plague thee for this rudeness.
BELFOREST Come, set forward to the church.
    Exeunt [*all except*] *Sebastian*
SEBASTIAN And verify the proverb: the nearer the church, the   135
further from God. Poor wench! For thy sake may his ability° die
in his appetite, that thou beest not troubled with him thou lovest
not. May his appetite move thy desire to another man, so he shall
help to make himself cuckold. And let that man be one that he
pays wages to, so thou shalt profit by him thou hatest. Let the   140
chambers be matted,° the hinges oiled, the curtain° rings silenced,
and the chamber-maid hold her peace at his own request, that he
may sleep the quietlier; and in that sleep let him be soundly
cuckolded. And when he knows it, and seeks to sue a divorce, let

him have no other satisfaction than this: 'he lay by and slept; the   145
law will take no hold of her because he winked at° it.'

 Exit

[2.1]

Music. A banquet, in the night. Enter D'Amville, Belforest,
Levidulcia, Rousard, Castabella, Languebeau Snuffe at one
door; at the other door Cataplasma and Soquette, ushered by
Fresco

LEVIDULCIA Mistress Cataplasma, I expected you an hour since.

CATAPLASMA Certain ladies at my house, madam, detained me; otherwise I had attended your ladyship sooner.

LEVIDULCIA We are beholding to you for your company. My lord, I pray you bid these gentlewomen welcome; th'are my invited friends. 5

D'AMVILLE Gentlewomen, y'are welcome; pray sit down.

LEVIDULCIA Fresco, by my Lord D'Amville's leave I prithee go into the buttery. Thou sha't find some o' my men there; if they bid thee not welcome, they are very loggerheads.°

FRESCO If your loggerheads will not, your hogsheads shall, madam, 10
if I get into the buttery.

Exit [Fresco]

D'AMVILLE That fellow's disposition to mirth should be our present example. Let's be grave and meditate when our affairs require our seriousness. 'Tis out of season to be heavily disposed.

LEVIDULCIA We should be all wound up° into the key of mirth. 15

D'AMVILLE The music there!

[Music begins to play again]

BELFOREST Where's my Lord Montferrers? Tell him here's a room attends him.

Enter Montferrers

MONTFERRERS Heaven give your marriage that I am deprived of—joy. 20

D'AMVILLE My Lord Belforest, Castabella's health!

D'Amville drinks

Set ope the cellar doors, and let this health
Go freely round the house.—Another to
Your son, my lord, to noble Charlemont.
He is a soldier. Let the instruments 25
Of war congratulate his memory.°

Drums and trumpets [sound]. Enter a servant

SERVANT My lord, here's one i' th'habit of a soldier says he is newly returned from Ostend,° and has some business of import to speak.

D'AMVILLE Ostend! Let him come in. My soul foretells
    He brings the news will make our music full.°   30
    My brother's joy would do 't, and here comes he
    Will raise it.
        Enter Borachio disguised
MONTFERRERS O my spirit, it does dissuade
    My tongue to question him, as if it knew
    His answer would displease.
D'AMVILLE   Soldier, what news?
    We heard a rumour of a blow you gave   35
    The enemy.
BORACHIO   'Tis very true, my lord.
BELFOREST Canst thou relate it?
BORACHIO   Yes.
D'AMVILLE   I prithee do.
BORACHIO The enemy, defeated of a fair
    Advantage by a flatt'ring stratagem,°
    Plants all th'artillery against the town,   40
    Whose thunder and lightning made our bulwarks shake,
    And threatened in that terrible report°
    The storm wherewith they meant to second it.°
    Th'assault was general; but for the place
    That promised most advantage to be forced,°   45
    The pride of all their army was drawn forth
    And equally divided into front
    And rear. They marched, and coming to a stand,
    Ready to pass our channel at an ebb,°
    W'advised it for our safest course to draw   50
    Our sluices up and make't unpassable.
    Our governor opposed, and suffered 'em°
    To charge us home e'en to the rampire's foot,
    But when their front was forcing up our breach
    At push o' pike, then did his policy°   55
    Let go the sluices and tripped up the heels
    Of the whole body of their troop that stood
    Within the violent current of the stream.
    Their front, beleaguered 'twixt the water and
    The town, seeing the flood was grown too deep   60
    To promise them a safe retreat, exposed
    The force of all their spirits, like the last
    Expiring gasp of a strong-hearted man,

Upon the hazard of one charge, but were
Oppressed and fell. The rest that could not swim   65
Were only drowned, but those that thought to 'scape
By swimming were by murderers that flankered
The level of the flood both drowned and slain.°
D'AMVILLE Now by my soul, soldier, a brave service.
MONTFERRERS O what became of my dear Charlemont?   70
BORACHIO Walking next day upon the fatal shore,
Among the slaughtered bodies of their men
Which the full-stomached sea had cast upon
The sands, it was m'unhappy chance to light
Upon a face, whose favour when it lived   75
My astonished mind informed me I had seen.
He lay in's armour as if that had been
His coffin, and the weeping sea, like one
Whose milder temper doth lament the death
Of him whom in his rage he slew, runs up   80
The shore, embraces him, kisses his cheek,
Goes back again, and forces up the sands
To bury him, and ev'ry time it parts
Sheds tears upon him, till at last (as if
It could no longer endure to see the man   85
Whom it had slain, yet loath to leave him) with
A kind of unresolved unwilling pace,
Winding her waves one in another, like
A man that folds his arms or wrings his hands
For grief, ebbed from the body and descends,   90
As if it would sink down into the earth
And hide itself for shame of such a deed.
D'AMVILLE And, soldier, who was this?
MONTFERRERS   O Charlemont!
BORACHIO Your fear hath told you that whereof my grief
Was loath to be the messenger.
CASTABELLA   O God.   95
       Exit Castabella
D'AMVILLE Charlemont drowned? Why, how could that be, since
It was the adverse party that received
The overthrow?
BORACHIO His forward spirit pressed into the front,
And, being engaged within the enemy   100
When they retreated through the rising stream,
I' the violent confusion of the throng

Was overborne and perished in the flood.
And here's the sad remembrance of his life,
      [*He produces*] *the scarf*
Which for his sake I will forever wear.   105
MONTFERRERS Torment me not with witnesses of that
Which I desire not to believe, yet must.
D'AMVILLE Thou art a screech-owl, and dost come i' night°
To be the cursèd messenger of death.
Away! Depart my house or, by my soul,   110
You'll find me a more fatal enemy
Than ever was Ostend. Be gone! Dispatch!
BORACHIO Sir, 'twas my love—
D'AMVILLE   Your love to vex my heart
With that I hate? Hark, do you hear,   you knave?°
[*Aside to Borachio*] O th'art a most delicate,° sweet, eloquent   115
   villain.
BORACHIO [*aside to D'Amville*] Was't not well counterfeited?
D'AMVILLE [*aside to Borachio*] Rarely. [*Aloud*] Be gone; I will not
   hear reply.°
BORACHIO Why, then, farewell. I will not trouble you.
         Exit [*Borachio*]
D'AMVILLE [*aside*] So. The foundation's laid. Now by degrees   120
The work will rise and soon be perfected.°
[*Aloud*] O this uncertain state of mortal man!
BELFOREST What then? It is th'inevitable fate
Of all things underneath the moon.
D'AMVILLE   'Tis true.°
Brother, for health's sake overcome your grief.   125
MONTFERRERS I cannot, sir. I am uncapable
Of comfort. My turn will be next. I feel
Myself not well.
D'AMVILLE   You yield too much to grief.
LANGUEBEAU All men are mortal. The hour of death is uncertain.
Age makes sickness the more dangerous, and grief is subject to   130
distraction.° You know not how soon you may be deprived of the
benefit of sense. In my understanding, therefore, you shall do
well if you be sick to set your state in present order. Make your
will.
D'AMVILLE [*aside*] I have my wish.   135
[*Aloud*] Lights for my brother!
MONTFERRERS   I'll withdraw a while,
And crave the honest counsel of this man.

BELFOREST With all my heart. I pray attend him, sir.
    Exeunt Montferrers and [Languebeau] Snuffe
  This next room, please your lordship.
D'AMVILLE   Where you will.
    Exeunt Belforest and D'Amville
LEVIDULCIA My daughter's gone! Come, son, Mistress Cataplasma,   140
    come; we'll up into her chamber.° I'd fain see how she entertains
    the expectation of her husband's bedfellowship.
ROUSARD 'Faith, howsoever she entertains it, I shall hardly please
    her; therefore let her rest.
LEVIDULCIA Nay, please her hardly, and you please her best.°   145
    Exeunt

[2.2]

*Enter three servants [carrying torches], drunk, drawing in
Fresco*

FIRST SERVANT Boy! Fill some drink, boy.
FRESCO Enough, good sir; not a drop more by this light.°
SECOND SERVANT Not by this light? Why then, put out the candles,
    and we'll drink i' th' dark an t'wou't,° old boy.
FRESCO No, no, no, no, no.   5
THIRD SERVANT Why then, take thy liquor. A health, Fresco!
    [Servants] kneel°
FRESCO Your health will make me sick, sir.
FIRST SERVANT Then 'twill bring you o' your knees I hope, sir.
FRESCO May I not stand and pledge it,° sir?
SECOND SERVANT I hope you will do as we do.   10
FRESCO Nay then, indeed I must not stand, for you cannot.
    [Fresco kneels]
THIRD SERVANT Well said, old boy.
FRESCO Old boy! You'll make me a young child anon, for if I
    continue this, I shall scarce be able to go alone.°
FIRST SERVANT My body is as weak as water, Fresco.   15
FRESCO Good reason, sir. The beer has sent all the malt up into your
    brain and left nothing but the water in your body.
    *Enter D'Amville and Borachio, closely observing their
    drunkenness*
D'AMVILLE Borachio, seest those fellows?
BORACHIO   Yes, my lord.

D'AMVILLE Their drunkenness that seems ridiculous
   Shall be a serious instrument to bring   20
   Our sober purposes to their success.
BORACHIO I am prepared for th'execution, sir.
D'AMVILLE Cast off this habit and about it straight.
BORACHIO
   Let them drink healths and drown their brains i' the flood;
   I'll promise them they shall be pledged in blood.   25
      Exit [Borachio]
FIRST SERVANT You ha' left a damnable snuff° here.
SECOND SERVANT Do you take that in snuff, sir?
FIRST SERVANT You are a damnable rogue then.
      [They fall] together by th' ears°
D'AMVILLE *[aside]* Fortune, I honour thee. My plot still rises
   According to the model of mine own desires.   30
   [Aloud] Lights for my brother! What, ha' you drunk yourselves
   mad, you knaves?
FIRST SERVANT My lord, the jacks abused me.°
D'AMVILLE *[to the First Servant]* I think they are the jacks° indeed
   that have abused thee. Dost hear? That fellow is a proud knave.   35
   He has abused thee. As thou goest over the fields by and by in
   lighting my brother home, I'll tell thee what sha't do: knock him
   over the pate with thy torch; I'll bear thee out in't.°
FIRST SERVANT I will singe the goose by this torch.
      Exit [First Servant]
D'AMVILLE *[to the Second Servant]* Dost hear, fellow? Seest thou that   40
   proud knave? I have given him a lesson for his sauciness. H'as
   wronged thee. I'll tell thee what sha't do: as we go over the fields
   by and by, clap him suddenly o'er the coxcomb° with thy torch;
   I'll bear thee out in't.
SECOND SERVANT I will make him understand as much.   45
      Exit [Second Servant]. Enter Languebeau Snuffe
D'AMVILLE Now, Monsieur Snuffe, what has my brother done?
LANGUEBEAU Made his will, and by that will made you his heir, with
   this proviso, that as occasion shall hereafter move him, he may
   revoke or alter it when he pleases.
D'AMVILLE *(aside)* Yes, let him if he can. I'll make it sure   50
   From his revoking.
      Enter Montferrers and Belforest, attended [by First and
      Second Servants] with lights
MONTFERRERS   Brother, now good night.
D'AMVILLE The sky is dark; we'll bring you o'er the fields.

[*Aside*] Who can but strike wants wisdom to maintain;°
He that strikes safe and sure has heart and brain.
    Exeunt

[2.3]

    Enter Castabella
CASTABELLA O love! thou chaste affection of the soul,
    Without th'adult'rate mixture of the blood,°
    That virtue which to goodness addeth good,
    The minion of Heaven's heart. Heaven, is't my fate
    For loving that thou lov'st, to get thy hate?   5
    Or was my Charlemont thy chosen love,
    And therefore hast received him to thyself?
    Then I confess thy anger's not unjust:
    I was thy rival. Yet to be divorced
    From love has been a punishment enough,   10
    Sweet Heaven, without being married unto hate,
    Hadst thou been pleased. O double misery!
    Yet since thy pleasure hath inflicted it,
    If not my heart, my duty shall submit.
        Enter Levidulcia, Rousard, Cataplasma, Soquette, and Fresco
        with a lantern
LEVIDULCIA Mistress Cataplasma, good night. I pray when your   15
    man has brought you home, let him return and light me to my
    house.
CATAPLASMA He shall instantly wait on your ladyship.
LEVIDULCIA Good, Mistress Cataplasma, for my servants are all
    drunk; I cannot be beholding to 'em for their attendance.   20
        Exeunt Cataplasma, Soquette, and Fresco
    O here's your bride.
ROUSARD   And melancholic too, methinks.
LEVIDULCIA How can she choose? Your sickness will
    Distaste th'expected sweetness o' the night.
    That makes her heavy.
ROUSARD   That should make her light.°
LEVIDULCIA Look you to that.
CASTABELLA   What sweetness speak you of?   25
    The sweetness of the night consists in rest.
ROUSARD With that sweetness thou shalt be surely blest

Unless my groaning wake thee. Do not moan.°
LEVIDULCIA Sh'ad rather you would wake and make her groan.
ROUSARD Nay, troth, sweetheart, I will not trouble thee. 30
    Thou shalt not lose thy maidenhead tonight.
CASTABELLA O might that weakness ever be in force,
    I never would desire to sue divorce!
ROUSARD Wilt go to bed?
CASTABELLA   I will attend you, sir.
ROUSARD Mother, good night.
LEVIDULCIA   Pleasure be your bedfellow. 35
    Exeunt Rousard and Castabella
    Why, sure their generation was asleep°
    When she begot those dormice, that she made°
    Them up so weakly and imperfectly.
    One wants desire, the t'other ability—
    When my affection even with their cold bloods, 40
    As snow rubbed through an active hand does make°
    The flesh to burn, by agitation is
    Inflamed! I could unbrace and entertain°
    The air to cool it.
    Enter Sebastian
SEBASTIAN   That but mitigates
    The heat; rather embrace and entertain 45
    A younger brother; he can quench the fire.
LEVIDULCIA Can you so, sir? Now I beshrew your ear.°
    Why, bold Sebastian, how dare you approach
    So near the presence of your displeased father?
SEBASTIAN Under the protection of his present absence. 50
LEVIDULCIA Belike you knew he was abroad then?
SEBASTIAN   Yes.°
    Let me encounter you so; I'll persuade°
    Your means to reconcile me to his love.°
LEVIDULCIA Is that the way? I understand you not.
    But for your reconcilement, meet m'at home; 55
    I'll satisfy your suit.
SEBASTIAN   Within this half hour?
LEVIDULCIA Or within this whole hour. When you will.
    Exit Sebastian
    A lusty blood! H'as both the presence and the spirit of a man. I
    like the freedom of his behaviour. Ho! Sebastian! Gone? H'as set
    my blood a-boiling i' my veins. And now, like water poured upon 60

the ground that mixes itself with every moisture it meets, I could
clasp with any man.
>   *Enter Fresco with a lantern*
O Fresco, art thou come?
[*Aside*] If t'other fail, then thou art entertained.
Lust is a spirit which whosoe'er doth raise,   65
The next man that encounters boldly, lays.°
>   *Exeunt*

[2.4]

>   *Enter Borachio warily and hastily over the stage,° with a
>   stone in either hand*

BORACHIO Such stones men use to raise a house upon,°
> But with these stones I go to ruin one.
>   [*Borachio*] *descends° [into the gravel pit]. Enter two Servants,
>   drunk, fighting with their torches; D'Amville, Montferrers,
>   Belforest and Languebeau Snuffe*

BELFOREST Passion o' me, you drunken knaves, you'll put the lights
out.
D'AMVILLE No, my lord, th'are but in jest.   5
FIRST SERVANT Mine's out.
D'AMVILLE [*aside to First Servant*] Then light it at his head; that's
light enough.°
>   [*Servants continue to fight, extinguishing both torches*]
'Fore God, th'are out. You drunken rascals, back and light 'em.
>   *Exeunt servants*
BELFOREST 'Tis exceeding dark.
D'AMVILLE   No matter;   10
> I am acquainted with the way. Your hand.
> Let's easily walk. I'll lead you till they come.
MONTFERRERS My soul's oppressed with grief. 'T lies heavy at my
heart. O my departed son, ere long I shall be with thee.
>   *D'Amville thrusts him down into the gravel pit*
D'AMVILLE Marry, God forbid!   15
MONTFERRERS O, O, O.
D'AMVILLE Now all the host of Heaven forbid!
>   [*Calls offstage*]
>   Knaves! Rogues!

BELFOREST Pray God he be not hurt! He's fallen into the gravel pit.
D'AMVILLE Brother, dear brother!
　　　　[*Calls offstage*]
　　　　　　　　　　　　　　Rascals, villains, knaves!
　　　　Enter the servants with lights
　　Eternal darkness damn you; come away.　　　　　　　　　20
　　Go round about into the gravel pit,
　　And help my brother up.
　　　　[*Exeunt servants*]
　　　　　　　　　　　　Why, what a strange
　　Unlucky night is this! Is't not, my lord?
　　I think that dog that howled the news of grief,°
　　That fatal screech-owl, ushered on this mischief.　　　　25
　　　　Enter [servants] with the murdered body [of Montferrers]
LANGUEBEAU Mischief indeed, my lord. Your brother's dead.
BELFOREST He's dead.
FIRST SERVANT　　　　He's dead.
D'AMVILLE　　　　　　　　Dead be your tongues! Drop out
　　Mine eye-balls, and let envious Fortune play
　　At tennis with 'em. Have I lived to this?
　　Malicious Nature, hadst thou born me blind,　　　　　　30
　　Th'adst yet been something favourable to me.
　　No breath? No motion? Prithee tell me, Heaven,
　　Hast shut thine eye to wink at murder, or
　　Hast put this sable garment on to mourn
　　At's death?°　　　　　　　　　　　　　　　　　　35
　　Not one poor spark in the whole spacious sky
　　Of all that endless number would vouchsafe
　　To shine? You viceroys to the king of Nature,
　　Whose constellations govern mortal births,°
　　Where is that fatal planet ruled at his　　　　　　　　40
　　Nativity? That might ha' pleased to light
　　Him out, as well into th'world, unless
　　It be ashamed t'ave been the instrument
　　Of such a good man's cursèd destiny!
BELFOREST Passions transports you. Recollect yourself.°　　　45
　　Lament him not. Whether our deaths be good
　　Or bad, it is not death but life that tries.°
　　He lived well, therefore questionless well dies.
D'AMVILLE Aye, 'tis an easy thing for him that has
　　No pain to talk of patience. Do you think　　　　　　　50

That Nature has no feeling?
BELFOREST   Feeling? Yes.°
  But has she purposed anything for nothing?
  What good receives this body by your grief?
  Whether is't more unnatural not to grieve°
  For him you cannot help with it, or hurt   55
  Yourself with grieving and yet grieve in vain?
D'AMVILLE Indeed, had he been taken from me like
  A piece o' dead flesh, I should neither ha' felt it
  Nor grieved for 't. But come hither, pray look here.
  Behold the lively tincture of his blood!   60
  Neither the dropsy nor the jaundice in't,
  But the true freshness of a sanguine red,°
  For all the fog of this black murd'rous night°
  Has mixed with it. For anything I know,
  He might ha' lived till doomsday, and ha' done   65
  More good than either you or I. O brother!
  He was a man of such a native goodness,
  As if regeneration had been given°
  Him in his mother's womb; so harmless°
  That rather than ha' trod upon a worm   70
  He would ha' shunned the way; so dearly pitiful°
  That ere the poor could ask his charity
  With dry eyes, he gave 'em relief wi' tears—
     [Weeps]
  With tears—yes, faith, with tears.
BELFOREST   Take up the corpse.
  For wisdom's sake, let reason fortify   75
  This weakness.
D'AMVILLE   Why, what would you ha' me do?
  Foolish Nature will have her course in spite
  O' wisdom. But I have e'en done.
  All these words were but a great wind, and now
  This shower of tears has laid it, I am calm again.°   80
  You may set forward when you will.
  I'll follow you like one that must and would not.
LANGUEBEAU Our opposition will but trouble him.
BELFOREST The grief that melts to tears by itself is spent;
  Passion resisted grows more violent.   85
     Exeunt [all except] D'Amville. Borachio ascends° [from the
     gravel pit]

D'AMVILLE Here's a sweet comedy. 'T begins with '*O Dolentis*'°
  And concludes with 'ha, ha, he'.
BORACHIO   Ha, ha, he.
D'AMVILLE O my echo! I could stand
  Reverberating this sweet musical air
  Of joy till I had perished my sound lungs°   90
  With violent laughter. Lovely night-raven!
  Th'ast seized a carcass.
BORACHIO   Put him out on's pain.
  I lay so fitly underneath the bank
  From whence he fell, that ere his falt'ring tongue
  Could utter double 'O', I knocked out's brains   95
  With this fair ruby, and had another stone°
  Just of this form and bigness ready, that
  I laid i' th' broken skull upon the ground
  For's pillow, against the which they thought he fell
  And perished.   100
D'AMVILLE Upon this ground I'll build my manor house,
  And this shall be the chiefest corner-stone.
BORACHIO 'T has crowned the most judicious murder that°
  The brain of man was e'er delivered of.
D'AMVILLE Aye, mark the plot. Not any circumstance   105
  That stood within the reach of the design,
  Of persons, dispositions, matter, time,
  Or place, but by this brain of mine was made
  An instrumental help; yet nothing from
  Th'induction to th'accomplishment seemed forced   110
  Or done o' purpose, but by accident.
BORACHIO First, my report that Charlemont was dead,
  Though false, yet covered with a mask of truth.
D'AMVILLE Aye, and delivered in as fit a time,
  When all our minds so wholly were possessed   115
  With one affair, that no man would suspect
  A thought employed for any second end.
BORACHIO Then the precision to be ready, when
  Your brother spake of death, to move his will.
D'AMVILLE His business called him thither, and it fell   120
  Within his office, unrequested to't.
  From him it came religiously and saved
  Our project from suspicion, which if I
  Had moved had been endangered.

BORACHIO   Then your healths,
   Though seeming but the ordinary rites   125
   And ceremonies due to festivals—
D'AMVILLE Yet used by me to make the servants drunk,
   An instrument the plot could not have missed.°
   'Twas easy to set drunkards by the ears;
   Th'ad nothing but their torches to fight with,   130
   And when those lights were out—
BORACHIO   Then darkness did
   Protect the execution of the work
   Both from prevention and discovery.
D'AMVILLE Here was a murder bravely carried through
   The eye of observation, unobserved.°   135
BORACHIO And those that saw the passage of it made
   The instruments, yet knew not what they did.
D'AMVILLE That power of rule philosophers ascribe
   To him they call the supreme of the stars,°
   Making their influences governors°   140
   Of sublunary creatures, when their selves°
   Are senseless of their operations—
      Thunder and lightning

                 What!°
   Dost start at thunder? Credit my belief;
   'Tis a mere effect of Nature,
   An exhalation hot and dry, involved   145
   Within a wat'ry vapour i' the middle
   Region of the air, whose coldness°
   Congealing that thick moisture to a cloud,
   The angry exhalation shut within
   A prison of contrary quality   150
   Strives to be free; and with the violent
   Eruption through the grossness of that cloud
   Makes this noise we hear.
BORACHIO   'Tis a fearful noise.°
D'AMVILLE 'Tis a brave noise, and methinks graces our
   Accomplished project as a peal of ordnance   155
   Does a triumph; it speaks encouragement.°
   Now Nature shows thee how it favoured our
   Performance, to forbear this noise when we
   Set forth, because it should not terrify
   My brother's going home, which would have dashed   160
   Our purpose—to forbear this lightning

In our passage, lest it should ha' warned him°
O' the pitfall. Then propitious Nature winked
At our proceedings; now it doth express
How that forbearance favoured our success.   165

BORACHIO You have confirmed me; for it follows well°
That Nature, since herself decay doth hate,
Should favour those that strengthen their estate.

D'AMVILLE Our next endeavour is—since on the false
Report that Charlemont is dead depends   170
The fabric of the work—to credit that°
With all the countenance we can.

BORACHIO   Faith, sir,°
Even let his own inheritance, whereof
Y'ave dispossessed him, countenance the act.
Spare so much out of that to give him a   175
Solemnity of funeral; 'twill quit
The cost, and make your apprehension of°
His death appear more confident and true.

D'AMVILLE I'll take thy counsel. Now⸱farewell black night,
Thou beauteous mistress of a murderer;   180
To honour thee, that hast accomplished all,
I'll wear thy colours at his funeral.
          Exeunt

[2.5]

          Enter Levidulcia into her chamber, manned° by Fresco

LEVIDULCIA Th'art welcome into my chamber, Fresco. Prithee shut
the door. [*He starts to leave*] Nay, thou mistakest me. Come in and
shut it.

FRESCO 'Tis somewhat late, madam.

LEVIDULCIA No matter. I have somewhat° to say to thee. What, is   5
not thy mistress towards° a husband yet?

FRESCO Faith, madam, she has suitors, but they will not suit her,
methinks. They will not come off lustily,° it seems.

LEVIDULCIA They will not come on lustily, thou wouldst say.

FRESCO I mean, madam, they are not rich enough.   10

LEVIDULCIA But I, Fresco, they are not bold enough. Thy mistress
is of a lively attractive blood, Fresco, and in troth she's o' my mind
for that. A poor spirit is poorer than a poor purse.° Give me a

fellow that brings not only temptation with him, but has the
activity of wit and audacity of spirit to apply every word and   15
gesture of a woman's speech and behaviour to his own desire, and
make her believe she's the suitor herself, never give back till he has
made her yield to it.

FRESCO Indeed among our equals, madam, but otherwise we shall be
put horribly out o' countenance.°   20

LEVIDULCIA Thou art deceived, Fresco. Ladies are as courteous as
yeomen's wives, and methinks they should be more gentle.° Hot°
diet and soft ease makes 'em, like wax always kept warm, more
easy to take impression. Prithee untie my shoe. What, art thou
shamefaced too? Go roundly to work, man. My leg is not gouty;°   25
'twill endure the feeling,° I warrant thee. Come hither, Fresco;
thine ear.
     [*Levidulcia kisses Fresco*]
'Sdainty,° I mistook the place; I missed thine ear and hit thy lip.

FRESCO Your ladyship has made me blush.

LEVIDULCIA That shows th' art full o' lusty blood and thou knowest   30
not how to use it. Let me see thy hand. Thou shouldst not be
shamefaced by thy hand, Fresco. Here's a brawny flesh and a hairy
skin, both signs of an able body. I do not like these phlegmatic,
smooth-skinned, soft-fleshed fellows. They are like candied suckets
when they begin to perish, which I would always empty my closet   35
of and give 'em my chamber-maid. I have some skill in palmistry;
by this line that stands directly against me° thou shouldst be near
a good fortune, Fresco, if thou hadst the grace to entertain it.

FRESCO O what is that, madam, I pray?

LEVIDULCIA No less than the love of a fair lady, if thou dost not lose   40
her with faint-heartedness.

FRESCO A lady, madam? Alas, a lady is a great thing; I cannot
compass° her.

LEVIDULCIA No? Why? I am a lady. Am I so great I cannot be
compassed? Clasp my waist and try.   ·   45

FRESCO I could find i' my heart, madam—
     Sebastian knocks within

LEVICULCIA 'Uds body, my husband! Faint-hearted fool, I think
thou wert begotten between the North Pole and the congealed
passage!° Now, like an ambitious coward that betrays himself with
fearful delay, you must suffer for the treason you never com-   50
mitted.° Go, hide thyself behind yond arras, instantly.
     Fresco hides himself. Enter Sebastian

Sebastian! What do you here so late?

SEBASTIAN Nothing yet, but I hope I shall.

Sebastian kisses Levidulcia

LEVIDULCIA Y'are very bold.

SEBASTIAN And you very valiant, for you met me at full career.°   55

LEVIDULCIA You come to ha' me move your father's reconciliation.
I'll write a word or two i' your behalf.

SEBASTIAN A word or two, madam? That you do for me will not be
contained in less than the compass of two sheets.° But in plain
terms, shall we take the opportunity of privateness?   60

LEVIDULCIA What to do?

SEBASTIAN To dance the beginning of the world after the English
manner.°

LEVIDULCIA Why not after the French or Italian?

SEBASTIAN Fie, they dance it preposterously,° backward.   65

LEVIDULCIA Are you so active° to dance?

SEBASTIAN I can shake my heels.

LEVIDULCIA Y'are well made for't.

SEBASTIAN Measure me from top to toe, you shall not find me differ
much from the true standard of proportion.   70

Belforest knocks within

LEVIDULCIA I think I am accursed. Sebastian, there's one at the door
has beaten opportunity away from us. In brief, I love thee, and it
shall not be long before I give thee a testimony of it. To save thee
now from suspicion, do no more but draw thy rapier, chafe°
thyself, and when he comes in rush by without taking notice of   75
him. Only seem to be angry, and let me alone for° the rest.

Enter Belforest

SEBASTIAN Now by the hand of Mercury!

Exit Sebastian

BELFOREST What's the matter, wife?

LEVIDULCIA Ooh, ooh, husband!

BELFOREST Prithee what ail'st thou, woman?   80

LEVIDULCIA O feel my pulse. It beats, I warrant you. Be patient a
little, sweet husband; tarry but till my breath come to me again,
and I'll satisfy you.

BELFOREST What ails Sebastian? He looks so distractedly!

LEVIDULCIA The poor gentleman's almost out on's° wits, I think.   85
You remember the displeasure his father took against him about
the liberty of speech he used even now when your daughter went
to be married?

BELFOREST Yes, what of that?

LEVIDULCIA 'T has crazed him sure. He met a poor man i' the street   90
even now. Upon what quarrel I know not, but he pursued him so
violently that if my house had not been his rescue, he had surely
killed him.

BELFOREST What a strange desperate young man is that!

LEVIDULCIA Nay, husband, he grew so in rage when he saw the man   95
was conveyed from him that he was ready even to have drawn his
naked weapon° upon me. And had not your knocking at the door
prevented him, surely h'ad done something to me.

BELFOREST Where's the man?

LEVIDULCIA Alas, here. I warrant you the poor fearful soul is scarce   100
come to himself again yet. [*Aside*] If the fool have any wit he will
apprehend me. [*To Fresco*] Do you hear, sir? You may be bold to
come forth; the Fury that haunted you is gone.

Fresco peeps fearfully forth from behind the arras

FRESCO Are you sure he is gone?

BELFOREST He's gone; he's gone, I warrant thee.   105

FRESCO I would I were gone too. H' as shook me almost into a dead
palsy.°

BELFOREST How fell the difference between you?

FRESCO I would I were out at the back door.

BELFOREST Th'art safe enough. Prithee tell's the falling out.   110

FRESCO Yes sir, when I have recovered my spirits. My memory is
almost frighted from me. O, so, so, so. Why, sir, as I came along
the street, sir, this same gentleman came stumbling after me and
trod o' my heel. I cried 'O'. 'Do you cry, sirrah?' says he. 'Let me
see your heel; if it be not hurt, I'll make you cry for something.'   115
So he claps my head between his legs and pulls off my shoe. I
having shifted no socks in a sennight, the gentleman cried, 'Foh,'
and said my feet were base and cowardly feet; they stunk for fear.
Then he knocked my shoe about my pate, and I cried 'O', once
more. In the meantime comes a shag-haired° dog by and rubs   120
against his shins. The gentleman took the dog in shag-hair to be
some watchman in a rug gown,° and swore he would hang me up
at the next door with my lantern in my hand, that passengers
might see their way as they went without rubbing against
gentlemen's shins. So, for want of a cord, he took his own garters   125
off, and as he was going to make a noose, I watched my time° and
ran away. And as I ran, indeed, I bid him hang himself in his own
garters.° So he, in choler, pursued me hither as you see.

BELFOREST Why, this savours of° distraction.

LEVIDULCIA Of mere distraction.   130
FRESCO [*aside*] Howsoever it savours, I am sure it smells like a lie.
BELFOREST Thou may'st go forth at the back door, honest fellow;
  the way is private and safe.
FRESCO So it had need, for your fore-door,° here, is both common°
  and dangerous.°   135
     Exit Belforest
LEVIDULCIA Good night, honest Fresco.
FRESCO Good night, madam. If you get me kissing o'ladies again—
     Exit Fresco
LEVIDULCIA This falls out handsomely.
  But yet the matter does not well succeed
  Till I have brought it to the very deed.   140
     Exit

[2.6]

     Enter Charlemont in arms, a Musketeer, and a Sergeant
CHARLEMONT Sergeant, what hour o' the night is 't?
SERGEANT About one.
CHARLEMONT I would you would relieve me, for I am
  So heavy that I shall ha' much ado°
  To stand out my perdu.
     Thunder and lightning
SERGEANT   I'll e'en but walk   5
  The round, sir, and then presently return.
MUSKETEER For God's sake, sergeant, relieve me. Above five hours
  together in so foul a stormy night as this!
SERGEANT Why, 'tis a music, soldier. Heaven and earth are now in
  consort,° when the thunder and the cannon play one to an-   10
  other.
     Exit Sergeant
CHARLEMONT I know not why I should be thus inclined
  To sleep; I feel my disposition pressed
  With a necessity of heaviness.
  Soldier, if thou hast any better eyes,   15
  I prithee wake me when the sergeant comes.
MUSKETEER Sir, 'tis so dark and stormy that I shall
  Scarce either see or hear him ere he comes
  Upon me.

CHARLEMONT I cannot force myself to wake.
     [Charlemont] sleeps. Enter the Ghost of Montferrers
GHOST Return to France, for thy old father's dead   20
  And thou by murder disinherited.
  Attend with patience the success of things,°
  But leave revenge unto the King of kings.
     Exit [Ghost]. Charlemont starts and wakes
CHARLEMONT O my affrighted soul! what fearful dream
  Was this that waked me? Dreams are but the raised   25
  Impressions of premeditated things,
  By serious apprehension left upon
  Our minds, or else th'imaginary shapes
  Of objects proper to th'complexion or°
  The dispositions of our bodies. These°   30
  Can neither of them be the cause why I
  Should dream thus, for my mind has not been moved
  With any one conception of a thought
  To such a purpose, nor my nature wont
  To trouble me with fantasies of terror.   35
  It must be something that my Genius would°
  Inform me of. Now gracious Heaven forbid!
  O, let my spirit be deprived of all
  Foresight and knowledge ere it understand
  That vision acted, or divine that act   40
  To come. Why should I think so? Left I not°
  My worthy father i' the kind regard°
  Of a most loving uncle?—Soldier, saw'st
  No apparition of a man?
MUSKETEER   You dream,
  Sir; I saw nothing.
CHARLEMONT   Tush, these idle dreams   45
  Are fabulous. Our boiling fantasies
  Like troubled waters falsify the shapes
  Of things retained in them, and make 'em seem
  Confounded when they are distinguished. So°
  My actions daily conversant with war,   50
  The argument of blood and death, had left,
  Perhaps, th'imaginary presence of
  Some bloody accident upon my mind,
  Which, mixed confusedly with other thoughts,
  Whereof th'remembrance of my father might   55

Be one, presented all together seem
Incorporate, as if his body were
The owner of that blood, the subject of
That death, when he's at Paris and that blood
Shed here. It may be thus. I would not leave   60
The war, for reputation's sake, upon
An idle apprehension, a vain dream.
    Enter the Ghost
MUSKETEER Stand! Stand, I say! No? Why then, have at thee!
  Sir, if you will not stand, I'll make you fall.
    [*Fires his musket at the Ghost*]
  Nor stand, nor fall? Nay, then the devil's dam   65
  Has broke her husband's head, for sure it is a spirit.°
  I shot it through, and yet it will not fall.
    Exit [*Musketeer*]. *The Ghost approaches Charlemont. He*
    fearfully avoids it
CHARLEMONT O pardon me! My doubtful heart was slow°
  To credit that which I did fear to know.
    Exeunt

[3.1]

Enter [D'Amville with] the funeral of Montferrers
D'AMVILLE Set down the body. Pay earth what she lent,
But she shall bear a living monument°
To let succeeding ages truly know
That she is satisfied what he did owe,°
Both principal and use, because his worth°   5
Was better at his death than at his birth.
    A dead march. Enter the funeral of Charlemont as a soldier,
    [escorted by musketeers]
And with his body place that memory°
Of noble Charlemont, his worthy son,
And give their graves the rites that do belong
To soldiers. They were soldiers both. The father   10
Held open war with sin, the son with blood;
This in a war more gallant, that more good.
    [Musketeers fire] the first volley
There place their arms, and here their epitaphs,°
And may these lines survive the last of graves:
    [D'Amville reads]
                  The Epitaph of Montferrers   15
        Here lie the ashes of that earth and fire
        Whose heat and fruit did feed and warm the poor;
        And they, as if they would in sighs expire
        And into tears dissolve, his death deplore.°
    — *He did that good freely, for goodness' sake,*   20
        Unforced, for gen'rousness he held so dear
        That he feared none but Him that did him make,
        And yet he served Him more for love than fear.
            So's life provided that though he did die°
            A sudden death, yet died not suddenly.°   25
                  The Epitaph of Charlemont
        His body lies interred within this mould,°
        Who died a young man, yet departed old,°
        And in all strength of youth that man can have
        Was ready still to drop into his grave.   30
        For aged in virtue, with a youthful eye
        He welcomed it, being still prepared to die;

And living so, though young deprived of breath,
He did not suffer an untimely death,
But we may say of his brave blest decease: 35
He died in war, and yet he died in peace.
    [Musketeers fire] the second volley
O might that fire revive the ashes of
This phoenix! Yet the wonder would not be°
So great as he was good, and wondered at
For that. His life's example was so true 40
A practique of religion's theory
That her divinity seemed rather the
Description than th'instruction of his life,
And of his goodness was his virtuous son
A worthy imitator. So that on 45
These two Herculean pillars, where their arms°
Are placed, there may be writ *Non ultra*. For
Beyond their lives, as well for youth as age,
Nor young nor old, in merit or in name,
Shall e'er exceed their virtues or their fame. 50
    [Musketeers fire] the third volley
'Tis done. [*Aside*] Thus fair accompliments make foul
Deeds gracious. Charlemont, come now when t'wou't,°
I've buried under these two marble stones
Thy living hopes and thy dead father's bones.
    Exeunt [D'Amville and the funeral attendants]. Enter
    Castabella mourning, to the monument of Charlemont
CASTABELLA O Thou that knowest me justly Charlemont's, 55
Though in the forced possession of another,
Since from Thine own free spirit we receive it
That our affections cannot be compelled,
Though our actions may, be not displeased if on
The altar of his tomb I sacrifice 60
My tears. They are the jewels of my love
Dissolvèd into grief, and fall upon
His blasted spring as April dew upon
A sweet young blossom shaked before the time.
    Enter Charlemont with a servant
CHARLEMONT Go see my trunks disposed of. I'll but walk 65
A turn or two i'th'church and follow you.°
    Exit Servant
O, here's the fatal monument of my

Dead father first presented to mine eye.
What's here? In memory of Charlemont?
Some false relation has abused belief.°   70
I am deluded. But I thank thee, Heaven;
Forever let me be deluded thus.
My Castabella mourning o'er my hearse?
Sweet Castabella, rise; I am not dead.

CASTABELLA O Heaven defend me!
      [*Castabella*] *falls in a swoon*

CHARLEMONT   I beshrew my rash   75
And inconsid'rate passion—Castabella!—
That could not think—my Castabella!—that
My sudden presence might affright her sense.
I prithee, my affection, pardon me.
            Castabella rises
Reduce thy understanding to thine eye.°   80
Within this habit which thy misinformed
Conceit takes only for a shape, live both°
The soul and body of thy Charlemont.

CASTABELLA [*touching him*]
I feel a substance warm and soft and moist,
Subject to the capacity of sense.°   85

CHARLEMONT Which spirits are not, for their essence is
Above the nature and the order of
Those elements whereof our senses are
Created. Touch my lip. Why turn'st thou from me?

CASTABELLA Grief above griefs! That which should woe relieve, 90
Wished and obtained, gives greater cause to grieve.

CHARLEMONT Can Castabella think it cause of grief
That the relation of my death proves false?

CASTABELLA The presence of the person we affect,
Being hopeless to enjoy him, makes our grief   95
More passionate than if we saw him not.

CHARLEMONT Why not enjoy? Has absence changed thee?

CASTABELLA   Yes,
From maid to wife.

CHARLEMONT   Art married?

CASTABELLA   O, I am.

CHARLEMONT Married! Had not my mother been a woman,
I should protest against the chastity   100
Of all thy sex. How can the merchant or

The mariner, absent whole years from wives
Experienced in the satisfaction of
Desire, promise themselves to find their sheets
Unspotted with adultery at their   105
Return, when you that never had the sense
Of actual temptation could not stay
A few short months?
CASTABELLA   O, do but hear me speak.
CHARLEMONT But thou wert wise, and didst consider that
A soldier might be maimed and so perhaps   110
Lose his ability to please thee.
CASTABELLA   No.
That weakness pleases me in him I have.
CHARLEMONT What, married to a man unable too?
O strange incontinence! Why? was thy blood
Increased to such a pleurisy of lust   115
That of necessity there must a vein
Be opened, though by one that had no skill°
To do 't?
CASTABELLA Sir, I beseech you hear me.
CHARLEMONT   Speak.
CASTABELLA Heav'n knows I am unguilty of this act.
CHARLEMONT Why, wert thou forced to do't?
CASTABELLA   Heav'n knows I was.   120
CHARLEMONT What villain did it?
CASTABELLA   Your uncle D'Amville.
And he that dispossessed my love of you
Hath disinherited you of possession.°
CHARLEMONT Disinherited? Wherein have I deserved
To be deprived of my dear father's love?   125
CASTABELLA Both of his love and him. His soul's at rest,
But here your injured patience may behold
The signs of his lamented memory.
            Charlemont finds his father's monument
H'as found it. When I took him for a ghost
I could endure the torment of my fear   130
More eas'ly than I can his sorrows hear.
            Exit [Castabella]
CHARLEMONT Of all men's griefs must mine be singular?
Without example? Here I met my grave,
And all men's woes are buried i' their graves

But mine. In mine my miseries are born.   135
I prithee, sorrow, leave a little room
In my confounded and tormented mind
For understanding to deliberate
The cause or author of this accident;
A close advantage of my absence made   140
To dispossess me both of land and wife,
And all the profit does arise to him
By whom my absence was first moved and urged.
These circumstances, uncle, tell me you
Are the suspected author of those wrongs,   145
Whereof the lightest is more heavy than
The strongest patience can endure to bear.
    Exit

[3.2]

Enter D'Amville, Sebastian, and Languebeau Snuffe

D'AMVILLE Now, sir! Your business?
SEBASTIAN   My annuity.
D'AMVILLE Not a denier.
SEBASTIAN   How would you ha' me live?
D'AMVILLE Why, turn crier. Cannot you turn crier?°
SEBASTIAN Yes.
D'AMVILLE   Then do so; y'ave a good voice for't.
   Y'are excellent at crying of a rape.   5
SEBASTIAN Sir, I confess in particular respect to yourself I was
   somewhat forgetful. General honesty possessed me.
D'AMVILLE Go, th'art the base corruption of my blood,
   And like a tetter grow'st unto my flesh.°
SEBASTIAN Inflict any punishment upon me. The severity shall not   10
   discourage me if it be not shameful, so you'll but put money i'my
   purse. The want of money makes a free spirit more mad than the
   possession does an usurer.
D'AMVILLE Not a farthing.
SEBASTIAN Would you ha' me turn purse-taker? 'Tis the next° way   15
   to do't. For want is like the rack;° it draws a man to endanger
   himself to the gallows rather than endure it.
     Enter Charlemont. D'Amville counterfeits to take him for a
     ghost

D'AMVILLE What art thou? Stay! Assist my troubled sense.
  My apprehension° will distract me. Stay!
          Languebeau Snuffe avoids [Charlemont] fearfully
SEBASTIAN What art thou? Speak!
CHARLEMONT   The spirit of Charlemont.   20
D'AMVILLE O stay! Compose me. I dissolve.°
LANGUEBEAU No, 'tis profane. Spirits are invisible. 'Tis the fiend i'
  the likeness of Charlemont.° I will have no conversation with
  Satan.
          Exit Languebeau Snuffe
SEBASTIAN The spirit of Charlemont? I'll try that.   25
          Strike[s] Charlemont, and the blow [is] returned
  'Fore God, thou sayest true; th'art all spirit.°
D'AMVILLE Go call the officers.
          Exit D'Amville
CHARLEMONT Th'art a villain and the son of a villain.
SEBASTIAN You lie.
          [They] fight. Sebastian is down
CHARLEMONT *[about to kill Sebastian]* Have at thee.
          Enter the Ghost of Montferrers
  Revenge, to thee I'll dedicate this work.   30
GHOST Hold, Charlemont!
  Let Him revenge my murder and thy wrongs
  To whom the justice of revenge belongs.
          Exit [Ghost]
CHARLEMONT You torture me between the passion of
  My blood, and the religion of my soul.   35
          Sebastian rises
SEBASTIAN A good honest fellow.
          Enter D'Amville [and Borachio] with Officers
D'AMVILLE What, wounded? Apprehend him. Sir, is this
  Your salutation for the courtesy
  I did you when we parted last? You ha'
  Forgot I lent you a thousand crowns. *[To the Officers]* First let   40
  Him answer for this riot. When the law°
  Is satisfied for that, an action for°
  His debt shall clap him up again. *[To Charlemont]* I took
  You for a spirit, and I'll conjure you°
  Before I ha' done.
CHARLEMONT   No. I'll turn conjurer. Devil!   45
  Within this circle, in the midst of all°
  Thy force and malice, I conjure thee do

293

Thy worst.

D'AMVILLE   Away with him.

Exeunt Officers with Charlemont

SEBASTIAN   Sir, I have got
A scratch or two here for your sake. I hope
You'll give me money to pay the surgeon.   50

D'AMVILLE   Borachio, fetch me a thousand crowns!

[*Exit Borachio*]

                                                                    I am

Content to countenance the freedom of°
Your spirit when 'tis worthily employed.
A' God's name, give behaviour the full scope
Of gen'rous liberty, but let it not   55
Disperse and spend itself in courses of
Unbounded licence.

       [*Enter Borachio with the money*]
                          Here, pay for your hurts.

SEBASTIAN   I thank you, sir.

       [*Exeunt*] D'Amville [*and Borachio*]

'Gen'rous liberty'—that is to say, freely to bestow my abilities to
honest purposes. Methinks I should not follow that instruction   60
now if, having the means to do an honest office for an honest
fellow, I should neglect it. Charlemont lies in prison for a thousand
crowns, and here I have a thousand crowns. Honesty tells me
'twere well done to release Charlemont. But discretion says I had
much ado to come by this, and when this shall be gone I know not   65
where to finger any more, especially if I employ it to this use,
which is like to endanger me into my father's perpetual displeasure. And then I may go hang myself, or be forced to do that will
make another save me the labour. No matter. Charlemont, thou
gav'st me my life, and that's somewhat of a purer earth than gold,   70
as fine as it is. 'Tis no courtesy I do thee, but thankfulness. I owe
thee it and I'll pay it. He fought bravely, but the officers dragged
him villainously. Arrant knaves! For using him so discourteously,
may the sins o' the poor people be so few that you sha' not be able
to spare so much out o' your gettings° as will pay for the hire of   75
a lame starved hackney to ride to an execution, but go a-foot to
the gallows and be hanged. May elder brothers° turn good
husbands° and younger brothers° get good wives, that there be no
need of debt-books nor use of sergeants. May there be all peace
but i' the war and all charity but i' the devil, so that prisons may   80

be turned to hospitals,° though the officers live o' the benevolence.° If this curse might come to pass, the world would say,
'Blessed be he that curseth.'
    Exit

[3.3]

    Enter Charlemont in prison
CHARLEMONT I grant thee, Heaven, thy goodness doth command
    Our punishments, but yet no further than
    The measure of our sins. How should they else°
    Be just? Or how should that good purpose of
    Thy justice take effect by bounding men   5
    Within the confines of humanity,
    When our afflictions do exceed our crimes?°
    Then they do rather teach the barb'rous world
    Examples that extend her cruelties
    Beyond their own dimensions, and instruct   10
    Our actions to be more, more barbarous.
    O my afflicted soul, how torment swells
    Thy apprehension with profane conceit
    Against the sacred justice of my God!
    Our own constructions are the authors of°   15
    Our misery. We never measure our
    Conditions but with men above us in
    Estate, so while our spirits labour to
    Be higher than our fortunes, th'are more base.
    Since all those attributes which make men seem°   20
    Superior to us are man's subjects and
    Were made to serve him, the repining man
    Is of a servile spirit to deject°
    The value of himself below their estimation.
    Enter Sebastian with the Keeper
SEBASTIAN [*to the Keeper*] Here, take my sword. [*To Charlemont*]   25
    How now, my wild swaggerer, y'are tame enough now, are you
    not? The penury of a prison is like a soft consumption.° 'Twill
    humble the pride o' your mortality and arm your soul in complete
    patience to endure the weight of affliction without feeling it. What,
    hast no music in thee? Th'ast trebles and basses enough, treble°   30

injury and base usage. But trebles and basses make poor music
without means.° Thou want'st means, dost? What, dost droop? Art
dejected?

CHARLEMONT   No, sir. I have a heart above the reach
Of thy most violent maliciousness,   35
A fortitude in scorn of thy contempt—
Since Fate is pleased to have me suffer it—
That can bear more than thou hast power t'inflict.
I was a baron; that thy father has
Deprived me of. Instead of that, I am   40
Created king. I've lost a signory
That was confined within a piece of earth,
A wart upon the body of the world.
But now I am an emp'ror of a world,
This little world of man. My passions are°   45
My subjects, and I can command them laugh,
Whilst thou dost tickle 'em to death with misery.

SEBASTIAN   'Tis bravely spoken, and I love thee for 't. Thou liest
here for a thousand crowns. Here are a thousand to redeem
thee—not for the ransom o' my life thou gav'st me; that I value   50
not at one crown. 'Tis none o' my deed; thank my father for 't.
'Tis his goodness. Yet he looks not for thanks, for he does it
underhand,° out of a reserved° disposition to do thee good without
ostentation.
       [Holds out the money]
Out o' great heart you'll refuse't now, will you?   55

CHARLEMONT   [taking the money]
No. Since I must submit myself to Fate,
I never will neglect the offer of
One benefit, but entertain them as
Her favours and th'inductions to some end   60
Of better fortune, as whose instrument
I thank thy courtesy.

SEBASTIAN   Well, come along.
       Exeunt

[3.4]

Enter D'Amville and Castabella

D'AMVILLE Daughter, you do not well to urge me. I
  Ha' done no more than justice. Charlemont
  Shall die and rot in prison, and 'tis just.
CASTABELLA O father, mercy is an attribute
  As high as justice, an essential part 5
  Of His unbounded goodness, whose divine
  Impression, form, and image man should bear.
  And, methinks, man should love to imitate
  His mercy, since the only countenance°
  Of justice were destruction, if the sweet 10
  And loving favour of His mercy did
  Not mediate between it and our weakness.
D'AMVILLE Forbear. You will displease me. He shall rot.
CASTABELLA Dear sir, since by your greatness you
  Are nearer Heav'n in place, be nearer it 15
  In goodness! Rich men should transcend the poor
  As clouds the earth, raised by the comfort of
  The sun to water dry and barren grounds.
  If neither the impression in your soul
  Of goodness, nor the duty of your place 20
  As goodness' substitute can move you, then°
  Let Nature, which in savages, in beasts,
  Can stir to pity, tell you that he is
  Your kinsman.
D'AMVILLE   You expose your honesty
  To strange construction. Why should you so urge 25
  Release for Charlemont? Come, you profess
  More nearness to him than your modesty
  Can answer. You have tempted my suspicion.
  I tell thee he shall starve, and die, and rot.
    Enter Charlemont and Sebastian
CHARLEMONT Uncle, I thank you.
D'AMVILLE   Much good do it you. 30
  Who did release him?
SEBASTIAN   I.
    Exit Castabella
D'AMVILLE [*aside to Sebastian*] You are a villain.

SEBASTIAN [*aside to D'Amville*] Y'are my father.
    Exit Sebastian
D'AMVILLE [*aside*]   I must temporize.°
    [*To Charlemont*] Nephew, had not his open freedom made°
    My disposition known, I would ha' borne
    The course and inclination of my love   35
    According to the motion of the sun,°
    Invisibly enjoyed and understood.
CHARLEMONT That shows your good works are directed to
    No other end than goodness. I was rash,
    I must confess, but—
D'AMVILLE   I will excuse you.   40
    To lose a father and, as you may think,
    Be disinherited, it must be granted,
    Are motives to impatience. But for death,
    Who can avoid it? And for his estate,
    In the uncertainty of both your lives   45
    'Twas done discreetly to confer 't upon
    A known successor, being the next in blood,
    And one, dear nephew, whom in time to come
    You shall have cause to thank. I will not be
    Your dispossessor, but your guardian.   50
    I will supply your father's vacant place,
    To guide your green improvidence of youth
    And make you ripe for your inheritance.
CHARLEMONT Sir, I embrace your gen'rous promises.
        [*Charlemont embraces D'Amville.*] *Enter Rousard sick,*
        and Castabella
ROUSARD Embracing? I behold the object that   55
    Mine eye affects. Dear cousin Charlemont!
D'AMVILLE My elder son! He meets you happily,
    For with the hand of our whole family
    We interchange th'indenture of our loves.°
CHARLEMONT And I accept it, yet not joyfully   60
    Because y'are sick.
D'AMVILLE   Sir, his affection's sound
    Though he be sick in body.
ROUSARD   Sick indeed.
    A gen'ral weakness did surprise my health
    The very day I married Castabella,
    As if my sickness were a punishment   65

That did arrest me for some injury
I then committed. [*To Castabella*] Credit me, my love,
I pity thy ill fortune to be matched
With such a weak unpleasing bedfellow.

CASTABELLA Believe me, sir, it never troubles me.   70
I am as much respectless to enjoy°
Such pleasure as ignorant what it is.

CHARLEMONT Thy sex's wonder. [*Aside*] Unhappy Charlemont!

D'AMVILLE Come, let's to supper. There we will confirm
The eternal bond of our concluded love.°   75

     Exeunt

[4.1]

Enter Cataplasma and Soquette with needlework

CATAPLASMA Come, Soquette, your work! let's examine your work.
What's here? A medlar with a plum tree growing hard by it,° the
leaves o' the plum tree falling off, the gum issuing out o' the
perished joints,° and the branches some of 'em dead and some
rotten, and yet but a young plum tree. In good sooth, very pretty.   5

SOQUETTE The plum tree, forsooth, grows so near the medlar that
the medlar sucks and draws all the sap from it and the natural
strength o' the ground, so that it cannot prosper.

CATAPLASMA How conceited you are! But here th'ast made a tree to
bear no fruit. Why's that?   10

SOQUETTE There grows a savin tree° next it, forsooth.

CATAPLASMA Forsooth, you are a little too witty in that.

Enter Sebastian

SEBASTIAN [*embracing her*] But this honeysuckle° winds about this
whitethorn° very prettily and lovingly, sweet Mistress Cataplasma.   15

CATAPLASMA Monsieur Sebastian! In good sooth, very uprightly°
welcome this evening.

SEBASTIAN What, moralizing upon this gentlewoman's needlework?
Let's see.

CATAPLASMA No, sir, only examining whether it be done to the true   20
nature and life o' the thing.

SEBASTIAN Here y'ave set a medlar with a bachelor's button° o' one
side and a snail° o' th' t'other. The bachelor's button should have
held his head up more pertly towards the medlar; the snail o' th'
t'other side should ha' been wrought with an artificial° laziness,   25
doubling his tail and putting out his horn but half the length, and
then the medlar falling, as it were, from the lazy snail and inclining
towards the pert bachelor's button, their branches spreading and
winding one within another as if they did embrace. But here's a
moral. A poppering pear° tree growing upon the bank of a river,   30
seeming continually to look downwards into the water as if it were
enamoured of it, and ever as the fruit ripens lets it fall for love, as
it were, into her lap; which the wanton stream, like a strumpet, no
sooner receives but she carries it away and bestows it upon some
other creature she maintains, still seeming to play and dally under   35

300

the poppering so long that it has almost washed away the earth from the root, and now the poor tree stands as if it were ready to fall and perish by that whereon it spent all the substance° it had.

CATAPLASMA Moral for you that love those wanton running waters.

SEBASTIAN But is not my Lady Levidulcia come yet?   40

CATAPLASMA Her purpose promised us her company ere this. *Lirie,*° your lute and your book.

SEBASTIAN Well said. A lesson o' th' lute to entertain the time with till she comes.

[Soquette plays upon the lute]

CATAPLASMA *Sol, fa, mi, la.*—*Mi, mi, mi.*—'Precious!° Dost not see   45
mi° between the two crotchets?° Strike me full there. So—for-ward.—This is a sweet strain,° and thou finger'st it beastly. *Mi* is a large° there, and the prick° that stands before *mi* a long; always halve your note.—Now—run your division° pleasingly with those quavers.° Observe all your graces° i' the touch. Here's a sweet   50
close°—strike it full; it sets off your music delicately.

Enter Languebeau Snuffe and Levidulcia

LANGUEBEAU Purity be in this house.

CATAPLASMA 'Tis now entered, and welcome with your good lady-ship.

SEBASTIAN Cease that music. Here's a sweeter instrument.   55

[Tries to embrace Levidulcia]

LEVIDULCIA *[aside to Sebastian]* Restrain your liberty! See you not Snuffe?

SEBASTIAN What does the stinkard here? Put Snuffe out.° He's offensive.

LEVIDULCIA No. The credit of his company defends my being   60
abroad from the eye of suspicion.

CATAPLASMA Will 't please your ladyship go up into the closet?° There are those falls and tires° I told you of.

LEVIDULCIA Monsieur Snuffe, I shall request your patience. My stay will not be long.   65

LANGUEBEAU My duty, madam.

Exit [Levidulcia] with Sebastian

[Aside] Falls and tires? I begin to suspect what falls and tires you mean. My lady and Sebastian the fall and the tire, and I the shadow.° I perceive the purity of my conversation is used but for a property to cover the uncleanness of their purposes. The very   70
contemplation o' th' thing makes the spirit° of the flesh begin to wriggle in my blood. And here my desire has met with an object

already. This gentlewoman, methinks, should be swayed with the
motion,° living in a house where moving example is so common.
Temptation has prevailed over me, and I will attempt to make it   75
overcome her. [*Aloud*] Mistress Cataplasma, my lady, it seems, has
some business that requires her stay. The fairness o' the evening
invites me into the air; will it please you give this gentlewoman
leave to leave her work and walk a turn or two with me for honest
recreation?   80

CATAPLASMA With all my heart, sir. Go, Soquette, give ear to his
instructions. You may get understanding° by his company, I can
tell you.

LANGUEBEAU In the way of holiness, Mistress Cataplasma.

CATAPLASMA Good Monsieur Snuffe!—I will attend° your re-   85
turn.

LANGUEBEAU [*to Soquette*] Your hand, gentlewoman.
    [*Aside*] The flesh is humble till the spirit move it,
    But when 'tis raised it will command above it.°
        Exeunt

[4.2]

    Enter D'Amville, Charlemont, and Borachio

D'AMVILLE Your sadness and the sickness of my son
    Have made our company and conference
    Less free and pleasing than I purposed it.

CHARLEMONT Sir, for the present I am much unfit
    For conversation or society.   5
    With pardon I will rudely take my leave.

D'AMVILLE Good night, dear nephew.
        Exit Charlemont
                            Seest thou that same man?

BORACHIO Your meaning, sir?

D'AMVILLE   That fellow's life, Borachio,
    Like a superfluous letter in the law,°
    Endangers our assurance.

BORACHIO   Scrape him out.°   10

D'AMVILLE Wou't do't?

BORACHIO   Give me your purpose; I will do't.°

D'AMVILLE Sad melancholy has drawn Charlemont,

With meditation on his father's death,
Into the solitary walk behind the church.
BORACHIO The churchyard? This the fittest place for death.   15
Perhaps he's praying. Then he's fit to die.
We'll send him charitably to his grave.
D'AMVILLE No matter how thou tak'st him. First take this.
        [*Gives Borachio a*] *pistol*
Thou knowest the place. Observe his passages,
And with the most advantage make a stand,°   20
That, favoured by the darkness of the night,
His breast may fall upon thee at so near
A distance that he sha' not shun the blow.
The deed once done, thou may'st retire with safety.
The place is unfrequented, and his death   25
Will be imputed to th'attempt of thieves.
BORACHIO Be careless. Let your mind be free and clear.
This pistol shall discharge you of your fear.°
        Exit [*Borachio*]
D'AMVILLE But let me call my projects to account:
For what effect and end I have engaged   30
Myself in all this blood. To leave a state
To the succession of my proper blood.°
But how shall that succession be continued?
Not in my elder son, I fear. Disease
And weakness have disabled him for issue.   35
For th' t'other, his loose humour will endure°
No bond of marriage—and I doubt his life,
His spirit is so boldly dangerous.
O pity that the profitable end
Of such a prosp'rous murder should be lost!   40
Nature forbid. I hope I have a body°
That will not suffer me to lose my labour
For want of issue, yet. But then 't must be
A bastard. Tush, they only father bastards
That father other men's begettings. Daughter!   45
Be it mine own, let it come whence it will.
I am resolved. Daughter!
        Enter Servant
SERVANT   My lord.
D'AMVILLE I prithee call my daughter.
        Enter Castabella

CASTABELLA Your pleasure, sir?
D'AMVILLE   Is thy husband i' bed?
CASTABELLA Yes, my lord.
D'AMVILLE   The evening's fair. I prithee   50
   Walk a turn or two.
CASTABELLA   Come, Jaspar.
D'AMVILLE   No.
   We'll walk but to the corner o' the church;
   And I have something to speak privately.
CASTABELLA No matter; stay.
     Exit Servant
D'AMVILLE [*aside*]   This falls out happily.
     Exeunt

[4.3]

Enter Charlemont, Borachio dogging him in the churchyard.
The clock strikes twelve

CHARLEMONT Twelve.
BORACHIO [*aside*] 'Tis a good hour; 'twill strike one anon.°
CHARLEMONT How fit a place for contemplation
   Is this dead of night, among the dwellings
   Of the dead. This grave—perhaps th'inhabitant   5
   Was in his lifetime the possessor of
   His own desires. Yet in the midst of all
   His greatness and his wealth, he was less rich
   And less contented than in this poor piece
   Of earth, lower and lesser than a cottage,   10
   For here he neither wants nor cares. Now that
   His body savours of corruption,
   He enjoys a sweeter rest than e'er he did
   Amongst the sweetest pleasures of this life,
   For here there's nothing troubles him. And there,   15
   In that grave lies another. He, perhaps,
   Was in his life as full of misery
   As this of happiness; and here's an end
   Of both. Now both their states are equal. O,
   That man with so much labour should aspire   20
   To worldly height, when in the humble earth

The world's condition's at the best! Or scorn
Inferior men, since to be lower than
A worm is to be higher than a king!
BORACHIO Then fall and rise.
   Discharges [*the pistol, which*] *gives false fire*
CHARLEMONT   What villain's hand was that?°   25
Save thee or thou shalt perish.°
   They fight
BORACHIO Zounds, unsaved, I think.
   [*Borachio*] *fall*[*s*]
CHARLEMONT What, have I killed him? Whatsoe'er thou beest,
I would thy hand had prospered, for I was
Unfit to live and well prepared to die.
What shall I do? Accuse myself, submit   30
Me to the law, and that will quickly end
This violent increase of misery?
But 'tis a murder to be accessory
To mine own death. I will not. I will take   35
This opportunity to 'scape. It may
Be Heav'n reserves me to some better end.
   Exit Charlemont. Enter Languebeau Snuffe and Soquette into
   the churchyard
SOQUETTE Nay, good sir, I dare not. In good sooth I come of a
generation both by father and mother that were all as fruitful as
costermongers'° wives.   40
LANGUEBEAU Tush, then a tympany is the greatest danger can be
feared. Their fruitfulness turns but to a certain kind of phlegmatic
windy disease.°
SOQUETTE I must put my understanding to your trust, sir. I would
be loath to be deceived.   45
LANGUEBEAU No, conceive° thou sha't not. Yet thou shalt profit by
my instruction too. My body is not every day drawn dry, wench.
SOQUETTE Yet methinks, sir, your want of use should rather make
your body like a well: the lesser 'tis drawn, the sooner it grows dry.°
LANGUEBEAU Thou shalt try that instantly.   50
SOQUETTE But we want place and opportunity.
LANGUEBEAU We have both. This is the back side of the house
which the superstitious call Saint Winifred's church, and is verily
a convenient unfrequented place,
Where under the close curtains of the night—   55
SOQUETTE You purpose i' the dark to make me light.

[Languebeau Snuffe] pulls out a sheet, a hair,° and a beard
But what ha' you there?

LANGUEBEAU This disguise is for security sake, wench. There's a
talk, thou know'st, that the ghost of old Montferrers walks. In this
church he was buried. Now if any stranger fall upon us before our   60
business be ended, in this disguise I shall be taken for that ghost
and never be called to examination,° I warrant thee. Thus we shall
'scape both prevention and discovery. How do I look in this habit,
wench?

SOQUETTE So like a ghost that, notwithstanding I have some fore-   65
knowledge of you, you make my hair stand almost on end.

LANGUEBEAU I will try how I can kiss in this beard. O, fie, fie, fie.
I will put it off, and then kiss, and then put it on. I can do the rest
without kissing.

*Enter Charlemont doubtfully,° with his sword drawn; [he] is
upon them before they are aware. They run out divers ways
and leave the disguise*

CHARLEMONT What ha' we here? A sheet? A hair? A beard?   70
What end was this disguise intended for?
No matter what. I'll not expostulate
The purpose of a friendly accident.°
Perhaps it may accommodate my 'scape.
I fear I am pursued. For more assurance,   75
I'll hide me here i' th' charnel house,
This convocation-house of dead men's skulls.

*To get into the charnel house he takes hold of a death's head;
it slips and staggers him°*

Death's head, deceiv'st my hold?
Such is the trust to all mortality.

*[Charlemont] hides himself in the charnel house. Enter
D'Amville and Castabella*

CASTABELLA My lord, the night grows late. Your lordship spake   80
Of something you desired to move in private.

D'AMVILLE Yes, now I'll speak it. Th'argument is love.
The smallest ornament of thy sweet form,
That abstract of all pleasure, can command
The senses into passion, and thy entire   85
Perfection is my object; yet I love
Thee with the freedom of my reason. I
Can give thee reason for my love.

CASTABELLA   Love me,

My lord? I do believe it, for I am
The wife of him you love.
D'AMVILLE 'Tis true. By my 90
Persuasion thou wert forced to marry one
Unable to perform the office of
A husband. I was author of the wrong.
My conscience suffers under't, and I would
Disburden it by satisfaction.
CASTABELLA How? 95
D'AMVILLE I will supply that pleasure to thee which
He cannot.
CASTABELLA Are y' a devil or a man?
D'AMVILLE A man, and such a man as can return
Thy entertainment with as prodigal°
A body as the covetous desire 100
Of woman ever was delighted with;
So that, besides the full performance of
Thy empty husband's duty, thou shalt have
The joy of children to continue the
Succession of thy blood; for the appetite 105
That steals her pleasure, draws the forces of
The body to an united strength and puts
'Em altogether into action,
Never fails of procreation.°
All the purposes of man 110
Aim but at one of these two ends, pleasure
Or profit, and in this one sweet conjunction
Of our loves they both will meet. Would it
Not grieve thee that a stranger to thy blood
Should lay the first foundation of his house 115
Upon the ruins of thy family?
CASTABELLA Now Heav'n defend me! May my memory
Be utterly extinguished, and the heir
Of him that was my father's enemy
Raise his eternal monument upon 120
Our ruins, ere the greatest pleasure or
The greatest profit ever tempt me to
Continue it by incest.
D'AMVILLE Incest? Tush.°
These distances affinity observes
Are articles of bondage cast upon° 125

Our freedoms by our own subjections.°
Nature allows a gen'ral liberty
Of generation to all creatures else.
Shall man, to whose command and use all creatures
Were made subject, be less free than they?°   130

CASTABELLA   O God,
Is Thy unlimited and infinite
Omnipotence less free because Thou dost
No ill? Or if you argue merely out
Of Nature, do you not degenerate   135
From that, and are you not unworthy the
Prerogative of Nature's masterpiece,
When basely you prescribe yourself
Authority and law from their examples°
Whom you should command? I could confute   140
You, but the horror of the argument
Confounds my understanding. Sir, I know
You do but try me in your son's behalf,
Suspecting that my strength and youth of blood
Cannot contain themselves with impotence.°   145
Believe me, sir,
I never wronged him. If it be your lust,
O quench it on their prostituted flesh,
Whose trade of sin can please desire with more
Delight and less offence.
          [D'Amville tries to kiss her]
                            The poison of   150
Your breath, evaporated from so foul a soul,
Infects the air more than the damps that rise°
From bodies but half rotten in their graves.

D'AMVILLE   Kiss me. I warrant thee my breath is sweet.
These dead men's bones lie here of purpose to   155
Invite us to supply the number of°
The living. Come, we'll get young bones and do't.°
I will enjoy thee. No? Nay then invoke
Your great supposed protector. I will do't.

CASTABELLA   Supposed protector? Are y' an atheist? Then   160
I know my prayers and tears are spent in vain.
O patient Heav'n, why dost thou not express
Thy wrath in thunderbolts, to tear the frame
Of man in pieces? How can earth endure

The burden of this wickedness without   165
An earthquake, or the angry face of Heav'n
Be not inflamed with lightning?
D'AMVILLE   Conjure up
The devil and his dam; cry to the graves;
The dead can hear thee; invocate their help.°
CASTABELLA O would this grave might open, and my body   170
Were bound to the dead carcass of a man°
Forever, ere it entertain the lust°
Of this detested villain.
D'AMVILLE   Tereus-like,°
Thus I will force my passage to—
CHARLEMONT   The devil!
    Charlemont rises in the disguise and frights D'Amville away
Now, lady, with the hand of Charlemont!   175
I thus redeem you from the arm of lust.
My Castabella!
CASTABELLA   My dear Charlemont!
CHARLEMONT For all my wrongs I thank thee, gracious Heav'n;
Th'ast made me satisfaction, to reserve°
Me for this blessèd purpose. Now, sweet death,   180
I'll bid thee welcome. Come, I'll guard thee home,
And then I'll cast myself into the arms
Of apprehension, that the law may make°
This worthy work the crown of all my actions,
Being the best and last.
CASTABELLA   The last? The law?   185
Now Heav'n forbid, what ha' you done?
CHARLEMONT   Why, I have killed
A man—not murdered him, my Castabella;
He would ha' murdered me.
CASTABELLA   Then, Charlemont,
The hand of Heav'n directed thy defence.
That wicked atheist, I suspect his plot.   190
CHARLEMONT My life he seeks. I would he had it, since
He has deprived me of those blessings that
Should make me love it. Come, I'll give it him.
CASTABELLA You sha' not. I will first expose myself
To certain danger than for my defence   195
Destroy the man that saved me from destruction.
CHARLEMONT Thou canst not satisfy me better than

To be the instrument of my release
From misery.

CASTABELLA   Then work it by escape.
Leave me to this protection that still guards°   200
The innocent, or I will be a partner
In your destiny.

CHARLEMONT   My soul is heavy. Come, lie down to rest;
These are the pillows whereon men sleep best.

> *Charlemont and Castabella lie down with either of them a*
> *death's head for a pillow. Enter Languebeau Snuffe seeking*
> *Soquette*

LANGUEBEAU   Soquette, Soquette, Soquette! O art thou there?   205
> *He mistakes the body of Borachio for Soquette*

Verily thou liest in a fine premeditate readiness for the purpose.
Come, kiss me, sweet Soquette. [*Kisses the body*] Now purity
defend me from the sin of Sodom!° This is a creature of the
masculine gender. [*Touches the body*] Verily the man is blasted.
Yea, cold and stiff! Murder, murder, murder!   210
> *Exit Languebeau Snuffe. Enter D'Amville distractedly; he*
> *starts at the sight of a death's head*

D'AMVILLE   Why dost thou stare upon me? Thou art not
The skull of him I murdered. What hast thou
To do to vex my conscience? Sure thou wert
The head of a most doggèd usurer,
Th'art so uncharitable. And that bawd,   215
The sky there, she could shut the windows and
The doors of this great chamber of the world,
And draw the curtains of the clouds between
Those lights and me about this bed of earth,
When that same strumpet, Murder, and myself   220
Committed sin together. Then she could
Leave us i' th' dark till the close deed
Was done; but now that I begin to feel
The loathsome horror of my sin and, like
A lecher emptied of his lust, desire   225
To bury my face under my eyebrows and°
Would steal from my shame unseen, she meets me
I' the face with all her light corrupted eyes°
To challenge payment o' me. O behold!°
Yonder's the ghost of old Montferrers in   230
A long white sheet, climbing yond lofty mountain

To complain to Heav'n of me. Montferrers!
'Pox o' fearfulness. 'Tis nothing but°
A fair white cloud. Why, was I born a coward?
He lies that says so. Yet the count'nance of   235
A bloodless worm might ha' the courage now
To turn my blood to water. The trembling motion
Of an aspen leaf would make me, like
The shadow of that leaf, lie shaking under 't.
I could now commit a murder, were   240
It but to drink the fresh warm blood of him
I murdered, to supply the want and weakness
O' mine own, 'tis grown so cold and phlegmatic.°
LANGUEBEAU (*within*) Murder, murder, murder!
D'AMVILLE Mountains o'erwhelm me—the ghost of old Montferrers 245
  haunts me.
LANGUEBEAU [*within*] Murder, murder, murder!
D'AMVILLE O were my body circumvolved°
  Within that cloud, that when the thunder tears
  His passage open, it might scatter me   250
  To nothing in the air!
              Enter Languebeau Snuffe with the Watch
LANGUEBEAU   Here you shall find
  The murdered body.
D'AMVILLE   Black Beelzebub
  And all his hell-hounds come to apprehend me?
LANGUEBEAU No, my good lord, we come to apprehend
  The murderer.
[D'AMVILLE]   The ghost, great Pluto, was   255
  A fool, unfit to be employed in any
  Serious business for the state of hell.
  Why could not he ha' suffered me to raise
  The mountain o' my sins with one as damnable
  As all the rest, and then ha' tumbled me   260
  To ruin? But apprehend me e'en between
  The purpose and the act, before it was
  Committed!
WATCH Is this the murderer? He speaks suspiciously.°
LANGUEBEAU No, verily. This is my Lord D'Amville, and his   265
  distraction, I think, grows out of his grief for the loss of a faithful
  servant, for surely I take him to be Borachio that is slain.
D'AMVILLE Ha! Borachio slain? Thou look'st like Snuffe, dost not?

LANGUEBEAU Yes, in sincerity, my lord.

D'AMVILLE Hark thee—sawest thou not a ghost?   270

LANGUEBEAU A ghost? Where, my lord? [*Aside*] I smell a fox.°

D'AMVILLE Here i' the churchyard.

LANGUEBEAU Tush, tush, their walking spirits are mere imaginary
    fables. There's no such thing *in rerum natura*.° Here is a man slain,
    and with the spirit of consideration° I rather think him to be the   275
    murderer got into that disguise than any such fantastic toy.°

D'AMVILLE My brains begin to put themselves in order.
    I apprehend thee now. 'Tis e'en so.
       [*Looks at the body*]
    Borachio! I will search the centre, but°
    I'll find the murderer.   280

WATCH [*noticing Charlemont and Castabella*] Here, here, here.

D'AMVILLE Stay! Asleep? So soundly? And so sweetly
    Upon death's heads? And in a place so full
    Of fear and horror? Sure there is some other
    Happiness within the freedom of the   285
    Conscience than my knowledge e'er attained to.
    Ho, ho, ho!

CHARLEMONT [*waking*] Y'are welcome, uncle. Had you sooner come,
    You had been sooner welcome. I'm the man
    You seek. You sha' not need examine me.°   290

D'AMVILLE My nephew! And my daughter! O my dear
    Lamented blood, what fate has cast you thus
    Unhappily upon this accident?

CHARLEMONT You know, sir, she's as clear as chastity.°

D'AMVILLE As her own chastity. The time, the place,   295
    All circumstances argue that unclear.

CASTABELLA Sir, I confess it, and repentantly
    Will undergo the selfsame punishment
    That justice shall inflict on Charlemont.

CHARLEMONT Unjustly she betrays her innocence.   300

WATCH But, sir, she's taken with you, and she must
    To prison with you.

D'AMVILLE   There's no remedy;
    Yet were it not my son's bed she abused,
    My land should fly but both should be excused.°
       Exeunt

[4.4]

Enter Belforest and a Servant

BELFOREST Is not my wife come in yet?

SERVANT   No, my lord.

BELFOREST Methinks she's very affectedly inclined°
To young Sebastian's company o' late,
But jealousy is such a torment that
I am afraid to entertain it. Yet   5
The more I shun by circumstance to meet
Directly with it, the more ground I find
To circumvent my apprehension. First,°
I know sh'as a perpetual appetite,
Which being so oft encountered with a man   10
Of such a bold luxurious freedom as
Sebastian is, and of so promising
A body, her own blood, corrupted, will
Betray her to temptation.'
        Enter Fresco closely°

FRESCO [*aside*] 'Precious! I was sent by his lady to see if her lord were   15
in bed. I should ha' done 't slyly without discovery, and now I am
blurted upon 'em before I was aware.
        Exit [Fresco]

BELFOREST Know not you the gentlewoman my wife brought home?

SERVANT By sight, my lord. Her man was here but now.

BELFOREST Her man? I prithee run and call him quickly.   20
        [*Exit Servant*]
This villain, I suspect him ever since
I found him hid behind the tapestry.
        [*Enter Fresco with Servant*]
Fresco! Th'art welcome, Fresco.—Leave us.
        [*Exit Servant*]
Dost hear, Fresco? Is not my wife at thy mistress's?

FRESCO I know not, my lord.   25

BELFOREST I prithee tell me, Fresco; we are private, tell me. Is not
thy mistress a good wench?

FRESCO How means your lordship that? A wench o' the trade?°

BELFOREST Yes faith, Fresco, e'en a wench o' the trade.

FRESCO O no, my lord. Those falling diseases° cause baldness, and   30
my mistress recovers° the loss of hair, for she is a periwig maker.

BELFOREST And nothing else?

FRESCO Sells falls and tires and bodies° for ladies, or so.

BELFOREST So, sir, and she helps my lady to falls and bodies now
and then, does she not?   35

FRESCO At her ladyship's pleasure, my lord.

BELFOREST Her pleasure, you rogue? You are the pander to° her
pleasure, you varlet, are you not? You know the conveyances°
between Sebastian and my wife. Tell me the truth, or by this hand
I'll nail thy bosom to the earth. Stir not, you dog, but quickly tell 40
the truth.

FRESCO (speak[s] *like a crier*) O yes!°

BELFOREST Is not thy mistress a bawd to my wife?

FRESCO O yes!

BELFOREST And acquainted with her tricks and her plots and her   45
devices?

FRESCO O yes! If any man, court, city or country,° has found my
Lady Levidulcia in bed but my Lord Belforest, it is Sebastian.

BELFOREST What, dost thou proclaim it? Dost thou cry it, thou
villain?   50

FRESCO Can you laugh° it, my lord? I thought you meant to proclaim
yourself cuckold.

    Enter the Watch

BELFOREST The watch! Met with my wish. I must request th'assistance of your offices.

    Fresco runs away

'Sdeath, stay that villain; pursue him.   55

    Exeunt

[4.5]

    Enter Languebeau Snuffe importuning Soquette

SOQUETTE Nay, if you get me any more into the churchyard—

LANGUEBEAU Why, Soquette, I never got thee there yet.

SOQUETTE Got me there? No, not with child.

LANGUEBEAU I promised thee I would not, and I was as good as my word.

SOQUETTE Yet your word was better then than your deed. But steal   5
up into the little matted° chamber o' the left hand.

LANGUEBEAU I prithee let it be the right hand; thou left'st me
before, and I did not like that.

SOQUETTE 'Precious, quickly! So soon as my mistress shall be in bed
   I'll come to you.   10
      Exit [Languebeau] Snuffe. Enter Sebastian, Levidulcia
      and Cataplasma
CATAPLASMA I wonder Fresco stays so long!
SEBASTIAN Mistress Soquette, a word with you.
      Whisper[s to Soquette, aside]
LEVIDULCIA If he brings word my husband is i' bed, I will adven-
   ture° one night's liberty to lie abroad. My strange affection to this
   man! 'Tis like that natural sympathy which e'en among the   15
   senseless creatures of the earth commands a mutual inclination and
   consent. For though it seems to be the free effect of mine own
   voluntary love, yet I can neither restrain it, nor give reason for 't.
   But now 'tis done, and in your power it lies to save my honour or
   dishonour me.   20
CATAPLASMA Enjoy your pleasure, madam, without fear. I never will
   betray the trust you have committed to me, and you wrong
   yourself to let consideration of the sin molest your conscience.
   Methinks 'tis unjust that a reproach should be inflicted on a
   woman for offending but with one, when 'tis a light offence in   25
   husbands to commit° with many.
LEVIDULCIA So it seems to me.—Why, how now, Sebastian, making
   love to that gentlewoman? How many mistresses ha' you i' faith?
SEBASTIAN In faith, none, for I think none of 'em are faithful; but
   otherwise, as many as clean shirts. The love of a woman is like a 30
   mushroom: it grows in one night and will serve somewhat
   pleasingly next morning to breakfast, but afterwards waxes ful-
   some° and unwholesome.
CATAPLASMA Nay, by Saint Winifred, a woman's love lasts as long
   as winter fruit.°   35
SEBASTIAN 'Tis true: till new come in—by my experience no longer.
      Enter Fresco running
FRESCO Somebody's doing has undone us, and we are like pay.dearly
   for 't.
SEBASTIAN Pay dear? For what?
FRESCO Will 't not be a chargeable reckoning,° think you, when here 40
   are half a dozen fellows coming to call us to account, with ev'ry
   man a several° bill° in his hand that we are not able to discharge?
      Knock at the door
CATAPLASMA Passion o' me, what bouncing's° that? Madam, withdraw yourself.

LEVIDULCIA Sebastian, if you love me, save my honour.   45
        Exeunt [all except Sebastian]
SEBASTIAN What violence is this? What seek you?
        Enter Belforest and the Watch
    Zounds, you shall not pass.
BELFOREST Pursue the strumpet!
        [*Exeunt Watch*]
                                            Villain, give me way,
    Or I will make my passage through thy blood.
SEBASTIAN My blood will make it slippery, my lord.   50
    'Twere better you would take another way;
    You may hap fall else.
            They fight. Both [are mortally wounded]. Sebastian falls first
                I ha't i' faith.°
            [*Sebastian*] *dies. While Belforest is staggering, enter*
            Levidulcia. [Belforest falls and dies.]
LEVIDULCIA O God! My husband! My Sebastian! Husband!
    Neither can speak; yet both report my shame.
    Is this the saving of my honour, when   55
    Their blood runs out in rivers, and my lust
    The fountain whence it flows? Dear husband, let
    Not thy departed spirit be displeased
    If with adult'rate lips I kiss thy cheek.
    Here I behold the hatefulness of lust,   60
    Which brings me kneeling to embrace him dead,
    Whose body living I did loathe to touch.
    Now I can weep! But what can tears do good?
    When I weep only water, they weep blood.
    But could I make an ocean with my tears,   65
    That on the flood this broken vessel of
    My body, laden heavy with light lust,
    Might suffer shipwreck and so drown my shame,
    Then weeping were to purpose; but alas!
    The sea wants water enough to wash away   70
    The foulness of my name. O, in their wounds
    I feel my honour wounded to the death.
    Shall I outlive my honour? Must my life
    Be made the world's example? Since it must,
    Then thus in detestation of my deed,   75
    To make th'example move more forcibly
    To virtue, thus I seal it with a death
    As full of horror as my life of sin.

Enter the Watch with Cataplasma, Fresco, Languebeau
Snuffe, and Soquette

WATCH Hold, madam!

[Levidulcia] stabs herself [and dies]

Lord, what a strange night is this!

LANGUEBEAU May not Snuffe be suffered to go out of himself?°   80

WATCH Nor you, nor any. All must go with us.

O with what virtue lust should be withstood,
Since 'tis a fire quenched seldom without blood!

Exeunt

[5.1]

Music. A closet discovered.° A servant sleeping with lights and money before him. Enter D'Amville

D'AMVILLE What, sleep'st thou?

SERVANT   No, my lord—nor sleep nor wake,
But in a slumber troublesome to both.

D'AMVILLE Whence comes this gold?

SERVANT   'Tis part of the revenue
Due to your lordship since your brother's death.

D'AMVILLE To bed. Leave me my gold.

SERVANT   And me my rest.   5
Two things wherewith one man is seldom blest.
    Exit [Servant]

D'AMVILLE Cease that harsh music. W'are not pleased with it.
    He handles the gold
Here sounds a music whose melodious touch
Like angels' voices ravishes the sense.
Behold, thou ignorant astronomer,°   10
Whose wand'ring speculation seeks among
The planets for men's fortunes! With amazement
Behold thine error and be planet-struck.°
These are the stars whose operations make
The fortunes and the destinies of men.   15
Yond lesser eyes of Heav'n, like subjects raised°
Into their lofty houses when their prince
Rides underneath th'ambition of their loves,
Are mounted only to behold the face
Of your more rich imperious eminence   20
With unprevented sight. Unmask, fair queen;°
    Unpurses the gold
Vouchsafe their expectations may enjoy
The gracious favour they admire to see.
These are the stars, the ministers of fate,
And man's high wisdom the superior power   25
To which their forces are subordinate.
    [D'Amville] sleeps. Enter the Ghost of Montferrers

GHOST D'Amville, with all thy wisdom th'art a fool,
Not like those fools that we term innocents,

But a most wretched miserable fool,
Which instantly, to the confusion of   30
Thy projects, with despair thou shalt behold.
          Exit Ghost. D'Amville starts up
D'AMVILLE What foolish dream dares interrupt my rest
    To my confusion? How can that be, since
    My purposes have hitherto been borne
    With prosp'rous judgement to secure success?   35
    Which nothing lives to dispossess me of
    But apprehended Charlemont, and him
    This brain has made the happy instrument
    To free suspicion, to annihilate
    All interest and title of his own,   40
    To seal up my assurance and confirm°
    My absolute possession by the law.
    Thus while the simple, honest worshipper
    Of a fantastic providence groans under°
    The burden of neglected misery,   45
    My real wisdom has raised up a state
    That shall eternize my posterity.
          Enter Servants with the body of Sebastian
    What's that?
SERVANT   The body of your younger son,
    Slain by the Lord Belforest.
D'AMVILLE   Slain? You lie.
    Sebastian! Speak, Sebastian! H'as lost
    His hearing. A physician presently!   50
    Go call a surgeon.
ROUSARD (*within*)   O.
D'AMVILLE   What groan was that?
    How does my elder son? The sound came from
    His chamber.
SERVANT   He went sick to bed, my lord.
ROUSARD (*within*) O.   55
D'AMVILLE The cries of mandrakes never touched the ear°
    With more sad horror than that voice does mine.
          Enter a Servant, running
SERVANT If ever you will see your son alive—
D'AMVILLE Nature forbid I e'er should see him dead.
          [*The servants draw forth*] a [*curtained*] *bed with Rousard*
    Withdraw the curtains. O how does my son?   60

SERVANT Methinks he's ready to give up the ghost.
D'AMVILLE Destruction take thee and thy fatal tongue.
    Death, where's the doctor? Art not thou the face
    Of that prodigious apparition stared upon
    Me in my dream?
SERVANT   The doctor's come, my lord.   65
    Enter Doctor
D'AMVILLE Doctor, behold two patients in whose cure
    Thy skill may purchase an eternal fame.
    If thou hast any reading in Hippocrates,°
    Galen, or Avicen, if herbs or drugs°
    Or minerals have any power to save,   70
    Now let thy practice and their sovereign use
    Raise thee to wealth and honour.
DOCTOR   If any root
    Of life remains within 'em capable
    Of physic, fear 'em not, my lord.
ROUSARD   O.
D'AMVILLE His gasping sighs are like the falling noise   75
    Of some great building when the groundwork breaks.
    On these two pillars stood the stately frame
    And architecture of my lofty house.
    An earthquake shakes 'em; the foundation shrinks.°
    Dear Nature, in whose honour I have raised   80
    A work of glory to posterity,
    O bury not the pride of that great action
    Under the fall and ruin of itself.
DOCTOR My lord, these bodies are deprived of all
    The radical ability of Nature.°   85
    The heat of life is utterly extinguished.
    Nothing remains within the power of man
    That can restore them.
D'AMVILLE   Take this gold; extract°
    The spirit of it, and inspire new life°
    Into their bodies.
DOCTOR   Nothing can, my lord.   90
D'AMVILLE You ha' not yet examined the true state
    And constitution of their bodies. Sure,
    You ha' not. I'll reserve their waters till°
    The morning. Questionless, their urines will
    Inform you better.

DOCTOR   Ha, ha, ha!

D'AMVILLE   Dost laugh,   95
  Thou villain? Must my wisdom that has been
  The object of men's admiration now
  Become the subject of thy laughter?

ROUSARD   O.

    [Rousard] dies

[DOCTOR AND SERVANTS] He's dead.

D'AMVILLE   O there expires the date°
  Of my posterity! Can Nature be   100
  So simple or malicious to destroy
  The reputation of her proper memory?
  She cannot. Sure there is some power above
  Her that controls her force.

DOCTOR   A power above Nature?
  Doubt you that, my lord? Consider but   105
  Whence man receives his body and his form:
  Not from corruption like some worms and flies,°
  But only from the generation of
  A man, for Nature never did bring forth
  A man without a man; nor could the first   110
  Man, being but the passive subject, not
  The active mover, be the maker of
  Himself; so of necessity there must
  Be a superior power to Nature.

D'AMVILLE Now to myself I am ridiculous.   115
  Nature, thou art a traitor to my soul.
  Thou hast abused my trust. I will complain
  To a superior court to right my wrong.
  I'll prove thee a forger of false assurances.°
  In yond Star Chamber thou shalt answer it.°   120
  Withdraw the bodies. O, the sense of death°
  Begins to trouble my distracted soul.
    Exeunt

[5.2]

[A raised judges' bench and a scaffold are brought out.]
Enter Judges and Officers.

FIRST JUDGE Bring forth the malefactors to the bar.
    Enter Cataplasma, Soquette and Fresco [guarded]
  Are you the gentlewoman in whose house
  The murders were committed?

CATAPLASMA   Yes, my lord.

FIRST JUDGE That worthy attribute of gentry which
  Your habit draws from ignorant respect°   5
  Your name deserves not, nor yourself the name
  Of woman, since you are the poison that
  Infects the honour of all womanhood.

CATAPLASMA My lord, I am a gentlewoman, yet
  I must confess my poverty compels   10
  My life to a condition lower than
  My birth or breeding.

SECOND JUDGE   Tush, we know your birth.

FIRST JUDGE But under colour to profess the sale
  Of tires and toys for gentlewomen's pride,
  You draw a frequentation of men's wives°   15
  To your licentious house, and there abuse
  Their husbands.

FRESCO   Good my lord, her rent is great.
  The good gentlewoman has no other thing
  To live by but her lodgings; so she's forced
  To let her fore-rooms out to others, and°   20
  Herself contented to lie backwards.

SECOND JUDGE   So.

FIRST JUDGE Here is no evidence accuses you
  For accessaries to the murder; yet
  Since from the spring of lust which you preserved
  And nourished ran th'effusion of that blood,   25
  Your punishment shall come as near to death
  As life can bear it. Law cannot inflict
  Too much severity upon the cause
  Of such abhorred effects.

SECOND JUDGE   Receive your sentence.
  Your goods, since they were gotten by that means   30
  Which brings diseases, shall be turned to th'use°

Of hospitals; you carted through the streets°
According to the common shame of strumpets,
Your bodies whipped till with the loss of blood
You faint under the hand of punishment.   35
Then, that the necessary force of want
May not provoke you to your former life,
You shall be set to painful labour, whose
Penurious gains shall only give you food
To hold up nature, mortify your flesh,   40
And make you fit for a repentant end.
[CATAPLASMA, SOQUETTE, FRESCO] O good my lord!
FIRST JUDGE   No more; away with 'em.
        Exeunt [Cataplasma, Soquette, and Fresco, guarded].
        Enter Languebeau Snuffe, [guarded]
SECOND JUDGE Now, Monsieur Snuffe, a man of your profession
    Found in a place of such impiety!
LANGUEBEAU I grant you the place is full of impurity; so much the   45
    more need of instruction and reformation. The purpose that
    carried me thither was with the spirit of conversion to purify their
    uncleanness, and I hope your lordship will say the law cannot take
    hold o' me° for that.
FIRST JUDGE No, sir, it cannot; but yet give me leave   50
    To tell you that I hold your wary answer
    Rather premeditated for excuse
    Than spoken out of a religious purpose.
    Where took you your degrees of scholarship?°
LANGUEBEAU I am no scholar, my lord. To speak the sincere truth,   55
    I am Snuffe the tallow-chandler.
SECOND JUDGE How comes your habit to be altered thus?
LANGUEBEAU My Lord Belforest, taking a delight in the cleanness
    of my conversation, withdrew me from that unclean life and put
    me in a garment fit for his society and my present profession.   60
FIRST JUDGE His lordship did but paint a rotten post,
    Or cover foulness fairly. Monsieur Snuffe,
    Back to your candle-making! You may give
    The world more light with that than either with
    Instruction or th'example of your life.   65
LANGUEBEAU Thus the Snuffe is put out.
        Exit Languebeau Snuffe. Enter D'Amville distractedly
D'AMVILLE Judgement, judgement!
SECOND JUDGE   Judgement, my lord? In what?
D'AMVILLE Your judgements must resolve me in a case.°

Bring in the bodies!
  [*Servants bear in the hearses of Sebastian and Rousard*]
                Nay, I will ha't tried.
This is the case, my lord: my providence,   70
E'en in a moment, by the only hurt
Of one, or two, or three at most—and those
Put quickly out o' pain too, mark me; I
Had wisely raised a competent estate
To my posterity; and is there not   75
More wisdom and more charity in that,
Than for your lordship, or your father, or
Your grandsire to prolong the torment and
The rack of rent from age to age upon°
Your poor penurious tenants, yet perhaps   80
Without a penny profit to your heir?
Is 't not more wise, more charitable? Speak!
FIRST JUDGE He is distracted.
D'AMVILLE   How? Distracted? Then
You ha' no judgement. I can give you sense
And solid reason for the very least   85
Distinguishable syllable I speak.
Since my thrift was more charitable, more
Judicious than your grandsire's, why, I would
Fain know why your lordship lives to make
A second generation from your father,   90
And the whole fry of my posterity
Extinguished in a moment, not a brat
Left to succeed me: I would fain know that.
SECOND JUDGE Grief for his children's death distempers him.
FIRST JUDGE My lord, we will resolve you of your question.   95
  In the meantime vouchsafe your place with us.
D'AMVILLE I am contented, so you will resolve me.
        [*D'Amville*] *ascends* [*to the bench*]. *Enter Charlemont and*
        Castabella, [*guarded*]
SECOND JUDGE Now, Monsieur Charlemont. You are accused
  Of having murdered one Borachio that
  Was servant to my Lord D'Amville. How can   100
  You clear yourself? Guilty or not guilty?
CHARLEMONT Guilty of killing him, but not of murder.
  My lords, I have no purpose to desire
  Remission for myself.

D'Amville descends to Charlemont

D'AMVILLE   Uncivil boy!
  Thou want'st humanity to smile at grief.   105
  Why dost thou cast a cheerful eye upon
  The object of my sorrow, my dead sons?
FIRST JUDGE O good my lord, let charity forbear
  To vex the spirit of a dying man.
  A cheerful eye upon the face of death   110
  Is the true count'nance of a noble mind.
  For honour's sake, my lord, molest it not.
D'AMVILLE Y'are all uncivil. O, is't not enough
  That he unjustly hath conspired with Fate
  To cut off my posterity, for him   115
  To be the heir to my possessions, but
  He must pursue me with his presence, and
  In the ostentation of his joy
  Laugh in my face and glory in my grief?
CHARLEMONT D'Amville, to show thee with what light respect   120
  I value death and thy insulting pride,
  Thus, like a warlike navy on the sea,
  Bound for the conquest of some wealthy land,
  Passed through the stormy troubles of this life
  And now arrived upon the armèd coast,   125
  In expectation of the victory
  Whose honour lies beyond this exigent,
  Through mortal danger, with an active spirit,
  Thus I aspire to undergo my death.
    [Charlemont] leaps up [onto] the scaffold. Castabella leaps
    after him
CASTABELLA And thus I second thy brave enterprise.   130
  Be cheerful, Charlemont. Our lives cut off
  In our young prime of years are like green herbs
  Wherewith we strew the hearses of our friends;
  For as their virtue gathered when th'are green,
  Before they wither or corrupt, is best,   135
  So we in virtue are the best for death
  While yet we have not lived to such an age
  That the increasing canker of our sins
  Hath spread too far upon us.
D'AMVILLE   A boon, my lords;
  I beg a boon.

FIRST JUDGE   What's that, my lord?   140
D'AMVILLE His body when 'tis dead
  For an anatomy.
SECOND JUDGE   For what, my lord?°
D'AMVILLE Your understanding still comes short o' mine.
  I would find out by his anatomy
  What thing there is in Nature more exact°   145
  Than in the constitution of myself.
  Methinks my parts and my dimensions are
  As many, as large, as well composed as his,
  And yet in me the resolution wants
  To die with that assurance as he does.   150
  The cause of that in his anatomy
  I would find out.
FIRST JUDGE   Be patient and you shall.
D'AMVILLE I have bethought me of a better way.
  Nephew, we must confer. Sir, I am grown
  A wondrous student now o' late. My wit   155
  Has reached beyond the scope of Nature; yet,
  For all my learning, I am still to seek
  From whence the peace of conscience should proceed.
CHARLEMONT The peace of conscience rises in itself.
D'AMVILLE Whether it be thy art or nature, I   160
  Admire thee, Charlemont. Why, thou hast taught
  A woman to be valiant. I will beg°
  Thy life. [To the Judges] My lords, I beg my nephew's life.°
  [To Charlemont] I'll make thee my physician. Thou shalt read
  Philosophy to me. I will find out   165
  Th'efficient cause of a contented mind;°
  But if I cannot profit in 't, then 'tis
  No more, being my physician, but infuse
  A little poison in a potion when
  Thou giv'st me physic, unawares to me.   170
  So I shall steal into my grave without
  The understanding or the fear of death;
  And that's the end I aim at, for the thought
  Of death is a most fearful torment, is't not?
SECOND JUDGE Your lordship interrupts the course of law.   175
FIRST JUDGE Prepare to die.
CHARLEMONT   My resolution's made.
  But ere I die, before this honoured bench,

With the free voice of a departing soul,
I here protest this gentlewoman clear
Of all offence the law condemns her for.   180
CASTABELLA I have accused myself. The law wants power
    To clear me. My dear Charlemont, with thee
    I will partake of all thy punishments.
CHARLEMONT Uncle, for all the wealthy benefits
    My death advances you, grant me but this: 185
    Your mediation for the guiltless life
    Of Castabella, whom your conscience knows
    As justly clear as harmless innocence.
D'AMVILLE Freely. My mediation for her life,
    And all my int'rest in the world to boot,   190
    Let her but in exchange possess me of
    The resolution that she dies withal.
    The price of things is best known in their want.
    Had I her courage, so I value it,
    The Indies should not buy't out o' my hands.°   195
CHARLEMONT Give me a glass of water.
D'AMVILLE   Me, of wine.°
    This argument of death congeals my blood.
    Cold fear, with apprehension of thy end,
    Hath frozen up the rivers of my veins.
        [*A servant pours him*] *a glass of wine*
    I must drink wine to warm me and dissolve   200
    Th'obstruction, or an apoplexy will
    Possess me. Why, thou uncharitable knave,
    Dost bring me blood to drink? The very glass
    Looks pale and trembles at it.
SERVANT   'Tis your hand, my lord.
D'AMVILLE Canst blame me to be fearful, bearing still   205
    The presence of a murderer about me?
        [*Servant gives Charlemont*] *a glass of water*
CHARLEMONT Is this water?
SERVANT   Water, sir.
CHARLEMONT Come, thou clear emblem of cool temperance,
    Be thou my witness that I use no art
    To force my courage, nor have need of helps   210
    To raise my spirits, like those weaker men
    Who mix their blood with wine, and out of that
    Adulterate conjunction do beget

A bastard valour. Native courage, thanks.
Thou lead'st me soberly to undertake   215
This great hard work of magnanimity.°
D'AMVILLE Brave Charlemont, at the reflection of
Thy courage my cold fearful blood takes fire,
And I begin to emulate thy death.°
        [Enter Executioner]
Is that thy executioner? My lords,   220
You wrong the honour of so high a blood
To let him suffer by so base a hand.°
JUDGES He suffers by the form of law, my lord.
D'AMVILLE I will reform it. Down, you shag-haired cur.
The instrument that strikes my nephew's blood   225
Shall be as noble as his blood. I'll be
Thy executioner myself.
        [D'Amville climbs onto the scaffold and seizes the axe from
        the Executioner]
FIRST JUDGE Restrain his fury! Good my lord, forbear!
D'AMVILLE [brandishing the axe]
I'll butcher out the passage of his soul
That dares attempt to interrupt the blow.   230
SECOND JUDGE My lord, the office will impress a mark
Of scandal and dishonour on your name.
CHARLEMONT The office fits him; hinder not his hand,
But let him crown my resolution with
An unexampled dignity of death.   235
Strike home. Thus I submit me.
        [Charlemont kneels and makes] ready for execution
CASTABELLA   So do I.
        [Castabella prepares for execution]
In scorn of death thus hand in hand we die.
D'AMVILLE I ha' the trick on 't, nephew. You shall see
How eas'ly I can put you out of pain. O!
        As he raises up the axe, [D'Amville] strikes out his own
        brains. [He] staggers off the scaffold
EXECUTIONER In lifting up the axe, I think h'as knocked   240
His brains out.
D'AMVILLE   What murderer was he
That lifted up my hand against my head?
[FIRST] JUDGE None but yourself, my lord.
D'AMVILLE   I thought he was

A murderer that did it.
[FIRST] JUDGE   God forbid.
D'AMVILLE Forbid? You lie, judge; he commanded it,   245
    To tell thee that man's wisdom is a fool.
    I came to thee for judgement, and thou think'st
    Thyself a wise man. I outreached thy wit
    And made thy justice murder's instrument
    In Castabella's death and Charlemont's,   250
    To crown my murder of Montferrers with
    A safe possession of his wealthy state.
CHARLEMONT I claim the just advantage of his words.
[SECOND] JUDGE Descend the scaffold and attend the rest.
D'AMVILLE There was the strength of natural understanding.   255
    But Nature is a fool. There is a power
    Above her that hath overthrown the pride
    Of all my projects and posterity,
    For whose surviving blood I had erected
    This proud monument, and struck 'em dead   260
    Before me, for whose deaths I called to thee
    For judgement. Thou didst want discretion for
    The sentence, but yond power that struck me knew
    The judgement I deserved, and gave it. O!
    The lust of death commits a rape upon me,   265.
    As I would ha' done on Castabella.
        [D'Amville] dies
[FIRST] JUDGE Strange is his death and judgement. With the hands
    Of joy and justice I thus set you free.
        [Helps Charlemont and Castabella down from the scaffold]
    The power of that eternal providence
    Which overthrew his projects in their pride   270
    Hath made your griefs the instruments to raise
    Your blessings to a greater height than ever.
CHARLEMONT Only to Heav'n I attribute the work,°
    Whose gracious motives made me still forbear
    To be mine own revenger. Now I see   275
    That *patience is the honest man's revenge.*
[FIRST] JUDGE Instead of Charlemont that but e'en now
    Stood ready to be dispossessed of all,
    I now salute you with more titles, both
    Of wealth and dignity, than you were born to.   280
    And you, sweet madam, Lady of Belforest,

You have that title by your father's death.

CASTABELLA With all the titles due to me increase
The wealth and honour of my Charlemont,
Lord of Montferrers, Lord D'Amville, Belforest,   285
And for a close to make up all the rest,
    Embrace[s Charlemont]
The lord of Castabella. Now at last
Enjoy the full possession of my love,
As clear and pure as my first chastity.

CHARLEMONT The crown of all my blessings! I will tempt   290
My stars no longer, nor protract my time
Of marriage. When those nuptial rites are done,
I will perform my kinsmen's funerals.

[FIRST] JUDGE The drums and trumpets! Interchange the sounds
Of death and triumph for these honoured lives,°   295
Succeeding their deservèd tragedies.°
    [Drum and trumpet sound]

CHARLEMONT Thus by the work of Heav'n the men that thought
To follow our dead bodies without tears
Are dead themselves, and now we follow theirs.
    Exeunt, [bearing the body of D'Amville]

EXPLANATORY NOTES

The Spanish Tragedy

Dramatis Personae. marshal: knight marshal, an officer of the royal household with judicial authority over the palace and its environs.

1.1.8 *prime and pride*: spring-time; flourishing.

14 *divorce*: separation.

15 *late conflict with Portingale*: recounted in *The First Part of Hieronimo*, which describes the love affair between Bel-imperia and Don Andrea and the onset of the war between Spain and Portugal (Portingale). The only text we have of this 'prequel' is obviously incomplete and corrupt; some have even doubted that it is Kyd's work.

19 *Acheron*: a river in Hades, the classical underworld, over which dead souls must pass. The Ghost's description of Hades is adapted from Virgil, *Aeneid* vi, the first of many references to classical literature in the play.

20 *Charon*: the ferryman who takes dead souls over the Acheron.

23 *Sol*: the sun.

Thetis: a sea nymph; the sea.

29 *Avernus*: a lake in Hades that serves as the gateway to the underworld.

30 *Cerberus*: a three-headed dog who guards Hades.

33 *Minos, Aeacus, and Rhadamanth*: judges in Hades, who decide the fates of dead souls.

36 *graven leaves of lottery*: the judge takes from an urn pages describing the deeds 'allotted' to Andrea on earth.

44 *myrtle . . . cypress*: emblematic of love and death respectively.

48 *Hector*: in the *Iliad*, greatest of the Trojan heroes, killed by Achilles.

49 *Achilles' Myrmidons*: in the *Iliad*, the notoriously remorseless followers of Achilles, the greatest of the Greek heroes.

50 *censor*: judge.

52 *infernal king*: Pluto, the god of the underworld.

53 *doom*: judge.

66 *Ixion*: who lusted after Juno, queen of the gods, and was punished on a wheel in Hades.

73 *Elysian green*: the Elysian fields, where the spirits of the virtuous live on after death.

81 *rounded*: whispered.

82 *gates of horn*: the gates from which, according to *Aeneid* vi, prophetic dreams proceed.

87 *author*: perpetrator.

90 *mystery*: events with hidden significance.

91 *Chorus*. Revenge and Andrea probably remain onstage throughout the play, very likely overlooking the events from the 'upper stage' or balcony.

1.2.9 *wonted homage*. The Portuguese viceroy, as a feudal subordinate of the Spanish king, is obliged publicly to declare his fealty.

14 *O multum . . . iuris*: O much favoured by God, heaven fights for you, and people who plot against you submit, kneeling: victory is the sister of justice.

20 *deeper wage*: larger reward.

21 *blissful chivalry*: felicitous skill at arms.

23 *bound*: boundary.

27 *sundry colours of device*: various heraldic banners.

32 *battles*: forces.

   squadron form: square formation.

33 *wings of shot*: soldiers with firearms on the outer edges of the squadron.

34 *push of pike*: hand-to-hand combat.

56 *Pede pes . . . viro*: foot to foot and lance to lance; arms clash against arms, and man is attacked by man.

73 *insulting*: triumphing.

76 *Pricked*: spurred.

82 *carbines*: troops equipped with light firearms.

86 *argument*: token.

96 *frolic*: rejoice.

99 S.D. *tucket*: trumpet salute.

107 *demonstration*: visual display.

109 *enriched*: by ransoms and by traditional perquisites of the victors, e.g. armour of defeated soldiers.

120 *over-cloying*: excessive; overpowering.

122 *staying*: stopping.

136 *measure*: treatment.

139 *controlled*: restrained; overpowered.

140 *it boots not ask*: it is not worth asking.

142 *colours*: flag.

157 *enjoyed*: possessed.

159 *privilege*: royal prerogative.

160 *whether*: which.

161 *him*: Lorenzo.

  this: Horatio.

164 *wan*: won.

167 *difference*: dispute.

172 *He hunted . . . beard*: proverbial sayings.

174 *want no right*: lack nothing he deserves.

175 *abide the censure of my doom*: accept my decision.

177 *sit beside my right*: forgo what I deserve.

186 *estate*: social position.

188 *substance*: wealth.

190 *him*: Horatio.

1.3.12 *image of melancholy*: because the ground is 'low'.

17 *Qui iacet . . . obesse magis*: He who lies on the ground has nowhere further to fall. Fortune has exhausted its power to wound me; nothing remains to harm me more.

20 *sable weed*: black garment, suitable for mourning.

25 *wilful-mad*: insanely obstinate.

29 *Whose foot [is] standing on a rolling stone*: as the goddess Fortuna was traditionally depicted.

53 *author*: source.

57 *battery*: assault.

58 *at large*: in full.

66 *colour*: appearance.

82 *Terceira*: an island in the Azores, a Portuguese province.

93 *envious*: spiteful.

1.4.16 *Nemesis*: goddess of retribution against those whom the pagan gods resented for their merits.

20 *As Pallas was before proud Pergamus*. At the destruction of Troy, as related in *Aeneid* ii, Athena appeared in arms on the towers of Pergamus, one of the citadels of Troy.

22 *paunched*: stabbed in the belly, a breach of the chivalric code of arms.

27 *just remorse*: righteous indignation.

34 *wound*: embraced.

36 *dewed*: moistened.

47 *favour*: love-token.

55 *if your good liking stand thereto*: if you approve.

71 *disdain*: indignation.

80 *argues*: is evidence that.

82 *conceit*: imagination.

84 *enlarge*: release.

85 *to gage*: as a pawn.

86 *that*: what

92 *boots*: use is.

96 *aspect*: face (accented on the second syllable).

98 *words of course*: clichés.

99 *device*: trickery.

S.D. *glove*. An aristocratic woman's gloves, elaborately bejewelled and embroidered, were valuable items. They were considered a suggestive love-token for a woman to give a man, hence Balthazar's and Horatio's reaction.

107 *Let me alone*: leave it to me.

118 *pleasure*: delight.

127 *cheer*: hospitality.

130 *wait thou upon our cup*: pour my wine for me; a significant sign of favour for a man of Horatio's birth, which at the same time distinguishes him sharply from Lorenzo and Balthazar, guests at the King's banquet.

137 *pompous jest*: elaborate entertainment.

S.D. *Drum*: drummer.

139 *sound*: fathom.

142 *bore sway in Albion*: ruled in England. Hieronimo's masque, displaying fictional English triumphs over the Spanish and Portuguese, caters to the sentiments of the actual audience, the London theatregoers, rather than to those of the King and Viceroy Hieronimo is purportedly trying to please. England was hostile to Spain during the latter part of the sixteenth century; its defeat of the Spanish Armada in 1588 was an occasion of great patriotic pride.

145 *Saracen*: Moor.

149 *late*: recent.

171 S.D. *of*: from.

174 *Pledge*: toast.

176 *we sit . . . delicate*: we are spending more time at dinner than the food deserves.

1.5.4 *league*: alliances.

2.1.3 *sustains*: bears.

  4 *haggard hawks will stoop to lure*: wild hawks will fly down to the bait.

  8 *sufferance*: patient endurance.

  13 *feature is not to content*: features do not please.

  14 *work*: cause.

  15 *lines*: in love letters or poems.

  16 *Pan and Marsyas*: in classical mythology, rude satyrs who challenged Apollo, the god of art, to a musical competition; they represent poor taste and artistic incompetence.

  20 *slandered*: discredited.

  25 *uprear her state*: improve her status.

  31 *lets you not be*: prevents you from being.

  36 *sound the bottom of this doubtful theme*: discover the truth about this uncertain matter.

  41 *Vien qui presto*: come here quickly (Italian).

  47 *conveyance*: acting as a go-between.

  53 *living*: means of support.

    dignities: titles.

  58 *If case it lie in me*: if it is possible for me.

  71 *stay*: stop; wait.

  82 *liberal*: generous.

  85 *Full-fraught*: laden.

  87 *cross*: formed by the hilt of the sword.

  91 *unjust*: untrue.

  94 *for me*: as far as I am concerned.

  100 *sort*: way.

  103 *advance thy state*: improve your situation; because Lorenzo, as a man, is more powerful than his sister.

  107 *tam . . . ingenio*: translated in the following line.

  126 *limed*: lit. coated with birdlime, a sticky material used to snare birds; i.e. made into a trap.

  131 *captivate*: capture.

  136 *remove*: removal.

2.2.4 *contents*: sources of pleasure.

  7 *My heart . . . ship at sea*. Kyd implies that Bel-imperia is taking the sexual initiative by having her voice her emotions first, and by putting

into her mouth figures of speech that men conventionally use to court women in Renaissance love poetry.

14 *make resort*: take refuge.

20 *joys*: enjoys; possesses.

23 *fond*: foolish; loving.

26 *whereon*: on what.

30 *Dangers . . . love*: the metaphor of love as war pervades Renaissance love poetry.

37 *countercheck*: arrest by counteraction; reply to.

41 *villain*. Originally, a villain was a man of low birth; Balthazar's term of opprobrium suggests not merely his jealousy of Horatio but his sense that Bel-imperia's love violates class boundaries.

48 *Happily*: perhaps.

50 *singing with the prickle at her breast*. Although Bel-imperia does not seem to realize it, her image is an ominous one. According to classical myth, Philomela turned into a nightingale after revenging herself on a brother-in-law that had raped her; the nightingale was supposed to thrust a thorn into its breast to remind herself of the suffering her song commemorates. For the Renaissance, Philomela symbolized the closeness of artistic beauty to terror and violence.

2.3.3 *coy it as becomes her kind*: pretend reluctance as is appropriate for her sex.

5 *stoop*: submit.

10 *make this marriage up*: confirm this marriage plan.

18 *in case*: provided that.

19 *released*: cancelled.

22 *motion*: proposal.

23 *work it*: bring it about.

29 *king*: i.e. viceroy.

37 *pitched*: settled.

42 *will*: stubbornness.

43 *friends*: relatives.

44 *amiable*: lovable.

50 *give back*: refuse.

2.4.7 *controls*: overpowers.

10 *without*: outside.

20 *misdoubt*: trepidations.

28 *record*: repeat their songs.

31 *frame sweet music to Horatio's tale*: compose sweet music to accompany Horatio's speech.

32 *Venus*: goddess of love and mother of Cupid, the god of erotic love; also, a planet ('star').

34 *Mars*: god of war, Venus's lover.

37 *ruder*: rougher.

40 *ward*: guard.

41 *retort*: throw back.

45 *compassed*: surrounded; conquered.

47 *dies*. The word 'die' could mean 'experience orgasm'; a common Renaissance pun, but especially ominous in this context.

52 *forbear*: i.e. to struggle.

tried: shown, in battle and in the sexual encounter with Bel-imperia.

53 S.D. *in the arbour*: perhaps upon a stage-prop tree, which might remain onstage for Hieronimo's and Isabella's subsequent visits to the arbour, or even double as Pedringano's gallows in 3.6. The title-page of the 1615 quarto shows a trellis which might serve some of the same functions. Lorenzo and Balthazar have Horatio hanged because it was considered a humiliating form of execution suitable for lower-class criminals; thus Hieronimo considers the corpse 'dishonoured' (l. 83). Hanging could take a long time, however, so the murderers stab their victim in order to make sure he is dead.

54 *fruits*: a pun, because Horatio is hanging from a tree; cf. Hieronimo in 3.13 and Isabella in 4.2.

62 S.D. *shirt*: nightshirt.

63 *naked bed*: Elizabethans slept either nude or lightly clothed.

90 *misdone*: done wrong.

111 *glasses*: windows.

113 *handkercher*: small scarf; perhaps the same one Horatio took from the dead Andrea's arm, originally a favour from Bel-imperia.

118 *spent*: exhausted.

124 *practice*: plot.

142 *O aliquis . . . sequatur*: O, let someone blend for me those herbs that the lovely spring brings forth, and let a medicine be given for my grief; or else let someone provide juices, if there be any, that bring forgetfulness of years. I myself shall gather, from all over the wide world, whatever herbs the sun brings up into the realms of light. I myself shall drink whatever poison the wise woman concocts, and whatever herbs her incantation combines with hidden power. I shall persist through everything, even death, until all the feelings in my breast are dead for once

and for all. So, my life, shall I never see your eyes again? Has perpetual sleep extinguished your light? I shall perish with you: thus, thus it would delight me to go into the shadows. But nevertheless I shall resist surrendering to a swift death, since in that case no revenge might follow your death.

2.5.2 *looked*: expected.

11 *heavy case*: in a bad situation; in a coffin.

3.1.2 *helpless doubts*: irremediable fears.

17 *works*: outcomes; relationships to deeds.

18 *there's no credit in the countenance*: men's faces cannot be trusted.

21 *consorted*: accompanied.

23 *hourly coasts the centre*: hour by hour coasts around the earth (believed the centre of the universe in pre- Copernican astronomy.)

30 S.D. *Halberts*: guards armed with halberds.

31 *extremes*: hopeless situations.

36 *infect*: infected.

37 *yield . . . mould*: give me faith in anyone in this world.

46 *suggestion*: false accusation. The ending 'ion' is often, as here, sounded as two syllables.

47 *When*: hurry.

50 *Phlegethon*: river of fire in hell.

52 *maliced*: behaved maliciously.

55 *lake*: i.e. Phlegethon.

57 *injurious*: calumnious.

65 *entreated*: treated.

66 *commends*: sends greetings.

75 *intimate these ills*: suggest these bad things.

79 *quital for thy discontent*: repayment for your suffering.

80 *in kindness*: by your nature.

81 *fact*: deed.

89 *misconceived*: suspected.

95 *preferred*: promoted.

98 *mean*: small.

105 *articulated*: proposed in articles.

3.2.2 *lively form of death*: death with the appearance of life.

12 *secretary*: confidant.

16 *of*: from.

17 *frame*: direct.

18 *fear*: terrify.

23 S.D. *A letter falleth*: the letter is presumably dropped from the upper stage, perhaps by Bel-imperia herself, who will later appear there 'imprisoned'. 'Red ink' indicates that it should be written in red letters visible to the audience.

26 *writ*: writing.

34 *malign?*: treat badly.

36 *mean*: perpetrator.

48 *circumstances*: circumstantial evidence.

51 *close*: meet.

62 *suit unto her*: request for her.

74 *Admit*: even admitting.
   condition's: nature is.

76 *humour*: temperament.

84 *hard by*: nearby.

93 *mount*: rise in status; but Lorenzo also implies 'ascend the gallows'.

94 *Che le Ieron!*: gibberish; 'perhaps a corruption of the page's name' (F. Boas, (ed.), *Works of Thomas Kyd*, 1901).

101 *cast*: planned.

102 *spread the watch*: deploy the night-watchmen.

113 *dealt for*: accounted for.

116 *base companions*: low-born associates ('companion' was frequently a contemptuous term in Renaissance English).

117 *hazard our good haps*: risk our good fortune.

118 *fear their faith*: worry about their trustworthiness.

3.3.2 *hold on*: keep on the same course.

4 *shift*: manage by myself.

6 *adventure*: take risks.

10 *fail*: be unsuccessful; go bankrupt.

11 *wishing, want*: desiring wealth, have to go without.

15 *suspect*: suspicion.

20 *watch and ward*: patrol.

22 *somewhat in't*: something to it.

23 *stay thy pace*: stand still.

27 *close with*: ambush.

29 *play the man*: i.e. by behaving violently. Since Pedringano's part was

apparently played by a short adult or a boy (cf. 3.6.63–64), the idiom would seem doubly significant in performance.

37 *priest*: i.e. to give him 'last rites'.

3.4.2 *preventing*: averting.

10 *fault*: crime.

31 *exasperate*: make harsh; intensify.

35 *hardly shall deny*: with difficulty shall deny my request.

43 *hopeful*: ambitious.

44 *look like fowlers*: act like bird-hunters, i.e. predators.

46 *reaching fatch*: far-reaching contrivance.

56 *stand good lord*: support him, as a lord ought.

58 *may*: are able to do.

60 *like wax*: i.e. easily.

63 *advised*: careful.

66 *delivery*: liberation.

69 *turnèd off*: cast off the gallows ladder to be hanged.

70 *uttermost be tried*. Lorenzo seems to say that no effort will be omitted on Pedringano's behalf, although Pedringano will have to wait until the last moment for his reprieve; but he implies that 'Pedringano will experience the worst'.

73 *an if*: if.

74 *unknown*: to himself.

77 *cleanly*: efficiently.

82 *list not*: prefer not to.

86 *lie too open to advantages*: eagerly await opportunities to gain a position of superiority.

88 *E quel . . . mi basterà*: And what I want, no one knows; I understand, that is enough for me (Italian).

3.5.3 *men's-kind in our minority*: male minors.

4 *uncertainty*: untrustworthiness.

that: that which.

11 *audience*: the people who come to see him executed.

descant: comment.

of: upon.

14 *warrant*: licence.

16 *sort*: way.

3.6.1 *extremes*: hardships.

7 *know the cause*: perhaps 'know who has caused Horatio's death' (Hieronimo does not yet believe Bel-imperia's information); perhaps 'perform the revenge'.

8 *toils*: exhausts.

16 *here*: at his heart, where he keeps Horatio's handkerchief as a reminder. S.D. *Enter Officers*. Perhaps the officers bring onstage the gallows upon which Pedringano is hanged later in the scene; or perhaps the gallows is a fixed prop that doubles as a tree in the scenes in Hieronimo's garden. The latter staging option would emphasize causal and symbolic connections between Horatio's death and Pedringano's.

17 *set*: in session.

20 *nearer*: more secret; more incriminating.

23 *gear*: business; apparatus.

39 *approvèd*: proven.

45 *disfurnish me of my habit*: the clothes of the executed person were the hangman's perquisite.

47 *boot*: compensation (with a pun).

48 *flat*: final.

50 *up*: go up the gallows ladder.

55 *turned off*: pushed off the ladder.

68 *companion*: fellow.

71 *truss*: both 'close-fitting garment' and 'noose'. 'To truss up' is to hang.

82 *Is your roguery become an office*. Pedringano mocks the hangman's use of the genteel word 'office' (vocation, career) in connection with his unsavoury occupation.

83 *seal it*: lend it your authority (the hangman is saying 'Takes one to know one').

91 *set so light*: considered so trivial.

95 *intercepts itself of*: cuts itself off from.

100 *soft*: not so fast.

104 *Stand you*: do you rely (with a joke about Pedringano's precarious position on the ladder).

3.7.1 *breathe abroad*: express publicly.

20 *merry conceits*: jokes.

23 *passport*: pardon; the illiterate hangman mistakes Pedringano's letter to Lorenzo for an official document.

26 *stand between the gallows and me*. The pardon the hangman believes Pedringano to have obtained would authorize punishment of anyone who executed the sentence in defiance of its order. The hangman wants

Hieronimo to protect him from any such consequences. Hieronimo's acceptance of responsibility contrasts with Lorenzo's treatment of subordinates.

29 *somewhat nearer me concerns*: something concerns me more intimately.

33 *labour my delivery*: arrange my liberation.

54 *accident*: circumstance.

65 *banned*: cursed.

69 *plain me*: complain.

72 *purchase*: obtain.

3.8.1 *purge*: cure.

  5 *recure*: recover.

  11 *whipstalk*: whip handle, used as a toy. Isabella remembers Horatio as a small child, still wearing the 'gowns' that boys wore before the age of about seven years.

21 *greet*: honour.

22 *mirror*: model for imitation.

3.9.3 *notice*: information.

  9 *that thou sawest*. As the theatre spectators are aware and Bel-imperia of course is not, Andrea in the company of Revenge is looking on at this moment, most likely from a few feet away on the same balcony.

12 *force perforce*: like it or not.

13 *apply me to the time*: submit to circumstances.

3.10.7 *enlarged*: set free.

  11 *nine-day's wonder*: short-lived sensation.

13 *time*: about time.

19 *salve*: calm.

  soothe me up: back up my story.

20 *hap to stand on terms*: chance to be difficult.

28 *company*: companion.

31 *clap*: shut.

45 *matters . . . determinèd*: property or political power to which the viceroy was relinquishing claim.

48 *next in sight*: nearest to them.

56 *so meanly accompanied*: accompanied by a person of such low origins.

58 *forth*: out of.

62 *entreateth of*: describes.

63 *forged*: devised; with the double meaning 'counterfeited'.

69 *exasperate*: made harsher.

71 *give his fury place*: give his anger room to dissipate.

74 *Aetna*: active volcano on the island of Sicily.

84 *politic*: shrewd in a worldly, amoral way; cf. Lorenzo's pride in his 'policy' in 3.4.38.

88 *Ariadne's twines*. Ariadne used a thread to guide Theseus out of the Minotaur's labyrinth; but Balthazar associates Bel-imperia's 'twines' with bondage, not freedom.

89 *surprised*: captured.

102 *Et tremulo . . . opus*: And I feared to join panic to trembling terror—a vain work of foolish treachery.

103 *an*: if.

105 *lodestar*: the North Star, by which travellers calculate their direction. Cf. 'Ariadne's twines' above; what ought to be images of assurance and liberation become for Balthazar metaphors for disorientation and imprisonment.

108 *Incertain to effect*: uncertain whether he will be able to complete.

3.11.10 s.d. *out at another*. The back wall of the Renaissance stage had two permanent doors for exits and entrances.

14 *list*: listen.

20 *baleful humours*. Melancholy was associated with black bile, one of the four 'humours' or fluids that combined to produce different human temperaments. Excess of melancholy led to suicidal depression.

uphold: continue in.

30 *him*: himself.

34 *passing*: exceedingly

3.12.4 *toys*: trivialities.

6 *trudge*: move on.

10 *firebrand*: torch that lights the way.

16 *This way, or that way?*. Hieronimo is trying to decide whether to commit suicide by stabbing himself with the poniard or hanging himself in the noose.

Soft and fair: slow down; easy now.

22 *I'll be with thee to bring*: you'll have to reckon with me.

24 *there goes the hare away*: the hunt is underway.

31 *go by!*: be careful.

42 *myrrh or incense*: traditionally burned as propitiatory offerings to the gods.

46 *inexplicable*: unbreakable.

75 *pickaxe*: to dig down into the underworld.

79 *outrage*: outburst.

82 *Needs must he go that the devils drive*: proverbial; the 'devils' here are both Lorenzo and the others who prevent Hieronimo from presenting his case, and Hieronimo's own vengeful obsessions, which are driving him insane.

83 *happed*: happened to.

84 *demean*: behave; demean himself.

101 *exempt the place*: refrain from replacing Hieronimo in the position.

3.13.1 *'Vindicta mihi'*: Hieronimo quotes the first part of a verse from Romans 12: 19: 'Vengeance is mine; I will repay, saith the Lord.'

6 *Per scelus . . . iter*: the safe way to crime is always through crimes (from Seneca's *Agamemnon*).

8 *conductors*: conduits.

9 *the worst of resolution*: the worst possible consequence of resolving to take revenge.

10 *contend*: strive to attain.

13 *Fata . . . sepulchrum*: translated and applied to Hieronimo's own situation in lines 14–19.

21 *Not as the vulgar wits of men*: not as ordinary people would proceed.

23 *As*: but.

24 *kindship*: friendliness.

26 *Closely*: secretly; precisely.

time: particular circumstances.

27 *extremes . . . time*: i.e. in desperate straits opportunities will not occur.

35 *Remedium malorum iners est*: is a useless remedy for evils.

36 *menace*: threaten.

38 *bear me down*: overcome me.

43 *cap*: which he will remove respectfully in the presence of his superiors.

45 *what coil is that you keep*: what is the noise you are making.

49 *actions*: cases.

60 *battery*: assault.

Give place: let another go ahead of you (because crimes against persons take precedence over property issues).

61 *action of the case*: case not within the court's usual jurisdiction, requiring a special writ.

62 *ejectione firmae by a lease*: a writ to reject a tenant before his lease expires.

66 *band*: bond.

67 *silly*: simple; pathetic.

72 *Corsic*: of Corsica, a rocky Mediterranean island.

    ruthful: merciful.

77 *blood*: passion; blood-relationship.

85 *lively*: living.

    S.D. *napkin*: scarf.

91 *But here . . . thine.* Hieronimo gives the old man money and perhaps articles of his attire.

92 *all as one are our extremities*: we are in the same terrible situation.

99 *lesser things*: people of lower rank (Don Bazulto is poorer than Hieronimo).

100 *meaner wits*: less exalted intelligences.

105 *o'erturneth . . . deep*: a difficult passage: perhaps, the raging sea 'turns over the top layer of the water, making the waves race, while the layers below are also agitated'. Hieronimo seems to be comparing his own, relatively exalted, social station with that of the humbler Old Man, in order to excoriate himself for not having taken more effective action heretofore.

111 *Alcides*: Hercules, whose last and greatest labour was to enter Hades by force and bind Cerberus, its three-headed watchdog.

114 *triple-headed porter*: Cerberus.

116 *Thracian poet*: Orpheus, legendary poet and musician whose songs convinced the gods to allow him to enter the underworld to find his dead wife, Euridyce.

118 *thou canst*: you know.

119 *sound the burden*: play the bassline or refrain; express the heavy load.

122 *rent*: rip.

150 *favour*: features; good fortune.

170 *stay*: support.

172 *Three parts in one*: a common sixteenth-century contrapuntal musical texture.

3.14.6 *sometimes*: formerly. In fact, in the late sixteenth century Portugal remained a major colonial power.

8 *brave*: excellent.

28 *marriage*: trisyllabic here.

35 *nature strives in him*: natural emotions overcome him.

37 *extremities*: extreme emotions.

39 *Or*: either.

50 *intercept*: hinder.

60 *answer for thee*: justify your behaviour.

61 *common*: general.

67 *exclaim against*: denounce; complain about.

74 *vulgar, liberal of their tongues*: common people prone to gossip.

75 *small advantage makes a water-breach*: a tiny crack in a dam becomes a large hole.

80 *ill beseemed*: was inappropriate for.

81 *for*: because.

106 *salute*: greet.

117 *trow*: do you believe.

118 *Pocas palabras*: few words (Spanish).

125 *short*: little to say.

149 *pause*: let it rest.

151 *homely*: hospitable.

158 *lovely*: delightful.

167 *Pha!*: an expression of disgust.

169 *Chi mi . . . mi vuole*: He who displays uncustomary love for me either has betrayed me or wants to betray me.

3.15.1 *Erichtho*: a sorceress.

3 *Erebus*: deity of primeval darkness.

16 *Thus . . . upon*: thus mortals base their beliefs upon what they have merely imagined.

18 *mood*: rage.

24 *instance*: example.

26 s.d. *dumb show*: mime.

28 *nuptial torches*: carried in the wedding procession to symbolize desire.

31 *sable*: black, colour of death.

saffron: deep yellow, symbolic of fertility in classical Roman wedding ceremonies.

4.1.15 *ingratitude*: unkindness.

19 *tendered*: pampered.

20 *in respect of thee*: compared to you.

23 *bear it out for fashion's sake*: pretend for the sake of appearances.

31 *applies our drift*: consents to our scheme.

38 *care*: caution.

39 *Nor think I thoughtless think upon a mean*: nor think I am not concerned to think of a way.

40 *at full*: fully.

49 *grace my practices*: look with favour on, and participate in, my plans.

50 *For why*: because.

57 *assure yourselves of*: rely upon.

61 *study*: library; mind.

62 *first night's sport*. The entertainment associated with royal and aristocratic weddings could go on for more than a week.

64 *motion*: entertainment (trisyllabic here).

67 *I'll fit you*: I'll give you what you need; I'll give you what you deserve.

70 *professor*: practitioner.

73 *quick*: impatient; perhaps with a pun on 'alive'.

82 *plausible*: worth applauding; realistic (since the tragedy will involve actual deaths).

83 *tragedy*. Aristocratic marriages were normally celebrated with comic performances, and the actors were not the newlyweds themselves, but professionals of lower social rank.

84 *Nero*: Roman emperor notorious not only for cruelty but for insisting upon performing in a public theatre, usually an occupation for slaves. This dubious precedent hints at Hieronimo's opinion of Balthazar, and also perhaps at Hieronimo's plan to combine theatre and violence.

86 *experience*: trial.

90 *I'll make one*: I, for one, will participate.

99 *tell what*: know how.

102 *country manner*: the custom of our country.

103 *argument*: plot.

104 *roundly*: fully; right away.

105 *knight of Rhodes*: a member of a military and religious order founded at the time of the Crusades. Conflict between pagan and Christian warriors over a beautiful maiden is a stock plot of Renaissance chivalric romance.

109 *Soliman*: the Turkish emperor.

113 *break*: divulge.

130 *conceited*: decided.

138 *Turkish cap*: fez.

142 *Phoebe, Flora, or the Huntress*: the goddess of the moon, the goddess of flowers, or Diana, the goddess of chastity.

144 *I'll look to one*: I'll provide a costume.

153 *comedies . . . tragedy*. Hieronimo's distinction between the subject-matter of comedy and tragedy originates with Aristotle and becomes commonplace in Renaissance literary theory.

154 *Tragoedia cothurnata*: formal Greek tragedy, performed by actors wearing *cothurni*, thick-soled laced boots.

155 *matter*: serious matter.

162 *Italian tragedians . . . French tragedians*. Continental actors were famous for their improvisatory skill in the *commedia dell'arte*, a kind of extemporaneous comedy involving stock characters; Hieronimo and Lorenzo claim that they applied the same techniques to the performance of tragedy.

164 *rests*: remains.

186 *soothe his humours up*: humour him.

188 *ply this gear*: work on this thing.

189 *fall of Babylon*: Revelations 18 describes the destruction of Babylon, the city of sinful luxury. Hieronimo conflates Babylon with the Tower of Babel, erected to challenge God's supremacy; God punished its builders by making them speak mutually unintelligible languages.

4.2.5 S.D. *cuts down the arbour*. If the 'arbour' is a trellis covered with greenery, Isabella may strip off the leaves; or she may overturn a property tree upon which Horatio was hanged.

13 *complot*: garden plot; conspiracy.

17 *eastern wind*: proverbially bleak and unhealthy.

   noisome: stinking. Diseases were thought to be carried by such air: cf. *mal aria*, 'bad air'.

20 *passengers*: passersby.

27 *cited*: summoned; incited.

30 *to hold excused | Thy negligence*: to have thy negligence excused.

4.3. S.D. *knocks up*: hastily arranges. The curtain may be hung over one of the entrance-doors or in front of the 'inner stage', an alcove at the back of the stage.

1 *fellows*: associates.

7 *argument*: plot.

14 *title*. In the Renaissance theatre a title-board announced the name, setting, and time of the play.

4.4.3 *of pleasure*: at their pleasure.

8 *bookkeeper*: the person in charge of the script.

11 S.D. *largely*: fully. Possibly the 'play in sundry languages' was actually staged in a variety of foreign languages, or perhaps it was performed in

English and this stage direction is adapted from an introduction by Hieronimo.

18 *wait*: serve.

28 *influence of her lights*: emanations or 'influences' of an ethereal fluid from the stars were imagined to affect human destinies; Soliman attributes this power to Perseda's eyes ('lights').

50 *wit*: understand.

54 *favour*: beauty; love.

57 *released*: alleviated.

76 *fabulously counterfeit*: fictional pretence.

86 *urge instance*: demand proof.

102 *sorted leisure*: arranged their time.

109 *soonest*: quickest.

111 *Through-girt*: struck through.

117 *Marched in a net*: acted with little concealment, although expecting to escape notice.

118 *rated*: reproved.

143 *him*: Horatio.

147 *his latest fortune*: the rope with which he intends to hang himself.

156 *Break ope the doors*: which Hieronimo has locked with the key he obtained from Castile.

214 *Scylla*: a legendary monster-woman identified with a treacherous rock in the Mediterranean, sometimes imagined as accompanied by dogs or as a sea-nymph metamorphosed into a bitch. The Viceroy confuses her with Charybdis, a similar monster who drowns sailors in a whirlpool nearby.

4.5.5 *quaint*: cunning.

10 *Dido*: in *Aeneid* iv, Dido commits suicide after Aeneas abandons her; according to legend, by doing so she avoids marriage with Iarbas, another suitor.

14 *doom*: decree, not necessarily hostile.

18 *inured*: practised.

22 *vestal virgins*: in classical Rome, virgins consecrated to the service of Vesta, goddess of the hearth, and famous for their incorruptible chastity. They are perhaps not Bel-imperia's most appropriate companions.

28 *bugs*: hobgoblins.

31 *Tityus*: like Ixion and Sisyphus, a symbol of what happens to mortals who disregard laws laid down by the gods. The casually ferocious punishment of the innocent Castile suggests the disproportionate, amoral quality of Andrea's final triumph.

36 *Chimaera*: a fire-breathing monster.

First Addition

14 *assure*: ensure.

18 *presently*: immediately.

33 *persuasions*: evidences.

37 *mischief*: evil; the word suggests graver harm in Renaissance than in modern English.

41 *apprehension*: understanding; mental grasp.

52 *waste of grief*: with a pun on 'waist'.

54 *put me in the mind*: remind me.

Second Addition

9 *troth*: truth.

nothing: no importance.

Third Addition

3 *wide*: off the mark.

7 *bred up*: developed.

12 *breeds*: grows.

14 *go*: walk.

17 *young bacon*: piglet.

23 *unsquared, unbevelled*: rude; unfinished.

25 *Strikes . . . mad riots*: destroys their equanimity with his crazy excesses.

35 *back*: end.

42 *whips*: wielded by devils who punish evildoers in hell.

48 *confusion*: destruction.

Fourth Addition

30 *burn daylight*: waste time (proverbial); but also literal in this context.

46 *she*: the moon.

47 *book*: almanac.

53 *when mischief doth . . . say to mischief*: how do we reproach evil when it is committed unintentionally.

63 *set it of a kernel*: planted it from a seed.

65 *the infant and the human sap*: the sap of the baby tree, reacting to heat the way human beings do.

74 *none lives but painted comfort*: all comfort is merely apparent, not real.

96 *weigh*: balance; outweigh.

110 *tricks*: hallucinations.

118 *matted*: with a dull (matte) finish. Renaissance group portraits often

included family members posthumously, or represented them younger or older than they were at the time the painting was made. Narrative sequences were commonly depicted by showing several different episodes side-by-side in a single painting. As Hieronimo's demands upon the painter continue, however, they become more and more unrealistic; suggesting perhaps the superior representational power of the theatrical medium.

120 *speaking*: meaningful.

127 *Seemingly*: i.e. I can paint a person who seems to be crying.

134 *Judas his own colour*: Judas, the disciple who betrayed Christ, was reputed to be red-haired.

143 *alley*: garden path.

146 *jarring*: ticking.

148 *tottering*: swinging.

149 *weave*: sway.

with a trice: instantly.

152 *Priam*: King of Troy, as depicted at the destruction of the city in *Aeneid* ii.

160 *brave*: fine.

abuseth: deceives.

Fifth Addition

8 *secure*: confident.

16 *ride*: float.

28 *grew inward with*: became intimate with.

48 *Nunc iners cadat manus!*: Now may my hand fall idle!

49 *rupture*: breaking.

The Revenger's Tragedy

Dramatis Personae: the character's Italian names have allegorical significance. Lussurioso: lecherous. Spurio: bastard. Ambitioso: ambitious. Supervacuo: superfluous. Vindice: revenger. Piato: hidden. Dondolo: idiot. Nencio: dolt. Sordido: corrupt. Gratiana: grace. Castiza: chastity.

1.1 s.D. *skull*: the skull is that of Vindice's late beloved, Gloriana (glorious). The stage directions in the quarto leave it unclear whether Vindice reveals the skull immediately or later in the scene.

4 *do*: have sex with.

5 *characters*: 'character' in Renaissance English means 'symbol', 'type', or 'appearance' rather than 'personality'; here it suggests the unequivocal way the persons of the play instantiate their emblematic names.

7 *heat*: the sexual drive is associated with heat, normally a property of youth, but here arising from hellish desires in an old man.

13 *fret*: anger; a ridge on a stringed instrument that controls fingering.

15 *My study's ornament*: a decoration in Vindice's study; also, a subject of his thought.

20 *unsightly*: ugly; unseeing.

28 *told*: counted.

38 *'Age . . . covetous'*: a *sententia* or proverb. Vindice frequently resorts to pithy, traditional sayings in order to summarize or make sense of his own experience. His respect for proverbial wisdom was likely to have been shared by the original audience of *The Revenger's Tragedy*, since collections of such sayings were highly popular in the English Renaissance.

39 *quit-rent*: literally, rent paid in lieu of services required of a tenant; here, a form of repayment.

42 *determined*: judged.

44 *kept touch*: held up her end of the bargain.

46 *three-piled flesh*: three-piled velvet was an expensive plush fabric with a high nap.

48 *goes by clay*: is ascertained by fleshly bulk.

52 *braver*: showier.

55 *bald madam.*The figure of Opportunity was traditionally represented as a winged woman, bald except for hair growing from her forehead, so that she could be grasped only as she approached, never as she was leaving; hence 'seize opportunity by the forelock'.

59 *Give me to taste*: let me know what it is.

61 *turned out*: dismissed.

63 *guess at that.* Hippolito suggests that the Duchess's sexual interest in him may have kept him his job.

72 *Up in their built houses*: inside the head; perhaps with a reference to the commonplace Renaissance notion of the memory as a building.

74 *scope of his intent*: extent of his plan.

75 *conjuring*: importuning.

76 *strange-digested*: unsettled; oddly composed. Renaissance medicine held that human beings were composed of four fluids or 'humours': black bile, blood, phlegm, and yellow bile. Differences among individuals, as well as many mental and physical disorders, were ascribed to differences or imbalances in the way these four elements were combined.

fellow: a more derogatory term in Renaissance than in modern English, usually denoting a man of the lower classes.

78 *grooms*: men (contemptuous).

79 *stepmother's nuptials*: an unmarried widow often retained control over her late husband's estate and thus over his retainers and children from previous marriages; these people could suffer upon her remarriage.

81 *base-coined*: made of inferior metal; illegitimate.

82 *reach*: understand.

89 *Next to a skull*. Lussurioso only draws the line at dead women, although they may be healthier than some of the live women he desires.

93 *put on*: take the role of.

94 *right*: true (ironic).

a man o' th' time: a man of the world.

97 *prefer*: recommend.

100 *foretop*: see 1.1.55 n.

101 *French mole . . . and all*: syphilis, called the 'French disease' by the English, causes hair loss and tumours on the head.

102 *habit*: costume.

103 *coin*: counterfeit.

107 *Only . . . belief*: despite their virtue, Castiza and Gratiana, like all women, are credulous and will believe excuses.

115 *The law's a woman*: Justice, personified as female.

124 *deject*: humiliate.

125 *smothered in his spirit*: many diseases were ascribed to stoppages that prevented the natural flow of spirits and bodily fluids.

129 *secretary*: confidant.

1.2.6 *His violent . . . our tombs*: the rape has blackened (thrown ink on) the pre-eminent and most visible part of the dukedom and will become material for satirists after the Duke is dead.

7 *in our lives*: while we live.

10 *broad*: forthright; indecent.

11 *silver*: grey-haired.

14 *bowelled*: disembowelled, in preparation for burial.

15 *cered in*: sealed with wax, a preservative applied to the cerecloths or sheets in which a corpse was wrapped.

20 *fact*: deed.

24 *son-in-law*: stepson (the Duchess, punning, encourages the Duke to ignore the law).

33 *iron forehead*: unmoved countenance.

36 *corse*: corpse.

37 *fruitless*: without obtaining what she desires; without her child (because her son seems likely to receive a death sentence).

39 *low metal*: base metal; with a pun on 'low mettle', apathy.

42 *attempt*: assault.

46 *general-honest*: always virtuous.

49 *jest*: jest at.

65 *easier 'sessed*: given a lighter sentence.

75 *performance*: sexual performance.

81 *Hold, hold*: stop, stop.

82 *dad*: familiar term, disrespectful in this context.

83 *sitting*: court session.

85 *makes for thee*: is to your advantage.

90 *if judgement . . . will kill it*. Once outrage over the crime has time to cool, the judges can be flattered and bribed out of sentencing Junior Brother to death.

95 *easy*: compliant. Doctors were often suspected of poisoning their patients.

97 *keep church better*: attend church more regularly (since persons of high rank were buried in the church, the Duke will 'attend' all services after his death).

107 *in his forehead*: by committing adultery, which was supposed to cause the cuckolded husband to grow invisible horns.

117 *duty on your hand*: an inferior's mark of respect to a superior (here, a kiss on the hand) was called his 'duty'.

123 *hatted dame*: woman of the citizen class.

   answer: respond; suffice.

136 *ride a horse well*: suggestive of good sexual technique.

   shrewd: formidable.

138 *peeping over half-shut holiday windows*: Renaissance windows were commonly fitted with four shutters. People inside the house could obtain privacy without sacrificing light by closing the bottom pair of shutters and leaving the upper pair open. But the groom is tall enough to look over the shutters on holidays to see how the inhabitants spend their leisure time.

138 *desire him 'light*: ask him to dismount.

139 *penthouse*: awning.

140 *rid*: rode.

141 *check the signs, and clatter barbers'·basins*: bump into the signs over shops,

and rattle the metal shaving-dishes barbers hung out to advertise their services.

143 *beggar*. Spurio alludes to the proverb 'Set a beggar on horseback, and he'll ride at a gallop'; with sexual innuendo.

147 *bid fair for't*: gave it a good try.

151 *collet*: the part of the ring that holds the jewel.

156 *injury*: injure (a common Renaissance variant).

160 *seventh commandment*: against adultery.

163 *hot-backed*: lusty.

164 *mad*: madden.

    rough: disturbed.

172 *Earnest*: pledge; foretaste.

173 *picks open*: i.e. like a lock.

175 *woman's heraldry*: the horns of a cuckold.

179 *stirring*: stimulating.

180 *healths*: toasts.

182 *Their tongues . . . heels*: their tongues are 'short' because their speech becomes defective under the influence of alcohol. 'To have short heels' means 'to behave wantonly'.

183 *thick*: drunkenly pronounced.

197 *falsely sown*. Spurio suggests that although Lussurioso's mother was married to the Duke, his real paternity is as doubtful as his own.

199 *loose my days upon him*: devote my time to (troubling) him.

200 *draw*: inscribe, with reference to cuckold's horns.

1.3.1 *far*: different.

12 *scholar*: proverbially inexperienced in worldly matters.

13 *maid in the old time*: old-fashioned virgin.

14 *get good clothes*: improve her wardrobe. Extravagant attire was a favourite form of conspicuous consumption in early modern Europe, associated by satirists with a general corruption of moral standards, especially in women.

17 *reach out o' th' verge*: go out of bounds; are merely whimsical.

22 *politic siftings*: cunning inquiries.

23 *rare*: choice.

24 *This our age swims within him*: he is up-to-the- minute.

    Time: proverbially bald.

28 *blanks*: unsigned documents, or coins not yet stamped with a value.

33 *Push*: pish, a deprecatory expression.

34 *muskcat*: civet cat, from whose anal glands an expensive perfume was derived; figuratively, the foppish courtier who wore such perfume. Vindice's grossly indecorous language and behaviour to a man of far higher social position are a calculated attempt to convince Lussurioso that 'Piato' is a man who disregards convention; but the disguise conveniently allows him to express his genuine contempt for the heir apparent.

36 *Gather him into boldness*: encourage him to be familiar.

37 *familiar as an ague*: as intimately physical as a shaking fever.

40 *remember me*: remember who I am.

47 *to my hand*: for my purposes.

48 *scrivener*: agent.

49 *Fool*: accessory.

51 *patrimonies washed a-pieces*: inheritances ruined, as in a shipwreck.

53 *gravel a petition*: sand was dusted over the wet ink of legal documents to dry them quickly.

56 *Dutch*: drunken, uncouth; traits the English stereotyped as Dutch and German (Deutsch).

59 *cling*: embrace.
daughter-in-law: stepdaughter or daughter-in-law in the modern sense.

62 *rim*: limit; edge of the womb.

75 *fathomed into all estates*: informed about all modes and levels of social life.

76 *near employment*: job requiring discretion.

79 *disease o' th' mother*: here, talkativeness, considered a female vice; with a pun on a hysterical disorder called 'the mother'.

80 *close*: i.e. closed up, without 'leaky' orifices; figuratively, reserved, silent.

84 *confirmed in me*: taken into my confidence.

85 *enter*: initiate; but in the next line Vindice plays upon the word in the sense of demonic possession.
Indian: both the East and West Indies were proverbially sources of great mineral wealth.

92 *waxed lines*: letters sealed with wax.
neatest spirit: purest passion.

98 *repugnant*: resistant.

100 *blood*: lineage.

103 *friend*: mistress.

105 *What . . . night*: what is more disgusting than night after night.

112 *portion*: dowry.

114 *bring it into expense*: disburse it.

117 *gi'en 't the tang*: described it accurately.

122 *raise*: promote.

123 *late*: recent.

127 *bodkin will put a man in*: hairpin will suggest a topic for discussion (with obscene implication).

128 *wagging of her hair*: continuing the obscene innuendo.

136 *simple age*: innocent and foolish stage of life.

139 *wind up*: incite; prepare.

140 *work*: persuade.

142 *carried*: carried out.

152 *dainty*: rare.

153 *the name | Is so in league with age*: the name of bawd is so closely associated with old age.

154 *eclipse*: overpower.

157 *furnish thee*: give you what you need.

169 *disheir*: disinherit (by murdering him).

170 *angry froth is down in me*: my fury is under control.

171 *meanest*: most stupid.

175 *o'erwrought*: prevailed over.

179 *touch*: test (as gold was tested by rubbing it against a quartz 'touchstone').

180 *Venture my lands in heaven upon their blood*: stake my chance of salvation on their virtue.

1.4 S.D. *discovering*: showing, perhaps by removing a curtain to the 'inner stage', a small chamber at the back of the stage in which the body could be laid out as if in state.

4 *played a glorious act*: ironically representing rape as a dramatic character.

5 *strikes man out of me*: deprives me of my manly resolve.

11 *pledge her honour*: the lady's honour and life, personified, are imagined as relations drinking pledges (toasts) with poisoned wine.

14 *confection*: arrangement; preservative.

15 *leaf tucked up*: page folded over.

17 *'Melius . . . vivere'*: It is better to die in virtue than to live in disgrace.

18 *effectual*: pertinent.

21 *as to ourselves*: as for us.

23 *Curae . . . stupent*: Light sorrows speak out; heavy ones are silent.

31 *moth*: rapacious pest.

32 *Filled up a room*: took up a space.

33 *wearing*: clothing (continuing the metaphor of the moth from l. 31).

40 *Unfit but for relation to be spoke of*: unmentionable, were it not required for the narration.

43 *live upon damnation of both kinds*: make their living off the sins of both sexes.

46 *dowry for her name*: legacy for which her name may be remembered.

60 *sitting*: court session.

61 *Judgement . . . in gold*: the judges' decisions show that they have been bribed.

64 *We swear . . . it*: perhaps the men draw their own swords here, or perhaps swear upon the hilt of Hippolito's sword, held up to resemble a cross.

72 *court it*: display themselves at court.

2.1.1 *hardly*: severely.

2 *constant thoughts*: steadfast moral convictions.

7 *revenue*: stressed on the second syllable.

17 *dirty way*: literally, roundabout travelling; but Castiza is also reproving Dondolo's obscene innuendo.

21 *gentleman-usher*: a well-born servant to a person of superior rank.

23 *Yours be your own*: do it your way.

25 *affects*: loves.

34 *attorney*: middleman.

40 *box*: blow; also boxwood, a fragrant shrub.

41 *drawn-work cuff*: a pun, meaning both 'the lacy end of a sleeve' and the mark made by Castiza's hand slapping his face.

43 *take the wall*: occupy a privileged position. Since pavement close to buildings was cleaner than the heavily used middle of the street, socially superior pedestrians claimed the 'wall side' when walking with or passing their inferiors.

44 *above my tongue*: my words cannot describe my emotions.

45 *right honourable*: truly chaste; also, a courtesy title for aristocrats.

47 *approved*: both 'thought well of' and 'fully tested'.

50 *As my resolve in that point*: as I have already decided.

52 *siren's tongue*: sirens were mythical women whose beautiful voices lured sailors to their deaths.

59 *like to be our sudden duke*: likely to become duke suddenly.

60 *The . . . tide*: the crown is open to him at any moment. Since the grave is said to 'gape' for all men, Vindice's expression insinuates the imminent death of both the Duke and Lussurioso.

65 *ne'er be seen in't*: the difference would never be noticed.

68 *If you'd . . . daughter*: children in the womb were thought to be made out of the mother's blood.

69 *wheel comes about*: the wheel of fortune, which has reduced her means, is now raising her up.

71 *white*: white-haired; also, covered with mould.

78 *vex*: disturb by increasing.

80 *foolish country girl*: once again, moral rectitude is associated with an unsophisticated rural perspective.

84 *angels*: a common Renaissance pun on the name of a gold coin impressed with a representation of St Michael.

89 *dejected, scorned of greatness*: cast down, despised by the great.

91 *Spring with the dew o' th' court*: rise up by the court's invigorating power.

93 *raise my state*: improve my social situation.

97 *keep men after men*: keep men lined up (to request her patronage).

100 *though it be but some*: although only partially.

101 *bring you home*: bring you to your goal.

106 *touched me nearly*: spoke right to the point about my situation; also, tested me severely.

108 *turns edge*: is deflected or blunted.

122 *the mother*: hysterical disorder incident to women, supposed to arise from the womb; here also maternal feeling.

126 *precious side*: the outer side, that sees. Vindice associates the inward turn of his eyeballs with an *absence* of self-reflection; suggesting that he characteristically acquires his moral bearings not by introspection but by observing the effects of his actions in the world.

147 *rule*: both 'regulation' and 'straight edge for making measurements'; the double meaning is extended in the term 'square out'.

151 *shades*: both obscurity, and ghosts in contrast to flesh-and-blood men.

153 *You cannot . . . without fee*: you cannot come into the possession of yourselves without making a payment to another.

162 *It is a wise . . . mother*: a play on the saying, 'It is a wise child who knows his father.'

163 *I owe your cheek my hand*: you deserve to have your face slapped.

165 *'haviours*: behaviours.

166 *time*: opportunity.

169 *rich*: scarce, therefore costly, because no longer imported.

179 *keep*: maintain.

181 *charge*: expensive encumbrances.

183 *break up . . . friends*: sell her (sexual) belongings—with the implication of rupturing the virginal hymen—and depend upon 'friends' for her support.

185 *fall*: capitulate sexually.

187 *petitionary people*: those who come to court asking for favours.

189 *ravished*: delighted; sexually despoiled.

195 *stirring*: stimulating (and perhaps, still twitching; 'calvered' salmon, a delicacy, was cut up while still alive).

197 *quicken*: excite, become alive or pregnant; the word equates the 'meats' with the people who eat them.

200 *Bareheaded vassals . . . wear 'em*: the men seem to be bareheaded out of respect for their betters, keeping their hats hung up on hooks because they have no need of them; but Vindice suggests that the hats will not fit on their heads over their cuckold's horns.

210 *as useless as old men*: because pictures perform no actions.

213 *Walk . . . foreparts*. Vindice describes the selling off of inherited land to purchase expensive court garments. 'Forepart' is an ornamental breast covering.

215 *met again*: agreed.

216 *come up*: emerge; travel to court.

218 *mete by the rod*: measured by the rod (1/160 of an acre).

220 *foretops*: locks of hair growing on top of the head.

221 *head-tires*: elaborate headdresses. Here as elsewhere, Vindice describes courtliness as a replacement of the natural with the contrived or unnatural.

much untold: much remains unsaid.

232 *struck hot irons*: made her blush red, like hot iron.

233 *from*: away from.

234 *inward*: intimate with you; inseparable from you.

236 *mother a disease*: cf. 2.1.122 n.

237 *outgone*: gone beyond.

239 *crystal plaudities*: ringing applause.

246 *base-titled creatures that look downward*: beasts.

251 *lord's great kitchen*: the enormous kitchen of a manor-house.

2.2.2 *well read in*: a good judge of.

6 *Knave in your face, my lord—behind your back*. To insult someone 'in his face' is to insult him directly, which Hippolito dares not do to Lussurioso.

10 *seasoned . . . season*: ripened (Lussurioso); time [for revenge] (Hippolito).

19 *toward*: in the offing.

20 *Ravish*: delight; but with a continuing suggestion that Lussurioso is Vindice's sexual victim.

rare: unusually good at your job.

22 *woman*: i.e. proverbially malleable.

24 *courage*: optimism; sexual energy.

25 *made indifferent-honest naught*: ruined a more-or-less virtuous woman.

27 *white money*: silver coins of low denomination; here, a cheap prostitute.

28 *turned to Mahomet*: converted to Islam.

31 *flat*: lay flat.

32 *close*: impervious.

a doubt: doubtful.

38 *true*: truthful.

thou . . . proclaim. Lussurioso will not live long enough to tell others about Gratiana's perfidy.

43 *travel | Into unknown lands*: try something new.

straight: immediately.

44 *Golden spurs*: monetary incentives.

48 *mother for her age*: in the Renaissance orders of precedence in a procession, at dinner, etc. were strictly determined by age and rank.

53 *fool*: innocent.

70 *beg, leg*: beg by 'making a leg', bowing by bending one knee.

79 *fees . . . arras*: fees for setting up assignations behind the tapestry screens used to insulate palace rooms.

farthingales: petticoats. The costliness of Renaissance clothing created a thriving resale market; the wages of many personal servants were supplemented by the master's or mistress's castoff garments.

plump: all at once, with onomatopoeic suggestion.

80 *rushes*: used to cover floors.

84 *missed*: ignored.

88 *o' th' wrong side*: by stabbing him in the back.

94 *lessen not my days*: Exodus 20: 12 promises long life to those who honour their parents.

96 *use*: prostitution.

101 *go hard*: be difficult (with *double entendre*).

102 *ports sure*: her openings safe.

109 *linen*: nightclothes.

118 *inward*: acquainted.

130 *additions*: honorific titles (sarcastic).

131 *funeral herald's fees*: black drapery and insignia of mourning, which heralds were paid to display in public for important funerals.

134 *full sea*: high tide.

135 *juggling*: trickery.

136 *i' th' toll-book*: listed as whores. A toll-book described animals and merchandise for sale at fairs.

138 *by water*: by a back door which opens upon a river or canal.

140 *proclamation*: legally, public denunciation as a known prostitute; here, the squeaking of iron hinges.

142 *careful sisters*: diligent whores. 'Spin thread' is slang for sexual activity.

152 *season*: time.

157 *start*: startle.

160 *Shadows*: covers up.

163 *horn royal*: referring to the Duke's cuckoldry, with a play on the 'royal antler', the third prong from the base of a stag's antler.

164 *fruit of two beds*: consequence of adultery.

171 *wildfire*: a highly inflammable substance used in war.

173 *follow the event*: go to see the outcome.

2.3 S.D. *bed*: this could have been located in a recess at the back of the stage, or it could have been pushed on to the stage for the duration of the scene.

2 *twisted*: sexually united; also suggesting perversion.

4 *soft*: quiet.

5 *spleen*: supposed to be the seat of anger.

8 *upper guard*: guard of the bedchamber.

11 *penitential heaves*: sighs of repentance.

16 *nerves*: sinews.

17 *lawyers*: who will prosecute Lussurioso for treason, the penalty for which was decapitation.

19 *myself*: duke.

25 *file*: defile.

26 *abused*: deceived.

28 *from*: out of.

32 *without frightful word*. Vindice knows he ought not say that he wishes he had killed the Duke, but he says it anyhow.

37 *knaves' chins and harlots' tongues*. In Renaissance English, 'harlot' could signify a male criminal as well as a whore. But elsewhere in *The Revenger's Tragedy* the word is always used in its modern sense; and here Spurio seems to mean that his servants combine the unkempt beards of disreputable men and the untrustworthy talkativeness of disreputable women.

38 *damn you with*: condemn you to.

43 *out o' th' socket*: out of order.

45 *so saucy with his elbows*. The guard grips Lussurioso by the arms—standard treatment for suspected criminals, but a rudely familiar way to handle the heir apparent.

53 *best release*: best hope of release.

59 *Puritan*: hypocritical.

63 *The craftiest . . . breath*: the craftiest lawyer earns the most money by saying little.

64 *Set on*: get started.

78 *sound*: completed.

79 *corrupted favor*: mistaken favouritism.

82 *Honey? How's this?*: what kind of sweet words are these?

85 *gathers*: concludes.

87 *Here's no stepmother's wit*. Unlike their mother, Lussurioso's stepmother, the brothers can't feign concern successfully.

91 *peevish moon*: strange mood.

93 *beside your spleen*: without taking your anger into account.

99 *signet*: signet-ring, which the Duke lends the brothers so that the judges will know the command is genuine.

101 *All speed that may be*: as soon as possible.

105 *scarlet hid in lawn*: heavy dark-red fabric behind translucent linen.

108 *prevent their envies*: keep their hatred from having consequences.

111 *suddenly*: immediately.

124 *nod at*: overlook.

130 *turned to poison | In the denial*: poisoned when they spurned his advances.

131 *hot*: lustful.

3.1.2 *him*: Lussurioso.

6 *Faiths*: loyalties.

7 *skin of gold*: cover for financial transactions.

8 *set by*: disregard.

14 *puffed out*: extinguished.

16 *packed*: dispatched.

17 *wind*: manœuvre.

18 *lies in*: lies in prison; a phrase also used of women in childbed, suggesting Ambitioso's blindness to the difference between rape and procreation. Cf. Junior Brother's similar joke, 3.4.17–18.

24 *set an edge*: motivate; sharpen (his axe). Cf. Supervacuo's next line.

25 *Meet*: appropriate.

27 *thou*: Lussurioso.

3.2.3 *delivery*: liberation.

    But: only.

  5 *myself*: duke.

    thank: reward.

3.3.14 *that is least impudent*: he who offends the least (Supervacuo is either being ironic or trying hypocritically to convey regret).

16 *sound*: carried out properly.

20 *gaping people*: the spectators at a public execution.

22 *black*: in a state of sin.

24 *live to be*: attain to power.

30 *block*: executioner's block; blockhead; mould for a hat.

3.4.9 *be from*: leave.

11 *of good cheer*: optimistic; Junior Brother plays with the meaning 'hospitable welcome'.

13 *bankrupt*: person imprisoned for debt.

15 *trick*: perhaps playing upon the meaning 'hand of cards'.

18 *lie in*: remain in jail; undergo childbirth.

22 *discharged of*: released of an obligation to guard.

30 *Suffer*: undergo execution; Junior Brother plays with the meaning 'allow' in his reply.

43 *powerful token*: the Duke's signet-ring.

57 *citizen's son*: middle-class city dweller; i.e. landlubber.

59 *stinted*: dry.

64 *duns*: strained interpretation (after the medieval philosopher Duns Scotus, regarded in the Renaissance as a splitter of logical hairs.)

67 *trick*: a hand of cards in the game of primero.

79 *respect of sign*: before letting blood from their patients, Renaissance surgeons consulted astrological conditions.

3.5.4 *silver ceiling*: palace ceilings were sometimes decorated with precious metals; Vindice may also allude to the roof of the public theatre, painted to look like the sky.

5 *partake*: participate.

10 *Are cut out of one piece*: are consistent.

11 *by price*: for a fee.

14 *angle*: corner.

22 *circle*: the enchanted area in which wizards encounter the devil; but also suggesting the circular shape of the theatre.

25 *digested*: concocted.

26 *missed*: excluded.

29 *lost*: i.e. in the violence of his joy.

30 *in a throng of happy apprehensions*: full of delightful anticipations.

37 *stoop*: submit.

38 *common to be common*: usual to be promiscuous.

39 *private-common shadowing vices*: concealed but frequently committed sexual sins.

41 *bare*: with his hat off.

42 S.D. *tires*: masque apparel.

46 *shell*: empty husk; ironically addressed to a skull, itself a 'shell' of sorts.

47 *do it*: perform sexually.

51 *all-hid*: a child's game; hide-and-seek.

53 *quaint piece*: fine or oddly appropriate specimen; 'quaint' is also slang for the female genitals.

54 *action*: sexual activity.

60 *go whistle*: do what it will.

71 *yellow labours*: the yellow thread of the silkworm's cocoon.

73 *lordships*: peerages and the property associated with them.
ladyships: the expensive accoutrements of courtly women.

75 *falsify*: tamper with, when the 'fellow' turns highway robber.

76 *put his life between the judge's lips*: subject himself to a death sentence pronounced by the criminal court.

78 *beat their valours*: force themselves to put forth their whole strength, with the suggestion that valour is thereby 'beaten' in the sense of defeated or exhausted.

90 *forgetful feasts*: banquets that induce the participants to forget their moral principles.

93 *antic amble*: clownish dance.

100 *property*: stage prop.

101 *it*: its, a common Renaissance form of the possessive.

104 *in the like strain*: in a similar way.

108 *quaintness*: curious elaboration.

111 *sign*: token without substance.

112 *periwig*: used to conceal baldness.

116 *'Tis vain . . . the streets*: a mask is an unnecessary vanity when beauty still exists; and after beauty is gone, a masked skull is better suited for a grave than for public display. Many Renaissance moralists deplore women's use of masks on the grounds that they excite male desire.

117 *You have my voice*: I agree with you.

119 *absent 'em*: get rid of them.

126 *privately rid forth*: gone out alone on horseback; but the Duke unintentionally suggests the meaning 'secretly done away with'.

137 *Have at all*: go on!—a phrase used to begin a fight; also suggesting the duke's sexual indiscriminateness.

145 *white devil*: hypocrite; devil in disguise.

149 *last*: lately.

161 *closer*: with his mouth closed.

167 *upon the infection of thy frowns*: in consequence of your ill-treatment.

171 *stick*: pierce.

196 *brooking the foul object*: bearing the disgusting sight.

198 *like comets shine through blood*: comets were considered omens of disaster; cf. Ambitioso's comment at 5.1.107 and the 'blazing star' in 5.3.1.

200 *Whist*: psst.

206 *rubs*: revives the memory of.

207 *waxen fire*: candle, held by a servant to light their way.

211 *hasped*: carnally connected. A hasp is a lock that fastens a pin into a round opening.

216 *brook*: endure (Duke); rivulet (Vindice).

218 *'Tis . . . bleed*: it is stately for a duke to die with a musical accompaniment.

219 *though yet unknown*: though nobody knows it yet.

220 *they peep up*: the heirs arise.

3.6.6 *slip*: bypass.

in lesser compass: as a lesser bit of ingenuity.

12 *from you*: far from your thoughts.

17 *publish 't*: announce it, so as to receive credit (despite the danger involved).

19 *honest*: honourable; actual.

34 *desertless office*: unrewarding job no one deserves.

37 *grace our flattery*: make our deception seem more plausible.

39 *fluent*: flowing.

62 *spared no tongue*: omitted no speeches.

81 *women*: i.e. untrustworthy (with a pun on 'woe-man'.)

90 *Sirrah*: disrespectful address to the recently departed Lussurioso.

fast: i.e. as securely as you can.

4.1.11 *wittily elected*: wisely chosen (sarcastic).

15 *will*: intended.

27 *upon the stroke | Jars in my brother*: just as Lussurioso says the word 'stroke'—a word that can also refer to a musical downbeat—Vindice makes an unwelcome entrance.

35 *iron-age*: imprisonment, fetter. In classical myth, the Iron Age is the last and worst of the four ages of the world, characterized by depravity and oppression: the world, in other words, depicted in *The Revenger's Tragedy*.

36 *make a woman dumb*: silence even a woman.

37 *Missing . . . about*: i.e. the situation has changed now that both Lussurioso and Spurio have escaped Vindice's traps.

44 *apply*: spend.

50 *blood*: temperament; desires.

52 *in us*: in our power.

58 *succeed*: come after (since Vindice replaces himself); perform successfully.

61 *does himself work to undo him*: does he himself precipitate his downfall.

63 *abuse my spleen*: wrongly arouse my anger.

65 *heart*: confidential plans.

66 *slight*: untrustworthy.

68 *he shall speed him*: Hippolito's brother shall get rid of Piato.

70 *black condition*: melancholy temperament.

72 *grind him to an edge*: sharpen his motivation.

84 *sudden*: whimsical.

87 *light*: frivolous.

4.2.2 *shifts*: tricks; changes of attire.

5 *quainter fallacy*: odder, more delightful mistake.

12 *pile . . . breast*: i.e. to kill him with the accumulated pressure of my vengeful thoughts, as those who refused to respond to criminal charges in the Renaissance were 'pressed' to death by weights piled on their chests.

14 *clad in clay*: buried.

17 *joy*: enjoy.

21 *fetch about*: take a roundabout path; speculate irrelevantly.

in present: about our immediate situation.

25 *It . . . doubtful*: it is not the least important aspect of good planning to take precautions.

26 *change tongue*: speak differently.

28 *heavy-sounding wire*: thick strings that make low sounds.

31 *I . . . discontent*: I initially described you as discontented.

37 *presence*: demeanour.

42 *How don you? God you god den*: how are you? God give you good evening (rural dialect, consistent with Vindice's uncourtly persona and his need to 'change tongue' before Lussurioso).

44 *in fire*: ardently.

46 *stood on't*: tolerated. Blasphemy is common at court, but respectful references to God are unendurable.

50 *black buckram*: a stiff fabric from which lawyer's bags were made.

52 *anno quadragesimo secundo . . . anno sextagesimo tertio*: the forty-second and sixty-third year of the sovereign's reign. The figures are practically impossible, even for a very long-lived monarch.

53 *three and twenty*: mathematics does not appear to be among Lussurioso's talents.

57 *terms*: words (the meanings of which are strained by lawyers); also the four terms each year in which courts were in session: Hilary, Easter, Trinity, and Michaelmas.

59 *canvassed*: brought before the court.

60 *Barbary*: barbarous.

61 *in law*: in legal jargon.

62 *writ of error*: a writ brought to reverse a judgment on grounds of error.

63 *sasarara*: English corruption of the Latin term *certiorari*, a writ issued by a superior court when someone appeals the verdict of a lower court.

65 *meets round in the same bent*: goes in the same direction.

69 *the bell*: which invites parishioners to pray.

73 *forfeitures and obligations*: liabilities and contracts.

76 *conceit a-coming in picture*: an idea for a picture dawning on me. Moral pictures were popular in the Renaissance.

77 *la*: there now (rural dialect).

81 *published bountiful*: reputed generous.

86 *pared*: cut (because Vindice obliquely represents Lussurioso's situation, although Lussurioso himself fails to make the connection).

93 *cloth-of-gold*: very expensive fabric woven with gold threads; probably what Lussurioso is wearing in this scene.

95 *pockets*: of the breeches; i.e. Vindice has misunderstood his point.

96 *draw*: depict; pull.

99 *cry you . . . mercy*: ask for forgiveness.

101 *in colours*: in a picture.

107 *hits*: has an effect.

109 *feed on those*: make them feed me.

114 *affect*: relish.

122 *kept it here*: withheld it.

130 *strongly wrought with me*: tried hard to persuade me.

133 *He . . . it*: Vindice's words ironically apply both to Lussurioso and eventually to himself.

137 *that part . . . The eye*: a *double entendre*, since 'eye' was slang for female genitalia.

139 *fine*: formidable.

149 *for happy*: as if they were good.

160 *take full mark of*: get a good look at; shoot at point-blank range.

163 *wind*: entice.

175 *observe*: obey.

180 *in case*: fit.

183 *conveyed*: carried out.

189 *carried*: managed.

197 *kept up | In stock*: reserved. The thunder, like the comet in Act 5, hints at an ordering and judging power beyond the chaotic, amoral world depicted in the play.

198 *lose*: forget.

it: the solution to our problem (which requires Vindice to 'lose himself' in another sense).

203 *conveyed*: disposed of.

205 *closest husk*: most thorough concealment; cf. Vindice's final remarks in 5.3.110–17.

210 *published*: described.

216 *it is substantial*: the plan is consistent and solidly conceived.

220 *in grain*: dyed indelibly into the fabric.

221 *hold colour*: not wash out; remain plausible.

4.3 S.D. *seemeth*: acts.

1 *unlock yourself*: disentangle yourself from me.

3 *or this or these*: either this embrace or these kisses.

4 *deal*: distribute.

10 *bent*: inclined.

11 *sleep soft*: live in luxury.

12 *unequal*: i.e. in rank.

15 *waist*: with a pun on 'waste'.

16 *about*: in circumference.

4.4.5 *iron nipples*: the daggers, pointed at her breast.

8 *cut*: shorten; cf. 2.2.94.

14 *possible*. The quarto inserts the words 'Thou only', in italics, between 'possible' and 'you'. The change of typeface in an often unreliable text, the unmotivated metrical interruption, and the fact that the phrase renders incoherent an otherwise straightforward sentence, all suggest a mistaken interpolation.

17 *fellow of the world's condition*: a worldly villain.

19 *uncivilly*: savagely, without respect to the norms of civilized society.

32 *Tried*: tested.

35 *in tune*: i.e. to harmonize with evil.

40 *give aim to*: help an archer by guiding the shot; here, to direct Castiza's 'aim' at Lussurioso.

43 *you*: the dagger.

44 *blush and change to red*: rust (but also referring to the action of tears on Gratiana's hard heart, newly susceptible to shame).

53 *I'll rinse it in seven waters of mine eyes*: I'll cleanse it by extended weeping ('seven waters' suggests a ritual aspect to the purification).

54 *salt*: a biblical symbol of righteousness, used in holy water as a sign of its purity and healing powers.

62 *of easy wax*: easily manipulated.

64 *forehead*: the site, throughout the play, where boldness and humiliation

are made visible, as in 1.2.4 and in the numerous references to the Duke's cuckold's horns.

68 *Green-coloured maids*: anaemic virgins. An insufficiency of dietary iron made adolescent girls in early modern Europe susceptible to anaemia, an ailment attributed at that time to sexual frustration or repression.

69 *full of hire and baseness*: corrupted by money earned as a prostitute.

70 *boiling lead again*: i.e. another torment.

72 *cloth-o'-silver*: costly fabric woven with silver threads.

81 *'Break . . . more'*: the proverb manifests again Vindice's obsession with 'keeping the ports sure', maintaining fragile boundaries intact.

82 *Most certainly applied*: how very true in this case.

86 *holy-watered mead*: meadow sprinkled with holy water, i.e. watered by the tears of her piety.

87 *Our . . . lead*: i.e. our hearts are light that were heavy before.

96 *forehead*: boldness.

100 *what for*: in regards to.

104 *usury*: here, whoredom.

106 *That's . . . in*: i.e. that's not what you really think will improve your prospects (but the newly contrite Gratiana takes 'saved' in a religious rather than a material sense).

108 *I am . . . wrought*: 'I am just what you have made me, as hardened as marble' or 'I am just as hardened as you are.'

115 *Your blessing . . . your curse*: in renaissance England, even adult children habitually knelt to ask for their parents' blessing; parental curses were regarded as similarly effectual. Gratiana first tried to force Castiza into prostitution by denying her the blessing; when this didn't work, she proceeded to a positive curse, a more serious measure.

117 *Sons . . . lights*: sons come to bad ends (with a pun on 'suns'), and daughters lose their guiding principles.

123 *kind*: gentle one; one related to me by blood.

124 *sick in health*: ill now that I have recovered.

130 *reading*: i.e. of books exhorting to virtue.

138 *pitch*: hurl you, with the implication that a downward trajectory is more common than an upward one, and that pitch (tar) defiles.

140 *purchase*: profit.

154 *inherits*: possesses, dwells within.

157 *glass*: mirror, i.e. example.

5.1.3 *lay*: wager; also, the position of the Duke's body.

7 *returns*: different descriptions of the same situation. A 'return' is a

sheriff's report on actions taken upon directives from a court of law. Sheriffs were required to submit such reports eight times during Michaelmas term (2–25 November).

11 *flesh-flies*: literally, flies that feed on carrion; here, sycophants.

against: before.

15 *made my revenge familiar*: acquainted him with my revenge.

16 *politician*: conspirator.

17 *catastrophe*: conclusion; especially the conclusion of a tragedy.

21 *open in as fair faces*: present similarly attractive possibilities.

22 *paint*: apply cosmetics.

25 *I'm for any weather*: I'm ready for anything.

41 *stifle in*: hold.

55 *qush*: squish.

60 *bear us out*: keep us out of trouble.

63 *Sa, sa, sa!*: an expression used by fencers when thrusting an opponent.

67 *from your names*: inappropriate names.

75 *intended*: i.e. that we intended.

84 *clear*: unsuspected.

93 *deep*: intelligent; secretive.

97 *let blood*: made to bleed; alluding to the medical practice of therapeutic blood-letting.

99 *H'as lost*: alluding to the proverb, 'losers have leave to speak.'

110 *owes*: owns.

112 *these clothes*: a man wearing these clothes.

113 *i' th' country*: where, in contrast to the court, people habitually tell the truth.

118 *cast*: cast-off; scattered.

120 *tug in the new stream*: row in the new current; i.e. work hard (for my own interest) in the altered situation.

124 *gave that charge | Upon our lives*: commanded upon threat of death.

126 *that fellow*: i.e. Piato, the person who was wearing those clothes.

133 *stick*: keep quiet; an ironic comment given Vindice's eventual fate.

136 *hits | Past the apprehension of indifferent wits*: succeeds better than persons of mediocre intelligence could grasp.

140 *something bold*: somewhat eager, even impertinent (since courtiers are not supposed to request anything of their ruler).

148 *foreign markets go*. 'The proverb "You may know by the market men how the markets go" . . . perhaps helps to explain Vindice's point, that as the

duke behaves, his courtiers will follow suit' (R. A. Foakes (ed.), *The Revenger's Tragedy*, 1966). 'Foreign' suggests simultaneously the unfamiliar newness of Lussurioso's reign and more generally Vindice's alienation from the court world.

149 *feet o' th' nines, and tongues o' th' twelves*: size nine feet but size twelve tongues (punning on the tongues of shoes and the loquacious tongues of the noblemen).

154 *your own*: your rightful possession.

164 *Spread*: displayed.

165 *revels*: courtly entertainments are obviously inappropriate during what ought to be a period of mourning for a head of state; hence Vindice's amazement.

several falls: different kinds of incident.

166 *Griefs . . . funerals*: i.e. grief intensifies joy, and feasts dispel mourning.

168 *foully bent*: inclined to evil.

171 *we are firm yet*: our plans for revenge are still good.

173 *have at the fairest mark*: aim at the best target; 'mark' is also slang for 'female genitalia'.

176 *out*: at a loss; excluded.

187 *fair play*: equal treatment; enjoyable game.

5.2.1 *of*: made of.

3 *That flow . . . livers*: that are too gentle and cowardly.

4 *stab home*: give a mortal blow to.

7 *Wind up*: draw up, excite.

10 *toward*: about to occur.

13 *affect*: desire, perhaps with the additional implication of 'pretend'.

15 *take pattern*: note the pattern, in order to copy.

19 •*strain*: i.e. of music.

26 *Let that alone*: don't worry about that.

27 *By . . . down*: one by one they will be made drunk and ineffectual.

28 *action*: conspiracy.

5.3. S.D. *possessing*: coronation.

blazing star: a comet, a bad omen; cf. 3.5.198 and 5.1.107.

10 *subsidies*: taxes that help support a sovereign.

11 *We must not frown so soon*: it would be impolitic to begin a reign by punishing people.

19 *bushing*: with a comet-like tail.

20 *quake*: terrify.

21 *it appeared | Before it*: the comet appeared before my coronation.

24 *read*: learned.

33 *threescore . . . Fourscore . . . fivescore*: sixty, eighty, one hundred.

39 *quite anon*: right away.

49 S.D. *measure*: dance step.

53 *sped him*: done him in.

62 *wake | An old man's eyes bloodshot*: bring tears to an old man's eyes.

68 *Law you now*: expressive of doubt; equivalent to 'oh, really now'.

73 *marrow*: material to savour.

   I cannot be expressed: I am unable to describe my emotions.

76 *office*: commission.

77 *prate on't*: chatter about it.

83 *unlikely*: unpromising.

85 *silver age*: because whereas the Duke's white hair symbolized hypocrisy and decrepitude, Antonio's signifies the return of the legendary Silver Age, in which peace and justice prevail. Cf. 4.1.35.

93 *strangeliest carried*: most unusually carried out.

   not: never.

105 *Is 't come about?*: both 'is this really happening' and 'has the situation reversed itself?'.

106 *set*: finish our career, with a pun on 'sun'.

112 *tongueless brass*: the silent metal of the victims' tombs.

115 *sentence*: proverb.

118 *witch*: prophet.

119 *we are in forever*: we are already done for; we are already passing into eternity.

121 *list*: pleased.

   nobles clipped: the aristocratic accessories in the plot shorn of titles or beheaded; a pun on the illegal 'clipping' or paring off the edges of gold coins called 'nobles'.

124 *turned*: converted.

126 *closed*: completed; hidden.

The Revenge of Bussy d'Ambois

Prefatory Epistle. Thomas Howard, second earl of Arundel (1585–1646) was a prominent patron of the arts and a frequent performer at court masques. His Roman Catholicism and his personal unpopularity may have encouraged Chapman to believe that he would be sympathetic to both the politics and the reception of *The Revenge of Bussy d'Ambois*.

6 *made no doubt to prefer*: had no hesitation about offering.

8 *excitation*: encouragement.

17 *the balance of their side . . . will to no grain abide the outweighing*: the scale will not tip in their (the maligners') favour.

20 *material*: substantial.

21 *sententious*: meaningful.

22 *limits*: contours.

24 *whatsoever merit . . . account*: whatever reward of your complete patronage and good will this work fails to supply, I shall soon make up for in another work, widely considered more worthy.

27 *acceptation*: state of being held in high regard.

29 *judicial ingenuity*: judicious intelligence.

32 *most divine philosopher*: Plato, who argued for the immortality of the soul.

Dramatis Personae. Many of these characters appear in Chapman's earlier tragedy, *Bussy d'Ambois*. Bussy is a penniless but well-born soldier courageous and outspoken to the point of foolhardiness. The Monsieur, younger brother of the King and heir apparent to the throne, is initially Bussy's patron. The Monsieur introduces Bussy to court, where he offends the Guise by courting his wife publicly. Soon thereafter Bussy loses the support of the Monsieur by refusing to participate in a conspiracy to kill the King. Meanwhile he becomes sexually involved with Tamyra, wife of Montsurry. The suspicious Montsurry tortures Tamyra in order to learn the truth of the affair, and with the collusion of Bussy's other enemies eventually has the hero murdered.

Although *The Revenge* relies to some extent upon the earlier play, several characters have been significantly reconceived, and so has the course of the action. The first play ends as the dying Bussy forgives his murderers, and his mistress Tamyra seeks reconciliation with her husband. The sequel represents Bussy as having prophesied the downfall of his enemies in his final moments, and later having reappeared as a ghost to demand revenge; Tamyra is thoroughly unrepentant. In *Bussy d'Ambois*, the Guise is the enemy of the protagonist and an accessory to his murder, but in *The Revenge*, he is Clermont d'Ambois's patron and Chapman's exemplary aristocrat. Clermont d'Ambois, the younger brother of Bussy, does not appear in the earlier play.

Some of the characters in both plays are very loosely based on French historical personages of the 1580s, as noted below.

Henry: Henry III of France, 1551–89. In a reign marked by religious wars and dynastic struggles, Henry was unpopular for his extravagance, his licentiousness, and his refusal to acknowledge traditional aristocratic privileges.

Monsieur: Duc d'Anjou, 1554–84; the leader of a moderate Catholic faction called the 'politiques', and, until he predeceased him, heir apparent to the childless Henry III.

Guise: Henry I de Lorraine, duc de Guise, 1550–88. The leader of the Holy League of nobles in defence of the Catholic cause.

Chatillon: Gaspard II de Coligny, Seigneur de Chatillon, 1519–72. Admiral of France and leader of the Protestant cause in France, killed by Guise's mercenaries in the St Bartholomew's Day Massacre.

1.1.2 *Swingeing in every license*: indulging in every kind of lawlessness. 'Swinge', a favourite word with Chapman, can mean 'power', 'leeway', 'freedom', or 'prerogative', and hence sometimes by extension 'indulgence' or 'licentiousness'.

3 *Stupid permission of*: morally insensitive failure to prosecute.

4 *parallel*: equal.

6 *suffered*: allowed.

7 *fright adultery!*: frighten adulterers; Montsurry hired killers to dispose of Bussy after learning of his relationship with Tamyra.

8 *policy . . . capacity*: political cunning finally reduced to its own terms.

10 *Deliverances*: liberations from calamity.

13 *tied up*: so that their bells cannot ring.

   glory: self-aggrandizement.

14 *smooth applauses*: servile approbation.

16 *bounded*: delimited.

17 *forms of time*: customary procedures, hallowed by time.

19 *Rule in more regular motion*: sovereign power exerted more appropriately.

21 *mean*: humble.

25 *imitation*: of the brows.

30 *Managed with curbs*: controlled with restraints; a 'curb' is a severe bit used on a fractious horse.

31 *esteemed . . . their own*: believed that the subjects' virtues cast their own into the shade.

34 *Ends aught rewarded*: results in any kind of reward.

35 *all the palm wears*: overpowers everything; wreaths of palm leaves symbolized victory.

47 *be-painted*: with cosmetics, associated with prostitutes.

51 *well got or none*: earned by virtuous means or not at all.

54 *used*: practised.

57 *so barren | That their parts only stood*: so devoid of merit that their talents only manifested themselves.

58 *Who*: those who.

59 *Civil*: socially responsible.

60 *upland boors*: rude peasants.

63 *our first natures*: our original sinless condition.

64 *arts*: endeavours.

67 *Fashion and favour*: courtly pretence and social climbing.

70 *Yet . . . that*: but now no one is considered wise except he who thinks religion foolish, compared with wealth.

71 *greatest Guise*. Baligny praises Guise's virtue in his absence in order to gain Renel's trust.

73 *depressed*: impoverished.

78 *accident*: event (i.e. the revenge).

charge: obligation.

79 *brother*: brother-in-law.

80 *suit*: courtship.

83 *second*: younger.

84 *since his apparition and excitement*: since the ghost of Bussy appeared and incited him to revenge.

87 *will needs acquit | Me of*: must excuse me from.

92 *challenge*: formal written demand for a duel.

94 *barricadoed*: barricaded.

96 *strangely*: because of unusual circumstances.

97 *My last lands' . . . with him*: the sale of my last piece of land, which he has endeavoured earnestly to obtain, is presently being negotiated.

100 *cast*: imagine.

her: gain's.

103 *rosy*: bright.

105 *friend's*: lover's.

107 *on needles' points*: impatiently.

108 *haste of the revenge*: desire for swift vengeance.

109 *her brother's fire*: Bussy's passionate nature.

114 *past her sex*: beyond what is expected of women, who are supposed to be gentle.

120 *passage cleared*: access made possible.

121 *All restitution to your worthiest lordship*: may you regain all that you have lost.

125 *affected with*: partial to.

129 *spice it*: adulterate my account.

possessed: convinced.

131 *danger | Charged in it to his person*: threat that Clermont's spirit poses to the king's life.

134 *politicians*: cunning political manipulators.

137 *We work . . . kind*: we strive to cast suspicion on all aspects of character.

141 *And . . . searcheth*: and the more we succeed in making the best seem worse, the more probing our intelligence seems to be.

145 *Brabant*: a territory in present-day Belgium and Holland; the French heir apparent was declared Duke of Brabant in 1581, but the title remained a formality.

149 *In chief heat of his faction*: strenuously involved in the manœuvring of the hard-line Catholic faction, of which Guise was the head.

153 *doctrine of stability and freedom*: the Stoics taught that mental composure, the highest form of human happiness, was to be obtained by detaching oneself from the desire for external good fortune.

155 *vulgar great ones*: ignorant aristocrats.

158 *read to*: teach.

162 *Known for a covert practice*: recognized as deceit (by 'politic' people like the Monsieur).

163 *abused*: deceived.

they: Guise and Clermont.

167 *They . . . nothing*: the wives' faces do not reveal their adulteries even when they have just committed the act, as if they haven't transgressed at all, or have accustomed themselves to sin.

169 *learning*: philosophy (Roman ethical writers like Seneca and Cicero deplored philosophy that had no practical application).

172 *embracing*: showing favour to.

173 *in some*: by some people.

174 *held false for*: considered to be false because of.

175 *more cunning held*: considered cleverer.

177 *hardly*: with difficulty.

179 *part engend'ring virtue*: separate these two, who are generating virtue between them.

181 *breathes*: evinces.

temper: disposition.

186 *ravish*: steal.

192 *T'unclasp thy bosom*: to unlock your private thoughts.

193 *glass*: mirror.

194 *many-headed beast*: common people, considered as a group.

196 *new-upstarted state*: newly exalted status (as Duke of Brabant).

197 *higher aims*: in *Bussy d'Ambois*, the Monsieur had treasonable designs on his brother's throne.

202 *braved*: defied, as Bussy does in the previous play.

204 *teeth*: i.e. face.

205 *Discerned*: distinguished.

rising sovereign: king-to-be.

207 *gross-full*: disgusting.

214 *of spleen*: in angry irritation.

215 *ingenuous*: high-minded.

219 *toward*: future.

229 *entertain*: retain in my service.

230 *What turn I meant to serve with you*: what employment I intended for you.

232 *end*: purpose.

234 *decayed commanders*: indigent soldiers.

235 *French crown*: ecu, a coin of modest value.

236 *to anything*: to do anything.

238 *trunks*: chests of clothing; the Monsieur implies that Bussy and Clermont had no luggage of value.

240 *Epaminondas*: fourth century BC Theban general and statesman, famous for his martial prowess and incorruptible morals.

242 *both your studies*: the concern of both of you.

248 *T'eternize*: make eternal (since the cook's bill would never be paid).

score it up: get it on credit (the 'score' is the shopkeeper's tally of a customer's debts).

250 *gentry*: gentle birth.

253 *keel of sea-coal*: coal-barge.

256 *cast my cast wardrobe*: given my old clothes (a common gift from masters to servants).

260 *corruption of their names*: their nicknames.

261 *blown . . . bubble*: inflated you two for no reason.

264 *table*: i.e. dining-companion.

266 *emrods*: obscure; perhaps 'emerods', genital tumours—the Monsieur suffered from syphilis.

268 *answer*: suit.

276 *Swisser*: the Swiss often served as mercenaries in foreign courts.

execution: employment.

277 *But killing of the king*: with these words, Bussy had refused to commit regicide at the Monsieur's orders; the Monsieur taunts him for his reluctance in an extended scene in *Bussy d'Ambois*.

283 *no princely deeds | Ere you're born*. Clermont's remarks on merit and birth, like the sentiments he expresses elsewhere in the play, are often adapted from classical philosophical writing, especially Epictetus' *Discourses*, Seneca's *Moral Letters*, and Cicero's philosophical dialogues. Because many of the arguments are repeated by several writers, it is sometimes difficult or misleading to pinpoint a particular source.

290 *retorted*: turned back upon him.

294 *Made show . . . knowing virtues*: demonstrated, even to his dull eyes, to be inferior to the worthiness sought by knowledgeably virtuous men.

295 *a shade, a bubble*: an illusory and evanescent thing.

298 *for . . . purchase*: as if it were earned by their own worth.

299 *both*: both birth and inheritance.

301 *won to their hands*: gained for them by others without their exertion.

304 *proud tumours*: swelling self-conceit.

308 *their houses . . . less*. English Renaissance aristocrats were widely criticized for skimping upon the hospitality traditionally expected of them in order to have money to enlarge their manor houses.

309 *outside*: external wealth.

310 *in*: inside.

311 *drown their substance*: use up their wealth.

313 *Sisyphus*: condemned to push a stone uphill again and again; here compared to the aristocrat remodelling his mansion.

316 *lay . . . temple*: spend on a human being—God's creation, called the temple of the Holy Spirit—the same money that they now spend on a single dirty nook in their mansions.

318 *Brought upon stages*: shown in theatres. The moral potential of theatrical representation, as well as the supposed moral degradation of contemporary theatres, concerned numerous dramatists and pamphleteers in the English Renaissance.

322 *pied*: parti-coloured, like a fool's costume.

324 *Check at*: object to.

as being: considering it to be.

328 *fits*: befits.

333 *Greek moralist*: Epictetus, from whose *Discourses* Clermont adapts his argument.

342 *If . . . worth*: if it is only a matter of producing an externally glorious person, who is most proud of external things irrelevant to his real worth.

345 *borne*: presented; endured.

347 *innovating Puritan*: some Puritans, radical religious reformers, considered theatres idolatrous and called for their abolition.

348 *sweater-out of zealous envy*: one who sweats religious malice from his pores.

351 *for stages fitted*: rendered suitable for staging.

352 *splenative*: satiric; the Greek philosopher Democritus was supposed to have laughed at all human affairs.

356 *ridiculous humour*: inclination to laugh.

359 *swearing | Never so thriftily*: never so effectively insisting upon the quality of his products.

362 *impetuously*: zealously.

363 *insulting*: arrogant.

365 *their good*: the justice they should serve.

377 *friend*: relation.

382 *bring us the success*: tell us what happens.

1.2.1 *red*: from weeping; but eventually from blood.

3 *crown . . . laurel*: in classical times victorious generals were crowned with laurel wreaths.

5 *fly*: escape.

8 *constant*: inevitable.

9 *prevent that length*: abbreviate the time between crime and punishment.

10 *still*: immobile.

12 *drawn*. Tamyra claims that Bussy's corpse has left a bloody print on the earth where he fell.

17 *rarefying*: making even thinner.

18 *sphere of fire*: in geocentric (Ptolemaic) astronomy, a sphere that surrounded the earth above the atmosphere but below the moon; the highest and purest of the realms subject to mortality.

21 *thy rival's*: Montsurry's.

25 *Still on this haunt*: do you persist in this habit.

27 *cockatrice-like*: like the legendary serpent, thought to kill by its glance, and to hatch from a cock's egg.

   brood'st: sits upon, as a hen an egg; meditates upon.

28 *breed . . . thine*: effectively satisfy your desire (which was thought to emanate from the blood).

29 *for thy lust*: that your lust might be.

31 *witchlike*: witches were supposed to copulate with dead bodies.

36 *Strange cross . . . shamefaced*: i.e. since shame, like lust, lies in the blood, both maidenly virtue and sexual desire are signalled by blushing.

38 *meets | With one not common?*: experiences an emotion uncorrupted by lust.

40 *illiberal*: unrefined.

43 *vulgar guises*: any appearance of indecency.

44 *but fly out for change*: help seeking sexual variety.

45 *matter*: substance.

46 *adulterate*: mixed, as Montsurry has already described; soiled by adultery.

   true: consistently.

48 *show*: appearance.

49 *all ye seek of us*: what husbands actually demand of women.

50 *common*: promiscuous.

58 *earnests*: serious moods.

65 *conditions . . . contents*: extremely generous conditions of surrender.

70 *their*: the townspeople's.

71 *advantage*: self-interest.

   their: the soldiers'.

73 *my love before*: the love I had for you before you were unfaithful.

75 *tortured*: in *Bussy d'Ambois*, Montsurry stabs his wife and puts her on the rack to get her to reveal her affair with Bussy.

76 *law*: right to demand forgiveness.

84 *Outrageous*: violent.

86 *charged*: loaded.

91 *have*: get in return.

93 *prostitute*: morally degraded.

100 *stays*: awaits.

103 *dame*: lady (a title applied to a woman of rank).

106 *her respect is chief in this design*: this plot has her interests chiefly in mind.

117 *passionate*: upset. At the end of *Bussy d'Ambois*, Montsurry claims to have forgiven his wife but insists upon a separation.

123 *like yours*: when Montsurry had Bussy murdered.

125 *rude*. Renel and Baligny must conceal from Montsurry their collusion in the plot to deliver Clermont's challenge.

130 S.D. *Draws his sword*. Renel pretends to react to Baligny's insulting suggestion that he is a 'doorman', Renaissance slang for 'pander'.

134 *touch*. By accepting the letter in which Clermont has issued his challenge, Montsurry would commit himself to fighting a duel. Refusing to accept such a challenge was considered ungentlemanly cowardice.

141 *politician*. Renel's exclamation is unintentionally ironic, because the 'politic' Baligny is deceiving him.

2.1.7 *gathered into hold*: harvested; i.e. 'taken care of'; with a play on 'hold' = 'prison'.

9 *Exceeding capital*: very important (with a suggestion that he is guilty of treason, a capital crime).

14 *country swinge*: leeway for action only obtainable in the country.

15 *wrought*: convinced.

16 *Cambrai*: city in modern-day Belgium, then under French control.

19 *confines*: borders.

22 *train him to some muster*: lure him to an assembly of troops.

23 *him*: himself.

24 *battle*: battalions.

26 *your whole powers*: your entire army.

27 *work his apprehension*: bring about his arrest.

29 *honest*: trustworthy (ironic here).

32 *for*: on behalf of.

35 *in particular respects*: from the point of view of particular individuals.

36 *As*: insofar as.

37 *As*: just as.

38 *Rector's*: rule-giver's, i.e. God's.

39 *globes*: geocentric Renaissance astronomy posited an earth surrounded by successively larger spheres or globes of moon, sun, planets, and stars.

43 *Since they . . . wronged*: i.e. since the general decrees are designed to preserve the order and purposes of both the globe of heaven and the globe of earth, no man can correctly think himself wronged as an individual by such decrees.

49 *Nor . . . subject*: nor is it unseemly to compare the way particular men

may happen to suffer from a generally beneficent divine rule, with the way particular men may suffer as your subjects.

50 *Grudge at their*: resent his.

56 *of heaven for wrong to him*: that heaven wrongs him.

73 *government*: territory (Cambrai).

79 *creature*: servant (a person 'created' by a patron).

84 *all his parts*: all human capacities.

88 *for his valour's season*: to temper his courage.

89 *rapt with outrage*: carried away by anger.

97 *for*: despite.

102 *fount*: source of the stream of knowledge.

103 *Brutus*: Roman who participated in a conspiracy to kill his friend, Julius Caesar, when he saw him to be a threat to the Roman republic. The politics and morality of his action were much debated in the Renaissance, and it is relevant to this play in which any desire to limit monarchical power is labelled as treason.

104 *of industry*: industriously.

105 *Euphorbus*: Trojan hero; the Greek philosopher Pythagoras, who believed in reincarnation, claimed to have been Euphorbus during the Trojan War.

114 *Greek tragedian*: Sophocles, the author of *Antigone*.

115 *for*: about.

116 *on*: to.

119 *With*: equal with.

122 *bounded*: limited.

126 *not fit*: because the King, not Guise, is Baligny's commander.

133 *for*: on behalf of.

134 *Either*: both (kings and subjects).

exception: objection.

136 *shines in some authority*: is displayed in some high position.

140 *redundance past their continent ever*: always more than the smaller vessel can contain.

141 *virtuosi*: virtuous people.

142 *spinners*: spiders.

144 *these*: the virtuous.

145 *Make . . . her*: make arguments about virtue and its comforts.

147 *the place, the weapon*: the recipient of a challenge was supposed to specify these.

148 *Soft*: calm down.

150 *in his despite*: in spite of him.

153 *quick*: alive.

154 *They*: Montsurry and his ilk.

sepulchres: tombs (elaborate on the outside, hollow or rotten within).

157 *soft*: at ease. The comparison is from Epictetus, *Discourses*, 4.1.

158 *close*: caged.

159 *quite*: entirely.

161 *gross*: fat.

165 *Domitian-like*: like the tyrannical Roman emperor AD 51–96. In his disregard of senatorial prerogatives, his sexual excesses, his failure to produce an heir, and his distrust of philosophers (he expelled the Stoics, including Epictetus, from Rome), Domitian resembles Chapman's King Henry. Like Henry, he was assassinated by political opponents.

168 *peasants'*: because aristocrats were supposed to be above thinking about money.

174 *wanton*: heedless.

183 *being privilege to all things base*: sanctioning all kinds of ignominious behaviour.

184 *foolish poet*: Suffenus, a mediocre writer ridiculed by the Latin poet Catullus, from whose Ode 22 this passage is adapted.

185 *paper royal*: sheets of paper 24 × 19 inches.

186 *parchment ruled with lead*: expensive sheets of sheepskin marked with lines.

pumice: slightly abrasive stone used to smooth parchment and erase stray marks.

187 *strings*: attached to valuable books to keep the covers from falling open.

188 *blest*: blissfully happy.

189 *ape-loved issue*: foolishly cherished product.

192 *painted*: superficially flashy.

196 *fain*: gladly.

198 *tenth Worthy*: the nine Worthies were supposed to be the greatest heroes of the pagan, Hebrew, and Christian civilizations: Hector, Alexander, Julius Caesar, Joshua, David, Judas Maccabeus, Arthur, Charlemagne, and Geoffrey of Bouillon.

204 *Massacre*: the St Bartholomew's Day Massacre of French Protestants, on 24 August 1572, instigated by Guise's Catholic faction.

206 *brutish sense*: ignorant sensibility.

208 *tender | The vile part*: pamper the body and our senses (easily deceived by appearances).

the part divine: manly reason.

214 *Paris . . . Lacedaemon*: in the Trojan War the Greeks were attempting to recover Helen, Queen of Lacedaemon, from Paris, prince of the Trojans, who had stolen her from her husband, Menelaus.

215 *laws of hospitality*: Paris seduced Helen while a guest in her husband's palace.

217 *his*: truth's.

218 *flattered*: pampered.

221 *understanding rules*: intelligent regulation.

224 *wolf that nourished Romulus*: Romulus, founder of Rome, was left to die as an infant, but was adopted by a wolf.

228 *by that deed . . . nor forms*: the nourishing of Romulus shows that behaviour, not external appearances or names, makes the difference between what we consider human and what bestial.

231 *that been saved*: that crime not been committed. The philosopher is Epictetus, from whose *Discourses* the example of Helen is drawn.

232 *Iliads and Odysseys*: Homer's epic poems on the Trojan War and its aftermath, translated into English by Chapman.

233 *true religion*: Roman Catholicism.

236 *for my learning*: for the sake of my instruction.

241 *countess*: Tamyra.

242 *this*: the attempt to deliver the challenge to Montsurry.

243 *so brave command*: splendid territory.

244 *training out*: exercising.

246 *breathe*: exercise.

Scotch running horse: some of the fastest horses in Renaissance Europe were bred in Galloway in the Scottish Lowlands, for use in racing and border warfare.

253 *At all parts*: in all respects.

258 *reaches*: limits.

260 *at no part*: in no way.

261 *the worth . . . in him*: all the worth he attributes to others, actually contained in him.

263 *He may be well*: he may well do so.

264 *cross*: oppose.

265 *in which*: in doing which.

267 *Atlas' shoulders*: in classical mythology, Atlas was a giant who bore the world on his shoulders; but in this passage Clermont imagines him towering *over* the earth.

269 *Rich . . . wander*: rich men, poor in reasoning ability, wander aimlessly.

271 *rank*: foul; the breath was supposed to distil some of the essence of the soul.

273 *odours*: perfumes.

274 *For which he only loves me*: for which reason only he loves me; for which reason he alone loves me.

276 *whatever change can be*: no matter what happens.

277 *thou hast ruined me*: therefore, in the event of your downfall, I would also fall.

3.1.1 *with wings*: in battle formations; swiftly.

6 *th' insulting pillars | Of Bacchus and Alcides*: in classical times the pillars of Bacchus in India were supposed to mark the eastern limits of the known world; the pillars of Hercules (Alcides) at the Strait of Gibraltar the western limit; both warned travellers in an intimidating ('insulting') way against proceeding further.

9 *At such an instance*: for such a reason.

27 *taken up*: exalted (by being offered the review of the troops, a sign of royal favour); captured.

29 *her*: herself.

33 *breathe himself*: catch his breath.

40 *will have best*: prefer that the best men be.

42 *merit*: justification.

43 *he*: Clermont, now under suspicion because of Bussy's transgressions.

45 *blood*: family.

 clear: guiltless.

46 *bastarding*: corruption by adultery of.

49 *to the coupling ends*: with sexual aims.

50 *mine own . . . friend's*: since Maillard is a bachelor, he is joking that he only sleeps with the wives of friends.

51 *make bold*: take liberties.

 common: normal; promiscuous.

56 *even . . . society*: which sustains the good things that develop from human association as the sun sustains growing things.

58 *hold | Colours for*: conceal.

62 *pretend*: set forth; feign.

63 *bethink us*: think.

64 *main strength*: brute force (of greater numbers).

66 *make him sure*: bind him securely.

70 *lackey's coats*: footmen's uniforms.

73 *close may lodge*: may place in secret.

74 *What think you . . . from horse*: this strategy was actually employed to capture the Count d'Auvergne, Chapman's historical model for Clermont.

77 *choicest brace of all our bands*: best two men of our army (punning on 'brace' = 'clasp'; 'band' = 'bonds').

79 *make*: move.

81 *engage*: wager.

83 *The bombast . . . giant*: the padding Political Cunning stuffs into the inflated form of what it represents as a great threat (cf. Baligny's remarks in 1.1. 134–42).

86 *And all . . . made?*: and all because of some trivial and insubstantial incident which, if it seems to affect him, he pretends is a heinous crime.

87 *It . . . ever*: perhaps one such incident is indeed slight, but not when they continue to occur.

91 *held | The fautor's right hand*: considered the patron's right-hand man.
   his: Guise's.

93 *fall . . . most capital*: be considered more than a trivial matter, and is a serious capital crime.

100 *Such . . . consorts*: we are known by the company we keep.

101 *vein hath safest vent*: sentiments are most safely expressed.

103 *ply*: occupy ourselves with.

3.2 S.D. *Gentleman Usher*: gentleman who serves an aristocrat.
   shows: it was common in Renaissance England to welcome distinguished visitors with masques, expensive dramatic entertainments.

1 This: the masque.

3 *at first full*: as large as it was originally.

4 *something*: somewhat.

6 *th' affairs*: court business.

8 *lies*: resides; the King had several palaces.
   advice: information.

10 *well qualified*: people's hunger for news about matters that did not seem to concern them directly was frequently satirized in Renaissance England.

12 *Locrian princes*: rulers of Locri, a Greek colony in Italy, whose laws were described by the Greek author Plutarch.

16 *innovations*: new ideas, often considered dangerous by those in power.

18 *go*: walk.

19 *shun rebating of*: avoid blunting.

22 *vile and vulgar admirations*: marvelling at what is base and common.

33 *bewrays | More glory*: suggests more pride.

39 *such a thought . . . goodness*: thoughts characterized by so much virtue.

41 *Demetrius Phalerius*: an Athenian orator of the fourth century BC, described in Plutarch's 'Precepts of Statecraft'.

47 *Demades, that passed Demosthenes*: Demades, 380–319 BC, was an orator, diplomat, and adversary of Demosthenes. None of his speeches survive. Demosthenes, 384–322 BC; another Athenian orator and statesman, was considered one of the greatest speakers of classical antiquity.

passed: surpassed.

54 *hugeness . . . hate*: pre-eminence which made people envy them.

56 *Makes*: helps.

guard: safekeeping.

58 *braveries*: displays.

60 *given their places*: installed.

62 *foregate*: front gate.

67 *dear*: valuable.

thrifty husband: frugal manager.

68 *fit for a novation*: tantamount to a complete upheaval.

70 *shield*: forbid.

79 *sound one!*: likely story (sarcastic).

81 *your strength*: where you will be safe.

82 *as*: as if.

83 *will*: so choose.

86 *notice*: warning.

91 *ling'ring*: delaying.

97 *equal*: fair (Charlotte); similar (Clermont).

98 *reason*: reasoning.

102 *one borne*: one wrong suffered passively.

106 *time is found for facts*: opportunity is found for deeds.

107 *No time . . . virtue*: kings are not restrained by considerations of time; much less are virtuous actions.

114 *bring their blood . . . wreaked with good*: either 'train their passions to endure every evil that they cannot replace with good', or 'learn to endure all evil, rather than revenge themselves, which is never a good course of action'.

115 *cause*: matter of concern.

120 *allowed*: approved.

122 *makes him worthy of your worst advantage*: permits you, without dishonouring yourself, to use any tactics you choose.

123 *cast a project*: made a plan.

128 *practice*: work on.

131 *retailing maidenheads*: selling virginities one by one.

141 *lay't on*: spend lavishly; put on a lot of cosmetics.

142 *bounties*: money; virtues.

143 *check*: recoil.

146 *surprise*: ambush.

147 *mock*: joke.

152 *Arden*: Ardennes, a forest in France and hide-out for thieves.

155 *This is not . . . be true*: the anonymous message is not a consequence of my unfulfilled revenge; the revenge will be as sure to happen in the future as it is unfinished at present—even if the message turns out to be true.

159 *let my blood up to that thought*: allow my anger to arise by considering that thought.

164 *votist of*: vowed to.

165 *with a precedent*: as an example.

170 *tender | And full of sulphur*: painful and inflammatory or accursed (sulphur was supposed to be a component of hellfire).

this letter's truth: the plot described in this letter, if it turned out to be true.

171 *comprehends so black a circumstance*: summarizes so foul a situation.

179 *if it be true as rare*: if it is as true as it is unusual.

182 *What's th'affair*: what is your business.

184 *studied*: carefully prepared; with an unconscious play on 'pretended'.

185 *consists*: makes up.

192 *take*: capture.

204 *without his forfeit*: without his having given up his authority, perhaps as a penalty for some transgression.

214 *Reason must bear him*: reasonable people must endure his eccentricities.

223 *out of your witness*: from your observation.

230 *such rhubarb*: so disagreeable.

233 *spice*: disguise.

236 *office*: duty. Executioners conventionally asked, and were granted, forgiveness by condemned persons; hence Maillard's response.

238 *all's one*: it's the same thing.

244 *note and use*: observation and practical application.

245 *right*: straight.

249 *succeeding*: coming to pass.

251 *uncredited*: disbelieved.

252 *approve*: find out by experience.

253 *raged*: was insane.

3.3.1 *downwards fit for lackeys*: demoted to footmen's uniforms.

   2 *pieces*: weapons.

   3 *complete*: stressed on the first syllable (as also in the following line)

   6 *enter*: begin.

  11 *how show we?*: how do we look.

     at all parts: in every respect.

  13 *battles*: battalions.

  15 *join*: begin the war games.

  24 *Hercules*: legendary Greek hero of enormous strength; the phrase was proverbial.

  25 *haste him*: hurry him along.

3.4.5 *sustain*: keep.

   7 *my hand . . . be used.* Clermont offers to shake hands as a sign of his good faith. Maillard protests that his word is sufficient, and that even his mere preference will be respected.

  10 *native power*: inborn intuition.

  14 *passionate.* According to Aristotle the subject of Homer's *Iliad* was the anger of Achilles, the greatest of the Greek soldiers.

  17 *of industry*: on purpose.

  20 *disposing these*: regulating their passions.

  24 *extends | To*: brings about.

  28 *government's*: behaviour is.

  29 *Pompey*: Roman general and statesman who opposed Julius Caesar's attempt to consolidate his power; Caesar defeated him in 48 BC.

  32 *approve*: demonstrate.

40 *sustain it . . . our mettle*: our spirit shrank from believing it.

47 *the worst*: virtually no one of high rank arrested for treason in Renaissance England escaped conviction.

51 *birthright*: inheritance.

55 *run a mixed course*: live a life in which good and bad are mixed.

56 *common*: in common; proverbial with Seneca, Cicero, and other classical Roman writers.

57 *find | Things' outward care*: care for outward things.

59 *His parts to th' use of th' All*: [and made] the individual parts of the world for the sake of the greater purpose.

61 *importeth*: carries with it.

62 *without*: not in.

63 *range*: wander.

66 *frame*: construction.

70 *in his proper part*: within his assigned place.

71 *invert*: reverse.

73 *shivers with the sway*: shatters when he comes up against the greater power of the universe.

74 *crossing*: working contrary to.

75 *God hath . . . damned a birth*: adapted from Epictetus, *Discourses*, iv. 7.

78 *battles ranged*: battalions arrayed.

85 *famous earl*: Edward de Vere, 17th earl of Oxford, minor poet and patron of the arts in Elizabethan England.

90 *From whence . . . derived*. England was supposed to have been settled first by Brutus, son of Aeneas (the ancestor of the Romans).

91 *beside*: besides.

93 *or*: either.

94 *public weals*: commonwealths.

96 *Duke Casimir*: Count Palatine, ruler of territories in Rhineland Germany, and a Protestant leader in the sixteenth-century religious wars in Continental Europe.

106 *cast . . . world*: thought of it only as a temptation to delay, motivated by worldly concerns.

Nor did it fit: nor was it consistent with.

111 *that crossed the vulgar*: contradicted ordinary conceptions.

112 *Sir John Smith*: a military disciplinarian who made unpopular criticisms about the sloppiness of English troops in the 1580s and 1590s; for Clermont's purposes, exemplary of inappropriate punctiliousness.

115 *Affecting . . . observations*: pretending that such degraded rituals constitute the essence of nobility.

117 *as*: as if.

123 *out*: i.e. out of their way.

124 *right-hand*: proper.

125 *brave wits*: great minds (sarcastic); flashily clever persons.

130 *rot at their doors*: i.e. waiting to be admitted.

133 *Twelve rods*: the *fasces*, a bundle of rods borne before the Roman consul as an emblem of his power.

134 *sit 'fore the whole tribunal*: sit before the Roman tribunal, a plebeian governmental body.

135 *Exhibit Circene games*: provide chariot races and other spectacles.

138 *void of perturbation*: free of emotional turmoil, the Stoic ideal.

139 *for constancy*: to obtain mental stability.

140 *vex for*: fret over.

145 *with all endeavour*: by all means.

147 *take*: react to.

149 *speed*: prosper.

s.d. *like*: disguised as.

154 *expecting*: awaiting.

160 *equal | In my acceptance*: equally acceptable to me.

165 *die*: singular of 'dice'.

4.1 s.d. *Alarm*: call to arms.

s.d. *Excursions over the stage*: military sallies suggested by men running across the stage.

6 *make him guards*: act as if they were protecting, not attacking him.

8 *First Soldier*: evidently not one of the 'lackeys'.

entertain: receive.

10 s.d. *chambers*: small cannons.

12 *possessed*: i.e. by his spirit.

16 *bore*: exerted.

22 *showed*: looked.

24 *horns*: wings of the battalion; tips of the moon.

27 *But they . . . weight oppressed*: but the foes out of range, and the cannonball forced down by its own weight.

31 *softliest*: most slowly.

32 *shivers any let it proves*: shatters any obstacle it encounters.

36 *reaches*: range; stratagems.

39 *something sacred*: meteors were regarded as divine omens and fatal to anyone who touched them.

41 *bands*: bonds.

51 *damnèd crew*: group condemned to hellfire.

52 *impolitic*: incorporate; with a play on 'politic' = 'cunning'.

56 *property*: nature of the thing.

59 *oath and oath . . . extremely*: two oaths fall into the same general category, but their specific characters diverge widely.

flat: clear.

60 *turn*: purposes; sexual act.

64 *being public once*: once they are public.

66 *public*: prostitutes; Clermont implies that Maillard, in 'going public', has prostituted his moral standards.

67 *makes*: transforms.

being the public good: since it is in the public interest.

74 *for that*: for that reason.

76 *a paribus*: from like things.

shrewd: ingenious; wicked.

78 *Retain*: remember.

81 *Use ye*: are you accustomed.

85 *leave your coats*: remove your lackeys' uniforms.

87 *virtue lives . . . any ill*: virtue remains unseparated from vice in any bad situation.

96 *huge state act*: tremendous service to the state.

97 *great*: friendly.

98 *held dangerous*: considered likely to revolt.

99 *Made me . . . danger*: described me as the reckless accomplice in Guise's rebellion.

104 *Since . . . used*: cf. 1.1.64.

105 *other*: otherwise.

109 *trumpet's*: trumpeter's.

110 *heavily*: sadly.

114 *hapless service*: unfortunate treatment; unhappy devotion.

123 *Condition*: on condition that.

128 *space*: time.

129 *patience*: endurance.

130 *consequence*: occurrence.

133 *Cause*: God.

134 *match with His whole fabric*: fit in with His total design.

138 *manners*: moral conduct.

139 *join*: align.

143 *straits*: narrow passages.

 revert: turn away.

147 *as well refract as voluntary*: resistant as well as co-operative.

148 *Reduceth*: leads back.

149 *applause*: assent.

150 *crossing it no breath*: never speaking against it.

154 *art*: learning.

157 *appertains*: is akin.

4.2.1 *scandal*. Baligny pretends that Clermont's arrest took place without his knowledge or consent.

 7 *smocks his ensigns*: women's undergarments his military banners.

 8 *sails*: i.e. 'what keeps his government afloat'.

 9 *ways of venery*: sexual positions.

15 *belly-gods*: gluttons.

18 *Vile men . . . blood*: evil men raised to high office live off the blood of the commonwealth.

19 *Bounties*: generous acts.

21 *places*: positions of authority.

22 *as they . . . grace*: as they benefit from others' graciousness and generosity, be sure to practise the same virtues themselves.

25 *Take*: take back.

 Why are wealth and power: what are wealth and power for.

27 *swoll'n in mind*: puffed up with pride.

28 *wind*: because it moves the merchant's ships.

30 *Something . . . to go*: taking credit for doing something that would have happened anyway.

33 *sere*: dry, hence easily kindled. Those prone to anger were supposed to generate excess heat, which dried up their bodily fluids.

37 *Sicile gulf*: the straits of Sicily, very perilous to ships.

39 *looking*: thinking of going.

 Medea: in classical myth, a sorceress who aided Jason in his search for the Golden Fleece and later married him; upon discovering his infidelity, she murdered their children. The heroine of an influential revenge tragedy by Seneca.

42 *reform*: restore.

4.3.5 *break*: fail (to fulfil his promise).

8 *confer*: bring with me.

10 *charge*: responsibility; burden.

13 *do him that desire*: satisfy that request.

17 *ground*: foundation.

26 *hold*: remain silent.

33 *train him*: trick him into coming.

37 *guiltlessly*: without a penalty.

42 *keep*: maintain.

45 *Kings' precedents . . . no danger*: kings who disregard the law establish dangerous precedents (since their own authority derives from the law).

48 *Full in all right . . . for their right*: complete in all virtue, excessive in nothing, nor straining their prerogative past its proper limit.

58 *compass*: scope.

64 *in the like*: in like manner.

67 *for your servant*: as regards your lover.

69 *His*: the king's.

he: Clermont.

78 *bought his bands out*: ransomed himself from imprisonment.

83 *Hate . . . speak*: you should hate liars as you hate the mouth of hell.

86 *service*: message; assistance.

87 *cabinet*: casket of jewels.

90 *close contracted*: concentrated in a small space.

93 *my comforts*: the comforts I can provide; i.e. the jewels.

108 *This might . . . much charge*: enigmatic; perhaps 'if the Countess had preferred tears to jewels before this, she could have saved a lot of money'; or 'if she hadn't made such a fuss she could have sent off the jewels more expeditiously'.

4.4.5 *Coloured with*: given plausibility by.

9 *reverence*: form of deference.

11 *stick . . . fire*: resist and perform listlessly what they ought to do eagerly, of their own free will.

19 *In his . . . object*: in his refusal to give up anything he deems worthy, or to incline even slightly to that which is base, or does not serve his aims.

21 *In estimation of th' idolatrous vulgar*: as they are valued by ordinary people, who worship mere externals.

24 *kind*: habit.

25 *In spite of temporizing*: scorning evasion.

rising: elevation.

28 *present most hard*: offer extreme hardships.

29 *charge*: onslaught.

31 *tyrannous will to do*: desire to do anything oppressive.

32 *abjection*: ignobility.

34 *The flexibility . . . anger*: his ability to put aside his most extreme anger.

41 *observers*: sycophants.

42 *Senecal*: possessing the virtues that Seneca, the Roman Stoic philosopher, recommends in his essays and *Moral Letters*.

44 *the day and fortune*: all times and situations.

46 *one to all*: the same in all circumstances.

49 *Machiavellian*: amorally expedient, as described in Machiavelli's treatise on political theory, *The Prince*.

50 *Teucers*: in the *Iliad*, Teucer is a coward who hides behind the shield of the hero Ajax.

51 *Cacusses*: in classical mythology, Cacus is a giant who plunders the countryside until killed by Hercules; Chapman conflates him with Procrustes, a legendary robber who cuts his victims to fit the length of his bed.

57 *quick*: alive.

58 *property for state*: mere tool of state policy.

spoil to thrive: thrive by ruining others.

4.5.1 *chance*: fortune.

11 *What can . . . well*: what can affect him, to keep him from doing well.

14 *pretty*: clever.

Put: admit.

21 *stay*: quell.

27 *stay one*: restrain oneself.

28 *raps*: strikes; pulls.

30 *th' adulterer*: whom the wife allows into the house when her husband is asleep or absent.

32 *overflow*: passions were conceived as fluids moving within the body.

33 *many critics*. In his commentary on his translation of the *Iliad*, Chapman complains about the pedantry of some Homeric interpreters.

34 *stand*: focus upon.

35 *feet*: beats of the line.

36 *sink beneath*: go unnoticed.

37 *upright gasping*: complete exhaustion.

41 *getting*: acquiring.

47 *meat . . . you*: you are no more able to assimilate this than sick men are able to digest meat.

51 *bands*: fetters.

59 *This*: the arrest.

63 *redeem your bands*: pay your ransom.

67 *Lord Lieutenant*. Baligny, still pretending that Clermont's capture occurred behind his back, sarcastically accuses Maillard of having usurped his authority as Lord Lieutenant.

68 *usurp that style enforced*: was forced to take your authority upon myself.

74 *brought you down*: to Cambrai, with the covert implication 'ruined you'.

to much good purpose: with only good motives.

79 *issue*: end.

80 *countess*: Tamyra.

82 *please*: appease.

85 *apparition showed it*: ghost revealed it.

87 *use weighty*: important reason.

93 *this*: the casket.

99 *equal*: true.

101 *seconding*: because Guise was also included in the prophecy.

103 *in one*: in one of its parts.

5.1 S.D. *ascends*: from a trapdoor in the stage floor.

2 *whole digestion of the world*: cosmic order, which on some accounts was born out of chaos and destined to return to it eventually.

4 *bide*: endure.

8 *th' infliction*: the punishment.

chainèd shot: two cannonballs connected by a chain, used to destroy the sails of enemy ships.

9 *still*: always.

17 *leaving, but for supposition sake*: leaving aside, only for the sake of argument.

18 *body*: fundamental constituent.

20 *Cleft*: sliced in two. This gory image refers to the division of the Christian world into Protestant and Catholic faiths.

22 *whose observation*: the observation of which.

28 *Stands by proportion*: endures because it is balanced and ordered.

32 *his*: its.

s.D. *close*: hidden.

34 *prevent*: outstrip.

36 *dispatched*: out of the way.

37 *admirèd*: astonishing.

38 *barricadoes*: barricades.

39 *Rheims*: city where French kings were crowned. The historical Guise was ambitious to succeed to the throne by one means or another; in Chapman's play his intentions are unclear, but the king's anxiety about him seems exaggerated.

43 *sense common*: in Renaissance psychology, an internal faculty that received and interpreted the impressions conveyed to it by the five 'external' senses.

45 *vapours of o'erflowing humours*: emanations from the bodily 'humours' or fluids that were supposed to determine health, personality, and mood.

46 *spirits*: vital spirits, supposed to be intermediate between the material 'humours' and the ethereal soul.

48 *painfully*: vigorously.

50 *actuates*: activates.

his: its.

52 *So*: similarly.

53 *cause alike*: same process.

55 *th' advertisements*: the warnings.

58 *Lorraine and Savoy*: provinces in the north and south of France.

59 *catastrophe*: ending.

61 *dissolving all our counsels*: bringing all our plans to nothing.

63 *Archbishop of Lyons*: Guise's brother.

65 *occasion*: juncture.

67 *let that fall*: overthrow.

68 *exhale*: exalt.

72 *thrusting on . . . you off*: getting so far out on a limb that your best efforts cannot save you.

77 *Avarice of all*: desire to have everything.

78 *spur*: motive to action; lit., goad worn on a riding boot to move a horse forward.

79 *curb*: restraint; lit., bit which forces a horse to stop.

79 *respect not*: do not care about.

81 *present*: present moment.

84 *by true doctrine*: by true religion. When Bussy protests that Clermont stresses self-sufficiency instead of dependence upon God, he raises a Christian objection to Stoicism that originated with St Augustine's *City of God* and is often repeated in the Renaissance. But Bussy's complaint does not really apply to Clermont's version of the philosophy, with its emphasis upon fitting oneself into a universal order; and his conclusion, justifying the taking of revenge, is hardly consistent with Christianity.

90 *by death, is only*: because we die, is only attained by.

91 *fit*: suit.

92 *perfecting*: perfecting of.

108 *desert of me*: good deeds to me.

109 *let*: restraint.

111 *supply it*: make up for it.

113 *fleshy*: fleshly.

122 *only since*: if only because.

126 *(for... kings)*: for the sake of the counterfeit glory of the king's ephemeral approval.

132 *ends, truth's name doth sue in*: purposes, pleads his case in the name of truth.

133 *study ruin*: labour to destroy others.

139 *hurt*: because the Stoics teach that true injury can only come from within.

140 *makes*: conduces.

146 *nothing uttering*: in no way expressing.

150 *chance*: event.

157 *frail parts of my blood*: lust was thought to emanate from the blood.

158 *enjoyed*: obtained sexual satisfaction.

161 *sticking*: remaining.

162 *Though the desire ... be gone*: it was commonplace in the Renaissance to insist that pleasure diminished sharply after the first few sexual acts with the same person.

166 *Which must chance ... valuing least*: which must always happen, since when I compare what reason loves (i.e. the woman's merits) and what desire loves (i.e. her body) I always prefer the best (i.e. her merits); what most people love, I value the least.

175 *fat*: fatten.

180 *devour*: eat intemperately.

181 *in our most health is our most disease*: the source of our greatest health becomes the source of our worst illness.

183 *'Tis for society confined in reason*: it leads to an association based upon reason.

188 *chaste and masculine*: non-sexual friendships among men are considered the best and most rewarding form of human interaction by Aristotle, Cicero, Seneca, and other classical philosophers.

192 *precise*: scrupulous.

5.2.3 *fire*: anger.

4 *giantly austere*: monstrously inflexible.

8 *shady*: shadowing.

11 *commands*: sees below her.

12 *stays*: delays.

15 *who*: which.

17 *Powder*: explosive potential.

as: like.

20 *for not those . . . hope*: for not only do you disregard whether you are revealing sensitive information, but you open the way to the destruction of your best plans.

23 *take wind*: be revealed.

25 *their twinkling*: the blinking of your enemies' eyes.

27 *Confidence that lightens ere she die*: confidence that anticipates a bright future just before it meets unsuspected destruction.

31 *access*: approach.

34 *patrons*: saviours.

37 *lodge*: set up.

38 *thunder*: strike with thunder.

5.3.1 *sister*: kindred spirit; also, to the extent Tamyra considers Bussy her true spiritual mate, Charlotte is a sister-in-law.

9 *bribing*: corrupting.

17 *vault*: underground passageway; Renel and the Countess climb up through the trapdoor in the floor of the stage.

24 *At all parts*: in all respects.

29 *mortal quarry*: deadly attack.

41 *stand on such occurrents*: are contingent upon such chance events.

42 *hand*: handwriting.

52 *Up*: the ladies watch part of the ensuing duel from the balcony above the stage.

57 *state*: majesty.

5.4.2 *only*: mere.

3 *lotteries set up for*: predictions (apparently written on slips of paper) giving notice of.

5 *Knit*: tied up.

6 *enter*: attend the council meeting.

11 *slave*: i.e. body.

16 *sink*: cesspool.

21 *far*: as far.

24 *my false man by falsehood*: my false, carnal self by treachery.

25 *clear*: free.

29 *try*: prove.

30 *lay about him*: strike out vigorously.

32 *blood saved*: bloodshed avoided.

34 *Alcides*: Hercules; with reference to the proverb 'Two are enough to conquer Hercules.'

35 *to friend*: helping them out.

S.D. *enters*: the guards have been hiding in ambush behind the arras (tapestry screen).

36 *this is*: this is the result of.

41 *urge*: insist upon.

44 *woe | Of your so wounded faith*: regret for your blemished fidelity.

45 *of force*: strong enough.

49 *idolatry*: devotion to improper goals.

53 *fountain to*: source of.

56 *The present . . . shifters' purchases*: the present intolerance of due process, and the unprincipled expedients resorted to in the interests of the king's security, will turn out like thieves' bargains.

58 *rain a poisoned shower*: stars were supposed to emit ethereal streams that affected events on earth. Henry was himself assassinated by a fanatic friar only ten months after he had the Guise murdered.

62 *scarlet*: cardinals wore scarlet robes; but the word also implies iniquity.

5.5.5 S.D. *gulf*: stage trapdoor.

11 *confer*: bring with me (Montsurry hired a group of killers to dispatch Bussy).

26 *that*: because.

27 *prevent*: frustrate.

28 *of one base is base*: over a cowardly person is dishonourable.

33 *gave me*: in *Bussy d'Ambois*, 5.4.

37 *show your back*: flee.

41 *lapwing*: plover that calls far from its nest in order to mislead predators.

45 *abject!*: coward; from Latin *abjectus*, 'thrown down'.

46 *people's voice*: what people commonly say.

57 *bands*: fetters.

62 *aching foreheads*: cuckolds.

66 *relic of the D'Ambois gall*: remnant of the D'Ambois spirit and presumption.

67 *purple*: bloody.

70 *of yourself*: of your own accord.

76 *Change*: exchange.

79 *point*: spur.

80 *challenge*: demand.

83 *Her power, in me urged*: the power of Necessity, forced upon you by me.

85 *at all*: all or nothing.

87 *Stick in his hands*: procrastinate (Clermont refrains from killing Montsurry when he is defenceless).

s.d. *gets down*. Charlotte leaves the balcony, where she has been stationed with the Countess and Renel, through a door in the back of the upper stage and reappears shortly on the main stage downstairs.

89 *it*: my death blow.

100 *not I*: not unfair that I.

102 *proved what I presume on*: performed what I have claimed to be able to do.

104 *charge speed*: attack succeed.

106 *in fate*: appointed by fate.

124 *instant*: immediate.

128 *approve the act*: condone the Massacre.

130 *approve*: prove.

131 *as*: while.

133 *fables*: many Stoics disbelieved in ghosts; but Clermont has good reason to believe in their existence, and tries in the next few lines to reconcile his beliefs with his recent experience.

156 *in mine own hands being*: acting of my own volition.

160 *needful*: necessary.

161 *fear*: fear for.

162 *skill*: have knowledge.

164 *jar*: dissonance.

169 *coverts*: veils.

175 *th' other*: the mind and soul.

184 *my venture . . . bottom put*: (with) my whole fortune inside the vessel.

187 *far-removed shores to*: on shores far removed from.

188 *he*: Guise.

197 *his*: its.

208 *snaky head*. Tamyra is comparing herself, Charlotte, and the Countess— the audience to the duel and to Clermont's suicide—to the three mythical Fates who oversee the workings of divine justice; they have snakes instead of hair.

213 *amends*: amendment.

The Atheist's Tragedy

Dramatis Personae. D'Amville: base of soul, from French 'd'âme' and English 'vile'; with a suggestion, too, of 'damned'.

Levidulcia: light (unchaste) and sweet.

Castabella: chaste and beautiful.

Languebeau: fine tongue.

Snuffe: a candle-wick (referring to the character's original occupation as tallow-chandler); also, 'a thing of no value'.

Borachio: drunkard.

instrument: one who carries out the commands of another.

Cataplasma: poultice.

Fresco: fresh.

1.1.3 *read*: learned.

4 *Nature*: an important concept for D'Amville, signifying the material world in so far as it can be explained without reference to a deity, but often itself anthropomorphized and credited with powers Christians reserve to God.

large: wide-ranging.

6 *course | Of revolution*: cycle of changes.

7 *state*: prime of life.

9 *For th'better composition o' the two*: for being better concocted than beasts are.

16 *casts*: adds.

20 *insensible*: imperceptible.

23 *comprehends*: includes the whole of.

26 *our time runs home unto the length | Of Nature*: our life lasts as long as Nature allows.

40 *respect*: attend to.

41 *Thanks*: thanks to.

48 *present*: alert.

52 *husbandry*: prudent management.

56 *providence*: here, economic foresight. D'Amville employs the word to refer to various kinds of secular prudence. The use of spiritual terminology in a material sense is characteristic of D'Amville and other sinful characters, e.g. Levidulcia and Languebeau Snuffe, throughout the play.

67 *original*: source.

77 *troop of gentry*: throng of well-born men below the aristocratic rank; hence Charlemont's social inferiors.

82 *free*: noble.

83 *maintenance*: funds.

84 *habit*: both uniform and military equipment, which Renaissance aristocrats bought with their own funds.

85 *necessity*: restraint.

90 *principal*: capital investment (playing on 'principle').

95 *bond*: written promise of repayment.

99 *love doth always satisfy itself*: love is its own reward; proverbial.

100 *labour*: work to obtain.

109 *take*: understand.

110 *pregnant wit*: fertile intelligence.

112 *subject for commodious providence*: opportunity to exercise foresight; convenient way of obtaining property.

118 *trust | For undertaking*: reliability in executing dangerous tasks.

1.2.6 *addition*: mark of honour added to a coat of arms.

16 *as hereditary . . . my ancestry*: as much my inheritance from all my ancestors as my blood is.

28 *play upon*: joke about; humiliate.

35 *tenderness*: overprotectiveness.

40 *this*: Rousard.

that: Sebastian.

41 *competitor*: partner.

57 *success . . . worth*: success commensurate with their merits.

63 *favour*: kind action (of saying farewell).

64 *withheld him in the way*: detained him.

78 *Possess the entertainment of remembrance*: remain in the memory.

92 *incorporated*: embodied; joined.

93 *contracted*: betrothed; consolidated. The 'pre-contract' or betrothal promise was a very serious matter in Renaissance England; by asking Languebeau to witness their vows Charlemont and Castabella are taking a legally binding step towards marriage. Thus the wedding of Castabella and Rousard is not only morally repugnant but violates Jacobean marriage law.

94 *Or*: either.

103 *copulation*: coupling; sexual intercourse. Languebeau's speeches burlesque the language of the Puritans, regarded by their enemies as religious hypocrites.

114 *fatally*: as ordained by fate.

118 *event*: outcome.

122 *concupiscences*: lustful desires, a favourite Puritan word.

127 *your joining one for me*: i.e. if that's how you kiss good-by, I'd like to kiss you hello; with sexual play on 'joining'.

148 *take your friendship . . . your principal*: borrow your friendship as from a usurer, paying an exorbitant interest rate, so that I will repay you far more friendship than you will have to invest in me.

151 *familiarity*: acquaintance.

154 *entertainment*: treatment.

166 *small*: miniature.

168 *light*: with a pun on 'light' = 'unchaste'.

186 *second end*: ulterior motive.

193 *be most thankful to your trust*: amply repay your confidence in him.

197 *give the onset*: commence the battle, with sexual *double entendre*.

200 *will*: with a play on 'will' = 'genital'.

201 *gratuity*: kindness; payment.

204 *This*: the ring.

205 *precisely*: exactly; 'precise' was also synonymous with 'Puritan'.

206 *profession*: professed religious beliefs.

209 *compare 's profession with his life*: the corruption and hypocrisy of clergymen were often deplored as encouraging cynicism about religion among the laity.

213 *engross it to himself*: monopolize it.

224 *state*: not d'Amville's personal estate, since Rousard and not he will receive Castabella's dowry, but the fortunes of the family in general.

227 *point*: objective.

228 *policy*: prudence, plotting; often, as here, used to mean expedient contrivance without regard to moral or religious scruples.

1.3.4 *entertained me for thy servant*: acknowledged me as your suitor.

10 *favour*: love-token (Rousard); face (Castabella).

11 *eye*: with possible sexual *double entendre* on eye = aperture.

12 *go to buffets*: get in a fight.

14 *bitter*: satirical.

15 *gray-eyed*: conventionally described as the most beautiful colour for eyes in Renaissance love poetry; playing on the proverb 'By the morning one knows the day.'

18 *light*: little; sexually loose.

21 *bracelet o' thy hair*: a common 'favour'.

22 *want hair*: hair loss is a symptom of syphilis, the illness from which Rousard is implied to be suffering; 'hare' is slang for 'whore', an equivocation Rousard picks up in the following line.

27 *worn off*: worn away; worn by another person.

28 *sensible*: intelligent; sensually arousing.

30 *Smelling*: foul breath is another symptom of syphilis.

37 *bestow the keeping of it*: manage to hold on to it.

44 *equivocation*: pun; but Castabella picks up on the meaning 'deliberately misleading ambiguity'. The ethical acceptability of the latter kind of equivocation was an important issue for Renaissance moral and religious writers.

46 *in quiet for*: at peace from.

54 *stand to't*: persist; have an erection.

1.4.3 *moved*: suggested.

4 *savoured*: had the appearance of.

7 *affection*: sexual love.

8 *familiar*: intimate.

9 *apprehension*: understanding.

23 *contrary*: opposed to her father's will.

27 *instant*: very.

29 *desires your conference*: wishes to speak with you.

31 *Time cuts off circumstance*: there is no time for a detailed account.

48 *contracted to*: wedded to; focused upon.

50 *want pretence*: lack an excuse.

53 *of the Family of Love*: among the true lovers; the Family of Love was a radical Protestant sect that was rumoured to encourage sexual promiscuity among its worshippers.

54 *generous*: brave; noble; aristocratic.

62 *into*: to persuade; with a bawdy innuendo.

63 *blood*: thought to be the source of lustful desire.

74 *unkindly*: unnaturally.

79 *Where*: whereas.

86 *prodigal | Expense*: each act of sexual intercourse was imagined to use up some vital fluids of the participants and thus to shorten their lives.

101 *mother i'law*: stepmother.

110 *neglect*: punishment (by God).

128 *unsanctified member*: profane part; punning on the Puritan term for a church member who had not been granted saving grace.

136 *ability*: sexual potency.

141 *matted*: strewn with rushes, a common Renaissance floor-covering, so that footsteps are inaudible.

curtain: bed-curtain.

146 *winked at*: ignored; connived at.

2.1.9 *very loggerheads*: true blockheads.

15 *wound up*: tuned, like a stringed instrument.

26 *congratulate*: salute.

28 *Ostend*: a city in Belgium, under siege by the Spanish from 1601 to 1604.

30 *make our music full*: complete our festivities.

39 *flatt'ring*: deceptive.

42 *report*: sound of cannonfire.

43 *storm*: assault.

45 *promised most advantage to be forced*: seemed most vulnerable to an attack.

49 *channel at an ebb*: the river outside Ostend at low tide.

52 *opposed*: refused this advice.

55 *our breach | At push o' pike*: the gap in our fortifications by hand-to-hand combat. The sudden overthrow of an aggressor resembles the workings of God's justice later in the play.

68 *murderers that flankered | The level of the flood*: small cannon that guarded the banks of the river.

108 *screech-owl*: traditional harbinger of disaster.

114 *that*: what.

115 *delicate*: pleasing.

118 *Rarely*: beautifully.

121 *perfected*: accented on the first syllable in Renaissance English.

124 *underneath the moon*: in Ptolemaic astronomy, the earth was the centre of the universe and the moon was the closest planet orbiting around it. All things within the moon's sphere of orbit were subject to decay; all things beyond were permanent.

131 *subject to distraction*: likely to become insane.

141 *into her chamber*: it was standard practice for family and friends to escort the bride and groom into the bedroom at the close of the wedding festivities.

145 *hardly*: with bawdy pun.

2.2.2 *by this light*: a mild oath, which the second servant puns upon in the following line.

4 *an t'wou't*: if you'd like.

6 S.D. *kneel*: customary procedure when drinking toasts in London taverns.

9 *pledge it*: return the toast.

14 *go alone*: walk unsupported.

26 *snuff*: dregs left in the cup after drinking; *in snuff*: as an insult.

28 S.D. *fall . . . th'ears*: begin to fight.

33 *jacks abused me*: knaves treated me badly.

34 *jacks*: drinking vessels.

38 *bear thee out in't*: support you.

43 *coxcomb*: head (lit. fool's head-dress).

53 *maintain*: persevere.

2.3.2 *adult'rate*: corrupt; adulterous.

24 *heavy*: depressed.

light: cheerful; wanton.

28 *groaning*: with pain (Rousard); in sexual ecstasy (Levidulcia).

36 *their generation was asleep*: their conception occurred when their parents were not fully awake (thought in the Renaissance to result in dull children).

37 *dormice*: slothful people.

41 *active*: vigorously moving, with masturbatory implications.

43 *entertain*: hold entwined.

47 *I beshrew your ear*: devil take your eavesdropping.

51 *abroad*: away from home.

52 *encounter*: meet with; have sex with.

53 *persuade | Your means*: convince you to intercede.

66 *Lust . . . lays*. Levidulcia describes sexual excitation as the conjuring up and exorcism of a devil, with obscene *double entendre*. In Renaissance medicine the 'vital spirits' were bodily fluids derived from the blood, from which the male and female seed were in turn derived.

2.4 S.D. *over the stage*: crossing from one side of the stage to the other.

1 *raise a house upon*: use for the foundation or corner-stone of a building; in l. 2 Borachio puns on 'house' = 'family'.

2 S.D. *descends*: Borachio climbs down into the trapdoor in the platform stage, into the 'gravel pit'.

8 *light*: light-witted.

24 *dog*: the messenger who brought news of Charlemont's death (unlike Belforest, D'Amville knows that Borachio is both messenger and murderer).

35 *Dead be your tongues! . . . At's death?*. This passage echoes Hieronimo's lament for Horatio in the first addition to *The Spanish Tragedy*, lines 46-51. Ribner cites analogies for the tennis-ball metaphor from Webster's *Duchess of Malfi* and Sharpham's *Cupid's Whirligig*.

39 *govern*: by astrological influence.

45 *Recollect yourself*: pull yourself together.

47 *tries*: puts to the test.

51 *That Nature has no feeling*: that emotion is unnatural; that the force of Nature possesses nothing analogous to human feelings.

54 *Whether*: interrogative expressing doubt between alternatives.

62 *sanguine*: the healthy red colour of blood, which was supposed to be the predominant fluid in healthy and temperamentally stable individuals.

63 *For all*: even though.

68 *regeneration*: redemption from original sin.

69 *harmless*: fearful of doing harm.

71 *dearly pitiful*: affectionately prone to pity.

80 *laid*: allayed.

85 S.D. *ascends*: climbs back on to the stage platform.

86 *'O Dolentis'*: a song of sorrow.

90 *perished*: destroyed.

96 *ruby*: the blood-stained stone.

103 *judicious*: carefully plotted.

128 *missed*: omitted.

135 *bravely carried through | The eye of observation, unobserved*: admirably committed without being noticed, though seen.

139 *him they call the supreme of the stars*: God, whom D'Amville refers to in a typically circumlocutory way.

140 *influences*: ethereal substances imagined to stream forth from constellations and planets, affecting events on earth.

141 *sublunary*: beneath the orbit of the moon, hence mortal; cf. 2.1.124

142 *senseless of their operations*: the stars, being unconscious, do not intend the effects they produce.

147 *middle | Region of the air*: the atmosphere was imagined to consist of three layers; the bottom and the top were warm and the middle was cold.

153 *'Tis a mere effect . . . noise we hear*: D'Amville provides a scientific account derived from the classical naturalist-philosophers Aristotle and Lucretius. Others held that thunder was a sign of divine displeasure.

156 *triumph*: victory celebration.

162 *passage*: walking.

166 *confirmed me*: convinced me; restored my courage.

171 *fabric of the work*: construction of the plot.

172 *to credit that | With all the countenance*: make that believable with all the appearance of plausibility.

177 *apprehension*: conviction.

2.5 S.D. *manned*: accompanied.

5 *somewhat*: something.

6 *towards*: likely to obtain.

8 *come off lustily*: work out well.

13 *A poor spirit . . . poor purse*: proverbial.

20 *out o' countenance*: disconcerted.

22 *gentle*: yielding; of good birth.

Hot: rich and spicy, thought to conduce to lust.

25 *gouty*: painfully swollen.

26 *endure the feeling*: put up with being touched.

28 *'Sdainty*: God's dignity, a ladylike oath.

37 *line that stands directly against me*: line on your palm that is closest to me; with bawdy innuendo.

43 *compass*: obtain (Fresco); embrace (Levidulcia).

49 *congealed passage*: Northwest Passage from Europe to the Far East.

51 *treason you never committed*: treason was punishable by death whether the revolt was actually attempted or merely intended.

55 *full career*: top speed.

59 *sheets*: of paper; bedsheets.

63 *after the English manner*: the way the English do it. ' "The beginning of the world" was a popular dance tune' (I. Ribner (ed.), *The Atheist's Tragedy*, 1964).

65 *preposterously*: literally, with the back part forward, referring to supposed sexual practices on the Continent.

66 *active*: eager.

74 *chafe*: rub (to make yourself red).

76 *let me alone for*: let me take care of.

85 *on's*: of his.

97 *naked weapon*: unsheathed sword, with *double entendre*.

107 *dead palsy*: fit of paralysis.

120 *shag-haired*: shaggy.

122 *watchman in a rug gown*: constable in a rough wool coat.

126 *watched my time*: took my opportunity.

128 *hang himself in his own garters*: a common insult.

129 *savours of*: suggests; smells like.

134 *fore-door*: front door (with *double entendre*).

   common: open to all.

135 *dangerous*: hazardous; bold.

2.6.4 *heavy*: weary.

10 *consort*: harmony.

22 *success of things*: outcome of events.

29 *complexion*: composition, as determined by the proportion of the four 'humours' or bodily fluids.

30 *Dreams . . . bodies*: Charlemont's theory of the origin of dreams is a standard one in the Renaissance. Cf. *The Revenge of Bussy d'Ambois*, 5.1.42–53.

36 *Genius*: guardian angel.

41 *understand | That vision . . . to come*: find out that the dream is true, or will come true in the future.

42 *regard*: care.

49 *Confounded*: mingled.

66 *devil's dam . . . head*: i.e. some calamity has occurred.

68 *doubtful*: apprehensive; hesitating.

3.1.2 *living*: lifelike.

4 *satisfied*: adequately repaid.

5 *use*: interest (on the life earth 'loaned' Montferrers).

7 *memory*: since Charlemont's body is missing, his coffin must remain empty.

13 *There*: on the graves, to which mourners could attach eulogies.

19 *deplore*: lament.

24 *provided*: managed.

25 *suddenly*: unprepared.

27 *His body*: Charlemont's body is, of course, not in the tomb; D'Amville's apparently generous epitaph serves his own interests.

   mould: grave.

28 *old*: i.e. wise.

38 *phoenix*: legendary bird, of which only one was supposed to exist, which burned itself to death every 500 years and was reborn from its own ashes.

46 *Herculean pillars*: D'Amville compares the grave monuments to the pillars of Hercules, two rocks at the Strait of Gibraltar that were thought in classical times to mark the western boundary of the navigable world. They were inscribed with the Latin words *Non ultra*: no further.

52 *t'wou't*: you like.

66 *church*: churchyard.

70 *relation*: rumour; with unconscious play on 'relative'.

80 *Reduce . . . eye*: i.e. make your ideas consistent with what you see.

82 *shape*: ghost.

85 *Subject to the capacity of sense*: able to be perceived through the senses.

117 *a vein | Be opened*: for blood-letting, thought to relieve illness by removing excess fluids.

123 *possession*: of his father's estate.

3.2.3 *crier*: town crier, a lower-class occupation.

   9 *tetter*: eczema, thought to be caused by impure blood.

15 *next*: easiest.

16 *rack*: instrument of torture used to extract confessions from suspected felons, who were hanged if they admitted their guilt.

19 *apprehension*: perception.

21 *Compose*: calm.

23 *fiend i' the likeness of Charlemont*: Puritans believed that ghosts were disguised devils, not the spirits of departed souls.

26 *spirit*: ghost; courage.

41 *riot*: disturbance of the peace.

42 *action*: lawsuit (debtors were imprisoned until they paid their debts).

44 *conjure*: exorcise; i.e. get rid of.

46 *circle*. Charlemont, surrounded by officers, imagines himself as a conjurer protected from devilish powers by a magic circle. In effect, he tells D'Amville that no external misfortunes can intrude upon his spiritual equanimity.

52 *countenance*: encourage.

75 *gettings*: fees; law officers were paid a certain sum per arrest.

77 *elder brothers*: who inherited the bulk of the family estate.

78 *husbands*: managers of their resources; married men.

younger brothers: who inherited little, and therefore needed to marry wealthy women to prosper.

81 *hospitals*: charitable institutions for the needy.

82 *o' the benevolence*: by charitable donations, because they will have no income.

3.3.3 *they*: our punishments.

7 *Or how . . . crimes*: or how can your justice, which restricts the capacities of human beings, function as benevolently as you intend, when our punishments are greater than our sins.

15 *constructions*: interpretations.

20 *those attributes*: i.e. wealth, social position, and other kinds of good fortune.

23 *deject*: lower.

27 *soft consumption*: slow form of tuberculosis.

30 *trebles . . . treble*: high notes; triple.

32 *means*: alto or tenor notes; money.

45 *little world*: many Renaissance doctors, alchemists, and magicians believed that the structure of the human body (the 'microcosm' or little world) duplicated the structures of the universe as a whole, the 'macrocosm' or big world.

53 *underhand*: unobtrusively.

reserved: secret.

3.4.9 *countenance*: aspect.

21 *goodness' substitute*: great men, as God's proxies in this world, were supposed to imitate God's mercy and justice in their relations with their inferiors.

32 *father*. Since 'villain' was originally a term for a man of low birth, a villain's father is perforce a villain himself.

33 *open freedom*: frank generosity.

36 *According to*: like.

59 *indenture*: formal covenant.

71 *respectless*: unconcerned.

75 *concluded*: settled.

4.1.2 *medlar with a plum tree growing hard by it*: a medlar is a pear-tree the fruit of which is edible only after it has begun to rot; the pears are shaped like female genitalia. 'Plum tree' is slang for female genitals. 'Hard by' = just next to; Soquette's needlework allegorically describes the relation between a prostitute and her bawd.

4 *perished joints*: syphilis attacks the cartilagenous tissue in the joints.

11 *savin tree*: a kind of juniper, the poisonous berries of which induce abortion.

13 *honeysuckle*: fragrant vine, symbolic of love.

14 *whitethorn*: spring-blooming bush associated with young lovers.

16 *uprightly*: definitely, with *double entendre*.

22 *bachelor's button*: buttercup, supposed to bring good fortune in love, with *double entendre*.

23 *snail*: representing the impotent husband.

25 *artificial*: skilfully depicted.

30 *poppering pear*: a tree with fruit shaped like male genitalia.

38 *substance*: money; semen (with reference to the common notion that sexual intercourse shortened life).

41 *Lirie*: unexplained; perhaps a textual corruption, and perhaps a representation of singing, along the lines of 'tra la la'.

45 *'Precious*: By God's precious blood, an oath.

46 *mi*: musical note, with a pun on 'me'. The entire lute lesson is a series of puns on sexual foreplay and consummation.

crochets: quarter-notes, with *double entendre*.

47 *strain*: musical passage, close embrace.

48 *large*: whole note, open space.

prick: dotted note, with *double entendre*.

49 *division*: rapid melodic passage; crotch.

50 *quavers*: eighth-notes; vibrations.

graces: grace notes, with *double entendre*.

51 *close*: final note of a musical phrase; copulation; orgasm.

58 *Put Snuffe out*: send Snuffe away; put the candle out.

62 *closet*: private room.

63 *falls and tires*: veils and head-dresses, with *double entendre*.

69 *shadow*: border attached to a bonnet to protect the complexion.

Languebeau suggests that his presence provides a cover for his mistress's adultery.

71 *spirit*: lust.

74 *swayed with the motion*: persuaded by the suggestion, with *double entendre*.

82 *understanding*: instruction; a position underneath.

85 *attend*: await.

89 *The flesh . . . above it*: Languebeau Snuffe's blasphemous inversion of the biblical phrase 'the spirit is willing but the flesh is weak'.

4.2.9 *superfluous letter in the law*: an extra letter in a legal document that changes its meaning.

10 *Scrape him out*: erase him.

11 *Give me your purpose*: tell me your intention.

20 *with the most advantage make a stand*: take up the best position.

28 *discharge*: rid; with a play on discharge = 'shoot'.

32 *proper*: own.

36 *loose humour*: licentious temperament.

41 *Nature forbid*: 'God forbid' is the normal expression. In the early seventeenth century it was illegal to say God's name onstage. Tourneur turns censorship into an opportunity for characterization: D'Amville, being an atheist, makes Nature his final authority.

4.3.2 *one*: one o'clock; a person.

25 S.D. *gives false fire*: misfires.

26 *Save thee*: defend yourself; save yourself by retreating.

40 *costermongers*: apple-sellers, hence amply supplied with 'fruits'.

43 *phlegmatic windy disease*: accumulation of phlegm and intestinal gas, the consequence of eating fresh fruit.

46 *conceive*: comprehend; conceive a child.

49 *well . . . dry*: proverbial.

56 S.D. *hair*: wig.

62 *called to examination*: questioned by the authorities. If, however, Soquette were found copulating with what seemed to be a devil, she would be subject to the death penalty for witchcraft.

69 S.D. *doubtfully*: hesitantly.

73 *friendly accident*: fortunate occurrence.

77 S.D. *staggers him*: makes him stagger.

99 *prodigal*: spendthrift, because the body in sexual intercourse was imagined to be spending its vital resources.

109 *appetite . . . fails of procreation*. Renaissance medical treatises maintained

that the greater 'heat' engendered by passionate or illicit sexual activity helped induce conception.

123 *incest*: ecclesiastical law prohibited sex with relations by marriage as well as with blood relatives.

125 *articles*: provisions.

126 *subjections*: submissiveness.

130 *These distances . . . than they*. This rationalization is adapted from Ovid's *Metamorphoses* Book x.

139 *their examples*: Castabella characteristically objects to D'Amville's habit of seeking models for his behaviour in the animal world, which human beings ought to surpass, rather than looking upward to heaven.

145 *contain*: content.

152 *damps*: noxious gases, thought to produce disease.

156 *supply*: increase.

157 *get*: beget.

169 *invocate*: call upon.

171 *my body . . . a man*: one of the threats which the Roman rapist Tarquin used to prevail over his victim, Lucretia.

172 *entertain*: give reception to.

173 *Tereus-like*: like the mythological king of Thrace who raped his sister-in-law.

179 *made me satisfaction*: repaid me adequately.

183 *apprehension*: arrest.

200 *this protection*: i.e. God.

208 *sin of Sodom*: homosexuality.

226 *bury my face under my eyebrows*: hide my face.

228 *I' the face*: face to face.

light: wanton; bright.

229 *challenge*: demand.

233 *'Pox o' fearfulness*: a plague upon my cowardice.

243 *phlegmatic*: full of phlegm, one of the four basic bodily fluids, an excess of which was supposed to cause weakness and lethargy.

248 *circumvolved*: enveloped. D'Amville's plea for annihilation is adapted from the protagonist's final speech in Christopher Marlowe's popular Elizabethan play, *Doctor Faustus*.

264 *suspiciously*: in a way that raises suspicion.

271 *smell a fox*: am suspicious.

274 *in rerum natura*: in the order of nature.

275 *with the spirit of consideration*: upon reflection.

276 *fantastic toy*: foolish illusion.

279 *centre*: of the earth.

290 *examine*: interrogate.

294 *clear*: innocent.

304 *fly*: be sold.

4.4.2 *affectedly*: lovingly.

8 *The more . . . apprehension*: the more I try, by roundabout methods, to avoid directly confronting my suspicions, the more reasonable they appear.

14 S.D. *closely*: quietly, to avoid detection.

28 *wench o' the trade?*: prostitute.

30 *falling diseases*: literally, epilepsy; here, diseases acquired while lying down, i.e. syphilis, which caused baldness.

31 *recovers*: repairs.

33 *bodies*: bodices, with *double entendre*.

37 *pander to*: go-between for.

38 *the conveyances*: what goes back and forth.

42 *O yes*: Fresco makes his confirmation of Belforest's accusations sound like 'Oyez' (Fr. 'Hear!'), the call of the town crier.

47 *man, court, city or country*: parodying legal formulae used in public announcements.

51 *laugh*: laugh at; playing on Belforest's 'cry' of l. 52.

4.5.6 *matted*: carpetted with rushes.

14 *adventure*: risk.

26 *commit*: have sex with.

33 *waxes fulsome*: grows offensive.

35 *winter fruit*: preserved fruit.

40 *chargeable reckoning*: large payment due.

42 *a several*: his own.

bill: pole-axe borne by law officers; invoice for payment.

43 *bouncing's*: pounding is.

52 *ha't*: have my death blow.

80 *suffered to go out of himself*: allowed to leave of his own accord; playing on 'snuff' = 'candlewick'.

5.1 S.D. *A closet discovered*: a small room revealed; probably by pulling a curtain hung before the 'inner stage', a chamber at the back of the main stage platform.

10 *astronomer*: astrologer.

13 *planet-struck*: paralysed with awe; sudden paralysis was thought to be caused by the influence of planets. D'Amville suggests that the sight of gold produces the same effect.

16 *lesser eyes*: stars. The roofs of Renaissance theatres were often painted with stars.

21 *like subjects . . . unprevented sight*: D'Amville imagines a monarch riding through the streets, beheld by spectators from the upstairs windows of houses.

unprevented: unobstructed.

41 *seal up my assurance*: legally ratify my title to his property.

44 *fantastic providence*: imaginary god.

56 *mandrakes*: plants with roots shaped vaguely like human beings; they were supposed to shriek so horribly when pulled up that anyone who heard the sound would go insane.

68 *Hippocrates*: fourth-century BC Greek physician, 'The Father of Medicine'.

69 *Galen*: second-century AD Greek medical writer whose theories provided the basis of Renaissance medical practice.

Avicen: eleventh-century Arab physician and philosopher.

79 *shrinks*: collapses.

85 *radical ability*: the 'humour' or fluid essential to all living things.

88 *extract*: potions of gold were believed to have great curative powers; and D'Amville, whose respect for material wealth is unbounded, is especially likely to think so.

89 *inspire*: breathe.

93 *reserve their waters*: save their urine, used to diagnose disease.

99 *date*: duration.

107 *corruption*: decaying material was supposed to generate vermin spontaneously.

119 *assurances*: legal titles to property, as well as 'confidence'.

120 *Star Chamber*: Tudor and Jacobean high court, here with a play on the stars in heaven, denigrated by D'Amville earlier in the scene.

121 *sense*: awareness.

5.2.5 *ignorant respect*: respect of ignorant people.

15 *frequentation*: habitual attendance.

20 *let her fore-rooms*: rent her front rooms, with bawdy innuendo.

21 *backwards*: in the back part of the house, with innuendo.

31 *means | which brings diseases*: because prostitution spread syphilis.

32 *carted*: whores were punished by being dragged through town at the tail of a cart and whipped.

49 *take hold o' me*: prosecute me.

54 *degrees of scholarship*: academic degrees. Religious moderates and conservatives stressed the need for university training for clerics, while some radical Puritans claimed to rely upon inspiration rather than learning.

69 *resolve me in a case*: judge a case for me.

79 *rack of rent*: rack-rent was a high rent based on the actual value of the property rented, rather than the lower sum determined by custom. The distinction D'Amville makes between those whose income derives from landholding and those who make money as 'entrepreneurs' marks the difference in Renaissance England between the traditional aristocracy and the *nouveaux riches*.

142 *anatomy*: the bodies of executed criminals were sometimes given or sold to doctors and scientists for dissection.

145 *exact*: perfect.

162 *valiant*: women were not supposed to be courageous.

163 *beg | Thy life*: ask that your life be spared; suggesting 'I wish for a life like yours.'

166 *efficient cause*: in Aristotelian philosophy, that which gives something its form, as a sculptor makes a sculpture.

195 *Indies*: both the East and West Indies were renowned for mineral wealth.

196 *glass of water*: those about to be executed were allowed an alcoholic drink to steady themselves, but Charlemont's courage requires no reinforcement.

216 *magnanimity*: great-spiritedness, according to Aristotle the essential characteristic of the virtuous man.

219 *emulate thy death*: share your courage in the face of death.

222 *so base a hand*: executioners came from the lowest social classes.

273 *attribute*: stressed on the first and third syllables.

295 *these honoured lives*: Charlemont's and Castabella's.

296 *their*: D'Amville's, Sebastian's, and Rousard's.

GLOSSARY

absolute perfect; detached
abstract essence
abuse deceive
accompliment social formality
Acheron in classical myth, a lake in
    hell; sometimes imagined as a deity
adamant diamond, sometimes thought
    to have magnetic powers
admire wonder
afeared afraid
affect love, like, desire, incline to;
    pretend
affection love; passion; inclination
affinity relation of kinship
affright frighten
aglet spangle
alack, alack the day alas
ambage equivocation
ambuscado ambush
an if
annoy suffering
annuity allowance
apishness foolish affectation
apoplexy paralytic stroke
apprehend understand; perceive; arrest
apprehensive perceptive
argument subject
arrant absolute
arras tapestry screen
Atlas in classical mythology, a giant
    who bore the world on his shoulders
attend await; show; listen to
aught anything
authentical genuine
author perpetrator, originator
avail assistance
avaunt begone
aversation aversion
ballace ballast
balm cure
bane poison
bashaw pasha, Turkish nobleman
bate weaken; diminish
battalia battle formation
Beelzebub a devil

behove require, make incumbent upon
belike perhaps
Bellona the goddess of war
beshrew curse
betide happen to
betimes early; right away
bewray reveal, betray
blast kill
blasted withered; killed
'Blood by God's blood, an oath
blurt burst in
boon favour
boot use; 'what boots it': what's the
    use. 'to boot': in addition, as extra
    compensation
bootless useless
bounty generosity
bower arbour
brack rupture
brainpan skull
brake thicket
brave (noun) champion; hired assassin;
    (adj.) fine; flashy; bold
breach wound; interruption; gap
brook bear, endure
buffet blow
bugbear imaginary hobgoblin
bulwark fortification
buttery pantry
by this light an oath
camphor perfume
canker skin ulcer
careless untroubled
carrier porter
Cassandra Trojan princess whose
    prophecies of doom, though true,
    were never believed
charnel house mortuary chapel
chevalier horseman
child's-part inheritance
Chimaera in classical mythology, a
    fire-breathing monster
choler anger
clap strike; put; confine
clip embrace

close (adj.) secret, concealed
cloven cut in two
coil noise
colour pretence; flag
commix mingle
compact put together, make up
compass (verb) attain; embrace; (noun) space; boundary
complot plot
conceit (noun) imagination; idea; opinion; understanding; (verb) interpret; devise; express
conceited ingenious
condescent approval
confound confuse; corrupt; destroy; damn
conjure entreat; invoke; effect by magic
consort associate; partnership; harmony
conster construe, understand
construction interpretation
contemptful contemptible
control prevent
convocation-house place of assembly
cornet troop of cavalry
corregidor advocate
corse corpse
corsive corrosive
costermonger fruit-seller
countermured doubly fortified
courser war-horse
cozen cheat
creature dependant
credulous trusting
cross (verb) oppose; obstruct; (noun) confusion; hindrance
crown gold coin
cuckold man whose wife commits adultery
Cupid blind boy-god of love
dag pistol
dam mother
'Death by God's death, an oath
delivery liberation
denier French coin of low denomination
desert merit; reward
desertful meritorious
design, designment plot, plan
desperate reckless
despite, despiteful malice, malicious

device trick, plan
devise make plans
digression deviation
ding strike
direful dire
disburden relieve
discover reveal
disposure disposition
distain defile (i.e. of honour)
distaste make distasteful
distemper upset
distich couplet
distracted, distraction insane; insanity
distressful suffering or causing suffering
ditcher ditch-digger
divers several
divine conjecture; prophesy
doom (verb) judge; (noun) judgement
doublet waistcoat
doubt (verb) fear for; suspect; (noun) suspicion
doubtful fearful
drab whore
drave drove
dropsy abnormal retention of fluid
drossy worthless
drudge slave
ducat valuable gold coin
dumb show mime
durance confinement
durst dare
ecstasy frenzy
empyreal heavenly
encomium eulogy
engross monopolize
enlargement release
enow enough
entreat (verb) behave toward; request; describe; (noun) entreaty
envious spiteful
envy malice
ere before
event outcome
example precedent
exigent extremity
expectless unexpectedly
expostulate question
expulse expel
extemporal immediate

fabulous imaginary
fact deed
fain (verb) desire; (adv.) gladly
falchion scimitar
farthing quarter of a penny
fashionmonger fashion consultant
fautor patron
favour love-token; face; demeanour; goodwill
fell dreadful, cruel
fervent burning
Flora goddess of flowers
flout mock
fly-flop fly-swatter
fond loving; foolish
forfend avert, prevent
forsooth in truth
forthwith immediately
forward bold; zealous; precocious
fray scare
frolic (verb) make merry; (adj.) cheerful
front forehead
froward stubborn
fry offspring
Furies in classical mythology, female divinities who violently avenge crimes
geal congeal
gear business
golls hands
gossip old woman
gramercy thank goodness
great-spleened prideful; angry
gripe grasp
groundwork foundation
guerdon reward
habit attire
hackney rented horse
halberdier soldier or guard armed with a halberd, a long- handled axelike weapon
half-moon semi-circular battle formation
halter hangman's noose
handy hand-to-hand
hap, haply perhaps
hap luck
hapless unfortunate
hearten encourage
heartless timid

Hecate name of a goddess sometimes associated with Diana or the moon, and sometimes with hell and sorcery
here-hence in consequence
hie approach quickly
hight is called, was called
hire payment
hogshead liquor cask
holp helped
homely unpretentious but hospitable
honesty chastity
hospital institution for the poor, aged, or infirm
hugger-mugger secrecy
hugy huge
humor mood; impulse; notion
humorous moody; whimsical
Hymen god of marriage
Ilion Troy
impair detract from
imperious majestic
import (noun) importance; (verb) signify; convey; concern
impulsion momentum
inclamation exclamation
induction prologue
inexpected unexpected
infective infectious
infortunate unfortunate
innative inborn
innocent mentally retarded person
insatiate rapacious
insculption inscription
instantly immediately
instrument accessory; tool
intentive heedful
interdict forbid
issue children; end
Jove in classical mythology, king of the gods; sometimes used to mean 'God'
Judas the disciple who betrayed Christ
jutty jut
kind (adj.) forgiving; friendly; related by blood; (noun) relative; species; gender
'lack alack
lancier mounted soldier armed with a lance
largess royal bestowal of gifts upon a special occasion

leese lose

lime (noun) a sticky substance smeared on twigs to catch birds; (verb) to trap

list (verb) desire; listen

loggerhead blockhead

lording gentleman

Lucifer the most glorious of the angels, who became Satan when he revolted from God

Luna the moon

luxur lecher

luxurious lecherous, voluptuous

madding insane

madonna my lady, a form of address

maintenance livelihood

manless brutish

marry (as an exclamation) by Mary

Mars god of war and lover of Venus

marshal-sessions trial

martialist soldier

maskeries masquerades

masque masked entertainment, often an allegory about aristocratic virtue

Mass By the Mass, an oath

massy massive

maugre despite

measled diseased

meed reward

mere complete

mettle spirit

minion favourite

minority youth

mischance misfortune

misconster misinterpet

miscreant wretch

misterm call by the wrong name

mistrust suspect

moiety half

motion proposal; performance

move anger; arouse; motivate; suggest; persuade

mum quiet; used as an exclamation

murrain plague

Myrmidons in the *Iliad*, ruthless soldiers under the command of the Greek hero Achilles

nake make naked

naught nothing

Nemesis goddess of vengeance

nill will not

noblesse nobility

obsequy funeral ceremony

of my soul an exclamation

office employment

ope open

ordnance artillery

out on fie upon; an expression of disgust

overtopping climbing over

pallet resting place

parasite sycophantic dependant

Paris Trojan prince whose theft of Helen, queen of Lacedaemonia, resulted in war between the Trojans and the Greeks

parlous clever; dangerous

parts intelligence, ability

passing extremely

passion o' me an exclamation referring to Christ's passion

pate head

patrician aristocrat; aristocratic

perdu extremely hazardous sentry duty

pester infest

pestilent plague-ridden

Phoebus the sun; the sun-god

phoenix unique legendary bird, which was supposed to burn to death every 500 years and regenerate from its own ashes: a symbol of rarity and purity

physic cure; medicine

plebeian (adj.) ordinary; (noun) common people

pleurisy feverish excess

Pluto god of the underworld

policy cunning; strategy; expediency

politic (adj.) cunning; prudent; expedient

politician sly, worldly manipulator

poniard dagger

Portingale Portugal

post ride swiftly to deliver a message

post-horse mounted relay messenger

practice plot, stratagem; practical affair

practique practice

precisian Puritan

prefer promote; recommend

prefix arrange in advance

premeditate anticipatory
presage omen
present, presently immediate, immediately
presentment performance
prevent forestall; anticipate
privy secret
prodigious ominous; monstrous
proper own
property prop; instrument; nature
Proserpine queen of the underworld, Pluto's consort
puissant powerful
pullen poultry
puny novice
purchase profit
purse-taker thief
quaint clever
quarled curdled
quit, quite repay
quittance revenge
quoits tossing game similar to horseshoes
quoth says, said
rack instrument of torture that stretched the body
rampire rampart
rank strong; corrupt
rarefy make thin; purify
rase scratch
reave bereave
rebato stiff collar or the wire frame that goes under it
rebutter reproach
reck attend to
recompt count up again
remission pardon
repair visit
respectless unconcerned
revels, reveling aristocratic entertainments, involving plays, masquerades, and games
round vigorous; plain-spoken
ruthful piteous
sable black
salute greet
savour smell; show traces
'Sblood God's blood, an oath
scinder sunder
scurvy poor

scutcheon shield emblazoned with a coat of arms, which originally commemorated feats of war
'Sdeath God's death, an oath
secretary confidant
seld seldom; rare
self-affecting narcissistic
sennight week
sensible intelligent; perceptible
sensive conscious
seres talons
sergeant law officer who makes arrests
'Sfoot God's foot, an oath
shadows parasols
shift trick
shiver break
signior sir
signory domain
silly pathetic, innocent
singular unique
sirrah term of address to an inferior
Sisyphus in classical mythology, punished in Hades by having continually to roll a stone to the top of a hill; the stone would escape at the summit and roll back down again
sith since
slake extinguish
sleight trick, deception
'Slid God's eyelid, an oath
'Slud God's blood, an oath
sluggy sluggish
sluice floodgate
solicit appeal to; disturb
sooth truth
sort group
sovereign efficacious
spinner spider
sprite spirit
state estate (i.e. both property and social position); dignity
stay wait; stop; support
still always
stint finish
stomach appetite; courage
stoop swoop
straight immediately
strond shore
Styx river in the underworld, over which the dead must pass

subscribe sign one's name
substance wealth; material
sucket piece of preserved fruit
suffer permit
suit request
sup dine
superficies surfaces
supposure supposition
surcease cease
surcharged overloaded
surprise ambush
sway (verb) persuade; (noun) power; government
swindge power; leeway; freedom; indulgence
tallow-chandler candle-maker
Tantalus in classical mythology, a man afflicted in Hades with terrible hunger and thirst, tormented by the sight of fruit and water just out of reach
tax rebuke
thriftless unproductive
tickle delicate; decisive
tires headdresses; costumes
Tityus in classical mythology, a giant tortured in Hades by having his liver continually torn out by vultures
toy trifle; caress; whim
train (1) followers; (2) deceit, trap
translucent luminous
treacher traitor
trencher plate
troth truth; loyalty; contract; (as an exclamation) in truth
try test; exercise; prove
tucket trumpet flourish
twain two
twitch pull
tympany swelling
Ud's body God's body, an oath
unbowel disembowel
unbrace undress; disclose

unkind cruel; unnatural; not respecting the ties of kinship
unmanured uncultivated
usurer one who lends money at interest, considered a sinful practice in Renaissance England
usury lending money at interest; by extension, any income acquired by sinful means
valiancy valour
varlet villain
vaunts boasts
venge revenge
Venus goddess of love and mother of Cupid
veny bout
verily truly
Vesper the evening star
virago man-like woman
vizard mask
votist a person who has taken a vow
vouchsafe grant
wainscot wood panelling
wanton voluptuary
watchword signal
weld carry
wend proceed
whenas when
whiles while
whilom formerly
whisk rush around
whurl growl
wight creature
wind manœuvre, lure
wist knew
withal with that; nevertheless
wonted accustomed
worldling worldly person
wot know
wreak revenge
yeoman man of the servant or peasant class
Zounds God's wounds, an oath